The Universal Irish Song Book; a complete collection of the songs and ballads of Ireland, etc.

Anonymous

The Universal Irish Song Book; a complete collection of the songs and ballads of Ireland, etc.
Anonymous
British Library, Historical Print Editions
British Library
1884
504 p. ; 8°.
11602.f.15.

GUIDE TO FOLD-OUTS, MAPS and OVERSIZED IMAGES

In an online database, page images do not need to conform to the size restrictions found in a printed book. When converting these images back into a printed bound book, the page sizes are standardized in ways that maintain the detail of the original. For large images, such as fold-out maps, the original page image is split into two or more pages.

Guidelines used to determine the split of oversize pages:

• Some images are split vertically; large images require vertical and horizontal splits.
• For horizontal splits, the content is split left to right.
• For vertical splits, the content is split from top to bottom.
• For both vertical and horizontal splits, the image is processed from top left to bottom right.

Dec.ʳ 11 1832

THE

UNIVERSAL

IRISH SONG BOOK;

A COMPLETE COLLECTION

OF THE

SONGS AND BALLADS OF IRELAND.

ILLUSTRATED.

NEW YORK :

P. J. KENEDY, Publisher,

5 BARCLAY STREET.

1884.

SONG,

PREFACE.

The Publisher, in presenting this " Universal Irish Song Book," confidently asserts, that in no other collection in Ireland or America will be found so many of the Songs of Ireland as in this volume.

It embodies all the standard songs of the different classes: Amatory, National, Convivial, Martial and Sentimental that enthused or amused the Irish people in Ireland, and their children, the Irish-Americans, for generations, and which will always continue popular with them.

A selection of the best of that crude class mainly composed in the last century by country school-masters and others with a smattering of poetic taste, and which are generally designated "Come all Ye's," are included for the purpose of satisfying the wishes of some parties who having heard them in their youth, still retain a more pleasing recollection of them than their literary merit warrants.

Notwithstanding the magnitude of the work and its completeness in detail, it is placed at a price that it is hoped will cause it to supersede all the fractional collections heretofore issued.

P. J. KENEDY.

NEW YORK, February, 1884.

THE
UNIVERSAL
IRISH SONG BOOK

ON MUSIC.

AIR.—" Banks of Banna."

WHEN through life unblest we rove,
  Losing all that made life dear,
Should some notes we used to love,
  In days of boyhood, meet our ear,
Oh! how welcome breathes the strain!
  Wakening thoughts that long have slept,
Kindling former smiles again
  In faded eyes that long have wept.

Like the gale, that sighs along
  Beds of oriental flowers,
Is the grateful breath of song,
  That once was heard in happier hours;
Fill'd with balm the gale sighs on,
  Though the flowers have sunk in death;
So, when pleasure's dream is gone,
  Its memory lives in Music's breath.

Music, oh how faint, how weak,
  Language fades before thy spell!
Why should Feeling ever speak,
  When thou canst breathe her soul so well?
Friendship's balmy words may feign,
  Love's are even more false than they;
Oh! 'tis only music's strain
  Can sweetly soothe, and not betray.

SONG OF THE BATTLE EVE.

Air.—"Cruiskeen Lawn."

TO-MORROW, comrade, we
On the battle-plain must be,
  There to conquer, or both lie low!
The morning star is up—
But there's wine still in the cup,
  And we'll take another quaff, ere we go, boy, go;
  We'll take another quaff ere we go.

'T is true, in manliest eyes
A passing tear will rise,
  When we think of the friends we leave lone;
But what can wailing do?
See, our goblet's weeping too!   [our own!
  With its tears we'll chase away our own, boy,
  With its tears we'll chase away our own.

But daylight's stealing on;
The last that o'er us shone
  Saw our children around us play;
The next—ah! where shall we
And those rosy urchins be?   [boy, away;
  But—no matter—grasp thy sword and away,
  No matter—grasp thy sword and away!

Let those who brook the chain
Of Saxon or of Dane,
  Ignobly by their firesides stay;
One sigh to home be given,
One heartfelt prayer to heaven,   [hurra!
  Then, for Erin and her cause, boy, hurra! hurra!
  Then, for Erin and her cause, hurra!

THE GROVES OF BLARNEY.

R. A. MILLIKEN. Born, 1767; Died, 1815.

THE groves of Blarney
They look so charming,
Down by the purling
  Of sweet silent streams;
Being banked with posies
That spontaneous grow there,
Planted in order
  By the sweet rock close.
'Tis there's the daisy
And the sweet carnation,
The blooming pink,
  And the rose so fair;
The daffodowndilly—
Likewise the lily,
All flowers that scent
  The sweet fragrant air.

'Tis Lady Jeffers
That owns this station;
Like Alexander,
  Or Queen Helen fair;
There's no commander
In all the nation,
For emulation,
  Can with her compare.
Such walls surround her,
That no nine-pounder
Could dare to plunder
  Her place of strength;
But Oliver Cromwell,
Her he did pommell,
And made a breach
  In her battlement.

There's gravel walks there,
For speculation,
And conversation
  In sweet solitude.
'Tis there the lover
May hear the dove, or
The gentle plover
  In the afternoon;

THE GROVES OF BLARNEY.—*Continued.*

And if a lady
Would be so engaging
As to walk alone in
   Those shady bowers,
'Tis there the courtier
He may transport her
Into some fort, or
   All under ground.

For 'tis there's a cave where
No daylight enters,
But cats and badgers
   Are for ever bred;
Being mossed by nature,
That makes it sweeter
Than a coach-and six,
   Or a feather bed.
'Tis there the lake is,
Well stored with perches,
And comely eels in
   The verdant mud;
Besides the leeches,
And grove of beeches,
Standing in order
   For to guard the flood.

There's statues gracing
This noble place in—
All heathen gods
   And nymphs so fair:
Bold Neptune, Plutarch,
And Nicodemus,
All standing naked
   In the open air!
So now to finish
This brave narration,
Which my poor geni
   Could not entwine;
But were I Homer,
Or Nebuchadnezzar,
'Tis in every feature
   I would make it shine.

THE BOWLD SOJER BOY.

SAMUEL LOVER.

OH, there's not a trade that's going,
Worth showing,
Or knowing,
Like that from glory growing,
        For a bowld sojer boy;
Where right or left we go,
Sure you know,
Friend or foe
Will have the hand—or toe,
        From a bowld sojer boy!
There's not a town we march through,
But the ladies, looking arch through
The window panes, will search through
        The ranks to find their joy;
While up the street,
Each girl you meet,
With look so sly,
Will cry
" My eye!
Oh! isn't he a darling— the bowld sojer boy!"

But when we get the route,
How they pout,
And they shout,
While to the right about
        Goes the bowld sojer boy!
'Tis then that ladies fair,
In despair
Tear their hair,
But the div'l a one I care,
        Says the bowld sojer boy;
For the world is all before us,
Where the landladies adore us,
And ne'er refuse to score us,
        But chalk us up with joy;
We taste her tap,
We tear her cap,
" Oh! that's the chap
For me,"
Says she,
" Oh, isn't he a darling—the bowld sojer boy."

THE BOWLD SOJER BOY.—*Continued.*

Then come along with me.
Gramachree,
And you'll see
How happy you will be
       With your bowld sojer boy;
Faith, if you're up to fun,
With me run,
'Twill be done
In the snapping of a gun,
       Says the bowld sojer boy;
And 'tis then that without scandal
Myself will proudly dandle
The little farthing candle
       Of our mutual flame, my joy;
May his light shine
As bright as mine,
Till in the line
He'll blaze
And raise
The glory of his cause, like a bowld sojer boy!

——o——

THE BANKS OF BANNA.

Rt. Hon. GEORGE OGLE.

SHEPHERDS, I have lost my love,
  Have you seen my Anna?
Pride of every shady grove
  Upon the banks of Banna.
I for her my home forsook,
  Near yon misty mountain,
Left my flocks, my pipe, my crook,
  Greenwood shade, and fountain.

Never shall I see them more
  Until her returning;
All the joys of life are o'er—
  From gladness chang'd to mourning.
Whither is my charmer flown?
  Shepherds, tell me whither?
Ah! woe for me, perhaps she's gone,
  For ever and for ever!

BARNEY BRALLAGHAN'S COURTSHIP.

'TWAS on a windy night,
  At two o'clock in the morning,
An Irish lad so tight,
  All wind and weather scorning,
At Judy Callaghan's door,
  Sitting upon the palings,
His love-tale he did pour,
  And this was part of his wailings—
      Only say
        You'll have Mister Brallaghan,
      Don't say nay,
        Charming Judy Callaghan.

Oh, list to what I say,
  Charms you've got like Venus;
Own your love you may,
  There's only the wall between us;
You lie fast asleep,
  Snug in bed and snoring,
Round the house I creep,
  Your hard heart imploring.
            Only say, &c.

I've got nine pigs and a sow,
  I've got a stye to keep 'em;
A calf and a brindled cow,
  And got a cabin to sleep in;
Sunday hose and coat,
  An old grey mare to ride on,
Saddle and bridle to boot,
  Which you may ride astride on.
            Only say, &c.

I've got an old Tom cat,
  Thro' one eye he's staring;
I've got a Sunday hat,
  Little the worse for wearing;
I've got some gooseberry wine—
  The trees had got no riper;
I've got a fiddle fine,
  Which only wants a piper.
            Only say, &c.

BARNEY BRALLAGHAN'S COURTSHIP.—*Continued.*

I've got an acre of ground,
  I've got it set with praties ;
I've got of backey a pound,
  And got some tay for the ladies ;
I've got the ring to wed,
  Some whiskey to make us gaily,
A mattress, feather bed,
  And handsome new shillelah.
                Only say, &c.

You've got a charming eye,
  You've got some spelling and reading ;
You've got, and so have I,
  A taste for genteel breeding ;
You're rich, and fair, and young,
  As everybody's knowing,
You've got a dacent tongue,
  Whene'er 'tis set a going.
                Only say, &c.

For a wife till death
  I am willing to take ye—
But, och, I waste my breath,
  The devil himself can't wake ye !
'Tis just beginning to rain,
  So I'll get under cover;
I'll come to-morrow again,
  And be your constant lover.
                Only say, &c.

————o————

DEAR LAND.

WHEN comes the day all hearts to weigh,
  If staunch they be, or vile,
Shall we forget the sacred debt
We owe our mother isle ?
My native heath is brown beneath,
  My native waters, blue ;
But crimson red o'er both shall spread,
  Ere I am false to you,
                Dear land—
  Ere I am false to you.

DEAR LAND.—*Continued.*

When I behold your mountains bold—
  Your noble lakes and streams—
A mingled tide of grief and pride
  Within my bosom teems.
I think of all your long dark thrall—
  Your martyrs brave and true;
And dash apart the tears that start—
  We must not *weep* for you,
      Dear land—
  We must not weep for you.

My grandsire died, his home beside;
  They seized and hanged him there;
His only crime, in evil time,
  Your hallowed green to wear.
Across the main his brothers twain
  Were sent to pine and rue;
And still they turn'd, with hearts that burn'd,
  In hopeless love to you
      Dear land—
  In hopeless love to you.

My boyish ear still clung to hear
  Of Erin's pride of yore,
Ere Norman foot had dared pollute
  Her independent shore:
Of chiefs, long dead, who rose to head
  Some gallant patriot few,
Till all my aim on earth became
  To strike one blow for you,
      Dear land—
  To strike one blow for you.

What path is best your rights to wrest
  Let other heads divine;
By work or word, with voice or sword,
  To follow them be mine.
The breast that zeal and hatred steel,
  No terrors can subdue;
If death should come, that martyrdom
  Were sweet, endured for you,
      Dear land—
  Were sweet, endured for you.

ERIN'S LOVELY HOME.

WHEN I was young and in my prime, my age just twenty-one,
I acted as a servant unto a gentleman;
I served him true and honest, and very well its known,
But cruelly he banished me from Erin's lovely home.

The reason he did banish me, I mean to let you hear,
I own I loved his daughter, and she loved me as dear;
She had a heavy fortune, but riches I had none,
And that's the reason I must go from Erin's lovely home.

It was in her father's garden, all in the month of June,
When viewing of those flowers, all in her youthful bloom.
She said, "My dearest William, if with me you will roam,
We'll bid adieu to all our friends, and Erin's lovely home."

That very night I gave consent along with her to go,
From her father's dwelling-place, which proved my overthrow;
The night being bright, by the moonlight we both set off alone,
Thinking we'd got safe away from Erin's lovely home.

When we came to Belfast, by the break of day,
My true-love she got ready our passage for to pay,
Five thousand pound she counted down, saying this shall be
       your own,
And never mourn for those you've left in Erin's lovely home.

But of our great misfortune, I mean to let you hear,
It was a few hours after her father did appear,
And marched me back to Omagh gaol, in the county of
       Tyrone,
From there I was transported from Erin's lovely home.

When I heard my sentence, it grieved my heart full sore,
And parting from my true-love, it grieved me ten times more;
I had seven links upon my chain, and every link a year,
Before I can return again to the arms of my dear.

Before the rout came to the gaol to take us all away,
My true-love came to me, and these words to me did say,
" Bear up your heart, don't be dismayed, I will not you disown,
Until you do return again to Erin's lovely home."

THE IRISH JAUNTING CAR.

My name is Larry Doolan, I'm a native of the soil;
If you want a day's diversion, I'll drive you out in style;
My car is painted red and green, and on the door a star,
And the pride of Dublin City is my Irish jaunting car.

CHORUS.

    Then, if you want to hire me, step into Mickey Maher,
    And ask for Larry Doolan and his Irish jaunting car.

When Queen Victoria came to Ireland her health to revive,
She asked the Lord Lieutenant to take her out to ride;
She replied unto his greatness, before they travelled far,
How delightful was the jogging of the Irish jaunting car.
    Then, if you want to hire me, &c.

I'm hired by drunken men, teetotalers, and my friends,
But a carman has so much to do, his duty never ends;
Night and day, both wet and dry, I travelled near and far,
And at night I count the earnings of my Irish jaunting car.
    Then, if you want to hire me, &c.

THE IRISH JAUNTING CAR.—*Continued.*

Some say the Russian bear is tough, and I believe it's true,
Though we beat him at the Alma and Balaklava too;
But if our Connaught Rangers would bring home the Russian
    Czar,
I would drive him off to blazes in my Irish jaunting car.
    Then, if you want to hire me, &c.

Some say all wars are over, and I hope to God they are;
For, you know full well they ne'er were good for a jaunting
    car;
But peace and plenty—may they reign here, both near and
    far;
Then we drive to feasts and festivals in an Irish jaunting car.
    Then, if you want to hire me, &c.

They say they are in want of men, the French and English,
    too.
And it's all about their commerce now they don't know what
    to do;
But if they come to Ireland our jolly sons to mar,
I'll drive them to the devil in my Irish jaunting car.
    Then, if you want to hire me, &c.

——o——

CUSHLA MA CHREE. *
From the Irish.

BEFORE the sun rose at yester-dawn,
I met a fair maid adown the lawn:
    The berry and snow
    To her cheek gave its glow,
And her bosom was fair as the sailing swan,
Then, pulse of my heart! what gloom is thine?

Her beautiful voice more hearts hath won
Than Orpheus' lyre of old had done;
    Her ripe eyes of blue
    Were crystals of dew,
On the grass of the lawn before the sun—
And, pulse of my heart! what gloom is thine?

*Vein, or pulse of my heart,

CATE OF ARAGLEN.

Air, " An Cailin Ruadh."

WHEN first I saw thee, Cate,
That summer evening late,
Down at the orchard gate
    Of Araglen,
I felt I ne'er before
Saw one so fair, *a-stor*,
I fear'd I'd never more
    See thee agen.
I stopp'd and gazed at thee,
My footfall, luckily
Reach'd not thy ear, tho' we
    Stood there so near ;
While from thy lips, a strain,
Soft as the summer rain,
Sad as a lover's pain,
    Fell on my ear.

I've heard the lark in June,
The harp's wild plaintive tune,
The thrush, that aye too soon
    Gives o'er his strain ;
I've heard, in hush'd delight
The mellow horn at night
Waking the echoes light
    Of wild Loch Lein ;
But neither echoing horn,
Nor thrush upon the thorn,
Nor lark at early morn
    Hymning in air,
Nor harper's lay divine,
E'er witch'd this heart of mine
Like that sweet voice of thine,
    That evening there.

And when some rustling, dear,
Fell on thy list'ning ear,
You thought your brother near,
    And nam'd his name,

CATE OF ARAGLEN.—*Continued.*

I could not answer—though,
As luck would have it so,
His name and mine, you know,
    Were both the same—
Hearing no answ'ring sound,
You glanced in doubt around,
With timid look and found
    It was not he;
Turning away your head
And, blushing rosy red,
Like a wild fawn you fled
    Far, far from me.

The swan upon the lake,
The wild rose in the brake,
The golden clouds that make
    The west their throne,
The wild ash by the stream,
The full moon's silver beam.
The evening star's soft gleam,
    Shining alone;
The lily rob'd in white—
All—all are fair and bright:—
But ne'er on earth was sight
    So bright, so fair,
As that one glimpse of thee
That I caught then, *ma chree,* *
It stole my heart from me
    That evening there.

And now you're mine alone,
That heart is all my own—
That heart, that ne'er hath known
    A flame before,
That form, of mould divine,
That snowy hand of thine,
Those locks of gold are mine
      For evermore.
Was lover ever seen
As blest as thine, Caitlin?
Hath ever lover been
    More fond, more true?

* My heart.

CRUISKIN LAWN.

Let the farmer praise his grounds,
Let the huntsman praise his hounds,
  The shepherd, his dew-scented lawn;
But I, more bless'd than they,
Spend each happy night and day
  With my charming little *cruiskin lawn.*

    Gra-ma-chree ma cruiskin,
    Slainte geal ma vourneen,
      Gra-ma-chree a coolin bawn.
    Gra-ma-chree ma cruiskin,
    Slainte geal ma vourneen,
    Gra-ma-chree a coolin, bawn, bawn, bawn,
      Gra-ma-chree a coolin bawn.

Immortal and divine,
Great Bacchus, god of wine,
  Create me by adoption your son,
In hope that you'll comply
That my glass shall ne'er run dry,
Nor my smiling little *cruiskin lawn.*

                Gra-ma-chree, &c.

And when grim Death appears,
In a few but pleasant years,
  To tell me that my glass has run;
I'll say, begone, you knave,
For bold Bacchus gave me leave
  To take another *cruiskin lawn.*

                Gra-ma-chree, &c.

Then fill your glasses high,
Let's not part with lips adry,
  Though the lark now proclaims it is dawn;
And since we can't remain,
May we shortly meet again,
  To fill another *cruiskin lawn.*

                Gra-ma-chree, &c.

GILLE MA CHREE.

GERALD GRIFFIN.

Gille ma chree,*
Sit down by me,
We now are joined, and ne'er shall sever,
This hearth's our own,
Our hearts are one,
And peace is ours for ever!

When I was poor,
Your father's door
Was closed against your constant lover.
With care and pain,
I tried in vain
My fortunes to recover.
I said, ' To other lands I'll roam.
Where fate may smile on me, love;'
I said, 'Farewell, my own old home!'
And I said, ' Farewell to thee, love!'
Sing *Gille ma chree*, &c.

I might have said,
My mountain maid,
Come live with me, your own true lover;
I know a spot,
A silent cot,
Your friends can ne'er discover,
Where gently flows the waveless tide
By one small garden only;
Where the heron waves his wings so wide,
And the linnet sings so lonely!
Sing *Gille ma chree*, &c.

I might have said,
My mountain maid,
A father's right was never given
True hearts to curse
With tyrant force,
That have been blest in heaven.

* Brightener of my heart.

But then, I said, "In after years,
When thoughts of home shall find her!
  My love may mourn with secret tears
Her friends, thus left behind her."
      Sing *Gille ma chree*, &c.

    " Oh, no," I said,
    " My own dear maid,
For me, though all forlorn for ever,
      That heart of thine
      Shall ne'er repine
O'er slighted duty—never.
From home and thee, though wandering far,
  A dreary fate be mine, love;
I'd rather live in endless war,
    Than buy my peace with thine, love."
      Sing *Gille ma chree*, &c.

      Far, far away,
      By night and day,
  I toil'd to win a golden treasure;
      And golden gains
      Repaid my pains
  In fair and shining measure.
I sought again my native land,
  Thy father welcomed me, love;
I poured my gold into his hand,
  And my guerdon found in thee, love.

      Sing *Gille ma chree*,
      Sit down by me,
We now are joined, and ne'er shall sever,
      This hearth's our own,
      Our hearts are one,
And peace is ours for ever!

THE BUGABOO.

Come, all you tender-hearted boys, wherever you may be,
And I'll tell you of the dangers upon the dark blue sea,
Of the dangers and the hardships, my boys, that I went
    through,
When I shipped as cook and steward, my boys, on board of
    the Bugaboo.
    (Repeat the last two lines of each verse.)

The day when first I joined her, she lay in James street canal;
She was large and stout and beautiful : forget her shape I nev-
    er shall—
The captain wore a large straw hat, knee breeches and a body
    coat so blue,
Arrah ! boys, he'd made a fine figure-head to ornament the
    Bugaboo.

We soon weighed anchor and set sail to plow the raging surf.
We were bound for the bog of Allan to get a load of turf,
We sailed until we passed the back of Richmond barracks so
    true,
When the gallant eighty-fourth fired a royal salute of bricks
    at the Captain of the Bugaboo.

We sailed three years, when a storm arose, and the sea ran
    mountains high :
The thunder rolled, the lightning flashed and lit the dark blue
    sky,
So the second mate gave orders to lower the sails and clew,
While the captain down below was smoking in his bed—he
    set fire to the Bugaboo.

When the captain found what he had done he loud for help
    did shout,
He called up through the chimney top for the helmsman to
    come and put it out :
But the helmsman was fast asleep, and to his post untrue,
And the fire burned so hard through the middle of the turf,
    they couldn't save the Bugaboo.

THE BUGABOO.—*Continued.*

When fifteen thousand miles from land, in latitude fifty-four,
The fire burned so hard one night, that it couldn't burn any
      more ;
So the captain he gave orders to lower the boats and save
      the crew,
While a thousand sods of turf and fifty thousand men were
      smothered in the Bugaboo.

———o———

I'M A RANTING, ROVING BLADE.

By Samuel Lover.

Whoo ! I'm a ranting, roving blade,
Of never a thing was I ever afraid :
I'm a gentleman born, and scorn a trade,
And I'd be a rich man, if my debts were paid.

But my debts are worth something, this truth instil—
That pride makes us fall, all against our will :
For, 'twas pride that broke me—I was happy, until
I was ruined all out by my tailor's bill.

I'm the finest guide that ever you see,
I know every place of curiosity,
From Ballinafad unto Tanderagee :
And if you're for sport, come along wid me.

I'll lade you sportin' round about :
We've wild ducks and widgeons, and snipe and throut,
And I know where they are, and what they are about,
And if they're not at home, then I'm sure they're out.

The miles in this country much longer be,
But that is a saving of time you see :
For, two of our miles is equal to three,
Which shortens the road in a great degree.

And the roads in this place is so plenty, we say,
That you have nothing to do, but find your own way :
If your hurry's not great, and you have time to delay,
You can go the short cut—that's the longest way.

THE IRISH SHORE.

By Una. (Mrs. A. Ford.)

"'Tis vain to hope, 'tis vain to dream,
 Your land can never rise;
With hate her children rend her heart,
 While low in dust she lies;
Forget her wrongs"—so says the world,
 As many did before.
But, Oh! how can we e'er forget
 Our dear old Irish shore?

Can we forget the glorious host
 Who scorned as slaves to live,
Who gave their lives to native land—
 What more could mortal give?
Or cease to venerate the soil
 Made holy by their gore?
Our hearts were clods, could we forget
 Our dear old Irish shore—

Can we forget that on our brows
 Is slavery's shameful brand—
That we are never truly free
 While fetters bind our land—
That Freedom on us seems to frown
 And murmur evermore:
"If true to me arise and free
 Your own green Irish shore."

When we forget to ope our eyes
 To meet the smile of day,
Forget to weep when those most dear
 Are shrouded in the clay—
Forget to look with love and trust
 To Him we now adore—
We may forget, but not till then,
 Our dear old Irish shore.

THE IRISH SHORE.—*Continued.*

'Tis vain to dream, but not to toil,
    O land we love, for thee ;
While hope remains and mem'ry lasts,
    Our dearest wish must be,
For thee to labor, plan and pray,
    And sleep, when life is o'er,
Beneath the sod that wraps thy breast,
    Our green old Irish shore.

——o——

THE BLACKBIRD.

ONCE on a morning of sweet recreation,
    I heard a fair lady a-making her moan,
With sighing and sobbing, and sad lamentation,
Aye singing, " My Blackbird for ever is flown !
He's all my heart's treasure, my joy, and my pleasure,
    So justly, my love, my heart follows thee ;
And I am resolved, in foul or fair weather,
    To seek out my Blackbird, wherever he be.

"I will go, a stranger to peril and danger,
    My heart is so loyal in every degree ;
For he's constant and kind, and courageous in mind,
    Good luck to my Blackbird, wherever he be !
In Scotland he's loved and dearly approved,
    In England a stranger he seemeth to be ;
But his name I'll advance in Ireland or France.
    Good luck to my Blackbird, wherever he be.

"The birds of the forest are all met together,
    The turtle is chosen to dwell with the dove,
And I am resolved in foul or fair weather,
    Once in the spring-time to seek out my love.
But since fickle Fortune, which still proves uncertain,
    Hath caused this parting between him and me,
His right I'll proclaim, and who dares me blame ?
    Good luck to my Blackbird, wherever he be."

IRISH SCHOOLMASTER.

Old Teddy O'Rourke kept a bit of a school
  At a place called Clarina, and made it a rule,
If the mind wouldn't mark, faith, he'd soon mark the back,
  And he'd give them their own, with a devilish crack.
His scholars were: Jerry, Big Billy and Ned,
  With Murrogh M'Carthy, Old Darby, and Ted,
Tall Dermot O'Clany, and Dennis O'Shea,
  Faith, all noble boys to drive learning away.

SPOKEN: Well, my boys, says old Ted, as you are all here, I'll just be calling your names over, to see if any of ye are missing. Gerald M'Shee.—I'm not here, sir.—Then where are you, agrah?—I'm astride of the door, sir.—Then come in, and I'll beat you. Corney O'Flaherty.—I'm here, but my brother Barney ain't.—Then where is your brother Barney? —Faith, sir, he's dead and they're going to WAKE him.—Poor fellow! I'm sorry he's gone HOME, for he was my own scholar; but do you go and sit down, and don't fall asleep, or I'll be after WAKING you.

So long life to old Teddy,
  For he's always ready
To kick up a row, or the whiskey to smack:
  With his drinking and eating,
  His birching and beating,
And his hubaboo, philaloo, row de dow whack.

Faith, Ted had a nose as big as a ton,
  And a chin too! och honey, but they were all one:
A grin too, he had, and if there was a noise,
  He'd just give a squint and frighten the boys;
A fortune he had, too:—his birch and his wig,
  A black ugly cow, and an old dirty pig,
A PRATTY plantation, a dog and a cat,
  And his head that he kept in an old greasy hat.

SPOKEN: Phelim O'Maheney, says he one day, before you sit down, stand up and say your alphabet: so keep your five fingers out of your head for a few minutes, and begin. What letter's that, sir?—I don't know, sir.—Arrah, botheration to you, what was it I said when I saw you blacking Pat Mooney's

THE IRISH SCHOOLMASTER.

eye?—Faith, sir, you said: Ah! you big blackguard.—Well, never mind the blackguard, but say Ah.—Ah.—Now, what letter's that?—Faith, sir, I don't know, you ought to know better than me.—What makes the honey, and hold your whist?—B.—That's a good boy. Now, what kind of a half-moon thing do you call that?—I don't know, sir.—Och! botheration, what do I do with my eyes?—He! he! he!—Well, what do you laugh at, sir? I ask you what do I do with my eyes?—You? you squint!—and what else, sir?—you see. —That's a good boy. Now go on.—D-E-F-G-H.—Well, why do you stop?—Because I can't go any further, sir.—What has your mother got at the corner of her nose?—A pimple, sir,— Och, my service t'ye, sir; and what else?—One eye.—Devil take you and don't be getting into figures now. Say I, without the one.—What's the next?—It's something, sir, but I don't know what.—What does your mother open the door with?—A string, sir, and sometimes her foot.—Well did you never have anything else?—Yes, sir, K.—That's a good boy; and now, as you have got to L, (hell) you may sit down and warm yourself—

So long life to old Teddy, &c.

———o———

DESERTER'S MEDITATION.
By J. P. Curran.

IF sadly thinking, with spirits sinking,
    Could more than drinking my cares compose,
A cure for sorrow from sighs I'd borrow,
    And hope to-morrow would end my woes.
But as in wailing there's nought availing,
    And Death unfailing will strike the blow,
Then for that reason, and for a season,
    Let us be merry before we go!

To joy a stranger, a way-worn ranger,
    In ev'ry danger my course I've run;
Now hope all ending, and Death befriending,
    His last aid lending, my cares are done:
No more a rover, or hapless lover,
    My griefs are over—my glass runs low:
Then for that reason, and for a season,
    Let us be merry before we go!

SWEET CASTLE HYDE.

As I roved out on a summer's morning,
  Down by the banks of Blackwater side,
To view the groves and the meadows charming,
  And the pleasant gardens of Castle Hyde.
'Tis there you'll hear the thrushes warbling,
  The dove and the partridge I now describe,
And lambkins sporting every morning,
  All to adorn sweet Castle Hyde.

There are fine walks in those pleasant gardens,
  And seats most charming in shady bowers,
The gladiator who is bold and daring,
  Each night and morning does watch the flowers.
There's a road for service to this fine arbor,
  Where the nobles in their coaches ride,
To view the groves and pleasant gardens,
  That front the palace of Castle Hyde.

If noble princes from foreign places
  Should chance to sail to our Irish shore,
'Tis in this valley they should be feasted,
  Where often heroes had been before.
The wholesome air of this habitation
  Would recreate your heart with pride:
There is no valley throughout this nation
  In beauty equal to Castle Hyde.

There are fine horses and stall-fed oxes,
  A den for foxes to play and hide,
Fine mares for breeding, and foreign sheep in
  With snowy fleeces in Castle Hyde.
The grand improvements that there are making,
  The trees all drooping with fruit beside,
The bees are humming the fields with music,
  Which yields more beauty to Castle Hyde.

SWEET CASTLE HYDE.—*Continued.*

The richest groves throughout this nation,
 And fine plantations you will see there,
The rose, the tulip, and the sweet briar,
 All vying with the lily fair.
The buck and doe, the fox and eagle,
 They skip and play by the river side,
The trout and salmon are always sporting
 In the clear streamlets of Castle Hyde.

——o——

THE DEAR IRISH BOY.

My CONNOR, his cheeks are as ruddy as morning,
 The brightest of pearls do but mimic his teeth :
While nature with ringlets his mild brows adorning,
 His hair Cupid's bow-strings, and roses his breath.
  Smiling, beguiling,
  Cheering, endearing,
Together how oft o'er the mountains we stray'd ;
  By each other delighted,
  And fondly united,
I have listened all day to my dear Irish boy.

No roebuck more swift could fly over the mountain,
 No veteran bolder meet danger or scars,
He's sightly, he's sprightly, he's clear as the fountain,
 His eyes beaming love, oh ! he's gone to the wars.
      Smiling, beguiling, &c.

The soft tuneful lark, his notes changed to mourning,
 The dark-screaming owl impedes my night's sleep,
While lonely I walk in the shade of the evening,
 Till my Connor's return I will ne'er cease to weep.
      Smiling, beguiling, &c.

The war being over, and he not returned,
 I fear that some dark envious plot has been laid ;
Or that some cruel goddess has him captivated,
 And left here to mourn his dear Irish maid.
      Smiling, beguiling, &c.

THE CROPPY BOY.

A Ballad of '98.

CARROLL MALONE.

The revolutionary party in Ireland of this period wore their hair short, like the round-heads of Cromwell's day—hence the term "crop," or "croppy." The dramatic spirit of this ballad imparts to it a strange interest.

"GOOD men and true! in this house who dwell,
  To a stranger *bouchal** I pray you tell
  Is the priest at home? or may he be seen?
  I would speak a word with Father Green."

" The priest's at home, boy, and may be seen;
  'Tis easy speaking with Father Green;
  But you must wait till I go and see
  If the holy Father alone may be."

The youth has entered an empty hall—
  What a lonely sound has his light foot-fall!
  And the gloomy chamber's chill and bare,
  With a vested priest in a lonely chair.

The youth has knelt to tell his sins:
  "*Nomine Dei*" the youth begins:
  At " *mea culpa*," he beats his breast,
  And in broken murmurs he speaks the rest.

" At the siege of Ross did my father fall,
  And at Gorey my loving brothers all.
  I alone am left of my name and race;
  I will go to Wexford† and take their place,

* Boy.

† The rebels made a desperate stand at Wexford, which was in their hands for some time; and there the sanguinary spirit of *both* parties was fearfully display-ed. It was not the first time Wexford beheld a massacre, for Cromwell, in 1649, placed a red letter before his name there in the page of history.

THE CROPPY BOY.—*Continued.*

" I cursed three times since last Easter day—
  At mass-time once I went to play ;
  I passed the churchyard one day in haste,
  And forgot to pray for my mother's rest.

" I bear no hate against living thing ;
  But I love my country above my king.
  Now, Father! bless me, and let me go
  To die, if God has ordained it so."

The priest said nought, but a rustling noise
  Made the youth look up in wild surprise ;
  The robes were off, and in scarlet there
  Sat a yeoman captain with fiery glare.

With fiery glare and with fury hoarse,
  Instead of blessing, he breathed a curse,—
" 'Twas a good thought, boy, to come here and shrive,
  For one short hour is your time to live.

" Upon yon river three tenders float,*
  The priest's in one if he isn't shot—
  We hold his house for our Lord the King,
  And, amen! say I, may all traitors swing!"

At Geneva Barrack† that young man died,
  And at Passage they have his body laid.
  Good people who live in peace and joy,
  Give a prayer and a tear for the Croppy Boy.

*Guard-ships were anchored off Wexford. which served as prisons for the cap-
tured rebels, or suspected persons.

† A military station in Wexford county.

THE IRISH GIRL.

ONE evening, as I strayed down the river's side,
Looking all around me, as an Irish girl I spied :
So red and rosy were her cheeks, and yellow was her hair,
And costly were the robes, which my Irish girl did wear.

Her shoes, of Spanish leather, were bound round with span-
            gles gay :
The tears came down her crystal eyes, and she began to say :
" Och, hone ! and, alas ! Astore Areen Machree,
Why should you go and leave me, and slight your own Molly ?

The first time that I saw my love, I was sick and very bad,
All the request I asked was that she might tie my head !
I asked her if one as bad as me could ever mend again—
For, love's a sore disorder—did you ever feel the pain ?

My love, she'll not come nigh me, for all the moan I make,
Nor either will she pity me, if my poor heart should break—
But was I of some noble blood, and she of low degree,
She would hear my lamentation, and come and pity me.

My only love is fairer than the lilies that do grow,
She has a voice that's clearer than any winds that blow :
She's the promise of this country, like Venus in the air
And let her go where'er she will, she's my joy and only dear !

Be it so or be it not, of her I take my chance :
The first time that I saw my love, she struck me in a trance—
Her ruby lips and sparkling eyes have so bewitched me
That, was I king of Ireland, queen of it she should be !

I wish I was a butterfly, on my love's breast I'd lie,
Or was I but a linnet, how I would sing and fly—
Or if I was a corn-creak, I'd sing till morning clear,
I would sit and sing for Molly—for, once I loved her dear !

If my love was a red rose in yonder garden fair,
And I to be the gardener, of her I would take care.
There's not a month throughout the year but my love would
            renew :
With flowers fine I'd garnish, with Sweet-William, Thyme and
            Rue.

THE IRISH GIRL.—*Continued.*

If I was in Monaghan, and sitting on the grass,
And in my hand a bottle, and on my knee a lass:
I'd call for liquors plenty, and I'd pay before I go:
"Come on, they say, my brave boys, let the wind blow
      high or low!

——o——

THE ANGEL'S WHISPER.

By SAMUEL LOVER.

A superstition of great beauty prevails in Ireland, that, when a child smiles in its sleep it is " talking with the angels."

A BABY was sleeping,
    Its mother was weeping,
For her husband was far on the wild raging sea,
    And the tempest was swelling
    Round the fisherman's dwelling,
And she cried, "Dermot, darling, oh! come back to me."

    Her beads while she numbered,
    The baby still slumbered,
And smiled in her face, as she bended her knee;
    Oh! bless'd be that warning,
    My child, thy sleep adorning,
For I know that the angels are whispering with thee.

    And while they are keeping
    Bright watch o'er thy sleeping,
Oh, pray to them softly my baby, with me,
    And say, thou would'st rather
    They'd watch o'er thy father!
For I know that the angels are whispering with thee.

    The dawn of the morning
    Saw Dermot returning,
And the wife wept with joy her babe's father to see,
    And closely caressing
    Her child, with a blessing,
Said, "I knew that the angels were whispering with thee."

COME BACK TO ERIN.

COME back to Erin, Mavourneen, Mavourneen,
　Come back, Aroon, to the land of my birth,
Come with the Shamrocks and spring-time, Mavourneen,
　And its Killarney shall ring with our mirth.
Sure, when we lent you to beautiful England,
　Little we thought of the lone winter days,
Little we thought of the hush of the Star shine
　Over the mountains, the Bluffs and the Brays!

CHORUS.

Come back to Erin, Mavourneen, Mavourneen,
　Come back again to the land of my birth,
Come back to Erin, Mavourneen, Mavourneen,
　And its Killarney shall ring with our mirth.

Over the green sea, Mavourneen, Mavourneen,
　Long shone the white sail that bore thee away,
Riding the white waves, that fair Summer mornin',
　Just like a May-flower afloat on the bay.
Oh! but my heart sank when clouds came between us,
　Like a gray curtain the rain falling down,
Hid from my sad eyes the path o'er the ocean,
　Far, far away where my Colleen had flown.
　　　　　　　　Come back to Erin, &c.

Oh! may the Angels, awakin' and sleepin',
　Watch o'er my bird in the land far away!
And it's my prayer will consign to their keepin'
　Care o' my jewel, by night and by day;
When by the fire-side, I watch the bright embers,
　Then all my heart flies to England and thee,
Cravin' to know if my darlin' remembers,
　Or if her thoughts may be crossin' to me.
　　　　　　　　Come back to Erin, &c.

EILEEN AROON.

GERALD GRIFFIN.

WHEN, like the early rose,
   Eileen aroon!
Beauty in childhood blows;
   Eileen aroon!
When like a diadem,
Buds blush around the stem,
Which is the fairest gem?
   Eileen aroon!

Is it the laughing eye,
   Eileen aroon!
Is'it the timid sigh,
   Eileen aroon!
Is it the tender tone,
Soft as the string'd harp's moan?
Oh, it is truth alone,
   Eileen aroon!

When, like the rising day,
   Eileen aroon!
Love sends his early ray,
   Eileen aroon!
What makes his dawning glow
Changeless through joy or woe?
Only the constant know—
   Eileen aroon!

I know a valley fair,
   Eileen aroon!
I knew a cottage there,
   Eileen aroon!
Far in that valley's shade,
I knew a gentle maid,
Flower of a hazel glade,
   Eileen aroon!

Who in the song so sweet?
   Eileen aroon!
Who in the dance so fleet?
   Eileen aroon!

EILEEN AROON.—*Continued.*

Dear were her charms to me,
Dearer her laughter free,
Dearest her constancy,
   Eileen aroon !

Were she no longer true,
   Eileen aroon !
What should her lover do?
   Eileen aroon !
Fly with his broken chain
Far o'er the sounding main,
Never to love again,
   Eileen aroon !

Youth must with time decay,
   Eileen aroon !
Beauty must fade away,
   Eileen aroon !
Castles are sacked in war,
Chieftains are scattered far,
Truth is a fixed star,
   Eileen aroon !

BRICKEEN BRIDGE.

THE COW ATE THE PIPER.

In the year '98, when our troubles were great,
  And it was treason to be a Milesian :
That black whiskered set we will never forget,
  Tho' history tells us they were Hessian.
In this troublesome time, oh ! 'twas a great crime,
  And murder never was riper—
At the side of Glenshee, not an acre from me,
  There lived one Denny Byrne a piper.

Neither wedding nor wake would be worth a shake,
  Where Denny was not first invited :
At squeezing the bags and emptying the kegs
  He astonished as well as delighted.
In these times poor Denny could not earn one penny,
  Martial law had him stung like a viper :
They kept him within till the bones and the skin
  Were grinning through the rags of the piper.

One evening in June as he was going home,
  After the fair of Rathangan,
What should he see from the branch of a tree,
  But the corpse of a Hessian there hanging—
Says Denny : " these rogues have boots, I've no brogues—"
  On the boots then he laid such a griper,
He pulled them with such might, and the boots were so tight,
  That legs and boots came away with the piper.

Then Denny did run, for fear of being hung,
  Till he came to Tim Kennedy's cabin ;
Says Tim, from within : " I can't let you in,
  You'll be shot if you're caught there a rapping."
He went to the shed, where the cow was in bed,
  With a wisp he began for to wipe her :
They laid down together, on a seven foot feather,
  And the cow fell a hugging the piper.

THE COW ATE THE PIPER.—*Continued.*

THEN Denny did yawn as the day did dawn,
  As he streeled off the boots of the Hessian,
The legs by the law he left them on the straw,
  And he gave them leg-bail for his mission.
When the breakfast was done, Tim sent out his son,
  To make Denny jump up like a lamplighter:
When the legs there he saw, he roared like a jack-daw:
  "Oh! daddy, the cow's ate the piper!"

"Musha bad luck to the beast—she'd a musical taste
  For to eat such a beautiful chanter:
Arrah! Patrick avic, take a lump of a stick,
  Drive her off to Glenhealy—we'll cant her."
Mrs. Kennedy bawled, the neighbors were called:
  They began for to humbug and gibe her:
To the church-yard Tim walked with the legs in a box,
  And the cow will be hung for the piper.

The cow she was drove a mile or two off,
  To the fair at the side of Glenhealy.
And there she was sold for four guineas in gold
  To the clerk of the parish, Tim Daley.
They went to a tent, the lucky penny was spent,
  The clerk being a jolly old swiper:
Who d'ye think there was there, playing the "Rakes of Kil-
      dare?"
  But poor Denny Byrne, the piper!

Then Tim gave a bolt, like a half-drunken colt,
  At the piper he gazed like a gommock—
He said: "By the powers! I thought these eight hours
  You were playing in Driman Dhu's stomach."
Then Denny observed how the Hessian was served,
  And they all wished their necks secured to the griper,
For grandure they met, their whistles they wet,
  And like devils they danced round the piper.

THE GALLANT HUSSAR.

A DAMSEL possessed of great beauty,
   She stood by her own father's gate:
The gallant Hussars were on duty,
   To view them this maiden did wait.
Their horses were capering and prancing,
   Their accoutrements shone like a star;
From the plains they were nearer advancing,
   She espied her young gallant Hussar.

Their pelisses were slung o'er their shoulders,
   So careless they seemed for to ride:
So warlike appeared those young soldiers,
   With glittering swords by their side;
To the barracks next morning so early,
   This damsel she went in her car,
Because that she loved him sincerely—
   Young Edward, the gallant Hussar.

It was there she conversed with her soldier,
   These words they were heard for to say—
Said Jane : " I've a heart none more bolder,
   For to follow my laddy away,"
"Oh fie!" said young Edward, " be steady,
   And think of the dangers of war,
When the trumpet sounds I must be ready—
   So wed not your gallant Hussar."

" For twelve months on bread and cold water,
   My parents confined me for you :
Oh! hard-hearted friends to their daughter,
   Whose heart it is loyal and true:
Unless they confine me for ever,
   Or banish me from you afar,
I will follow my soldier so clever,
   To wed with my gallant Hussar."

Said Edward : "Your friends you must mind them,
   Or else you are for ever undone:
They will leave you no portion behind them,
   So pray do my company shun."

THE GALLANT HUSSAR.—*Continued.*

She said: " If you will be true hearted,
　I have gold of my uncle's in store:
From this time no more we'll be parted,
　I will wed with my gallant Hussar."

As he gazed on each beautiful feature,
　The tears they did fall from each eye:
" I will wed with this beautiful creature,
　To forsake cruel war," he did cry.
So now they're united together,
　Friends think of them now they're afar,
Crying : " Heaven bless them now and for ever,
　Young Jane and her gallant Hussar."

——o——

CUSHLA MA CHREE.

JOHN PHILPOT CURRAN.

Air, " The Bank of Green Rushes."

DEAR Erin, how sweetly thy green bosom rises,
　An emerald set in the ring of the sea,
Each blade of thy meadows my faithful heart prizes,
　Thou queen of the west, the world's *cushla ma chree.**
Thy gates open wide to the poor and the stranger—
　There smiles hospitality, hearty and free ;
Thy friendship is seen in the moment of danger,
　And the wand'rer is welcomed with *cushla ma chree.*

Thy sons they are brave ; but, the battle once over,
　In brotherly peace with their foes they agree,
And the roseate cheeks of thy daughters discover
　The soul-speaking blush that says, *cushla ma chree.*
Then, flourish for ever, my dear native Erin,
　While sadly I wander, an exile from thee,
And, firm as thy mountains, no injury fearing,
　May Heaven defend its own *cushla ma chree!*

* Pulse of my heart.

SOGGARTH AROON.

JOHN BANIM. Born, 1798. Died, 1842.

AM I the slave they say,
    Soggarth aroon? *
Since you did show the way,
    Soggarth aroon,
Their slave no more to be,
While they would work with me
Ould Ireland's slavery,
    Soggarth aroon?

Why not her poorest man,
    Soggarth aroon,
Try and do all he can,
    Soggarth aroon,
Her commands to fulfil
Of his own heart and will,
Side by side with you still,
    Soggarth aroon?

Loyal and brave to you,
    Soggarth aroon,
Yet be no slave to you,
    Soggarth aroon,—
Nor, out of fear to you,
Stand up so near to you—
Och! out of fear to *you!*
    Soggarth aroon!

Who, in the winter's night,
    Soggarth aroon,
When the cowld blast did bite,
    Soggarth aroon,
Came to my cabin-door,
And, on my earthen-flure
Knelt by me, sick and poor,
    Soggarth aroon?

* Priest dear.

SOGGARTH AROON.—*Continued.*

Who, on the marriage-day,
    Soggarth aroon,
Made the poor cabin gay,
    Soggarth aroon—
And did both laugh and sing,
Making our hearts to ring,
At the poor christening,
    Soggarth aroon?

Who, as friend only met,
    Soggarth aroon,
Never did flout me yet,
    Soggarth aroon?
And when my hearth was dim,
Gave, while his eye did brim,
What I should give to him,
    Soggarth aroon?

——o——

ROBIN ADAIR.

WHAT'S this dull town to me? Robin's not near.
What was't I wished to see? what wished to hear?
Where's all the joy and mirth made this town heaven on earth?
Oh! they're all fled with thee, Robin Adair!

What made the assembly shine? Robin Adair!
What made the ball so fine? Robin was there!
What, when the play was o'er, what made my heart so sore?
Oh! it was parting with Robin Adair!

But now thou'rt cold to me, Robin Adair!
But now thou'rt cold to me, Robin Adair!
Yet he I loved so well, still in my heart shall dwell!
Oh! I can ne'er forget Robin Adair.

COLLEEN RUE.

As I roved out one summer's morning, speculating most cu-
    riously,
To my surprise, I soon espied, a charming fair one approaching
    me ;
I stood awhile in deep meditation, contemplating what
    should I do,
But recruiting all my sensations, I thus accosted the Colleen
    Rue :—

Are you Aurora, or the beauteous Flora, Euterpasia, or Venus
    bright,
Or Helen fair, beyond compare, that Paris stole from her
    Grecian's sight,
Thou fairest creature, you have enslaved me, I am intoxicated
    by Cupid's clue,
Whose golden notes and infatuation, deranged my ideas for
    you—Colleen Rue.

Kind sir, be easy, and do not tease me, with your false praise
    so jestingly,
Your dissimulations and invitations, your fantastic praises,
    seducing me,
I am not Aurora, or the beauteous Flora, but a rural maiden
    to all men's view,
That's here condoling my situation, and my appellation is the
    Colleen Rue.

Was I Hector, that noble victor, who died a victim of Grecian
    skill,
Or was I Paris, whose deeds were various, as an arbitrator
    on Ida's hill,
I would roam through Asia, likewise Arabia, through Pennsyl-
    vania seeking you,
The burning regions, like famed Vesuvius, for one embrace of
    the Colleen Rue.

Sir, I am surprised and dissatisfied, at your tantalizing inso-
    lence,
I am not so stupid, or enslaved by Cupid, as to be duped by
    your eloquence ;
Therefore desist from your solicitations, I am engaged, I
    declare 'tis true,
To a lad I love, beyond all earthly treasures, and he'll soon
    embrace his Colleen Rue.

———o———

THE FOUR-LEAVED SHAMROCK.

SAMUEL LOVER.

A four-leaved Shamrock is of such rarity that it is supposed to endue the find-
er with magic power.

I'LL seek a four-leaved Shamrock in all the fairy dells,
And if I find the charmed leaves, oh, how I'll weave my
    spells !
I would not waste my magic might on diamond, pearl, or gold,
For treasure tires the weary sense,—such triumph is but cold ;
But I would play the enchanter's part, in casting bliss
    around,—
Oh ! not a tear nor aching heart should in the world be found.

To worth I would give honor !—I'd dry the mourner's tears,
And to the pallid lip recall the smile of happier years ;
And hearts that had been long estrang'd, and friends that had
    grown cold,
Should meet again—like parted streams—and mingle as of old !
Oh! thus I'd play the enchanter's part, thus scatter bliss
    around,
And not a tear nor aching heart should in the world be found !

The heart that had been mourning o'er vanish'd dreams of
    love
Should see them all returning,—like Noah's faithful dove,
And Hope should launch her blessed bark on Sorrow's dark'n-
    ing sea,
And Mis'ry's children have an Ark, and saved from sinking be ;
Oh! thus I'd play the enchanter's part, thus scatter bliss
    around,
And not a tear nor aching heart should in the world be found.

THE PRETTY GIRL MILKING HER COW.

PRETTY GIRL MILKING HER COW.

'TWAS on a bright morning in summer,
I first heard his voice spakin' low,
As he said to a colleen beside me :
"Who's that purty girl milking her cow?"
Oh! many times afther ye met me,
An' vowed that I always should be
Your darlin' a Cushla, Alanna Mavourneen.
A Suilish Machree.

I haven't the manners or graces
Of the girls in the world where ye move,
I haven't their beautiful faces—
But oh! I've a heart that can love :
If it plaise ye, I'll dress me in satin,
An' jewels I'll put on my brow—
But, oh! don't be afther forgettin'
Your purty girl milking her cow.

——o——

I BREATHE ONCE MORE MY NATIVE AIR.

I BREATHE once more my native air,
    And hail each happy, happy scene,
That rises round me everywhere,
    As tho' I left but yester e'en.

CHORUS.—Oh! how I love thee Erin dear—
        When roaming on a foreign strand,
    In fancy still my steps were here—
        Home of my heart, my native land!
    In fancy still my steps were here,
        Home of my heart, my native land!

I've found the home so fondly sought,
    And weep—but these are joyous tears!
The rapture of a moment bought
    My long and weary absent years.
        Oh! how I love thee, &c.

PADDY HAGERTY'S OLD LEATHER BREECHES.

AT the sign of the Bell, on the road to Clonmel,
  Paddy Hagerty kept a nate shebeen:
He sold pig's-meat and bread, and had a fine lodging bed,
  And so well liked round had he been.
Himself and his wife, they struggled through life:
  On week days, Pat mended the ditches,
But on Sunday he dressed in a coat of the best,
  But his pride was his old Leather Breeches.

For twenty-one years or so, it appears
  His father these breeches had run in,
The night that he died, to his bed-side
  Called Paddy, his beautiful son, in.
The advice that he gave, ere he went to his grave,
  Was for him to take care of his riches ;
Says he : " It's no use to walk in my shoes,
  But I pray you jump into my Breeches."

Last winter's snow laid provisions low,
  That Paddy was ate out completely,
And the snow coming down, he could not get to town,
  So the hunger bothered him greatly,
One night as he lay dreaming away
  Of big dogs, frogs and witches,
He heard an uproar just outside of his door,
  And got up for to pull on his Breeches.

Says Brian McGurk, with the voice of a Turk:
  " Now, Paddy, come get us some eating,"
Says big Andy Moore: " I'll burst open the door:
  For, this is no night to be waiting."
Just as they spoke, the door in was broke,
  They crowded round Paddy like leeches,
They swore by Magog, that if he did not get them prog,
  That they would eat him right out of his Breeches.

PADDY HAGERTY'S OLD LEATHER BREECHES.

Continued.

Paddy in dread slipped into bed,
  That held Judy, his own darling wife, in,
Where he quickly agreed for to get them a feed,
  And he out and brought a big knife in.
He took up the waist of his breeches, the beast,
  And cut off the buttons and stitches,
Then cut them in stripes, by the way, they were tripes.
  And he boiled them his old Leather Breeches.

When the Breeches were stewed, on a dish they were strewed,
  The boys all cried out---Lord-be-thanked!
But Hagerty's wife, in dread of her life,
  She thought it high time for to shank it :
The boys they all smiled : for, they thought Pat had boiled
  Some mutton or beef of the richest ;
But little they knew it was leather burgoo,
  Made of Paddy's oid worn-out Breeches.

They walloped the stuff; says Darby ; " It's tough."
  Says Pat : " You're no judge of good mutton."
When Briny McGurk, on the point of a fork,
  Lifted up a big ivory button.
Says Andy ; " What's that? I thought it was fat."
  Brian jumps on his legs, and he screeches :
" By the powers above ! I'm striving to shove
  My teeth through the flap of his Breeches."

They all made at Pat, he was gone out of that ;
  For, he ran when he saw them all rising.
Says Darby ; " Make haste, and go for the priest
  By the holy jack-straws! I am poisoned."
In revenge for the joke, they up and they broke
  All the chairs, tables, and dishes ;
And ever since that night, they'll knock out your day light,
  If they catch you with the old Leather Breeches.

JOHNNY, I HARDLY KNEW YE.

WHEN on the road to old Athy, ahoo,
The harvest moon was in the sky;
I heard a dolorous damsel cry:
Och! Johnny, I hardly knew ye!

CHORUS.

Wid drums and guns, and guns and drums,
The enemy fairly slew ye;
My darling dear, you look so queer;
Och! Johnny, I hardly knew ye!

Where is your nose, ye pitiful crow, ahoo?
Ye had it when ye went to scatter the foe;
The loss of it has disfigured ye so:
Och! Johnny, I hardly knew ye!

CHORUS.

Where is your eye that looked so wild, ahoo,
When my poor heart ye first beguiled?
Why did you skedaddle from me and the child?
Och! Johnny, I hardly knew ye!

CHORUS.

It broke my heart to see you sail, ahoo,
And seeing ye here would raise a wail,
The cut in your head would embellish a tale—
Och! Johnny, I hardly knew ye!

CHORUS.

Yez haven't an arm and yez haven't a leg,
Ye're an eyeless, noseless, chickenless egg;
Ye'll have to be put with a bowl to beg;
Och! Johnny, I hardly knew ye!

CHORUS.

But sad as it is to see you so, ahoo,
And to think of you now as an object of woe;
Your Peggy will still keep you on as her beau,
Though, Johnny, I hardly knew ye.

CHORUS.

O'DONNELL ABU!

A. D. 1597—By. M. J. M'CANN. ESQ.

PROUDLY the note of the trumpet is sounding,
  Loudly the war-cries arise on the gale,
Fleetly the steed by Lough Swilly is bounding,
  To join the thick squadrons in Saimear's green vale.
      On, every mountaineer,
      Strangers to flight and fear!
    Rush to the standard of dauntless Red Hugh!
      Bonaght and Gallowglass
      Throng from each mountain-pass!
On for old Erin—O'Donnell abu!

Princely O'Neill to our aid is advancing,
  With many a chieftain and warrior-clan:
A thousand proud steeds in his vanguard are prancing,
  'Neath the borders brave from the banks of the Bann—
      Many a heart shall quail
      Under its coat of mail:
    Deeply the merciless foeman shall rue,
      When on his ear shall ring,
      Borne on the breeze's wing,
Tyrconnell's dread war-cry—O'Donnell abu!

Wildly o'er Desmond the war-wolf is howling,
  Fearless the eagle sweeps over the plain,
The fox in the streets of the city is prowling—
  All, all who would scare them are banished or slain!
      Grasp, every stalwart hand,
      Hackbut and battle-brand—
    Pay them all back the deep debt so long due:
      Norris and Clifford well
      Can of Tyrconnell tell—
Onward to glory—O'Donnell abu!

Sacred the cause that Clan-Conaill's defending—
  The altars we kneel at, and homes of our sires:
Ruthless the ruin the foe is extending—
  Midnight is red with the plunderer's fires!

O'DONNELL ABU.—*Continued.*

On, with O'Donnell, then!
Fight the old fight again,
Sons of Tyrconnell all valiant and true!
Make the false Saxon feel
Erin's avenging steel!
Strike for your country!—O'Donnell abu!

———o———

NED OF THE HILL.

By Samuel Lover.

Dark is the evening, and silent the hour,
Who is the minstrel by yonder lone tower?
His harp all so tenderly touching with skill;
Oh, who should it be, but Ned of the Hill?
Who sings, " lady love, come to me now,
Come and live merrily under the bough,
    And I'll pillow thy head,
    Where the fairies tread,
If thou wilt but wed with Ned of the Hill!"

Ned of the Hill has no castle nor hall,
Nor spearmen nor bowmen to come at his call;
But one little archer, of exquisite skill,
Has shot a bright shaft for Ned of the Hill,
Who sings, " lady love, come to me now,
Come and live merrily under the bough,
    And I'll pillow thy head,
    Where the fairies tread,
If thou wilt but wed with Ned of the Hill!"

'Tis hard to escape from that fair lady's bower,
For high is the window, and guarded the tower;
" But there's always a *way* where there is a *will*,"
So Ellen is off with Ned of the Hill!
Who sings, "lady love, thou art mine now!
We will live merrily under the bough,
    And I'll pillow thy head,
    Where the fairies tread,
For Ellen is wed to Ned of the Hill!"

THE IRISH STRANGER.

O, PITY the fate of a poor wretched creature,
That has wander'd thus far from his home,
I sigh for protection from want, woe, and danger,
But I know not which way for to roam;
I ne'er shall return to Hibernia's green bowers,
Where tyranny has trampled our sweetest of flowers,
They gave comfort to me in my loneliest hour,
But they're gone—I shall ne'er see them more.

With wonder I gaz'd on that high, lofty mountain,
As in grandeur it rose from its lord,
And with sorrow beheld my own garden yielding
The choicest of fruits for its board.
But where is my father's low cottage of clay,
Where I've spent many a long happy day?
Alas! has his lordship contriv'd it away?
Yes, 'tis gone—I shall ne'er see it more.

When the sloe and the berry hung ripe on the bushes,
I have gather'd them off without harm,
And I've gone to the fields where I've seen the green bushes,
Preparing for winter's cold storm;
I have sat by the fire on a cold winter's night,
Along with my friends, telling tales of delight,
Those days gave me pleasure, and I could invite,
But they're gone—I shall ne'er see them more.

O! Erin, sad Erin, it grieves me to ponder,
The wrongs of thine injured Isle,
Thy sons, many thousands, deploring do wander,
On shores far away, in exile.
But give me the power to cross o'er the main,
America might yield me some shelter from pain,
I'm only lamenting while here I remain,
For the joys I shall never see more.

THE IRISH STRANGER.—*Continued.*

Farewell, men of Erin, and those I left weeping
Upon this disconsolate shore,
Farewell to the grave where my father lies sleeping :
That ground I still dearly adore.
Farewell to each pleasure—I once had a home,
Farewell—now a stranger in England I roam,
O give me my freedom, or give me my tomb,
Friends, in pity—I'll ask for no more.

———o———

THE DAWNING OF THE DAY.

AT early dawn I once had been
   Where Lene's * blue waters flow,
When summer bid the groves be green,
   The lamp of light to glow—
As on by bower, and town, and tower,
   And wide-spread fields I stray,
I meet a maid in the greenwood shade,
   At the dawning of the day.

Her feet and beauteous head were bare,
   No mantle fair she wore,
But down her waist fell golden hair
   That swept the tall grass o'er ;
With milking-pail she sought the vale,
   And bright her charms' display,
Outshining far the morning star,
   At the dawning of the day !

Beside me sat that maid divine,
   Where grassy banks outspread—
" Oh, let me call thee ever mine,
   Dear maid," I sportive said.
" False man, for shame, why bring me blame?"
   She cried, and burst away—
The sun's first light pursued her flight,
   At the dawning of the day !

* *Lene,* Killarney.

GOD SAVE IRELAND.

HIGH upon the gallows tree,
Swung the noble-hearted three,
By the vengeful tyrant stricken in their bloom.
But they meet him face to face,
With the spirit of their race,
And they went with souls undaunted to their doom.
God save Ireland! said the heroes,
God save Ireland! said they all,
Whether on the scaffold high,
Or the battle field we die,
Oh! what matter, when for Erin dear we fall!

Girt around with cruel foes,
Still their courage proudly rose,
For they thought of hearts that loved them far and near.
Of the millions true and brave,
O'er the ocean's swelling wave.
And the friends in holy Ireland, ever dear.
God save Ireland! said they proudly,
God save Ireland! said they all,
Whether on the scaffold high,
Or the battle field we die,
Oh! what matter, when for Erin dear we fall!

Climb they up the rugged stair,
Rung their voices out in prayer,
Then, with England's fatal cord around them cast,
Close beneath the gallows tree,
Kissed like brothers lovingly,
True to home, and faith, and freedom to the last.
God save Ireland! said they proudly,
God save Ireland! said they all,
Whether on the scaffold high,
Or the battle field we die,
Oh! what matter, when for Erin dear we fall!

"God Save Ireland!"

GOD SAVE IRELAND.—*Continued.*

Never till the latest day,
  Shall the memory pass away,
Of the gallant lives thus given for our land ;
  But on the cause must go,
  Amidst joy, or weal or woe,
Till we've made our isle a nation, free and grand.
    God save Ireland ! say we proudly,
    God save Ireland ! say we all,
    If upon the scaffold high,
    Or the battle field we die,
Oh ! what matter, when for Erin dear we fall !

———o———

THE BOYS OF KILKENNY.

Air, " Meeting of the Waters."

OH ! the boys of Kilkenny are nate roving blades,
And whenever they meet with the dear little maids,
They kiss them, and coax them, and spend their money free ;
Oh ! of all towns in Ireland, Kilkenny for me.
          Oh ! of all towns, &c.

Through the town of Kilkenny there runs a clear strame,
In the town of Kilkenny there lives a fair dame,
Her cheeks are like roses—and her lips much the same—
Or a dish of ripe strawberries smothered in crame.
          Or a dish, &c.

Her eyes are as black as Kilkenny's famed coal,
And 'tis they through my heart have burnt a big hole ;
Her mind, like its river, is deep, clear, and pure,
But her heart is more hard than its marble I'm sure.
          But her heart, &c.

Oh ! Kilkenny's a fine town that shines where it stands,
And the more I think on it the more my heart warms ;
If I was in Kilkenny I'd feel quite at home,
For it's there I'd get sweethearts, but here I get none.
          For its there, &c.

THE WEXFORD HEROES.

COME, all you warriors and renowned nobles,
  Give ear, I pray, to my warlike theme;
And I will sing how Father Murphy
  Lately aroused from his sleepy dream.

Sure Julius Cæsar, nor Alexander,
  Nor brave king Arthur ever equalled him;
For armies formidable he did conquer,
  Though with two gunsmen he did begin.
Camolin cavalry he did unhorse them;
  Their first lieutenant he cut him down:
With shattered ranks, and with broken columns,
  They retreated home to Camolin town.

On the hill of Oulart, he displayed his valor,
  Where a hundred Corkmen lay on the plain;
At Enniscorthy his sword he wielded,
  And I hope he'll do it once more again.
The loyal townsmen gave their assistance;
  " We'll die or conquer," they all did say:
The yeoman cavalry made no resistance,
  For on the pavement their corpses lay:

When Enniscorthy became subject to him,
  'Twas then to Wexford we marched our men,
It's on the Three Rocks we took up our quarters,
  Waiting for daylight the town to win:
With drums a-beating the town did echo,
  And acclamations from door to door:
On the Windmill hill we pitched our tents,
  And we drank like heroes, but paid no score.

On Corrig-Rua for some time we waited,
  And next for Gorey we did repair;
At Tubberneering, we thought no harm,
  The bloody army was waiting there.

THE WEXFORD HEROES.—*Continued.*

The issue of it was a close engagement,
   While on the soldiers we played warlike pranks:
Through sheep-walks, hedge-rows, and shady thickets,
   There were mangled bodies and broken ranks.

The shuddering cavalry, I can't forget them;
   We raised the brushes on their helmets straight;
They turned about, and they bid for Dublin,
   As if they ran for a ten pound plate.
Some crossed Donnybrook, and more through Blackrock,
   And some up Shank-hill without wound or flaw,
And if Barry Lawless be not a liar,
   There's more went grousing up Luggielaw.

The streets of England were left quite naked
   Of all its army both foot and horse;
The Highlands of Scotland were left unguarded,
   Likewise the Hessians, the seas they crossed.
To the Windmill hill of Enniscorthy,
   The British fencibles they flew like deers;
And our ranks were tattered and sorely scattered,
   By the loss of Kyan and the Shelmaliers.

But if the Frenchmen they had reinforced us,
   Landed their transports in Bagenbun,
Father John Murphy would be their seconder,
   And sixteen thousand along with him come:
Success attend the sweet county Wexford,
   Threw off its yoke, and to battle run:
Let them not think we gave up our arms,
   For every man has a pike or gun.

THE EMIGRANT'S FAREWELL TO BALLYSHANNON.

ADIEU to Ballyshannon, where I was bred and born;
Go where I may, I'll think of you, as sure as night and morn;
The kindly spot, the friendly town, where every one is known,
And not a face in all the place but partly seems my own.
There's not a house or window, there's not a field or hill,
But East or West, in foreign lands, I'll recollect thee still;
I leave my warm heart with you, though my back I'm forced
      to turn,
So adieu to Ballyshannon and the winding banks of Erne.

No more on pleasant evenings we'll saunter down the Mall,
When the trout is rising to the fly, the salmon to the fall:
The boat comes straining on the net, and heavily she creeps,
Cast off! cast off! she feels the oars, and to her berth she
      sweeps;
Now stem and stern keep hawling, and gathering up the clue,
Till a silver wave of salmon rolls in among the crew;
Then they may sit and have their joke, and set their pipes to
      burn.
Adieu to Ballyshannon and the winding banks of Erne.

The music of the waterfall, the mirror of the tide,
When all the green hill'd harbor is full from side to side,
From Portnason to Ballybawns, and round the Abbey Bay;
From the little rocky island to Coolnargit's sandhills gray,
While far upon the southern line, to guard it like a wall,
The Leitrim mountains clothed in blue, gaze calmly over all;
And watch the ship sail up and down, the red flag at her
      stern,
Adieu to those, adieu to all, the winding banks of Erne.

Farewell to you, Kildoney lads, and them that pull the oar;
A lug-sail set, or haul a net, from the Point to Mullaghmore:
From Killybegs to Carrigan, with its ocean mountain steep,
Six hundred yards in air aloft, six hundred in the deep:
From Dooran to the Fairy Bridge, and round by Tullan strand,
Level and long, and white with waves, where gull and curlew
      stand,
Head out to sea, when on the lea, the breakers you discern,
Adieu to all the billowy coast and winding banks of Erne.

THE WINDING BANKS OF ERNE.

THE EMIGRANT'S FAREWELL TO BALLYSHANNON.

Continued.

Farewell to you, Bundoran and the summer crowds that run
From inland homes to see with joy the Atlantic's setting sun ;
To breath the buoyant, salted air, and sport among the
  waves ;
To gather shells on sandy beach, and tempt the gloomy
  caves :
To watch the flowing, ebbing tide—the boats, the crabs, the
  fish :
Young men and maids to meet and smile, and form a tender
  wish ;
The sick and old in search of health—for all things have their
  turn,
And I must quit my native shore and the winding banks of
  Erne.

Farewell to every white cascade, from the harbor to Belleek,
And every pool where fins may rest, and ivy-shaded creek :
The sloping fields, the lofty rocks, where ash and holly grow ;
The one split yew-tree gazing on the curving flood below ;
The lough that winds through islands, under Skean Mountain
  green ;
The Castle Caldwell's stretching woods, with tranquil bays
  between ;
And Breesie Hill and many a pond, among the heath and fern.
For I must say, adieu, adieu, to the winding banks of Erne.

The thrush will call through Camlin grove the live long sum-
  mer day,
The waters run by mossy cliff and bank with wild flowers
  gay :
The girls will bring their work, and sing beneath the twisted
  thorn,
Or stray with sweethearts down the path among the growing
  corn :
Along the river side they go, where I had often been ;
Oh! never shall I see again the days I once have seen,
A thousand chances are to one I never may return,
Adieu to Ballyshannon, and the winding banks of Erne.

THE EMIGRANT'S FAREWELL TO BALLYSHANNON.

Continued.

Now measure from the Commons down to each end of the Purt,
From the Red Barn to the Abbey, I wish no one any hurt ;
Search through the streets, and down the Mall and out to
              Portnason,
If any foes of mine are there, I pardon every one,
I hope that man and woman kind will do the same with me,
For my head is sore and heavy at voyaging the sea ;
My loving friends I'll bear in mind, and often fondly turn,
To think of Ballyshannon, and the winding banks of Erne.

Adieu to evening dances, where merry neighbors meet,
And the fiddle says to boys and girls, " Get up and shake your
              feet ;"
To *Shanachus* and wise old talk of Erin's days gone by,
Who trenched the rath on such a hill, and where the bones do
              lie
Of saint, or king, or warrior chief, with tales of fairy power,
And tender ditties sweetly sung, to pass the twilight hour,
The mournful song of exile is now for me to learn :
Adieu my dear companions on the winding banks of Erne.

If ever I'm a moneyed man, I mean, please God, to cast
My golden anchor in the place where youthful years were
              passed,
Though heads that now are black or brown must meanwhile
              gather gray ;
New faces rise by every hearth, and old ones pass away,
Yet dearer still that Irish hill than all the world beside—
It's home, sweet home, where'er I roam, through lands and
              waters wide ;
And, if the Lord allows me, I surely will return,
To my native Ballyshannon, and the winding banks of Erne.

THE EXILE OF ERIN.

There came to the beach a poor Exile of Erin,
    The dew on his thin robe was heavy and chill ;
For his country he sighed, when at twilight repairing
    To wander alone by the wind-beaten hill :
But the day-star attracted his eyes' sad devotion,
For it rose o'er his own native isle of the ocean,
Where once in the fire of his youthful emotion,
    He sang the bold anthem of "Erin go bragh."

" Sad is my fate," said the heart-broken stranger ;
    " The wild deer and wolf to a covert can flee ;
But I have no refuge from famine and danger,
    A home and a country remain not to me.
Never again in the green sunny bowers,
Where my forefathers lived, shall I spend the sweet hours,
Or cover my harp with the wild-woven flowers,
    And strike to the numbers of ' Erin go bragh.'

Erin, my country, tho' sad and forsaken,
    In dreams I revisit thy sea-beaten shore,
But, alas! in a far foreign land I awaken,
    And sigh for the friends who can meet me no more.
Oh cruel fate ! wilt thou never replace me
In a mansion of peace—where no perils can chase me ?
Never again shall my brothers embrace me !
    They died to defend me, or live to deplore !

Where is my cabin door, fast by the wild wood ?
    Sisters and sire, did you weep for its fall ?
Where is the mother that look'd on my childhood ?
    Where is the bosom-friend, dearer than all ?
Oh! my sad heart! long abandon'd by pleasure,
Why did it dote on a fast-fading treasure,
Tears, like the rain-drops, may fall without measure,
    But rapture and beauty they cannot recall.

THE EXILE OF ERIN.—*Continued.*

Yet, all its sad recollections suppressing,
 One dying wish my lone bosom can draw:
Erin! an exile bequeaths thee his blessing!
 Land of my forefathers! Erin go bragh!
Buried and cold, when my heart stills her motion,
Green be thy fields,—sweetest isle of the ocean,
And thy harp-striking bards sing aloud with devotion,
 Erin, ma vourneen! Erin go bragh!*

———o———

DUBLIN BAY—OR ROY NEILL.

They sailed away, in a gallant bark,
 Roy Neill and his fair young bride:
He had ventured all in that bounding ark,
 That danced o'er the silvery tide.
But his heart was young, and his spirit light,
 And he dashed the tear away,
As he watched the shore recede from sight,
 Of his own Sweet Dublin Bay.

Three days they sailed, and a storm arose,
 And the lightning swept the deep,
And the thunder-crash broke the short repose
 Of the weary sea-boys' sleep.
Roy Neill, he clasped his weeping bride,
 And he kissed her tears away—
"Oh! love, 'twas a fatal hour," she cried,
 " When we left Sweet Dublin Bay!"

On the crowded deck of the doomed ship
 Some stood in their mute despair:
And some, more calm, with a holy lip,
 Sought the God of the storm in prayer.
" She has struck on a rock!" the seamen cried,
 In the breath of their wild dismay—
And the ship went down, and the fair young bride,
 That sailed from Dublin Bay!

*Ireland, my darling! Ireland for ever!

THE MAID OF SWEET GORTEIN.

COME all you gentle muses, combine and lend an ear
Whilst I unfold the praises, of a comely lady fair,
The curling of her yellow locks, that stole away my heart,
And death I'm sure will be the cure, if she and I do part.

The praises of this lovely maid, I'm going to unfold,
Her hair hangs over her shoulders bare, like lovely links
of gold,
With a carriage neat, and limbs complete, which fractured
quite my brain,
Her skin more fairer than the swan, that swims on the parting
stream.

It was my cruel father, that caused all my woe,
He lock'd her in a close room, and would not let her go,
Her windows I did fairly watch, thinking she might be seen,
In hopes to get another sight of the maid of sweet Gortein.

My father, he came to me, and unto me did say,
Oh! son, oh! son, be advised by one, don't throw yourself
away,
To marry a poor servant girl, whose parents are so mean;
So stay at home, and do not roam, but alone with me remain.

Oh! father—dearest father, don't part me from my dear,
I would not part my darling girl, for ten thousand pounds a
year.
Was I possessed of William's crown, I would make her my
queen,
In high renown, to wear the crown, with the maid of sweet
Gortein.

My father in a passion flew, and unto me did say,
If that's the case, within this place, no longer she shall stay;
Mark what I say, from this very day, her face you never shall see,
I'll send her to some lonesome place, some place that's far away.

In two or three days after, a horse he did prepare,
He sent my darling far from me, to a place I know not where,
I may go to view my darling's house, where oft times she
has been,
But here in pain, I still remain, for the maid of sweet Gortein.

THE MAID OF SWEET GORTEIN.—*Continued.*

Now to conclude and make an end, I'll take my pen in hand,
John O'Brien is my name, and flowery is my land ;
My days are spent in merriment, since my darling I've first seen,
But her abode was near the road, in a place call'd sweet
        Gortein.

——o——

KATHLEEN O'MORE.

My love, still I think that I see her once more :
But, alas! she has left me her loss to deplore,
My own little Kathleen, my poor lost Kathleen,
              My Kathleen O'More.

Her hair glossy black, her eyes were dark blue,
Her color still changing, her smiles ever new :
So pretty was Kathleen, my sweet little Kathleen,
              My Kathleen O'More.

She milked the dun cow that ne'er offered to stir,
Though wicked to others, it was gentle to her ;
So kind was my Kathleen, my poor little Kathleen,
              My Kathleen O'More.

She sat by the door, one cold afternoon,
To hear the wind blow, and look at the moon,
So pensive was Kathleen, my poor little Kathleen,
              My Kathleen O'More.

Oh! cold was the night breeze that sighed round her bower,
It chilled my poor Kathleen, she drooped from that hour,
And I lost my poor Kathleen, my dear little Kathleen,
              My Kathleen O'More.

The bird of all birds that I love the best,
Is the robin that in the church-yard builds its nest :
For, he seems to watch Kathleen, hops lightly on Kathleen,
              My Kathleen O'More.

THE STAR OF SLANE.

You brilliant muses, who ne'er refuses,
   But still infuses in the poet's mind,
Your kind sweet favors to his poor endeavors,
   If his ardent labors but appear sublime.
Preserve my study from getting muddy,
   My ideas ready to inspire my brain,
My quill refine whilst I write these lines,
   On a nymph divine, called the Star of Slane.

In beautious spring, when the warblers sing,
   And their music rings thro' each silent grove,
Bright Sol did shine which did me incline,
   By the river Boyne for to go to rove.
I was contemplating and meditating,
   And ruminating as I paced the plain ;
When a charming fair one beyond compare,
   Did my heart ensnare, near the town of Slane.

Had Paris seen this young maid serene,
   The Grecian Queen he would soon disdain,
And straight embrace this virgin chaste,
   And peace would grace the Trojan plain.
If great Julius Cæsar would on her gaze, sir,
   He'd stand amazed for to view the dame.
Sweet Cleopather he would freely part her,
   And his crown he'd barter for the Star of Slane.

To praise her beauty, it is my duty,
   But alas, I'm footy in this noble part,
And to my sorrow, sly Cupid's arrow
   Full deep did burrow in my tender heart.
In pain and trouble, I still will struggle,
   Tho' sadly hobbled by my stupid brain,
Yet backed by nature, I will tell the features
   Of this lovely creature, called the Star of Slane.

Her eyes, 'tis true, are an azure blue,
   And her cheeks, the hue of the crimson rose;
Her hair, behold, does shine like gold,
   In fine flowing rolls it so nicely grows.

THE STAR OF SLANE.—*Continued.*

Her skin as white, as the snow by night,
  Straight and upright is her portly frame,
The chaste Diana, or fair Susanna,
  Are eclipsed in grandeur by the Star of Slane.

Her name to mention, might cause contention,
  And its my intention for to breed no strife,
But for to woo her, as I'm but pooer,
  Really I'm sure she won't be my wife;
In silent anguish I here must languish,
  Till time does banish my love-sick pain,
And my humble station I must bear with patience,
  Since great exaltation suits the Star of Slane.

———o———

MATILDE HERON'S CELTIC SONG.

COME to me, darling, I'm lonely without thee,
Come in the twilight when day's gone to rest ;
No rude eye shall witness me twining about thee,
As fondly I pillow thy head on my breast.
    Then come to me, darling, nor doubt I am true :
    For, my heart is but happy while thinking of you.

Come in the midnight, that procreant hour
When soul blends with soul in love's starlight bower :
When linked in long sweetness of exquisite bliss,
We murmur : good-night ! in a sweet, silent kiss.
    Then come to me, darling, nor doubt I am true :
    For, my heart is but happy while thinking of you.

Come in the twilight, or midnight, or day :
It's only my darkness when thou art away—
Then come to me, sweetheart, I languish, I pine
For one little smile to say : " Yes, I am thine ! "
    Then come to me, darling, nor doubt I am true :
    For, my heart is but happy while thinking of you.

THE BOYNE WATER.

JULY the first, of a morning clear, one thousand six hundred
    and ninety,
King William did his men prepare, of thousands he had thirty;
To fight King James and all his foes, encamped near the
    Boyne Water,
He little feared, though two to one, their multitudes to scatter.

King William called his officers; saying, "Gentlemen, mind
    your station,
And let your valor here be shown, before this Irish nation;
My brazen walls let no man break, and your subtle foes
    you'll scatter,
Be sure you show them good English play, as you go over
    the water."

    *   *   *   *   *   *

Both foot and horse they marched on, intending them to
    batter,
But the brave Duke Schomberg he was shot as he crossed
    over the water.
When that King William he observ'd the brave Duke
    Schomberg falling,
He rein'd his horse, with a heavy heart, on the Enniskil-
    leners calling ;

"What will you do for me, brave boys, see yonder men re-
    treating,
Our enemies encouraged are—and English drums are beat-
    ing;"
He says, "My boys, feel no dismay at the losing of one
    commander,
For God shall be our King this day, and I'll be general
    under."

    *   *   *   *   *   *   *   *

Within four yards of our fore-front, before a shot was fired,
A sudden snuff they got that day, which little they desired;
For horse and man fell to the ground, and some hung in
    their saddles,
Others turn'd up their forked ends, which we call coup de
    ladle.

THE BOYNE WATER.—*Continued.*

Prince Eugene's regiment was the next, on our right hand
    advanced,
Into a field of standing wheat, where Irish horses pranced—
But the brandy ran so in their heads, their senses all did
    scatter,
They little thought to leave their bones that day at the
    Boyne Water.

——o——

I LOVE MY LOVE IN THE MORNING.

GERALD GRIFFIN.

I LOVE my love in the morning
  For she like morn is fair,—
Her blushing cheek, its crimson streak,
  Its clouds, her golden hair.
Her glance, its beam, so soft and kind ;
  Her tears, its dewy showers ;
And her voice, the tender whispering wind
  That stirs the early bowers.

I love my love in the morning,
  I love my love at noon,
For she is bright, as the lord of light,
  Yet mild as autumn's moon :
Her beauty is my bosom's sun,
  Her faith my fostering shade,
And I will love my darling one,
  Till even the sun shall fade.

I love my love in the morning,
  I love my love at even ;
Her smile's soft play is like the ray,
  That lights the western heaven :
I loved her when the sun was high,
  I loved her when he rose ;
But, best of all when evening's sigh
  Was murmuring at its close.

THE BANKS OF CLODY.

DOWN by the banks of Clody I heard a maid complain,
Making sad lamentations for her false-hearted swain;
She says, " I'm deeply wounded, bound in the chain of love.
By a false-hearted young man who does inconstant prove."
I straightway stepped up to her, and put her in surprise;
I own she did not know me, I being in disguise.
I said, " My dearest jewel, my joy, and heart's delight,
How far have you to travel this dark and rainy night?"

Said she, " 'Tis too much freedom for to accost me so,
But as you have heard my secret, I'll also let you know—
I seek a faithless young man—young Johnny is his name—
And its on the banks of Clody I'm told he does remain."
" But don't depend on Johnny, he is a false young man;
Do not depend on Johnny, he will not meet you here;
But come with me to Green wood, no danger need you fear."

" If Johnny he was here to night, he'd keep me from all harm;
He's in the field of battle all in his uniform.
He's in the field of battle, and his foes he does defy,
Like the *rolling* king of honor, going to the wars of Troy.
Bould Sarsfield was not braver when Erin he did guard,
And when the war is over, his king will him reward;
He's crossing the main ocean for honor and for fame."
" No, no, fair maid, his ship was wrecked going by the coast
        of Spain."

When she heard that dreadful news she fell into despair,
A wringing of her hands, and a tearing of her hair;
" Since Johnny he is *drowned*, no man alive I'll take,
Through woods and lonesome valleys I'll wander for his sake."
So when he saw her loyalty, he could no longer stand,
He flew unto her arms, saying, " Bessy, I'm the man;
Bessy, I'm the young man—the cause of all your pain,
And since we met on Clody's banks, we'll never part again."

SHAN VAN VOGHT.

OH, I'm told that Anglesea,*
    Says the Shan Van Voght;
Oh, I'm told that Anglesea,
    Says the Shan Van Voght;
Oh, I'm told that Anglesea,
In the House of Lords one day,
Said the Papists he would slay,
    Says the Shan Van Voght.

But faith, at Waterloo
    Says the Shan Van Voght;
But faith, at Waterloo,
    Says the Shan Van Voght;
But faith, at Waterloo,
He'd have looked very blue,
Hadn't Paddy been there too,†
    Says the Shan Van Voght.

Yet, if he needs must fight,
    Says the Shan Van Voght;
Yet, if he needs must fight,
    Says the Shan Van Voght;
Yet, if he needs must fight,
Oh, he's always in the right
To keep Erin in his sight,
    Says the Shan Van Voght.

For Pat is fond of fun,
    Says the Shan Van Voght;
For Pat is fond of fun,
    Says the Shan Van Voght;
For Pat is fond of fun,
And was never known to run
From cannon, sword, or gun,
    Says the Shan Van Voght.

* The Marquis of Anglesea. Pronounced by the ballad-singers *Ang-gla-say.*

† This was suggested by a passage in a speech of Daniel O'Connell's at that time wherein he said that the Duke of Wellington kept all his objections against the Irish for his place in Parliament ; but that he had no objection to them on the field of Waterloo.

SHAN VAN VOGHT.—*Continued.*

And though Rock, alas, is gone,
    Says the Shan Van Voght;
And though Rock, alas, is gone,
    Says the Shan Van Voght ;
And though Rock, alas, is gone ,
I'll hold you ten to one
He'd be with us here anon,
    Says the Shan Van Voght.

But no Hussar* we'll see,
    Says the Shan Van Voght;
But no Hussar we'll see,
    Says the Shan Van Voght ;
But no Hussar we'll see
For old Erin shall be free,
And " So help me God " says she,
    The Shan Van Voght.

——o——

HE TELLS ME HE LOVES ME.

He tells me he loves me, and can I believe,
The heart he has won, he would wish to deceive ?
For ever and always, his sweet words to me
Are Aileen, mavourneen, acushlamacree!

Last night when we parted, his gentle good-bye
A thousand times said, and each time with a sigh,
And still the same sweet words he whispers to me,
My Aileen, mavourneen, acushlamacree!

The friend of my childhood, the hope of my youth,
Whose heart is all pure and whose words are all truth!
Oh, still the same sweet words he whispers to me,
Are Aileen, mavourneen, acushlamacree!

Oh! when will the day come, the dear happy day,
That a maiden may hear all a lover can say,
And he speaks out the words he now whispers to me,
My Aileen, mavourneen, acushlamacree!

*The Marquis of Anglesea, it may be remembered, was famous as a Hussar \
fficer ; or, I should rather say, *it can never be forgotten.*

PEGGY BAWN.

As I wandered o'er the Highland hills, to a farmer's house I
    came,
The night being dark and very wet, I ventured into the same ;
There I was kindly treated, and a pretty lass I espied,
Who asked me if I had a wife, but marriage I then denied.

There we conversed the live long night until near the dawn
    of day,
When frankly she said to me, 'Tis along with you I'll gae ;
For Ireland is a fine country, and the Scots unto you are kin ;
So I'll e'en gae along with you my fortune for to begin.

The morn been come and breakfast o'er, to the parlor I was
    ta'en,
Where the old man asked of me if I'd marry his daughter
    Jane ;
Five hundred marks I'll gie to her, besides a good piece of
    land.
But scarcely had he spoke these words when I thought of my
    Peggy Bawn.

Your offer, sir, is very good, and I thank you too, said I ;
But I cannot be your son-in-law, and I'll tell you the reason
    why :
In my own country there is a maid, who is constant to me
    and kind,
My very heart lies in her breast, she's the fairest of woman-
    kind.

Oh, Peggy Bawn, you are my dear, and my heart lies with-
    in your breast ;
And although you at a distance are, yet I love you ten times
    the best ;
Although you at a distance are, and the seas do between us
    roar,
Yet constant, dear Peggy Bawn, I'll be, now and for ever
    more !

LOUGH ERNE'S SHORE.

IT was on a summer's day, as carelessly I strayed,
   And straight I took my way down by Lough Erne's shore,
To meet a comely maid, who has my heart betrayed,
   Her beauty has betrayed me, none else can I adore.

She's the fairest of all creatures, beautiful in features,
   Her sweet and mild behavior has enchanted me;
You muses now assist me to ease my longing wishes,
   And petition Cupid that he may set her free.

I'll make no declaration of my inclination,
   There is no one in my station, either rich or poor,
Better could maintain her, if I could but gain her,
   So love, do not disdain me, acushla gal astore.

I always will endeavor by my daily labor,
   With kind and mild behavior I'll ever you adore;
Acres I have had waiting, for you my lovely creature,
   And valleys deck'd by nature, down by Lough Erne's shore.

Sweet, charming, lovely Molly, pity your dear Johnny,
   Who daily doats upon you, astoreen gal machree;
Each night as I slumber, of you, my dear, I ponder,
   I wake in greatest wonder, and think your face I see.

Not riches I admire, but you, my heart's desire,
   And all I do require is love and loyalty!
Grant me this, astore, and I will ask no more,
   Down by Lough Erne's shore, my bride you shall be.

I am now craving, and I am always raving,
   So readers, now excuse me what here I have said;
I never will disdain him that adores a female—
   Sweet, charming, lovely Molly has my heart betray'd.

Farewell, Lough Erne's shore—adieu for evermore!
   For to some distant shore I'll go and spend my days.
It grieves me to the heart, from Lough Erne's shore to part,
   Where fishes do divert, as they do sport and play.

LOUGH ERNE'S SHORE.—*Continued.*

My love from me is gone, and I'll end my days,
  I'll rove from town to town, some pleasure for to see;
Since Molly's proved unkind, and will not change her mind,
  Some other maid I'll find, to roam along with me.

I'll go to the fair of Castlefrench, to meet a comely wench,
  I'll treat her to punch, and with her I'll agree,
And as I go along, it shall be my constant song,
  Charming lovely Molly, you have wounded me.

———o———

COME TO ME, DARLING, I'M LONELY WITHOUT THEE.

By Joseph Brennan.

COME to me, darling, I'm lonely without thee,
Day-time and night-time I'm dreaming about thee:
Night-time and day-time in dreams I behold thee,
Unwelcome the waking which ceases to fold thee—
Come to me darling, my sorrows to lighten,
Come in thy beauty to bless and to brighten:
Come in thy womanhood meekly and lowly,
Come in thy lovingness, queenly and holy.

You have been glad when you knew I was gladdened:
Dear, are you sad to hear I am saddened?
Our hearts ever answer in tune and in time, love,
As octave to octave, or rhyme unto rhyme, love:
I cannot smile, but your cheek will be glowing:
You cannot weep, but my tears will be flowing:
You will not linger when I shall have died, love:
I could not live without you by my side, love.

Come to me, darling, ere I die of my sorrow,
Rise on my gloom like the sun of to-morrow:
Strong, swift and sweet, as the words which I speak, love,
With a song on your lip, and a smile on your cheek, love;
Come—for my heart in your absence is dreary:
Haste—for my spirit is sickened and weary:
Come to the arms which alone can caress thee,
Come to the heart which is throbbing to press thee.

BRENNAN ON THE MOOR.

IT's of a famous highwayman a story I will tell;
His name was Willy Brennan, in Ireland he did dwell;
And on the Kilworth mountains he commenced his wild career,
Where many a wealthy gentleman before him shook with fear.

CHORUS:

Brennan on the Moor, Brennan on the Moor,
Bold and undaunted, stood young Brennan on the Moor.

A brace of loaded pistols he carried night and day;
He never robbed a poor man upon the king's highway;
But what he'd taken from the rich, like Turpin and black Bess,
He always did divide it with the widow in distress.
Chorus—Brennan on the Moor, &c.

One night, he robbed a packman, by the name of Pedlar Bawn,
They travelled together till the day began to dawn;
The pedlar seeing his money gone, likewise his watch and chain,
He at once encountered Brennan and robbed him back again.
Chorus—Brennan on the Moor, &c.

Now, Brennan seeing the pedlar as good a man as he,
He says, "My worthy hero, will you come along with me?"
The pedlar, being stout-hearted, he threw his pack away,
And he proved a loyal comrade until his dying day.
Chorus—Brennan on the Moor, &c.

One day, on the highway, as Willy he sat down,
He met the Mayor of Cashel a mile out-side the town;
The Mayor, he knew his features—"I think, young man," said he,
"Your name is Willy Brennan—you must come along with me."
Chorus—Brennan on the Moor, &c.

As Brennan's wife had gone to town provisions for to buy,
When she saw her Willy, she began to weep and cry;
He says, "Give me that tenpenny." As soon as Willy spoke,
She handed him a blunderbuss, from underneath her cloak.
Chorus—Brennan on the Moor, &c.

BRENNAN ON THE MOOR.—*Continued.*

Then with his loaded blunderbuss—the truth I will unfold—
He made the Mayor to tremble, and robbed him of his gold;
One hundred pounds was offered for his apprehension there,
And he, with his horse and saddle, to the mountain did repair.
Chorus—Brennan on the Moor, &c.

Then Brennan being an outlaw, upon the mountain high,
With cavalry and infantry to take him they did try;
He laughed at them with scorn, until at length, it's said,
By a false-hearted woman he basely was betrayed.
Chorus—Brennan on the Moor, &c.

In the County Tipperary, at a place they call Clonmore,
Willy Brennan and his comrade that day did suffer sore:
He lay amongst the fern, which was thick upon the field,
And nine wounds he did receive before that he did yield.
Chorus—Brennan on the Moor, &c.

Then Brennan and his companion, when they were betrayed,
They with the mounted cavalry a noble battle made;
He lost his foremost finger, which was shot off by a ball,
So Brennan and his comrade were taken after all.
Chorus—Brennan on the Moor, &c.

So they were taken prisoners, in irons they were bound,
And conveyed to Clonmel Jail, strong walls did them surround;
They were tried and found guilty—the Judge made this reply:
" For robbing on the king's highway, you're both condemned
        to die."
Chorus—Brennan on the Moor, &c.

When Brennan heard his sentence, he made this reply:
" I own that I did rob the rich, and did the poor supply;
In all the deeds that I have done I took no life away;
The Lord have mercy on my soul against the judgment day."
Chorus—Brennan on the Moor, &c.

" Farewell unto my wife, and to my children three,
Likewise my aged father—he may shed tears for me;
And to my loving mother"—who tore her gray locks and cried,
Saying, " I wish, Willy Brennan, in your cradle you had died."
Chorus—Brennan on the Moor, &c.

THE MEMORY OF THE DEAD

By Professor Ingram.

Who fears to speak of Ninety-Eight?
　Who blushes at the name?
When cowards mock the patriot's fate,
　Who hangs his head for shame?
He's all a knave, or half a slave,
　Who slights his country thus;
But a *true* man, like you, man,
　Will fill your glass with us.

We drink the memory of the brave,
　The faithful and the few—
Some lie far off beyond the wave—
　Some sleep in Ireland, too;
All—all are gone—but still lives on
　The fame of those who died—
All true men, like you, men,
　Remember them with pride.

Some on the shores of distant lands
　Their weary hearts have laid,
And by the stranger's heedless hands
　Their lonely graves were made;
But, though their clay be far away
　Beyond the Atlantic foam—
In true men, like you, men,
　Their spirit's still at home.

The dust of some is Irish earth;
　Among their own they rest;
And the same land that gave them birth
　Has caught them to her breast;
And we will pray that from their clay
　Full many a race may start
Of true men, like you, men,
　To act as brave a part.

They rose in dark and evil days
　To right their native land:
They kindled here a living blaze
　That nothing shall withstand.

THE MEMORY OF THE DEAD.—*Continued.*

Alas! that Might can vanquish Right—
　　They fell and passed away ;
But true men, like you, men,
　　Are plenty here to-day.

Then here's their memory—may it be
　　For us a guiding light,
To cheer our strife for liberty,
　　And teach us to unite.
Through good and ill, be Ireland's still,
　　Though sad as their's your fate ;
And true men, be you, men,
　　Like those of Ninety-Eight.

——o——

COME ALL YOU YOUNG FELLOWS.

Come all you young fellows that follow the gun.
Beware of late shooting at the set of the sun.
With her white apron round her she looked like a fawn,
But alas to my grief, 'twas my own Molly Bawn!

I ran to my uncle with the gun in my hand,
Saying, Uncle, dear uncle, I scarcely can stand ;
My curse on you, Tony, that lent me your gun,
To go a late shooting at the set o' the sun!

I've a story to tell you which happened of late;
I loved Molly Bawn, and her beauty was great,
But I've shot my true lover—alas, I'm undone!
While she sat in the shade at the set of the sun.

I rubbed her fair temples, and found she was dead,
And a fountain of tears for my darling I shed,
A fountain of tears there I wept bitterly,—
So soon to be married to my darling Molly!

And now I'll be forced by the laws of the land,
For killing my darling, my trial to stand,
Oh! sad was the hour when I aimed at the fawn,
And I'll mourn till I die for my dear Molly Bawn.

THE FAITHLESS BRIDE.

I WAS of late at a noble wedding,
  The bridal of one that proved unkind
To him that loved her, but was forsaken;
  But now his image filled her mind.

Gay were the guests at that noble wedding,
  And bright the beauty assembled there;
As lovely as the star of evening.
  Or moonlight through the summer air.

But there was also her slighted lover,
  That day returned from the field of fight;
Great was his anger at the false bride,
  Who should be his this wedding night.

The wedding supper was now passed over,
  And every guest was to sing a song;
The first that sung was the slighted lover;
  The words to the false bride did belong.

How can you lie on a stranger's pillow
  You that have been my love so late;
And leave me here to wear the willow,
  Pining in sorrow for your sake!

But if I wear this woful willow,
  It will only be for a month or two;
And then I'll lay aside the willow,
  And change the old love for the new.

Here is the piece of gold that was broken;
  I kept it safe in a golden chain;
You gave it to me, a true-love token;
  No more with me it shall remain.

The bride, she sat at the head of the table;
  Each word he sung she marked right well;
To bear it longer she was unable;
  Down at the bridegroom's feet she fell.

THE FAITHLESS BRIDE.—*Continued.*

A small request I have to offer,
  This request I ask of you,
That I to-night may sleep with my mother,
  To-morrow night I'll sleep by you.

This request at last was granted;
  Sighing and sobbing she went to bed;
When they woke next morning early,
  There they found the young bride dead.

Now all young maids that hear this story,
  To your vows be firm and true;
Don't be led by lands or money,
  Nor change the old love for the new.

————o————

MOLLY BAWN.

Samuel Lover.

Oh, Molly Bawn, why leave me pining,
All lonely, waiting here for you?
  While the stars above are brightly shining,
Because they've nothing else to do.
  The flowers late were open keeping,
To try a rival blush with you;
  But their mother, Nature, set them sleeping,
With their rosy faces wash'd with dew.
                    Oh, Molly Bawn, &c.

Now the pretty flowers were made to bloom, dear,
  And the pretty stars were made to shine;
And the pretty girls were made for the boys, dear,
  And may be you were made for mine;
The wicked watch-dog here is snarling,
  He takes me for a thief you see;
For he knows I'd steal you, Molly, darling,
  And then transported I should be.
                    Oh, Molly Bawn, &c.

TERENCE'S FAREWELL.

LADY DUFFERIN.

So, my Kathleen, you're going to leave me
  All alone by myself in this place,
But I'm sure you will never deceive me,
  Oh no, if there's truth in that face.
Though England's a beautiful city,
  Full of illigant boys, oh what then—
You wouldn't forget your poor Terence,
  You'll come back to ould Ireland again.

Och, those English, deceivers by nature,
  Though maybe you'd think them sincere,
They'll say you're a sweet charming creature,
  But don't you believe them, my dear.
No, Kathleen, *agra !** don't be minding
  The flattering speeches they'll make,
Just tell them a poor boy in Ireland
  Is breaking his heart for your sake.

It's a folly to keep you from going,
  Though, faith, it's a mighty hard case—
For, Kathleen, you know there's no knowing
  When next I shall see your sweet face.
And when you come back to me, Kathleen,
  None the better will I be off, then—
You'll be spaking such beautiful English,
  Sure, I won't know my Kathleen again.

Eh, now, where's the need of this hurry—
  Don't flutter me so in this way—
I've forgot 'twixt the grief and the flurry,
  Every word I was maning to say ;
Now just wait a minute, I bid ye,—
  Can I talk if ye bother me so?
Oh, Kathleen, my blessing go wid ye,
  Ev'ry inch of the way that you go.

* My love.

"I'M SITTING ON THE STILE, MARY."

" And often in those grand old woods,
I'll sit and shut my eyes."

LAMENT OF THE IRISH EMIGRANT.

LADY DUFFERIN.

I'M sittin' on the stile, Mary,
  Where we sat side by side
On a bright May mornin' long ago,
  When first you were my bride:
The corn was springin' fresh and green,
  And the lark sang loud and high—
And the red was on your lip, Mary,
  And the love-light in your eye.

The *place* is little changed, Mary,
  The day is bright as then,
The lark's loud song is in my ear,
  And the corn is green again ;
But I miss the soft clasp of your hand,
  And your breath, warm on my cheek,
And I still keep list'ning for the words
  You never more will speak.

LAMENT OF THE IRISH EMIGRANT.—*Continued.*

'Tis but a step down yonder lane,
　And the little church stands near,
The church where we were wed, Mary,
　I see the spire from here.
But the grave-yard lies between, Mary,
　And my step might break your rest—
For I've laid you, darling! down to sleep,
　With your baby on your breast.

I'm very lonely now, Mary,
　For the poor make no new friends,
But, oh! they love the better still,
　The few our Father sends!
And you were all I had, Mary,
　My blessin' and my pride:
There's nothin' left to care for now,
　Since my poor Mary died.

Yours was the good, brave heart, Mary,
　That still kept hoping on,
When the trust in God had left my soul,
　And my arm's young strength was gone;
There was comfort ever on *your* lip,
　And the kind look on your brow—
I bless you, Mary, for that same,
　Though you cannot hear me now.

I thank you for the patient smile
　When your heart was fit to break,
When the hunger pain was gnawin' there,
　And you hid it, for *my* sake!
I bless you for the pleasant word,
　When your heart was sad and sore—
Oh! I'm thankful you are gone, Mary,
　Where grief can't reach you more!

I'm biddin' you a long farewell,
　My Mary—kind and true!
But I'll not forget *you*, darling!
　In the land I'm goin' to;

LAMENT OF THE IRISH EMIGRANT.—*Continued.*

They say there's bread and work for all,
    And the sun shines always there—
But I'll not forget old Ireland,
    Were it fifty times as fair !

And often in those grand old woods.
    I'll sit, and shut my eyes,
And my heart will travel back again
    To the place where Mary lies ;
And I'll think I see the little stile
    Where we sat side by side :
And the springin' corn, and the bright May morn,
    When first you were my bride.

——o——

THE BUNCHEEN OF LUCHAROE.

As I roved for recreation down by yon river clear,
Where transparent waters all by the sylvan forest steer,
The fields being spread with daisies, the fruit spontaneous
        seemed to grow,
Each bank being decorated with violets and green *lucharoe.*

I gazed with admiration, traversing through the shady grove,
Felicitating anglers as they the banks did gently rove,
Till I espied a fair one, more lovely than the falling snow,
As she was re-arranging her violets and green *lucharoe.*

As I perambulated, contemplating the works of Jove,
I thought she was Pandora, Fair Helen, or the Queen of Love,
Her notes were elevated, extirpated my grief and woe,
As she co-operated her violets and green *lucharoe.*

The radiance of her beauty so suited her majestic air,
I thought it too audacious or precarious to approach the fair ;
Her hair hung long and flowing, and did profusely seem to
        grow,
And her shape was in proportion to her violets and sweet
    lucharoe.

THE SHANDUINE. (OLD MAN.)

OH, pretty young girls, my ways never follow;
Don't take an old rogue with jaws toothless and hollow,
Who in bed by your side, than hard iron is colder,
Who is rough as the oak-root, and tougher and older.

> *Oh ro, my Shanduine, little I care for you;*
> *Oh ro, my Shanduine, black's my despair for you;*
> *You bitter old thief, I'm as mad as a hare for you;*
> *So crusty, so jealous, a miser and scold.*

They urged me to wed him with arguing and railing,
My parents, my friends, and the priest so prevailing;
The neighbors all gathered to flatter and feast 'em,
But seldom came after the *wrong way* I've blest 'em.
Same Chorus.

The match-making rogue met me out on the *high* way,
Advised me to marry, and said it was *my* way;
He cared not a thraneen when paid for his labors;
He made me the sneer of the boys and the neighbors.
Same Chorus.

If I had a stout *coppalcen* under my idol,
A stirrup of straw and a good hempen bridle,
I'd gallop him into a bog hole so cozy;
I'd not crooken a finger to rescue my Mosey.

> *Oh ro, my old man, I'll then end my sorrow;*
> *Oh ro, my old man, sweet joy will I borrow;*
> *Oh ro, my old man, I'll look for that morrow;*
> *For then I'll be single and wed a young man.*

And when he was drowned, from the bog-hole I'd take him;
And with a sad face, faith its joyful I'd wake him;
With tobacco and whiskey to make the boys funny,
Oh, wouldn't I put the wind under his money!
Same Chorus.

I ne'er can walk out but he's stuck close behind me;
I'm ne'er out of sight but he's jealous to find me;
If I dance he's afraid that some hundreds bespeak me;
He's afraid that the crows or the foxes will take me.
Same Chorus.

THE SHANDUINE. (OLD MAN.)—*Continued.*

But oh, in the dead of the night did you *watch* there,
His thin ashy hair, and his head on the *natch* there;
The blaze of the rush lighting up every wrinkle
In his old withered cheeks, while his ferret-eyes twinkle,
And he drawing the pipe—well, I'll do my endeavor,
But girls, machree, he'll be living for ever;"
Chorus as in first verse.

———o———

O! SAY, MY BROWN DRIMMIN.
J. J. CALLANAN.

O! SAY, my brown Drimmin, thou silk of the kine,
Where, where are thy strong ones, last hope of thy line?
Too deep and too long is the slumber they take;
At the loud call of freedom why don't they awake?

My strong ones have fallen—from the bright eye of day,
All darkly they sleep in their dwellings of clay,
The cold turf is o'er them—they hear not my cries,
And since Lewis no aid gives, I cannot arise.

O! where art thou, Lewis? our eyes are on thee—
Are thy lofty ships walking in strength o'er the sea?
In freedom's last strife if you linger or quail,
No morn e'er shall break on the night of the Gael.

But should the king's son, now bereft of his right,
Come proud in his strength, for his country to fight;
Like leaves on the trees, will new people arise,
And deep from their mountains shout back to my cries.

When the prince, now an exile, shall come for his own,
The isles of his father, his rights, and his throne,
My people in battle the Saxons will meet,
And kick them before, like old shoes from their feet.

O'er mountains and valleys they'll press on their rout,
The five ends of Erin shall ring to their shout;
My sons, all united, shall bless the glad day
When the flint-hearted Saxon they've chased far away.

WILLY REILLY.

" Oh! rise up, Willy Reilly, and come along with me,
I mean for to go with you and leave this counterie,
To leave my father's dwelling-house, his houses and free land;"
And away goes Willy Reilly and his dear *Coolen Bawn.**

They go by hills and mountains, and by yon lonesome plain,
Through shady groves and valleys all dangers to refrain;
But her father followed after with a well-arm'd band,
And taken was poor Reilly and his dear *Coolen Bawn.*

It's home then she was taken, and in her closet bound,
Poor Reilly all in Sligo jail lay on the stony ground,
'Till at the bar of justice before the Judge he'd stand,
For nothing but the stealing of his dear *Coolen Bawn.*

"Now, in the cold, cold iron, my hands and feet are bound,
I'm handcuffed like a murderer, and tied unto the ground,
But all the toil and slavery I'm willing for to stand,
Still hoping to be succored by my dear *Coolen Bawn.*"

The jailor's son to Reilly goes, and thus to him did say,
" Oh! get up, Willy Reilly, you must appear this day,
For great Squire Foillard's anger you never can withstand,
I'm afear'd you'll suffer sorely for your dear *Coolen Bawn.*"

Now Willy's drest from top to toe all in a suit of green,
His hair hangs o'er his shoulders most glorious to be seen;
He's tall and straight and comely as any could be found,
He's fit for Foillard's daughter, was she heiress to a crown.

" This is the news, young Reilly, last night that I did hear,
The lady's oath will hang you, or else will set you clear;"
" If that be so, " says Reilly, " her pleasure I will stand,
Still hoping to be succored by my dear *Coolen Bawn.*"

The Judge he said, " This lady being in her tender youth,
If Reilly has deluded her, she will declare the truth;
Then, like a moving beauty bright before him she did stand,
" You're welcome there my heart's delight and dear *Coolen
        Bawn.*"

* Fair young girl.

WILLY REILLY—*Continued.*

" Oh, gentlemen," Squire Foillard said, " with pity look on me,
This villain came amongst us to disgrace our family ;
And by his base contrivances this villany was planned,
If I don't get satisfaction I'll quit this Irish land."

The lady with a tear began, and thus replied she,—
" The fault is none of Reilly's, the blame lies all on me ;
I forced him for to leave his place and come along with me,
I loved him out of measure, which wrought our destiny ; "

Out bespoke the noble Fox, at the table he stood by,
" Oh ! gentlemen, consider on this extremity ;
To hang a man for love is a murder you may see,
So spare the life of Reilly, let him leave this counterie."

" Good, my lord, he stole from her, her diamonds and her rings,
Gold watch and silver buckles, and many precious things,
Which cost me in bright guineas more than five hundred
              pounds,—
I'll have the life of Reilly should I lose ten thousand pounds."

" Good, my lord, I gave them him as tokens of true love,
And when we are a-parting I will them all remove,
If you have got them, Reilly, pray send them home to me."
" I will, my loving lady, with many thanks to thee."

" There is a ring among them I allow yourself to wear,
With thirty locket diamonds well set in silver fair,
And as a true-love-token wear it on your right hand,
That you'll think on my poor broken heart when you're in a
              foreign land,"

Then out spoke the noble Fox, " You may let the prisoner go,
The lady's oath has cleared him, as the jury all may know ;
She has released her own true love, she has renewed his name,
May her honor bright gain high estate, and her offspring,
              rise to fame !"

GRA GAL MACHREE.

I AM a young lover that's sorely oppressed;
I'm inthralled by a fair one, and can find no rest;
Her name I'll not mention, though wounded I be
By Cupid's keen arrow—she's *Gra Gal Machree.*

I promised to tell that fair innocent dove
All by a fond letter that she was my love,
Expecting next morning with pleasure to see
Some token of love from my *Gra Gal Machree.*

But that false deceiver whom I did intrust—
Above all men breathing he's one of the worst—
He proved a deceiver and traitor to me,
For he ne'er gave my letter to *Gra Gal Machree.*

When he got the letter he ran out of hand
Unto her stern father, and told him the plan;
When the old man did read it he swore bitterly
That he'd alter the case with his *Gra Gal Machree.*

He called down his daughter with pride and disdain,
Saying "Here is a letter from your darling swain:
You cannot deny him—its plain you may see—
He titles you here his own *Gra Gal Machree.*"

This beautiful fair maid fell down on her knees,
Saying, "Father, dear father, now do as you please:
For if by wild horses I mangled should be,
I'll never deny he's my darling Johnny."

A horse was got ready without more delay,
And to some foreign country she was sent away,
But if I don't find her I'll mourn constantly,
And my last dying words shall be, *Gra Gal Machree.*

THE LADY AND THE FARMER.

THERE was a rich noble of late we do hear,
And he had one daughter was comely and fair;
A great many suitors admired his fair child;
But by none of these suitors her heart was beguiled.

Her father he died when she came of age;
To visit her workmen she rode in her chaise;
A handsome young farmer she there did espy,
And with rapture upon him she soon cast an eye.

He whistled so loud that the valleys did ring,
And his cheeks were like roses that bloom in the spring:
His features were comely, his hair a dark brown—
She never saw finer in country or town.

Home to her castle this lady she goes,
She dressed her fair person in officer's clothes,
With her sword by her side she went to the grove,
And the ploughman was pressed by the Captain of Love.

To the farmer so frightened the lady she said,
Come, come, jolly ploughman, and join the parade,
I'll leave you no longer to plough and to sow,
But abroad for a soldier with me you must go.

You are handsome and proper and fitted to shine,
With laced hat and feather, and scarlet so fine;
Abroad you will go, and your captain I'll be,
And a lady will court you of noble degree.

In a room in her castle her love she confined,
But she soon changed her clothes and she told him her mind
In his arms he embraced her, and solemnly swore
That the Captain of Love he would ever adore.

To the church went this couple the very next day,
And there they were married without more delay,
How happy's the ploughman, how altered is he,
From a farmer's estate a rich noble to be!

THE WIDOW'S PIG.

IT is not Morgan Rattler,
  Nor neither is it *Garraan Bui.*
The Royal Blackbird, Tristram Shandy,
  Nor that new thing called Langolee;
The sweet *Ceann Dhu*, the Bonnet Blue,
  The Colleen Rua, and the Irish Jig,
Must all be mute without dispute,
  Nor dare confute the Widow's Pig.

She was a beauty without paint,
  She was nate-made, both round and tight;
Her colors they were various—
  Of large spots both black and white;
With a circle round her neck,
  Tow'rds which the *bells* they did incline ;—
Dame Nature did endeavor
  To frame her the best of swine.

  As she roved out one morning,
    Her royal helpmate for to meet,
The cabin curs pursued her,
    And overtook her in the street.
Her ears they tore in ribbons,
    Her hams they fleeced with tooth and nail,
And in the gore they left her
    All from her snout unto her tail.

I placed her on the hearthstone,
  A sod beneath her head I laid,
In hopes she would come to herself,
  And keep the cabin o'er our head;
At last her eyes she opened,
  Saying "Mistress dear, will you sit still,
I'll make you the executor
  To my last testament and will.

My curse light on you, Tiger!
  And may the halter be your due!
Bad win to them that reared you,
  Or any of your murd'ring crew!

THE WIDOW'S PIG.—*Continued.*

My bristles give the *gracy*,
  For him to mend the naybours' brogues,
And make a halter of my skin
  To gibbet all sheep-stealing rogues.

My *crubeens* will be just the thing
  To hold the *thotheen* at the wakes,
And turn all that's left of me
  To puddings and the best pork-steaks."
She turned her face unto the wall,
  And passed away without a groan.
Good neighbors, all come round me,
  And sing with me her ullaghone!

————o————

DON'T MARRY.

BEFORE a maid is married,
  She's as mild as any nun ;
When marriage rites are over,
  She then lets loose her tongue.
She soon will prove an orator,
  And make the whole house ring ;
And why should I become your wife,
  To wash, to card, or spin?

*   *   *   *   *

There was a victim in a cart,
  Just going to be hanged,
When a reprieve came from the king,
  The horse and cart did stand.
It was that he should marry a wife,
  Or instantly should die ;
" For what should I corrupt my life?"
  The victim did reply ;
" They're crowding here from every port,
  'Twas wrong to interrupt the sport,
The bargain's bad of either sort,
  The wife's the worst—wheel on the cart."

THE REJECTED LOVER.

THE wheat and the rye they are turned out of shoot,
The blackbirds and thrushes are changing their notes,
The fields and the meadows have got a green coat,
   And love is the cause of my folly.

The week before Easter the moon did shine low,
And I to my false love a courting did go,
Where the young men and maidens did make a great show
   About me and my false-hearted lover.

When I saw my love as she sat at the meat,
I sat down beside her but nothing could eat ;
I loved her sweet company better than meat :
   But since she has wed with another.

When I saw my love and she dressed all in white,
She looked like an angel—she dazzled my sight;
I took up my hat and I wished her good night,
   And adieu to the false-hearted lady.

The next time I saw my love in the church stand
The ring on her finger, her love by the hand,
And now she's got mistress of houses and lands,
   And adieu to my false one for ever.

The last time I saw my love in the church bow,
Her bridesmaids around her, they made a great show ;
I kissed her soft hand, though my heart it was low,
   And after fell into a fever.

And now dig my grave both long, wide, and deep,
A stone at my head and a sod at my feet,
And there lay me down to take my last sleep,
   And adieu to my darling for ever !

THE SAILOR BOY.

OH ! the sailing trade is a weary life ;
It robs fair maids of their heart's delight,
Which causes me for to sigh and mourn,
For fear my true love will ne'er return.

       *   *   *   *

The grass grows green upon yonder lea,
The leaves are budding from ev'ry spray,
The nightingale in her cage will sing
To welcome Willy home to crown the spring.

I'll build myself a little boat,
And o'er the ocean 1 mean to float ;
From every French ship that *do* pass by,
I'll inquire for Willy, that bold sailor boy.

She had not sailed a league past three
Till a fleet of French ships she chanced to meet
" Come tell me, sailors, and tell me true,
If my love Willy sails on board with you."

" Indeed, fair maid, your love is not here,
But he is drowned by this we fear ;
'Twas yon green island as we passed by,
There we lost Willy, that bold sailor boy."

She wrung her hands and she tore her hair
Just like a lady that was in despair ;
Against the rock her little boat she run—
" How can I live, and my true love gone ? "

Nine months after, this maid was dead,
And this note found on her bed's head ;
How she was satisfied to end her life,
Because she was not a bold sailor's wife.

Dig my grave both large and deep,
Deck it over with lilies sweet,
And on my head-stone cut a turtle-dove,
To signify that I died for love.

MOLLY CAREW.

By Samuel Lover.

Ochone! and what will I do?
Sure, my love is all crost
Like a bud in the frost—
And there's no use at all in my going to bed,
For 'tis dhrames and not sleep, that comes into my head;
And 'tis all about you,
My sweet Molly Carew!
And indeed 'tis a sin and a shame!
You're complater than nature
In every feature,
The snow can't compare
With your forehead so fair;
And I rather would see just one blink of your eye
Than the purtiest star that shines out of the sky;
And by this and by that,
For the matter of that,
You're more distant by far than that same.
Ochone! *weirasthru!*
Ochone! I'm alone!
I'm alone in the world without you.

Ochone! but why should I spake
Of your forehead and eyes,
When your nose it defies
Paddy Blake, the schoolmasther, to put it in rhyme;
Tho' there's one Burke he says, that would call it *snub*lime!
And then for your cheek,
Troth, 'twould take him a week
Its beauties to tell, as he'd rather:
Then your lips! oh, Machree!
In their beautiful glow
They a patthern might be
For the cherries to grow;
'Twas an apple that tempted our mother, we know,
For apples were scarce, I suppose, long ago;
But at this time o'day,
'Pon my conscience, I'll say,
Such cherries might tempt a man's father!
Ochone! weirasthru!
Ochone! I'm alone!
I'm alone in the world without you.

MOLLY CAREW.—*Continued.*

Ochone! by the man in the moon,
　　You taze me all ways,
　　That a woman can plaze,
For you dance twice as high with that thief, Pat Magee,
As when you take share of a jig, dear, with me;
　　Though the piper I bate,
　　For fear the old chate
Wouldn't play you your favorite tune.
　　And when you're at mass
　　My devotion you crass,
　　For 'tis thinking of you
　　I am, Molly Carew;
While you wear, on purpose, a bonnet so deep
That I can't at your sweet purty face get a peep.
　　Och! lave off that bonnet,
　　Or else I'll lave on it
The loss of my wandherin' sowl!
　　Ochone! weirasthru!
　　Ochone! like an owl,
Day is night dear, to me, without you.

　　Ochone! don't provoke me to do it;
　　For there's girls by the score
　　That loves me—and more;
And you'd look mighty quare if some morning you'd meet
My wedding all marching in pride down the street;
　　Troth, you'd open your eyes,
　　And you'd die with surprise,
To think 'twasn't you was come to it;
　　And faith, Katty Naile,
　　And her cow, I go bail,
　　Would jump if I'd say
　　"Katty Naile name the day;"
And tho' you're fresh and fair as a morning in May,
While she's short and dark like a cowld winther's day,
　　Yet, if you don't repent
　　Before Easter, when Lent
Is over, I'll marry for spite.
　　Ochone! weirasthru!
　　And when I die for you,
My ghost will haunt you every night!

PADDY CAREY.

'TWAS in the town of nate Clogheen,
  That Sergeant Snapp met Paddy Carey;
A claner boy was never seen,
  Brisk as a bee, light as a fairy;
His brawny shoulders, four feet square,
  His cheeks like thumping red potatoes,
His legs would make a chairman stare!
  And Pat was loved by all the ladies,
Old and young, grave and sad,
  Deaf and dumb, dull or mad,
Waddling, twaddling, limping, squinting,
  Light, brisk and airy—

All the sweet faces at Limerick races,
  From Mullinavat to Magherafelt,
At Paddy's beautiful name would melt!
  The sowls would cry, and look so shy,
Och! Cushlamachree, did you never see
  The jolly boy, the darling joy, the ladies' toy,
Nimble-footed, black-eyed, rosy-cheeked,
  Curly-headed Paddy Carey!
Oh! sweet Paddy, beautiful Paddy!
  Nate little, tight little Paddy Carey.

His heart was made of Irish oak,
  Yet, soft as streams from sweet Killarney,
His tongue was tipped with a bit of the brogue,
  But the deuce a bit at all of the blarney.
Now Sergeant Snapp, so sly and keen,
  While Pat was coaxing duck-legged Mary,
A shilling slipped so nate and clane,
  By the powers, he 'listed Paddy Carey!
Tight and sound—strong and light—
  Cheek so round—eyes so bright—
Whistling, humming, drinking, drumming,
  Light, tight, and airy—
                    All the sweet faces, &c.

PADDY CAREY.—*Continued.*

The sowls wept loud, the crowd was great,
　When waddling forth came widow Leary ;
Though she was crippled in her gait,
　Her brawny arms clasped Paddy Carey!
"Och! Pat," she cried, "go buy the ring;
　Here's cash galore, my darling honey."
Says Pat, "My sowl, I'll do that thing."
　And clasped his thumb upon her money.
Gimlet eye—sausage nose—
　Pat so sly—ogle throws—
Learing, tittering, jeering, frittering,
　Sweet Widow Leary!
　　　　　　All the sweet faces, &c.

When Pat had thus his fortune made,
　He pressed the lips of Mistress Leary,
And mounting straight a large cockade,
　In captain's boots struts Paddy Carey ;
He grateful, praised her shape, her back,
　To others like a dromedary ; .
Her eyes, that seemed their strings to crack,
　Were Cupid's darts to Captain Carey!
Nate and sweet, no alloy—
　All complete—love and joy.
Ranting, roaring, soft, adoring,
　Dear Widow Leary!
　　　　　　All the sweet faces, &c.

From Mullinavat to Magherafelt,
　At Paddy's promotion sigh and melt :
The sowls all cry as the groom struts by,
　Och! Cushlamacree, thou art lost to me,
The jolly boy! the darling boy!
　The ladies' toy, the widow's joy!
Long sword girted, nate short skirted,
　Head cropped, whisker chopped Captain Carey!
Oh! sweet Paddy, beautiful Paddy!
　White-feathered, boot-leathered Paddy Carey!
　　　　　　All the sweet faces, &c.

THE WHISTLING THIEF.

By S. Lover.

WHEN Pat came o'er the hills his colleen fair to see,
His whistle, loud and shrill, his signal was to be;
"Oh! Mary," the mother cried, "there's some one whistling,
       sure."
"Oh! Mother, you know, its the wind that's whistling
       through the door."   (Whistles Garry Owen.)

" I've lived a long time, Mary, in this wide world, my dear,
But the wind to whistle like that, I never yet did hear."
" But Mother, you know, the fiddle hangs close behind the
       chink,
And the wind upon the strings is playing a tune, I think."
                 (Dog barks.)

" The dog is barking now, and the fiddle can't play that tune."
"But, Mother, you know that dogs will bark, when they see
       the moon."
"Now, how can he see the moon, when you know he's old
       and blind?
Blind dogs can't see the moon, nor fiddles be played by the
       wind.   (Pig grunts.)

And now, there is the pig uneasy in his mind."
"But, Mother, you know they say that pigs can see the wind."
" That's all very well in the day, but then I may remark
That pigs no more than we, can see anything in the dark.

Now, I'm not such a fool as you think; I know very well it is
       Pat:
Get out! you whistling thief, and get along home out o' that—
And you be off to your bed, and don't bother me with your
       tears:
For, tho' I've lost my eyes, I have not lost my ears."

MORAL.

Now, boys, too near the house don't courting go, d'ye mind?
Unless you're certain sure the old woman's both deaf and
       blind;
The days when they were young, forget they never can;
They're sure to tell the difference, 'twixt wind, fiddle, pig,
       dog, or man.

YOUNG RILEY.

As I was walking through the County of Cavan,
  All for to view the sweet charms of life,
There I beheld a most clever woman,
  She appeared to me to be an angel bright.

I said, " Fair maiden, now, could you fancy
  All ᴜr to be a young sailor's wife?"
Said she, "Kind sir, I would rather tarry,
  For I choose to live a single life."

I said, " Fair maiden, what makes you differ,
  From all the rest of your female kind?
For you are youthful, fair and handsome,
  All for to wed me pray be inclined."

Said she, ' Kind sir, if I must tell you,
  I have been married five years ago,
Unto one Riley, all in this country :
  'Tis he that proved my overthrow.

He was a young man of handsome fortune,
  He courted me both night and day,
Until he had my favor gained ;
  He left this country and fled from me."

I said, " Fair maiden, come let us travel
  Unto some far and distant shore,
Then we'll sail over to Pennsylvania,
  And bid adieu to Riley for evermore."

" If I should go to Pennsylvania,
  Or, if I should go to some distant shore,
Why, my poor heart would be always aching,
  For young Riley whom I adore."

It's youthful folly makes young folks marry,
  And when we are bound we must obey ;
What can't be cured, must be endured ;
  So farewell, Riley, till another day.

JOHN O'DWYER OF THE GLEN.

Translated from the Irish, by THOMAS FURLONG.

BLITHE the bright dawn found me,
Rest with strength had crown'd me,
Sweet the birds sang round me,
   Sport was all their toil.

The horn its clang was keeping,
Forth the fox was creeping,
Round each dame stood weeping,
   O'er the prowler's spoil.

Hark! the foe is calling,
Fast the woods are falling,
Scenes and sights appalling,
   Mark the wasted soil.

War and confiscation
Curse the falling nation;
Gloom and desolation
   Shade the lost land o'er.

Chill the winds are blowing,
Death aloft is going,
Peace or hope seems growing
   For our race no more.

Hark! the foe is calling,
Fast the woods are falling,
Scenes and sights appalling
   Throng the blood-stained shore.

Nobles, once high-hearted
From their homes have parted.
Scattered, scared, and started
   By a base-born band.

 *   *   *   *

Spots that once were cheering,
Girls beloved, endearing,
Friends from whom I'm steering,
   Take this parting tear.

Hark! the foe is calling,
Fast the woods are falling,
Scenes and sights appalling
   Plague and haunt me here.

MALLOW CASTLE.

THE RAKES OF MALLOW.

BEAUING, belling, dancing, drinking,
Breaking windows, damning, sinking,
Ever raking, never thinking,
   Live the rakes of Mallow.

Spending faster than it comes,
Beating waiters, bailiffs, duns,
Bacchus' true begotten sons,
   Live the rakes of Mallow.

One time naught but claret drinking,
Then like politicians thinking
To raise the sinking funds when sinking,
   Live the rakes of Mallow.

When at home with dadda dying,
Still for Mallow-water crying:
But where there is good claret plying
   Live the rakes of Mallow.

THE RAKES OF MALLOW.—*Continued.*

Living short but merry lives,
Going where the devil drives,
Having sweethearts, but no wives,
      Live the rakes of Mallow.

Racking tenants, stewards teasing,
Swiftly spending, slowly raising,
Wishing to spend all their days in
      Raking as at Mallow.

Then to end this raking life
They get sober, take a wife,
Ever after live in strife,
      And wish again for Mallow.

———-o———

KITTY CLARE.

GOLDEN hair and laughing eyes,
  Beaming on the gladdened sight,
Like an angel from the skies,
  Comes a fragile form of light.
Not a flower, 'mid all the bloom
  In that many lured parterre,
Half so sweet a presence has
  As my blushing Kitty Clare.

    CHORUS ;—Golden hair and laughing eyes, &c.

Romping, dancing all the day,
  Singing, gay as any bird,
Never 'mid celestial choirs
  Was a rarer cadence heard :
Turns she up two pouting lips,
  Then with laugh draws back the snare :
Never mind, I'll have her yet—
  Charming, teasing, Kitty Clare.
      Golden hair, &c.

WIDOW MACHREE.

By Samuel Lover.

Widow Machree, it's no wonder you frown,
Och, hone! widow Machree!
Faith! it ruins your looks, that same dirty black gown,
Och, hone! widow Machree!
How altered your air
With that close cap you wear!
'Tis destroying your hair,
Which should be flowing free:
Be no longer a churl,
Of its black silken curl
Och, hone! widow Machree!

Widow Machree, now the Summer is come,
Och, hone! widow Machree!
When ev'rything smiles, should a beauty look glum?
Och, hone! widow Machree!
See the birds go in pairs—
And the rabbits and hares—
Why even the bears
Now in couples agree;
And the mute little fish,
Though they can't speak, they wish.
Och, hone! widow Machree!

Widow Machree, and when Winter comes in,
Och, hone! widow Machree!
To be poking the fire, all alone, is a sin,
Och, hone! widow Machree!
Sure, the shovel and tongs
To each other belongs,
And the kettle sings songs
Full of family glee.
Yet alone with your cup,
Like a hermit you sup,
Och, hone! widow Machree!

Then, take my advice, darling widow Machree,
Och, hone! widow Machree!
And, with my advice, faith! I wish you'd take me,
Och, hone! widow Machree!

WIDOW MACHREE.—*Continued.*

You'd have me to desire
Then, to stir up the fire :
And sure hope is no liar
  In whispering to me
That the Ghosts would depart,
When you'd me near your heart,
  Och, hone ! widow Machree !

——o——

THE LOVELY LAND OF DREAMS.

By Samuel Lover.

There is a land where Fancy's twining
  Her flowers around life's fading tree,
Where light is ever softly shining,
  Like sunset o'er a tranquil sea.
'Tis there thou dwell'st in beauty's brightness,
  More fair than aught on earth e'er seems;
'Tis there my heart feels most of lightness,
  There, in the lovely Land of Dreams!

'Tis there, in groves, I often meet thee,
  And wander through the sylvan shade,
While I, in gentlest accents, greet thee,
  My own, my sweet and constant maid.
There, by some fountain fair reposing,
  Where all around so tranquil seems,
We wait the golden evening's closing,
  There, in the lovely Land of Dreams!

But when the touch of earthly waking
  Hath broken slumber's latest spell,
Those fabled joys, of Fancy's making,
  Are in my heart remembered well.
The day, in all its sunshine-splendor,
  Less fair to me than midnight seems,
When visions shed a light more tender
  Around the lovely Land of Dreams!

DRINANE DHUN.

OF late I'm captivated by a handsome young man,
I'm daily complaining for my own darling John,
I'll be roving all day until night does come on,
And I'll be shaded by the green leaves of the Drinane Dhun.

Next fair day I'll get a fairing from my handsome young man,
Twenty bright kisses from my own darling John,
Confuse them, consume them that say I'm not true ;
Through green groves and lofty mountains I'll rove with you.

My love is far fairer than a fine summer day,
His breath is far sweeter than the new mown hay :
His hair shines like gold when exposed to the sun,
He is fair as the blossom of the Drinane Dhun.

My love he is going to cross over the main,
May the Lord send him safe to his virtuous love again ;
He is gone and he's left me in grief for to tell,
O'er the green hills and lofty mountains between us to dwell.

I wish I had a small boat on the ocean to float,
I'd follow my darling wherever he did resort;
I'd sooner have my true-love to roll, sport, and play,
Than all the golden treasure by land or by sea.

I'm patiently waiting for my true-love's return,
And for his long absence I'll ne'er cease to mourn,
I'll join with the sweet birds till the summer comes on,
To welcome the blossoms of the Drinane Dhun.

Come all you pretty fair maids get married in time,
To some handsome young man that will keep up your prime ;
Beware of the winter morn, cold breezes come,
Which will consume the blossoms early of the Drinane Dhun.

THE SHAMROCK SHORE.

IN a musing mind with me combine,
 And grant me great relief,
Whilst here alone I sigh and moan,
 I'm overwhelmed with grief ;
Whilst here alone I sigh and moan,
 Away from friends at home,
With troubled mind, no rest can find,
 Since I left the Shamrock shore.

In the blooming spring, when small birds sing,
 And the lambs did sport and play,
My way I took, and friends forsook,
 Till I came to Dublin quay ;
I entered on board as passenger,
 To England I sailed o'er,
I bid farewell to all my friends,
 All round the Shamrock shore.

When young men all both great and small,
 Go to the fields to walk,
Whilst here alone I sigh and moan,
 To none of them can talk ;
Whilst I remain but to bewail,
 For the mold that I adore,
With a troubled mind, no rest can find,
 Since I left the Shamrock shore.

To Glasgow fair I did repair,
 Some pleasure for to find,
I own it was a pleasant place,
 Down by the flowery Clyde ;
I own it was a pleasant place,
 For rich attire they wore,
There's none so rare as can compare,
 To the girls of the Shamrock shore.

One evening fair to take the air,
 Down by yon shady grove,
I heard some lads and lasses gay,
 A making to them love ;

THE SHAMROCK SHORE.—*Continued.*

It grieved me so rejoiced to see,
  As I had once before,
Who had my heart betrayed,
  That I left on the Shamrock shore.

So now to conclude, and make an end,
  My pen begins for to fail,
Farewell my honored mother dear,
  And for me don't bewail.
Farewell my honored mother dear,
  And for me grieve no more,
When I think long I'll sing my song,
  In praise of the Shamrock shore.

——o——

LOVE NOT.

Hon. Mrs. Norton.

Love not, love not, ye hapless sons of clay!
  Hope's gayest wreaths are made of earthly flow'rs—
Things that are made to fade and fall away,
  When they have blossomed but a few short hours.
                                        Love not, love not!

Love not, love not! The thing you love may die—
  May perish from the gay and gladsome earth;
The silent stars, the blue and smiling sky,
  Beam on its grave as once upon its birth.
                                        Love not, love not!

Love not, love not! The thing you love may change;
  The rosy lip may cease to smile on you;
The kindly-beaming eye grow cold and strange;
  The heart still warmly beat, yet not be true.
                                        Love not, love not!

Love not, love not!—Oh, warning vainly said
  In present years, as in the years gone by;
Love flings a halo round the dear one's head,
  Faultless, immortal—till they change or die.
                                        Love not, love not!

UP FOR THE GREEN!

A song of the United Irishmen, 1796. Air, "Wearing of the Green."

'TIS the green—oh, the green is the color of the true,
And we'll back it 'gainst the orange, and we'll raise it o'er
 the blue!
For the color of old Ireland alone should here be seen—
'Tis the color of the martyr'd dead—our own immortal green.
  Then up for the green, boys, and up for the green!
  Oh! 'tis down to the dust, and a shame to be seen;
  But we've hands—oh, we've hands, boys, full strong enough
   I ween,
  To rescue and to raise again our own immortal green!

They may say they have power 'tis vain to oppose—
'Tis better to obey and live, than surely die as foes;
But we scorn all their threats, boys, whatever they may mean;
For we trust in God above us, and we dearly love the green.
  So we'll up for the green, and we'll up for the green!
  Oh, to *die* is far better than be curst as we have been;
  And we've hearts—oh, we've hearts, boys, full true enough,
   I ween,
  To rescue and to raise again our own immortal green!

They may swear, as they often did, our wretchedness to cure;
But we'll never trust John Bull again, nor let his lies allure.
No, we wont—no, we wont, Bull, for now nor ever more!
For we've hopes on the ocean,* and we've trust on the shore.
  Then up for the green, boys, and up for for the green!
  Shout it back to the Sasanach, " We'll *never* sell the green,
  For our TONE is coming back, and with men enough, I ween,
  To rescue and avenge us and our own immortal green!"

Oh, remember the days when their reign we did disturb,
At Limerick and Thurles, Blackwater and Benburb:
And ask this proud Saxon if our blows he did enjoy,
When we met him on the battle-field of France—at Fontenoy.
  Then we'll up for the green, boys, and up for the green!
  Oh, 'tis *still* in the dust, and a shame to be seen;
  But we've hearts and we've hands, boys, full strong enough
   I ween,
  To rescue and to raise again our own unsullied green!

*Alluding to the expected succor from France.

RORY OF THE HILLS.

THAT rake up near the rafters,
  Why leave it there so long?
The handle of the best of ash,
  Is smooth, and straight, and strong ;
And, mother, will you tell me,
  Why did my father frown,
When to make the hay, in summer-time,
  I climbed to take it down?
She looked into her husband's eyes,
  While her own with light did fill,
" You'll shortly know the reason, boy ! "
  Said Rory of the Hill.

The midnight moon is lighting up
  The slopes of Sliav-na-man—
Whose foot affrights the startled hares
  So long before the dawn?
He stopped just where the Anner's stream
  Winds up the woods anear,
Then whistled low and looked around
  To see the coast was clear.
A sheeling door flew open—
  In he stepped with right good will—
" God save all here, and bless your work,"
  Said Rory of the Hill.

Right hearty was the welcome
  That greeted him I ween,
For years gone by he fully proved
  How well he loved the Green;
And there was one amongst them
  Who grasped him by the hand—
One who through all that weary time
  Roamed on a foreign strand;
He brought them news from gallant friends
  That made their heart-strings thrill—
" My soul ! I never doubted them ! "
  Said Rory of the Hill.

RORY OF THE HILLS.—*Continued.*

They sat around the humble board,
  Till dawning of the day,
And yet no song nor shout I heard—
  No revellers where they;
Some brows flushed red with gladness,
  While some were grimly pale :
But pale or red, from out those eyes
  Flashed souls that never quail !
" And sing us now about the vow,
  They swore for to fulfil "—
" You'll read it yet in history,"—
  Said Rory of the Hill.

Next day the ashen handle,
  He took down from where it hung,
The toothed rake, full scornfully,
  Into the fire he flung ;
And in its stead a shining blade,
  Is gleaming once again—
(Oh ! for a hundred thousand of
  Such weapons and such men !)
Right soldierly he wielded it,
  And going through his drill—
" Attention, charge, front, point, advance! "
  Cried Rory of the Hill.

She looked at him with woman's pride,
  With pride and woman's fears;
She flew to him, she clung to him,
  And dried away her tears ;
He feels her pulse beat truly ;
  While her arms around him twine—
" Now God be praised for your stout heart,
  Brave little wife of mine."
He swung his first-born in the air,
  While joy his heart did fill—
" You'll be a Freeman yet, my boy,"
  Said Rory of the Hill.

Oh ! knowledge is a wondrous power,
  And stronger than the wind ;
And thrones shall fall, and despots bow
  Before the might of mind ;

RORY OF THE HILLS.—*Continued.*

The poet, and the orator,
  The heart of man can sway,
And would to the kind heavens
  That Wolfe Tone were here to-day !
Yet trust me, friends, dear Ireland's strength
  Her truest strength, is still,
The rough and ready roving boys,
  Like Rory of the Hill.

———o———

THE BANTRY GIRLS' LAMENT FOR JOHNNY.

OH who will plough the field, or who will sell the corn ?
Or who will wash the sheep, an' have 'em nicely shorn ?
The stack that's in the haggard, unthrashed it may remain,
Since Johnny went a-thrashing, the dirty King o' Spain.

The girls from the *bawnoge* in sorrow may retire,
And the piper and his bellows may go home and blow the
      fire :
For Johnny, lovely Johnny, is sailing o'er the main,
Along with other *pathriarchs*, to fight the King o' Spain.

The boys will sorely miss him when Moneyhore comes round,
And grieve that their bould captain is nowhere to be found ;
The *peelers* must stand idle against their will and grain,
For the valiant boy who gave them work now peels the
      King o' Spain.

At wakes or hurling-matches your like we'll never see
Till you come back again to us, asthore, gra-gal-machree !
And won't you throunce the buckeens that shows us much
      disdain,
Bekase our eyes are not as black as those you'll meet in
      Spain.

If cruel fate will not permit our Johnny to return,
His heavy loss we Bantry girls will never cease to mourn ;
We'll resign ourselves to our sad lot, and die in grief and pain,
Since Johnny died for Ireland's pride in the foreign land o'
      Spain.

THE RAMBLER FROM CLARE.

THE first of my courtship that ever was known,
I straight took my way to the County Tyrone,
Among the pretty fair maids they used me well there,
They called me the stranger or the rambler from Clare.
I straight took my way to the town of Tralee,
When I fell a courting young Sally McGee,
I first gained her favor, and then left her there,
And now they are in search of the rambler from Clare.
It's there I enlisted, in a town called Fermoy,
I had so many masters I could not comply;
I deserted next morning—the truth I declare—
And for Limerick, fair city, starts the rambler from Clare.

It's like a deserter my case to bewail,
I was taken and surrounded in a town called Rathkeale;
It's off to head-quarters I had to repair,
And in the black hole lay the rambler from Clare.
I took off my hat and made a low bow,
In hope that the Colonel would pardon me now,
The pardon he gave me was hard and severe,
Saying : "Bind him, confine him, he is the rambler from Clare."

When my aged mother heard this sudden surprise,
Both my loving brothers their shouts reached the skies;
"Brave boys," says my father, " your arms now prepare,
Bring me back my darling, he is the rambler from Clare."
It's there we assembled in a well armed band,
With our guns on our shoulders, being ten thousand strong;
The firing began, with our heroes in rear,
We broke the jail door, and freed the rambler from Clare.

We marched all along with our hats in our hands,
Our guns on our shoulders being a harmonious gang;
At the very next tavern we drank hearty there,
And made chief Commander of the rambler from Clare.
So it's now I have got the title of a united man,
I cannot stay at home in my own native land,
But off to America I have to repair:
He is gone, God be with him, he is the rambler from Clare.

THE RAMBLER FROM CLARE.—*Continued.*

Farewell to my mother wherever I may be,
Likewise to my sweetheart young Sally McGee,
Our ship it is ready and the wind it blows fair:
That the Lord may be with him, the rambler from Clare.

——o——

NORAH MACHREE.

Young Phelim O'Neale loved sweet Norah Machree,
The prettiest maiden in merry Tralee:
But though she looked on him with favoring eyes,
His love went no further than glances and sighs.
In sport or in broil none were bolder than he—
His heart then was dauntless as stout heart could be,
But when to her side he attempted to steal,
Faith! all in a flutter was Phelim O'Neale:
   "Oh! Norah Machree! sweet Norah Machree!
   Sure, you are the girl that's bewildering me:
   Oh! Norah Machree! sweet Norah Machree!
   Your bright eyes an' sure are bewildering me."

One day, Phelim thought he'd find courage to tell
Pretty Norah the love that within him did dwell:
He went to her cottage his suit to get heard,
But she so bewitched him, he spoke not a word.
The maid sweetly smiled, still he seemed in a dream:
So finding smiles useless, she gave a loud scream—
"Why, I never kissed you!" said Phelim, in fear.
Says she: "Ain't you going to, Phelim, my dear?"
            Oh! Norah Machree, &c.

Young Phelim thought twice, then he stole to her side
And asked her all trembling, to be his sweet bride.
Her answer you'll guess—for, a sharp, sudden sound—
I think 'twas a kiss—broke the silence around.
If men will be bashful, and dally like this,
A slight gentle hint, is not surely amiss:
So when pretty maidens, in such straits you be,
Then just take a lesson from Norah Machree.
            Oh! Norah Machree, &c.

THE LADS WHO LIVE IN IRELAND,

OR, WHERE THE APPLE PRATIES GROW.

My name is Ned O'Manney, I was born in sweet Killarney,
  I can fight, dance, or sing, I can plow, reap or mow;
And, if I meet a pretty girl, I never practice blarney;
  I've something more alluring, which perhaps you'd like to
      know:
I'm none of your Bulgrudderies nor other shabby families,
  But can unto my pedigree, a pretty title show:
Oh! I'm of the O's and Mac's, and likewise the sturdy Whacks.
  That live and toil in Ireland, where the Apple Praties grow;
  That live and toil in Ireland, where the Apple Praties grow.

I could a deal relate, if I could but trace my pedigree:
  My mother was a Hogan, but my father I don't know;
I've ninety-nine relations in a place they call Roscarberry,
  And each unto their name has a Mac or an O;
My Uncle was a Brallaghan, my Aunt she was a Callaghan:
  And as to my character, why, I can plainly show:
I'm a rantin' rovin' blade, and I never was afraid;
  For, I was born in Ireland, where the Apple Praties grow;
  For, I was born in Ireland, where the Apple Praties grow.

May Heaven still protect our hospitable country,
  Where first I drew my living breath, and heard its cocks
      to crow!
Adieu to its green hills, and its lovely Bay of Bantry!—
  Where, many a pleasant evening, my love and I did go—
Where shoals of fish, so pleasantly, did sport about so merrily,
  Beneath its glassy surface, their wanton tricks to show—
Oh! those scenes I did enjoy, like a gay unthinking boy,
  With the lads who live in Ireland, where the Apple Praties
     grow;
  With the lads who live in Ireland, where the Apple Praties
     grow.

St. Patrick was our saint, and a blessed man, in truth, was he;
  Great gifts unto our country he freely did bestow;
He banished all the frogs and toads, that sheltered in our
     country,
  And unto other regions it's they were forced to go:

THE LADS WHO LIVE IN IRELAND.—*Continued.*

There is one fact, undoubtedly, that cannot contradicted be :
  For, trace the Irish history, and it will painly show ;
Search the universe all round, tighter fellows can't be found
  Than the lads who live in Ireland, where the Apple Praties
        grow ;
  Than the lads who live in Ireland, where the Apple Praties
    grow.

—o—

TRUST TO LUCK.
By S. Lover.

TRUST to luck, trust to luck, stare fate in the face,
Sure the heart must be aisy when it's in the right place ;
Let the world wag away, let your friends turn to foes,
Let your pockets run dry, and thread-bare your clothes,
Should woman deceive when you trust to her heart,
Never sigh, 'twont relieve it, but add to the smart.

  Trust to luck, trust to luck, stare fate in the face,
  Sure the heart must be aisy when it's in the right place ;
  Trust to luck, trust to luck, stare fate in the face,
  Sure the heart must be aisy when it's in the right place.

Be a man, be a man, wheresoever you go,
Through the sunshine of wealth, or the tear drop of woe ;
Should the wealthy look grand, and the proud pass you by,
With the back of their hand, and scorn in their eye,
Snap your fingers and smile, as they pass on their way,
And remember the while, every dog has his day.
          Trust to luck, &c.

In love or in war, sure it's Irish delight,
He's good humored with both, the sweet girl and a fight ;
He coaxes, he bothers, he blarneys the dear,
To resist him she can't, and she's off when he's near ;
And when valor calls him, from his darling he'd fly
And for liberty fight, for Ould Ireland he'd die.
          Trust to luck, &c.

PATRICK SHEEHAN.

By Charles J. Kickham.

My name is Patrick Sheehan,
  My years are thirty-four,
Tipperary is my native place,
  Not far from Galtymore;
I came of honest parents—
  But now they're lying low—
And many a pleasant day I spent
  In the Glen of Aherlow.

My father died, I closed his eyes
  Outside our cabin door—
The landlord and the sheriff too
  Were there the day before—
And then my loving mother,
  And sisters three also,
Were forced to go with broken hearts
  From the Glen of Aherlow.

For three long months in search of work,
  I wandered far and near;
I went then to the poor-house
  For to see my mother dear;
The news I heard nigh broke my heart,
  But still, in all my woe,
I blessed the friends who made their graves
  In the Glen of Aherlow.

Bereft of home, and kith, and kin—
  With plenty all around—
I starved within my cabin,
  And slept upon the ground;
But cruel as my lot was,
  I ne'er did hardship know,
'Till I joined the English army,
  Far away from Aherlow.

" Rouse up there," says the Corporal,
  "You lazy Hirish hound,
Why don't you hear, you sleepy dog,
  The call 'to arms' sound?"

MUCKROSS ABBEY.

PATRICK SHEEHAN.—*Continued.*

Alas, I had been dreaming
  Of days long, long ago,
I woke before Sebastopol,
  And not in Aherlow.

I groped to find my musket—
  How dark I thought the night,
O blessed God, it was not dark,
  It was the broad daylight!
And when I found that I was *blind*,
  My tears began to flow,
I longed for even a pauper's grave
  In the Glen of Aherlow.

O blessed Virgin Mary,
  Mine is a mournful tale,
A poor blind prisoner here I am,
  In Dublin's dreary jail;
Struck blind within the trenches,
  Where I never feared the foe;
And now I'll never see again
  My own sweet Aherlow.

A poor neglected mendicant
  I wandered through the street,
My nine months' pension now being out,
  I beg from all I meet.
As I joined my country's tyrants,
  My face I'll never show
Among the kind old neighbors,
  In the glen of Aherlow.

Then Irish youths—dear countrymen—
  Take heed of what I say,
For if you join the English ranks
  You'll surely rue the day :
And whenever you are tempted
  A soldiering to go,
Remember poor blind Sheehan
  Of the Glen of Aherlow.

THE LOW-BACKED CAR.

Samuel Lover.

WHEN first I saw sweet Peggy,
  'Twas on a market day,
A low-backed car she drove, and sat
  Upon a truss of hay;
But when that hay was blooming grass,
  And decked with flowers of Spring,
No flow'r was there that could compare,
  With the blooming girl I sing.
As she sat in the low-backed car—
The man at the turnpike bar
  Never asked for the toll,
  But just rubbed his owld poll
And looked after the low-backed car.

In battle's wild commotion,
  The proud and mighty Mars,
With hostile scythes, demands his tithes
  Of death—in warlike cars;
While Peggy, peaceful goddess,
  Has darts in her bright eye,
That knock men down, in the market town,
  As right and left they fly—
While she sits in her low-backed car,
Than battle more dangerous far—
  For the doctor's art
  Cannot cure the heart
That is hit from the low-backed car.

Sweet Peggy, round her car, sir,
  Has strings of ducks and geese,
But the scores of hearts she slaughters
  By far out-number these;
While she among her poultry sits,
  Just like a turtle dove,
Well worth the cage, I do engage,
  Of the blooming god of love!
While she sits in her low-backed car,
The lovers come near and far,
  And envy the chicken
  That Peggy is pickin',
As she sits in the low-backed car.

THE LOW-BACKED CAR.—*Continued.*

O, I'd rather own that car, sir,
  With Peggy by my side,
Than a coach-and-four and goold *galore*,*
  And a lady for my bride;
For the lady would sit forninst † me,
  On a cushion made with taste,
While Peggy would sit beside me
  With my arm around her waist—
While we drove in the low-backed car,
To be married by Father Maher, ‡
  Oh, my heart would beat high
  At her glance and her sigh—
Though it beat in a low-backed car.

———o———

BILLY O'ROURKE.

I CUT my stick an' grazed my brogues
  In the latter end of May, sir,
And down to Dublin town I came,
  To cut the corn and hay, sir,
I paid the captain eight thirteens
  To carry me over to Parkgate;
And before the ship was half the way
  She went at a terrible hard gait.
      With my gilla chrue, and my heart so true,
      And Billy O'Rourke's the bouchal.

The captain he said, " To the bottom we'll go,"
  But I said, " I don't care a farden—
You promised to carry me to Parkgate,
  And I'll make you stick to your bargain."
Some fell upon their bended knees,
  The ladies all were fainting,
But I sat down to bread and cheese—
  I always minded the main thing.
      Chorus (as before).

* In plenty.   † Before.
‡ In defence of my rhyme, I must tell English readers that this name is pronounced as if written, Mar.

LAMENTATION OF GEN. JAMES SHIELDS.

BY DANIEL MORAN.

DRAW near all bold defenders of every race and clime,
Give ear to these few verses I hereby put in rhyme,
Concerning a brave warrior who fought on many fields,
A lion-hearted hero whose name is General Shields.

At eventide, the first of June, in Eighteen seventy-nine,
In Ottumwa's lovely city, fate's fiat cried " resign !"
The fight is o'er, the field is won, the Chieftain is at rest ;
And pœans of joy re-echo in mansions of the blest.

He emigrated to America when sixteen years old,
And for his adopted country fought vigorously and bold,
He proved to be a true citizen, as history relates,
And he fought many a hard battle for the United States.

He fought on bench and forum and in the field likewise,
And his love for truth and honor he never did disguise.
'Gainst the enemies of freedom he struck a manly blow,
And he raised our starry banner on the heights of Mexico.

He challenged Abraham Lincoln in Eighteen forty-two,
And showed the Western Hoosier what an Irishman could do;
He caused poor Abe to tremble, so the duel was soon o'er,
And brave Shields and honest Lincoln were friends for ever
        more.

A Hercules in intellect, a Bonaparte in skill,
A Hector on the war-path, a Hannibal in will ;
With Alexander's valor, and Spartan pluck and toil,
He vanquished Stonewall Jackson on old Virginia soil.

Descended from the noble stock of Ireland's glorious kings,
His Irish genius soared aloft on fame's immortal wings;
He loathed the cruel Sassanach and scorned old Albion's laws,
And stood in proud defiance of the British lion's claws.

He ranks with Dan O'Connell, with Grattan, Burke and Flood,
And Wellington and Brian Boru, and all such noble blood ;
So let every son of Erin breathe forth an honest prayer,
That with the Saints of Ireland James Shields may have a share.

LIMERICK RACES.

I'M a simple Irish lad, I've resolved to see some fun, sirs;
So, to satisfy my mind, to Limerick town I come, sirs;
Oh, murther! what a precious place, and what a charming city,
Where the boys are all so free, and the girls are all so pretty!
    Musha ring a ding a da.
     Ri too ral laddy, Oh!
    Musha ring a ding a da.
     Ri too ral laddy, Oh!

It was on the first of May, when I began my rambles,
When everything was there, both jaunting cars and jingles;
I looked along the road, that was lined with smiling faces,
All driving off ding-dong, to go and see the races.
    Musha ring a ding a da, &c.

So then, I was resolved to go and see the race, sirs,
And on a coach and four I neatly took my place, sirs,
When a chap bawls out; " behind! " and the coachman dealt
   a blow, sirs:
Faith! he hit me just as fair as if his eyes were in his poll, sirs.
    Musha ring a ding a da, &c.

So then, I had to walk, and make no great delay, sirs,
Until I reached the course, where everything was gay, sirs;
It's then I spied a wooden house, and in the upper story,
The band struck up a tune called : " Garry Owen and glory. "
    Musha ring a ding a da, &c.

There was fiddlers playing jigs, there was lads and lasses
   dancing,
And chaps upon their nags, around the course were prancing:
Some was drinking whiskey-punch, while others bawl'd out
   gaily:
"Hurrah, then, for the Shamrock green, and the splinter of
   shillelagh!
    Musha ring a ding a da, &c.

LIMERICK RACES.—*Continued.*

There was betters to and fro, to see who would win the race,
      sirs,
And one of the sporting chaps, of course, came up to me, sirs,
Says he: " I'll bet you fifty pounds, and I'll put it down this
      minute. "
" Ah then! ten to one," says I, "the foremost horse will win it."
      Musha ring a ding a da, &c.

When the players came to town, and a funny set were they,
I paid my two thirteens to go and see the play;
They acted kings and cobblers, queens, and everything so gaily,
But I found myself at home when they struck up: "Paddy
      Carey."
      Musha ring a ding a da, &c.

———o———

POTTEEN, GOOD LUCK TO YE, DEAR!

By Charles Lever.

Av I was a monarch in state,
   Like Romulus or Julius Caysar,
With the best of fine victuals to eat,
   And drink like great Nebuchadnezzar,
A rasher of bacon I'd have,
   And potatoes the finest was seen, sir;
And for drink, it's no claret I'd crave,
   But a keg of ould Mullen's potteen, sir,
     With the smell of the smoke on it still.

They talk of the Romans of ould,
   Whom, they say, in their own times was frisky;
But trust me to keep out of the cowld,
   The Romans at home here like whiskey.
Sure it warms both the head and the heart,
   It's the soul of all readin' and writin';
It teaches both science and art,
   And disposes for love or for fightin.'
     Oh! potteen, good luck to ye, dear!

SHANNON'S FLOWERY BANKS.

IN summer when the leaves were green, and blossoms decked
      each tree,
Young Teddy then declared his love, his artless love to me;
On Shannon's flowery banks we sat, and there he told his tale·
" O Patty! softest of thy sex! oh! let fond love prevail!
Ah! well-a-day, you see me pine in sorrow and despair,
Yet heed me not—then let me die, and end my grief and
      care."
" Ah! no, dear youth," I softly said, " such love demands my
      thanks,
And here I vow eternal truth—on Shannon's flowery banks."

And here we vowed eternal truth—on Shannon's flowery
      banks,
And then we gathered sweetest flowers, and played such art-
      less pranks:
But, woe is me! the press-gang came, and forced my Ted
      away,
Just when we named next morning fair to be our wedding-day.
" My love!" he cried, "they force me hence, but still my heart
      is thine:
Till peace be yours, my gentle Pat, while war and toil be mine:
With riches I'll return to thee—" I sobbed out words of
      thanks—
And then he vowed eternal truth—on Shannon's flowery banks.

And then he vowed eternal truth—on Shannon's flowery
      banks,
And then I saw him sail away, and join the hostile ranks.
From morn to eve, for twelve dull months, his absence sad I
      mourned;
The peace was made—the ship came back—but Teddy ne'er
      returned!
His beauteous face, his manly form, has won a nobler fair—
My Teddy's false, and I forlorn, must die in sad despair—
Ye gentle maidens, see me laid, while you stand round in ranks,
And plant a willow o'er my head—on Shannon's flowery banks!

PADDY'S WEDDING.

A COCKNEY IRISH SONG.

SURE, won't you hear what roaring cheer
    Was spread at Paddy's wedding, O!
And how so gay they spent the day,
    From the churching to the bedding, O!
    First, book in hand, came Father Quipes,
With the bride's dada, the bailey, O!
    While all the way to church the pipes
    Struck up a lilt so gaily, O!

Then there was Mat, and sturdy Pat,
    And merry Morgan Murphy, O!
And Murdock Mags, and Turlogh Skaggs,
    Maclochlan, and Dick Durfey, O!
    And then the girls dressed out in wipes,
Led on by Ted O'Reilly, O!
    All jigging, as the merry pipes
    Struck up a lilt so gaily, O!

When Pat was ask'd would his love last?
    The chancel echoed wid laughter. O!
"'Orrah, fait!" cried Pat, "you may say that,
    To the end of the world and after, O!"
    Then tenderly her hand he gripes,
And kisses her genteelly, O!
    While all in tune the merry pipes,
    Struck up a lilt so gaily, O!

Now a roaring set at dinner are met,
    So frolicsome and so frisky, O!
Potatoes galore, a skirraig or more,
    And a flowing madder of whiskey, O!
    To the bride's dear health round went the swipes,
That her joys might be nightly and daily, O!
    And still as they guttled, the merry pipes
    Struck up a lilt so gaily, O!

And then, at night, oh! what delight,
    To see them all footing and prancing, O!
An opera or ball were nothing at all
    Compared to the style of their dancing, O!

PADDY'S WEDDING.—*Continued.*

And then see old Father Quipes,
Beat time wid his shilaly, O !
    While the chanter wid his merry pipes,
    Struck up a lilt so gaily, O !

And now the lot so tipsy are got,
    They'll all go to sleep without rocking, O !
So the bridesmaids fair, now gravely prepare
    For throwing off the stocking, O !
    And round to be sure, didn't go the swipes
At the bride's expense so freely, O !
    While to wish them good night, the merry pipes
    Struck up a lilt so gaily, O !

———o———

THE STREAMS OF BUNCLODY.

WAS I at the moss-house where the birds do increase,
At the foot of Mount Leinster, or some silent place,
At the streams of Bunclody, where all pleasures do meet,
And all I require is one kiss from you, sweet.

The reason my love slights me, I do understand,
Because she has a freehold and I have no land;
A great store of riches, both silver and gold,
And everything fitting a house to uphold.

If I was a clerk who could write a good hand,
I'd write to my true love that she might understand,
That I'm a young man that's deeply in love,
That lived by Bunclody, and now must remove.

Adieu my dear father; adieu my dear mother;
Farewell to my sister, and likewise my brother;
I'm going to America, my fortune to try;
When I think on Bunclody, I'm ready to die.

THAT ROGUE REILLY.

By Samuel Lover.

THERE'S a boy that follows me every day,
  Although he declares that I use him vilely
But all I can do, he won't go away,
  That obstinate, ranting Reilly.
In every street 'tis him I meet:
  In vain the bye-way path I try;
The very shadow of my feet,
  I might as well attempt to fly
As that boy that follows me every day,
  Although he declares that I use him vilely:
But all I can say, he won't go away,
  That raking, ranting Reilly.

My mother she sent me ten miles away,
  In hopes that the fellow would never find me;
But the very next day, as we made the hay,
  The villain stood close behind me.
" For this," says I, " you'll dearly pay,
  How dare you such a freedom take?"
Says he : " I heard you were making hay,
  And I thought my dear, you'd want a rake:
And therefore I followed you here to-day,
  With your diamond eye and your point so wily,
Like a needle concealed in a bundle of hay,
  But I found you out," says Reilly.

I told him at last in a rage, to pack!
  And he fought for awhile after that more shyly;
But like a bad shilling, he still comes back,
  That counterfeit rogue, that Reilly.
To hunt me up he takes disguise ;
  Last week a beggar girl appears:
'Twas the rogue himself, but I knew his eyes,
  And didn't I box the rascal's ears!
Yet still he keeps following me every day,
  Plotting and planning so cute and slily;
There isn't a fox more tricks can play,
  Than raking, ranting Reilly.

THAT ROGUE REILLY.—*Continued.*

A nunnery, now, my old maiden aunt
   Declares for young women the best protection:
But shelter so very secure, I can't
   Consider without objection.
A plague on the fellows both great and small,
   They bother us so, till they find a wife;
Yet if we should never be bothered at all,
   I think 'twould be rather a stupid life.
So still the rogue follows me every day,
   And still I continue to use him vilely,
But the neighbors all say: till I'm burned to clay,
   I'll never get rid of Reilly.

——o——

THE MAID OF SKREEN.

THERE was a lad who loved a lass,
   Her dwelling was near Skreen;
Fair Flora in her beauty
   Could not equal this fair dame.
This lovely maid has me ensnared,
   And stole my tender heart,
By which indeed my veins do bleed:
   I'm burning with a love-sick dart.

When I'm alone I sigh and moan,
   And thus I often said—
I'd conquer men or *rifle* (rival?) swains,
   To gain this lovely maid.
I'd cross the deep without a ship
   (The mermaid would be my friend),
By land or say I'll spend my days
   Without the least content.

O! fairest of all womankind
   That e'er my eyes did see,
Take pity on your own true love,
   Prove kind, and marry me.
On mossy banks and purling streams,
   I'll wander and I'll rove,
Still raving and complaining
   For the loss of my true love.

THE IRISH WIFE.

I WOULD not give my Irish wife
   For all the dames of the Saxon land—
I would not give my Irish wife
   For the Queen of France's hand ;
For, she to me is dearer
   Than castles strong, or lands, or life—
An outlaw, so I'm near her
   To love till death my Irish wife.

Oh! what would be this home of mine—
   A ruined, hermit-haunted place,
But for the light that nightly shines
   Upon its walls from Kathleen's face ?
What comfort is a mine of gold—
   What pleasure in a royal life—
If the heart within lay dead and cold,
   If I could not have wed my Irish wife ?

When the law forbade the banns,
   I knew my king abhorred her race :
Who never bent before their clans,
   Must bow before their ladies' grace.
Take all my forfeited domain,
   I cannot wage with kinsmen strife,
Take knightly gear and noble name,
   And I will keep my Irish wife.

My Irish wife has clear blue eyes,
   My heaven by day, my stars by night ;
And twin like truth and fondness lie
   Within her swelling bosom white :
My Irish wife has golden hair ;
   Apollo's harp had once such strings :
Apollo's self might pause to hear
   Her bird-like carol when she sings.

I would not give my Irish wife
   For all the dames of the Saxon land—
I would not give my Irish wife
   For the Queen of France's hand :

THE IRISH WIFE.—*Continued.*

For, she to me is dearer
   Than castles strong, or lands, or life ;
In death I would be near her,
   And rise beside my Irish wife.

——o——

ENNISKILLEN DRAGOON.

A BEAUTIFUL damsel of fame and renown,
A gentleman's daughter of fame and renown,
As she rode by the barracks this beautiful maid,
She stood in her coach to see the dragoons parade.

They were all dressed out like gentlemen's sons,
With their bright shining swords and carbine guns,
With their silver-mounted pistols she observed them full soon,
Because that she loved her Enniskillen dragoon.

Yon bright son of Mars who stands on the right,
Whose armor doth shine like the bright stars of night,
Saying : " Willie, dearest Willie, you've listed full soon,
For to serve as a Royal Enniskillen dragoon. "

" O Flora, dearest Flora ! your pardon I crave :
It's now and forever I must be a slave—
Your parents they insulted me, both morning and noon,
For fear that you'd wed an Enniskillen dragoon. "

" Oh ! mind, dearest Willie, Oh ! mind what you say :
For, children are bound their parents to obey ;
For, when we're leaving Ireland, they will all change their
      tune,
Saying : " The Lord may be with you, Enniskillen dragoon !"

Fare you well, Enniskillen ! fare you well for a while,
And all round the borders of Erin's green Isle !
And when the war is over, he'll return in full bloom,
And they'll all welcome home the Enniskillen dragoon.

THE SAVAGE LOVES HIS NATIVE SHORE.

By James Orr. (The Poet of Ballycarry.)

THE savage loves his native shore,
  Though rude the soil and chill the air :
Then well may Erin's sons adore,
  Their isle which nature formed so fair.
What flood reflects a shore so sweet
  As Shannon great, or pastoral Bann?
Or, who a friend or foe can meet,
  So generous as an Irishman?

His hand is rash, his heart is warm,
  But honesty is still his guide ;
None more repents a deed of harm,
  And none forgives with nobler pride :
He may be duped, but won't be dared—
  More fit to practice than to plan ;
He dearly earns his poor reward,
  And spends it like an Irishman.

If strange or poor, for you he'll pay,
  And guide to where you safe may be ;
If you're his guest, the while you stay
  His cottage holds a jubilee.
His inmost soul he will unlock,
  And if he may your secrets scan,
Your confidence he scorns to mock,
  For faithful is an Irishman.

By honor bound in woe or weal,
  What'er she bids he dares to do ;
Try him with bribes—they won't prevail,
  Prove him in fire—you'll find him true.
He seeks no safety, let his post
  Be where it ought in danger's van ;
And if the field of fame be lost,
  It won't be by an Irishman.

Erin ! loved land, from age to age,
  Be thou more great, more famed and free,
May peace be thine, or, shouldst thou wage
  Defensive war—cheap victory.

THE SAVAGE LOVES HIS NATIVE SHORE.—*Continued.*

May plenty bloom in every field
  Which gentle breezes softly fan,
And cheerful smiles serenely gild,
  The home of every Irishman!

———0———

STEER MY BARK TO ERIN'S ISLE.

OH! I have roamed through many lands,
  And many friends I've met;
Not one fair scene or kindly smile,
  Can this fond heart forget.
But I'll confess that I'm content,
  No more I wish to roam;
Oh! steer my bark to Erin's isle,
  For Erin is my home.

In Erin's isle there's manly hearts,
  And bosoms pure as snow,
In Erin's isle there's right good cheer,
  And hearts that overflow.
In Erin's isle I'd pass my time,
  No more 1 wish to roam;
Oh! steer my bark to Erin's isle,
  For Erin is my home.

If England was my place of birth,
  I'd love her tranquil shore.
If bonny Scotland was my home,
  Her mountains I'd adore.
But pleasant days in both I've passed:
  I'd dream of days to come;
Oh! steer my bark to Erin's isle,
  For Erin is my home.

OULD IRELAND, YOU'RE MY DARLIN'

By John Brougham.

Ould Ireland, you're
  My jewel, shure,
My heart's delight and glory:
  Till time shall pass
His empty glass,
  Your name shall live in story;
And this shall be
  The song for me,
The first my heart was larnin',
  Before my tongue
One accent sung:
  Ould Ireland, you're my darlin'!

My blessin's on
  Each manly son
Of thine who will stand by thee;
  But hang the knave
And dastard slave
  So base as to deny thee—
Then bowld and free,
  While yet for me
The globe is 'round us whirlin',
  My song shall be:
Gra Galmachree,
  Ould Ireland, you're my darlin'!

Sweet spot of earth,
  That gave me birth,
Deep in my soul I cherish,
  While life remains
Within these veins,
  A love that ne'er can perish:
If it was a thing
  That I could sing
Like any thrush or starlin',
  In cage or tree,
My song should be:
  Ould Ireland, you're my darlin'!

HIBERNIA'S LOVELY JEAN.

WHEN parting from the Scottish shore,
  And the Highlands' mossy banks,
To Germany we all sailed o'er,
  To join the hostile ranks:
At length in Ireland we arrived,
  After a long campaign,
Where a bonny maid my heart betrayed—
  She's Hibernia's lovely Jean.

Her cheeks were of the roseate hue,
  With the bright blinks of her e'en,
Besparkling with the drops of dew
  That spangle the meadows green.
Jean Cameron ne'er was half so fair,
  No! nor Jessy of Dunblane,
No princess fine can her outshine—
  She's Hibernia's lovely Jean.

This bonny lass of Irish braw,
  Was of a high degree;
Her parents said, a soldier's bride
  Their daughter ne'er should be.
Overwhelmed with care, grief and despair,
  No hope does now remain,
Since the nymph divine cannot be mine,
  She's Hibernia's lovely Jean.

My tartan plaid I will forsake,
  My commission I'll resign,
I'll make this bonny lass my bride,
  If the lassie will be mine;
Then in Ireland, where the graces dwell,
  For ever I'll remain,
And in Hymen's band join heart in hand,
  Wi' Hibernia's lovely Jean.

Should war triumphant sound again,
  And call her sons to arms,
Or Neptune waft me o'er the flood,
  Far from Jeannie's charms;
Should I be laid in honor's bed,
  By a ball or dart be slain,
Death's pangs would cure the pains I bear
  For Hibernia's lovely Jean.

THE WEARING OF THE GREEN.

OH! Paddy dear, and did you hear the news that's going
round?
The Shamrock is forbid by laws, to grow on Irish ground.
No more St. Patrick's day we'll keep, his color can't be seen!
For, there's a bloody law agin the wearing of the Green!
Oh! I met with Napper-Tandy, and he took me by the hand,
And he says: "How is poor ould Ireland, and how does she
stand?
She's the most distressed country that ever I have seen:
For, they're hanging men and women, for the wearing of the
Green!

And since the color we must wear, is England's cruel red,
Ould Ireland's sons will ne'er forget the blood that they have
shed—
Then take the shamrock from your hat, and cast it on the sod:
It will take root, and flourish still, tho' under foot 'tis trod.

When the law can stop the blades of grass from growing as
they grow—
And when the leaves, in summer time, their verdure do
not show—
Then I will change the color I wear in my caubeen:
But, till that day, plaze God! I'll stick to the wearing of the
Green!

But, if at last, her colors should be torn from Ireland's heart,
Her sons, with shame and sorrow, from the dear old soil will
part:
I've heard whispers of a country that lies far beyond the sea,
Where rich and poor stand equal, in the light of Freedom's
day!

Oh, Erin! must we leave you, driven by the tyrant's hand?
Must we ask a mother's blessing, in a strange but happy land,
Where the cruel cross of England's thraldom is never to be seen,
But where, thank God! we'll live and die, still wearing of the
Green?

ADIEU TO INNISFAIL.

BY R. D. WILLIAMS

Air "The Cruiskeen Lawn."

ADIEU!—the snowy sail
Swells her bosom to the gale,
And our bark from Innisfail
          Bounds away.

While we gaze upon thy shore,
That we never shall see more,
And the blinding tears flow o'er,
          We pray.

Ma cuirneen! be thou long
In peace the queen of song—
In battle, proud and strong
          As the sea.

Be saints thine offspring still,
True heroes guard each hill,
And harps by ev'ry rill
          Sound free!

Though, round her Indian bowers,
The hand of nature showers
The brightest, blooming flowers
          Of our sphere:

ADIEU TO INNISFAIL.—*Continued.*

Yet not the richest rose
In an *alien* clime that blows,
Like the briar at home that grows
              Is dear.

Though glowing breasts may be
In soft vales beyond the sea,
Yet ever, *gra ma chree*,
              Shall I wail

For the heart of love I leave,
In the dreary hours of eve,
On thy stormy shores to grieve,
              Innisfail!

But mem'ry o'er the deep
On her dewy wing shall sweep,
When in midnight hours I weep
              O'er thy wrongs;

And brings me, steeped in tears,
The dead flowers of other years,
And waft unto my ears
              Home's songs,

When I slumber in the gloom
Of a nameless, foreign tomb,
By a distant ocean's boom,
              Innisfail!

Around thy em'rald shore
May the clasping sea adore,
And each wave in thunder roar,
              " All hail!"

And when the final sigh
Shall bear my soul on high,
And on chainless wing I fly
              Through the blue,

Earth's latest thought shall be,
As I soar above the sea,
" Green Erin, dear, to thee
              Adieu! "

WIDOW MALONE.

By Charles Lever.

Did you ever hear tell of the widow Malone, ohone,
Who lived in the town of Athlone, ohone?
　　Oh! she melted the hearts
　　Of the swains in them parts,
So lovely, the widow Malone, ohone!
So lovely, the widow Malone.

Of lovers she had a full score, or more,
And fortunes they all had galore, in store;
　　From the minister down
　　To the clerk of the crown,
All were courting the widow Malone, ohone!
All were courting the widow Malone.

But so modest was Mistress Malone, 'twas known
That no one could see her alone, ohone!
　　Let them ogle and sigh,
　　They could ne'er catch her eye,
So bashful the widow Malone, ohone!
So bashful the widow Malone.

Till one Mister O'Brien, from Clare, how-quare!
It's little for blushing they care down there,
　　Put his arm round her waist—
　　Gave ten kisses at laste—
"Oh!" says he, "you're my Molly Malone, my own!
Oh!" says he, "you're my Molly Molone."

And the widow they all thought so shy, my eye!
Ne'er thought of a simper or sigh, for why?
　　But "Lucius," says she,
　　"Since you've now made so free,
You may marry your Mary Malone, ohone!
You may marry your Mary Malone."

OH! ERIN, MY COUNTRY!

OH! Erin, my Country! altho' thy harp slumbers,
  And lies in oblivion near Tara's old hall,
With scarce one kind hand to awaken thy slumbers,
  Or sound a long dirge to the sons of Fingal:
The trophies of warfare they stand still neglected;
  For, cold lie the warriors to whom they were known;
But the harp of old Ireland shall be respected,
  While there lives but one bard to enliven its tone.

Oh! Erin, my Country! I love thy green bowers,
  No music to me like thy murmuring rill:
The shamrock to me is the fairest of flowers,
  And nothing more dear than thy daisy-clad hills;
Thy caves, whether used by warriors or sages,
  Are still sacred held in each Irishman's heart,
And thy ivy-crowned turrets, the pride of past ages,
  Tho' mould'ring in ruin, do grandeur impart.

Britannia may boast of her lion and armor,
  And glory, when she her old wooden walls views:
Caledonia may boast of her pibroch and clamor,
  And pride in her philibeg, kilt and hose:
But where is the nation can rival old Erin?
  Or, where is the country such heroes can boast?
In battle, they're fierce as the lion and tiger,
  And bold as the eagle that flies round her coast.

The breeze often shakes both the rose and the thistle,
  Whilst Erin's green shamrock lies hushed in the dale:
Contented it grows whilst the wintry wind whistles,
  And lies undisturbed in the moss of the vale:
Then hail, dearest island in Neptune's proud ocean,
  The land of my forefathers, my parents' agra!
Cold, cold must the heart be and devoid of emotion,
  That loves not the music of Erin-go-bragh.

KITTY TYRRELL.

You're looking as fresh as the morn, darling,
   You're looking as bright as the day;
But while on your charms I'm dilating,
   You're stealing my poor heart away:
But keep it and welcome, mavourneen,
   Its loss I'm not going to mourn;
Yet one heart's enough for a body,
   So pray give me yours in return,
     Mavourneen, mavourneen,
   Oh! pray give me yours in return.

I've built me a neat little cot, darling,
   I've pigs and potatoes in store;
I've twenty good pounds in the bank, love,
   And may be a pound or two more.
It's all very well to have riches,
   But I'm such a covetous elf,
I can't help still sighing for something,
   And, darling, that something's yourself,
     Mavourneen, mavourneen,
   And that something, you know, is yourself.

You're smiling, and that's a good sign, darling,
   Say "Yes," and you'll never repent,
Or, if you would rather be silent,
   Your silence I'll take for consent.
That good-natured dimple's a tell-tale,
   Now all that I have is your own,
This week you may be Kitty Tyrrell,
   Next week you'll be Mistress Malone,
     Mavourneen, mavourneen,
   You'll be my own Mistress Malone.

SINCE I'VE BEEN IN THE ARMY:

OR, THE GENTLEMAN OF THE ARMY.

I'M Paddy Whack of Ballyhack,
  Not long ago turned soldier :
In grand attack, in storm or sack,
  None will than I be bolder.
With spirits gay I march away,
  I please each fair beholder :
And now they sing ! " He's quite the thing,
  Och ! what a jovial soldier ! "
In Londonderry, or London merry,
  Och ! faith ! ye girls I charm ye :
And there ye come at beat of drum,
  To see me in the army—

CHORUS.

Rub a dub dub, and pilli li loo,
  Whack ! fal de lal la and trilli li loo :
I laugh and sing : aye that's the thing,
  Since I've been in the army !

The lots of girls my train unfurls,
  Would form a pleasant party ;
There's Kitty Lynch, a tidy wench,
  And Suke, and Peg M'Carthy :
Miss Judy Baggs, and Sally Maggs,
  And Martha Scraggs all storm me :
And Molly Maghee is after me,
  Since I've been in the army !
The Sallys and Pollys, the Kittys and Dollys,
  In numbers would alarm ye :
E'en Mrs. White, who's lost her sight,
  Admires me in the army—
                              Rub a dub dub, &c.

The roaring boys who made a noise,
  And thwacked me like the devil,
Are now become before me dumb,
  Or else are mighty civil :
There's Murphy Roarke, who often broke
  My head, now daresn't harm me :

SINCE I'VE BEEN IN THE ARMY.—*Continued.*

But bows and quakes and off he sneaks,
   Since I've been in the army—
And if one neglect to pay me respect,
   Och! another tips the blarney
With " Whist! my friend, and don't offend
   A gentleman of the army."
                    Rub a dub dub, &c.

My arms are bright: my heart is light,
   Good-humor seems to warm me:
I've now become with every chum
   A favorite in the army.
If I go on as I've begun,
   My comrades all inform me
They soon shall see that I will be
   A general in the army.
Delightful notion to get promotion:
   Then, ladies, how I'll charm ye!
For, 'tis my belief: Commander-in-Chief
   I shall be in the army.
                    Rub a dub dub, &c.

——o——

NORAH, THE PRIDE OF KILDARE.

As beauteous as Flora, is charming young Norah,
The joy of my heart and the Pride of Kildare,
I ne'er will deceive her; for, sadly 'twould grieve her,
To find that I sighed for another, less fair.

   Her heart with truth teeming, her eyes with smiles
       beaming,
   What mortal could injure a blossom so rare
   As Norah, dear Norah, the Pride of Kildare?

Where'er I may be, love, I'll ne'er forget thee, love;
Though beauties may smile and try to ensnare,
No, nothing shall ever my heart from thine sever,
Dear Norah, sweet Norah, the Pride of Kildare!
       Her heart with truth beaming, &c.

THE NEW ST. PATRICK'S DAY.

IT was one lovely morning, all in the month of May,
Down by a crystal fountain I carelessly did walk,
It's I being very tired and weary, I laid myself down to rest,
For to listen to the notes of the blackbird and thrush.

It's I being tired and weary, I laid myself down,
In silence to repose, and my sorrows to drown,
Up stepp'd a man, approaching without any more delay,
When I awoke from my slumber, it was St. Patrick's day.

There is this advice I'll give you, and mind it while you live ;
To the rose and thistle your secrets don't give,
For the catholics of Ireland are generous you know,
And they are always ready to face the daring foe.

There is another advice I'll give you, and mind it while you can,
And never trust your secrets to any other man,
For if that you do, they will surely you betray,
And will laugh at your downfall on St. Patrick's day.

It's have you not heard of this new invented plan,
How they all join together in the voice of a man,
For like the Bethel unions in the year ninty-four,
When the shamrock joined the thistle, boys, it grieves their
            hearts full sore.

O, Erin, dear loved country, oppressed—but not bowed down,
Thou yet shalt rise in splendor, with honor and renown ;
Thy hardy sons shall aid thee, in spite of all thy foes,
The war-like mountain thistle, or the over-reaching rose.

O mourn not, blooming shamrock, thy sorrows soon shall end,
Justice hears thy wailing, and succor soon shall send,
Like Mars, the god of battle, thou shalt put forth thy might,
The nations that surround thee, shall own thy cause as right.

A toast unto the Shamrock and famed St. Patrick's day,
And every true-bred Irishman this welcome tribute pay ;
Success to the brave patriots, who for their country died,
Still shall the four-leaved shamrock of nations be our pride.

IRISH MOLLY.

A Street Ballad.

OH ! who is that poor foreigner that lately came to town,
And like a ghost that cannot rest still wanders up and down ?
A poor, unhappy Scottish youth :—if more you wish to know,
His heart is breaking all for love of Irish Molly O !

    She's modest, mild, and beautiful, the fairest I have
          known—
    The primrose of Ireland—all blooming here alone—
    The primrose of Ireland, for wheresoe'er I go,
    The only one entices me is Irish Molly O !

When Molly's father heard of it, a solemn oath he swore,
That if she'd wed a foreigner he'd never see her more.
He sent for young Mac Donald and he plainly told him so—
" I'll never give to such as you my Irish Molly O !"
                  She's modest, &c.

Mac Donald heard the heavy news—and grievously did say –
" Farewell, my lovely Molly, since I'm banished far away,
A poor forlorn pilgrim I must wander to and fro,
And all for the sake of my Irish Molly O !
                  She's modest, &c.

" There is a rose in Ireland, I thought it would be mine ;
But now that she is lost to me, I must for ever pine,
Till death shall come to comfort me, for to the grave I'll go,
And all for the sake of my Irish Molly O !
                  She's modest, &c.

" And now that I am dying, this one request I crave,
To place a marble tombstone above my humble grave !
And on the stone these simple words I'd have engraven so—
Mac Donald lost his life for love of Irish Molly O !"
                  She's modest, &c.

A PLACE IN THY MEMORY, DEAREST.

By Gerald Griffin.

A PLACE in thy memory, Dearest,
  Is all that I claim!
To pause and look back, when thou hearest
  The sound of my name!
Another may woo thee nearer,
  Another may win and wear—
I care not though he be dearer:
  So I am remembered there!
     Remember me not as a lover
      Whose hope has been cross't,
     Whose bosom can never recover
      The light it has lost.
     As the young bride remembers the mother
      She loves, though she never may see—
     As a sister remembers a brother,
      Oh! Dearest, remember me!

I'd be thy true lover, Dearest,
  Couldst thou smile on me!
I would be the fondest and nearest
  That ever loved thee!
But a cloud on my pathway is looming,
  That never must burst upon thine:
And Heaven that made thee all blooming,
  Ne'er made thee to wither or pine!
     Remember me, then; oh! remember
      My calm light love!
     Tho' bleak as the blasts of November
      My life may prove:
     That life will, though lonely, be sweet,
      If its brightest enjoyment should be
     A smile and kind word when we meet,
      And a place in thy memory!

THE IRISHMAN'S SHANTY.

DID you ever go into an Irishman's shanty ?
Ah! there, boys, you'll find the whiskey so plenty ;
With a pipe in his mouth, there sits Paddy so free,
No king in his palace is prouder than he.
    Hurrah! my honey.
 SPOKEN: Now then, boys, one for Paddy.
    Whack! Paddy's the boy. •
     Ah! Ah! Ah! Ah! Ah!

There's a three legged stool and a table to match,
And the door of the shanty is locked with a latch,
There's a nate feather mattress all bursting with straw,
For the want of a bedstead it lies on the floor.
    Hurrah! my honey.
 SPOKEN: Now then, boys, one for the mattress.
    Whack! Paddy's the boy, &c.

There's a nate little bureau, without paint or gilt,
Made of boards that were left when the shanty was built;
And a three cornered mirror that hangs on the wall,
But devil a picture's been in it all.
    Hurrah! my honey.
 SPOKEN: Now then, boys, one for the picture.
    Whack! Paddy's the boy, &c.

He has three rooms in one—kitchen, bedroom, and hall ;
And his chest, it is three wooden pegs on the wall,
He's two suits of clothes, 'tis a wardrobe complete,
One to wear in the shanty, the same in the street.
    Hurrah! my honey.
 SPOKEN: Now then, boys, one for the old clothes.
    Whack! Paddy's the boy, &c.

He's a pig in the sty, and a cow in the stable,
And feeds them on scraps that's left from the table.
They get sick if confined, so they roam at their ease,
And go into the shanty whenever they please.
    Hurrah! my honey.
 SPOKEN: Now then, boys, one for the pigs.
    Whack! Paddy's the boy, &c.

THE IRISHMAN'S SHANTY.—*Continued.*

He can relish good victuals as ever ye's ate,
But is always contented with praties and mate ;
He prefers them when cowld (if he can't get them hot),
And makes tay in a bowl, when he can't get a pot.
        Hurrah ! my honey.
    SPOKEN : Now then, boys, one for the praties.
            Whack ! Paddy's the boy, &c.

He heeds not the rain, though it comes in a flood :
For, the roof of the shanty is shingled with mud.
There's a hole at one end that makes a chimney so neat
For the smoke and the sparks from the fire to retreat.
        Hurrah ! my honey.
    SPOKEN : Now then, boys, one for the roof.
            Whack ! Paddy's the boy, &c.

There is one who partakes of his sorrows and joys,
Who attends to the shanty, the girls and the boys ;
The brats he thinks more of than gold that's refined,
But Biddy's the jewel that's set in his mind.
        Hurrah ! my honey.
    SPOKEN : Now then, boys, one for Biddy.
            Whack ! Paddy's the boy, &c.

The rich may divide their enjoyments alone,
With those who have riches as great as their own :
But Pat hangs the latch-strings outside of his door,
And will share his last cent with the needy and poor.
        Hurrah ! my honey.
    SPOKEN : Now then, boys, one for Pat's generosity.
            Whack ! Paddy's the boy, &c.

TIM FINIGAN'S WAKE.

TIM FINIGAN lived in Walker Street,
  A gentleman Irishman—mighty odd—
He'd a beautiful brogue, so rich and sweet,
  And to rise in the world, he carried the hod.
But, you see, he'd a sort of a tipling way:
  With a love for the liquor poor Tim was born:
And, to help him through his work, each day,
  He'd a drop of the creatur' every morn.

CHORUS.

Whack, hurrah! blood and 'ounds! ye sowl ye,
  Welt the flure, ye're trotters shake,
Isn't it the truth I've tould ye?
  Lots of fun, at Finigan's wake?

One morning, Tim was rather full;
  His head felt heavy, which made him shake,
He fell from the ladder, and broke his skull:
  So they carried him home a corpse to wake.
They rolled him up in a nice clean sheet,
  And laid him out upon the bed,
With fourteen candles around his feet,
  And a couple of dozen around his head.

His friends assembled at his wake:
  Missus Finigan called out for the lunch,
First, they laid in tay and cake;
  Then, pipes and tobacky, and whiskey-punch.
Miss Biddy O'Brien began to cry;
  "Such a purty corpse did ever you see?
Arrah! Tim avourneen, an' why did ye die?"
  "Och, none of your gab," sez Judy Magee.

Then Peggy O'Connor took up the job:
  "Arrah! Biddy," says she, "ye're wrong, I'm shure"—
But Judy, then, gave her a belt on the gob,
  And left her sprawling on the flure.
Each side in the war did soon engage:
  'Twas woman to woman and man to man;
Shillelah-law was all the rage—
  An' a bloody ruction soon began.

TIM FINIGAN'S WAKE.—*Continued.*

Mickey Mulvaney raised his head,
  When a gallon of whiskey flew at him:
It missed him—and hopping on the bed,
  The liquor scattered over Tim!
Bedad! he revives! see how he raises!
  An' Timothy, jumping from the bed,
Cries, while he lathered around like blazes ;—
  " Bad luck to yer souls! d'ye think I'm dead?"

——o——

THE FLAMING O'FLANNIGANS.

OH! now I'm of age, and come into my property,
  Devil a ha'porth I'll think of but fun!
'Tis myself 'll be putting the ladies in joppardy,
  Just for to prove I'm my daddy's own son.
Och me! Miss Malone, I'll tache you civility:
  Judy O'Doddy, escape—if you can ;
I'm that 'll show yez the sweet sensibility,
  Lovin' most women, and fearin' no man.
    For, that was the way wid all the O'Flannigans,
      From the first bud of them down to myself:
    And wasn't my mother, besides, of the Bralagans?
      Why shouldn't I be a comical elf?

Oh! the racing and coorsing, and hunting and shooting,
  The clattering of glasses, and batt'ring of skulls:
The dances where I'll be upon the best footing
  With Irish Miss Murphies and English Miss Bulls:
The nate little parties of pleasure we'll rowl to,
  The rows and the ructions, and devil knows what—
The Dunns that I'll bate black and blue, by my soul, too,
  And the duels, that 'll ind wid the very first shot.
    For, that was the way with the Flaming O'Flannigans,
      From the first illigant boys of the name ,
    And wasn't my mother, besides, of the Bralagans?
      Why shouldn't I be a cock of the game?

THE RISING OF THE MOON.

Oh! then, tell me, Shane O'Farrell, tell me where you hurry so?
Hush, ma bouchal! hush and listen—and his cheeks were all
   aglow—
I bear orders from the Captain; get you ready quick and soon;
For, the pikes must be together by the risin' of the moon.

Chorus.

By the risin' of the Moon, by the risin' of the Moon;
For, the pikes must be together by the risin' of the Moon.

Oh! then, tell me, Shane O'Farrell, where the gatherin' is
   to be?
In the ould spot, by the river, right well-known to you and me.
One word more: for signal-token whistle up the marchin' tune,
With your pike upon your shoulder, by the risin' of the Moon.
   By the risin' of the Moon, &c.

Out from many a mud-wall cabin, eyes were watching thro'
   that night;
Many a manly heart was throbbing for that blessed warning
   light;
Murmurs passed along the valley, like a banshee's lonely croon;
And a thousand pikes were flashing by the risin' of the Moon.
   By the risin' of the Moon, &c.

Down along yon singing river, that dark mass of men was
   seen;
High above their shining weapons floats their own beloved
   green.
Death to every foe and traitor! forward strike the marchin'
   tune!
And hurrah, my boys, for Freedom! 'tis the risin' of the Moon.
   'Tis the risin' of the Moon, &c.

Well they fought for poor Ould Ireland, and full bitter was
   their fate;
Oh! what glorious pride and sorrow fill the name of Ninety-
   eight!
But yet, thank God! there's beating hearts in manhood's
   burning noon,
Who will follow in their footsteps by the risin' of the Moon.
   By the risin' of the Moon, &c.

FERMOY.

MOLLY BRALLAGHAN.

AH ! then, mam dear, did you never hear of purty Molly Bral-
      laghan ?
Troth, dear ! I have lost her, and I'll never be a man again,
Not a spot on my hide will another summer tan again,
  Since Molly she has left me all alone for to die.
The place where my heart was, you might easy rowl a
      turnip in,
As big as any pavin' stone : and from Dublin to the Devil's
      Glen,
If she chose to take another, sure she might have sent mine
      back again,
  And not leave me here all alone for to die.

Mam dear, I remember, when the milking time was past and
      gone,
We went into the meadows where she swore I was the only
      man
That ever she could love—yet, oh ! the base, the cruel one,
  After all that, to leave me here alone for to die !
Mam dear, I remember as we came home the rain began,
I rolled her in my coat, tho' devil a waistcoat I had on,
And my shirt was rather fine-drawn : yet oh ! the base and
      cruel one,
  After all that, she left me here alone for to die !

I went and told my tale to Father M'Donnel, mam,
And thin I wint and axed advice of Counsellor O'Connell,
      mam ;
He tould me promise-breeches had been ever since the world
      began—
  Now, I have only one pair, mam, and they are corduroy !
Arrah ! what could he mean, mam, or what would you advise
      me to do ?
Must my corduroys to Molly go ? in troth, I'm bothered what
      to do.
I can't afford to lose both my heart and my breeches, too—
  Yet, what need I care, when I've only got to die ?

MOLLY BRALLAGHAN.—*Continued.*

Oh! the left side of my carcass is as weak as water-gruel,
    mam—
The devil a bit upon my bones, since Molly's proved so cruel,
    mam:
I wish I had a carabine, I'd go and fight a duel, mam,
  Sure, it's better far to kill myself than to stay here to die.
I'm hot and determined as a live salamander, mam,
Wont you come to my wake, when I go my long meander, mam?
Oh! I'll feel myself as valiant as the famous Alexander mam,
  When I hear yiz crying round me: "Arrah! why did ye
    die?"

——o——

MY EMMET'S NO MORE.

DESPAIR in her wild eye, a daughter of Erin
Appeared on the cliffs of the bleak rocky shore;
Loose in the wind flowed her dark streaming ringlets
And heedless she gazed on the dread surge's roar.
Loud rang her harp in wild tones of despairing;
The time passed away with the present comparing,
And in soul thrilling strains deeper sorrow declaring,
She sang Erin's woes and her Emmet no more.

O Erin, my country, your glory's departed;
For, tyrants and traitors have stabbed thy heart's core,
Thy daughters have laved in the streams of affliction,
Thy patriots have fled, or lie stretched in their gore:
Ruthless ruffians now prowl thro' thy hamlets forsaken,
From pale hungry orphans their last morsel have taken;
The screams of thy females no pity awaken;
Alas! my poor country, your Emmet's no more!

Brave was his spirit, yet mild as the Brahmin,
His heart bled in anguish the wrongs of the poor;
To relieve their hard sufferings he braved every danger,
The vengeance of tyrants undauntedly bore.
E'en before him the proud titled villains in power
Were seen, though in ermine, in terror to cower:
But alas! he is gone— he has fallen a young flower.
They have murdered my Emmet, my Emmet's no more!

YOU'LL SOON FORGET KATHLEEN.

OH! leave not your Kathleen there's no one can cheer her,
  Alone in the wide world, unpitied she'll sigh :
And scenes that were loveliest, when thou wert but near her,
  Recall the sad visions of days long gone by!
'Tis vain that you tell me you'll never forget me :
  To the land of the shamrock you'll ne'er return more :
Far away from your sight, you will cease to regret me!
  You'll soon forget Kathleen, and Erin go bragh !

Oh ! leave not the land, the sweet land of your childhood,
  Where joyously passed the first days of our youth,
Where gaily we wandered 'mid valley and wildwood :
  Oh ! those were the bright days of innocent truth !
'Tis vain that you tell me you'll never forget me :
  To the land of the shamrock you'll ne'er return more :
Far away from your sight, you will cease to regret me,
  You'll soon forget Kathleen, and Erin go bragh !

———o———

TELL ME, MARY.

TELL me, Mary, how to woo thee,
  Teach my bosom to reveal
All my passion, Sweet, unto thee,
  All the love my heart can feel.
No, when joy first brightened o'er me,
  'Twas not joy illumed her ray :
And when sorrow flies before me,
  'Twill not chase her smile away.
                    Tell me, Mary, &c.

Like the tree no winds can sever
  From the ivy round it cast,
Thus, the heart that loves thee ever,
  Loves thee, Mary, to the last.
Tell me, Mary, how to love thee,
  Teach my bosom to reveal
All its sorrow, Sweet, unto thee,
  All the love my heart can feel.
                    Tell me, Mary, &c.

THE SUIT OF GREEN.

COME, all you pretty, fair maids, and listen to my melody,
When you hear my lamentation, I am sure you will pity me;
'Tis once I loved a young man, as neat a youth as could be seen,
He was torn from my arms, for wearing a suit of green.

I was sent for by my master—a girl that I liked to see,
She took me up to Dublin, some fineries to show to me:
She took me to a shop, of the neatest cloth that could be seen,
Embroidered with gold lace, and she bought me a suit of green.

'Twas on a summer's evening, as my love and I chanced to
        rove,
Folded in each other's arms, we pass'd thro' shady groves;
He laid his head against my breast, and most feelingly to me
        did say,
" My love, my life is in danger, for wearing of a suit of green."

I said, " My dearest William, if what you say to me be true,
Pray take off those green clothes, and I'll buy you a suit of
        blue ; "
" Oh no, my charming girl," he said," such cowardice shall
        ne'er be seen,
I am a son to Granua, and always will adorn the green.

I am a son to Granua—suppose from me my life they tore,
It is my national color—the shamrock St. Patrick wore ;
For it ne'er shall falter, tho' thousands do owe me spleen,
For some of the Queen's army have their facings made of
        green."

It was on a Sunday evening, as my love and I sat in a room,
Not thinking of any harm, immediately the guards did come :
With their guns they broke the door, the moment my love
        they'd seen,
And they tore him from my arms, for wearing the suit of green.

My love was taken prisoner, and by a court-martial he was
        tried,
The colonel gave orders, at twelve o'clock next day he should
        die ,
He said, " I disregard you, if the rights of law you give to me,
For all the crime you have against me is for wearing a suit
        of green."

THE SUIT OF GREEN.—*Continued.*

My love went to the general, her case to him she did make
      known,
Imploring for his mercy, down on her bended knees did fall;
" Arise! my charming girl," he said, " your love to you I will
      set free,
I'll restore him to your arms, with leave to wear a suit of
      green."

So now my trial's over, thanks be to God that I am free,
May prosperity attend the man that gave my love to me;
'Tis now I'll wed my Mary—a faithful girl she has proved to
      have been,
I'll embroider her with gold lace, and her mantle shall be of
      green.

———o———

THE DEAR LITTLE SHAMROCK.

There's a dear little plant that grows in our Isle:
  'Twas St. Patrick himself, sure, that set it,
And the sun on his labor, with pleasure, did smile,
  And with dews from his eyes oft did wet it.
It thrives thro' the bog, thro' the brake, thro' the mireland,
  And he called it: the dear little Shamrock of Ireland.
      The sweet little Shamrock,
      The dear little Shamrock,
      The sweet little, green little Shamrock of Ireland.

This dear little plant still grows in our land
  Fresh and fair as the daughters of Erin,
Whose smiles can bewitch, whose eyes can command,
  In each climate that each shall appear in:
And shine thro' the bog, thro' the brake, thro' the mireland,
  Just like their own dear little Shamrock of Ireland.
      The sweet little Shamrock, &c.

This dear little plant that springs from our soil,
  When its three little leaves are extended,
Denotes from one stalk we together should toil,
  And ourselves by ourselves be befriended:
And still thro' the bog, thro' the brake, thro' the mireland,
  From one root should branch like the Shamrock of Ireland.
      The sweet little Shamrock, &c.

NORAH O'NEAL.

Oh! I'm lonely to-night, love, without you,
    And I sigh for one glance of your eye ;
For, sure, there's a charm, love, about you,
    Whenever I know you are nigh.
Like the beam of that star when 'tis smiling
    Is the glance which your eye can't conceal,
And your voice is so sweet and beguiling,
    That I love you, sweet Norah O'Neal.

CHORUS : Oh! I don't think that ever I'll doubt you,
            My love I will never conceal ;
        Oh! I'm lonely to-night, love, without you,
            My darling, sweet Norah O'Neal!

Oh! the nightingale sings in the wild-wood,
    As if every note that he knew
Were learned from your sweet voice in childhood,
    To remind me, sweet Norah, of you ;
But I think, love, so often about you,
    And you don't know how happy I feel—
But I'm lonely to-night, love, without you,
    My darling, sweet Norah O'Neal.
                                    CHORUS.

Oh! why should I weep tears of sorrow ?
    Or why to let hope lose its place ?
Won't I meet you, my darling, to-morrow,
    And smile on your beautiful face ?
Will you meet me? Oh! say, will you meet me
    With a kiss, at the foot of the lane ?
And I'll promise whenever you greet me,
    That I'll never be lonely again.
                                    CHORUS.

THE GREEN FLAG.

A.. D. 1647.

By M. J. Barry.

Boys! fill your glasses,
Each hour that passes
Steals, it may be, on our last night's cheer;
The day soon shall come, boys,
With fife and drum, boys,
Breaking shrilly on the soldier's ear.
Drink the faithful hearts that love us—
'Mid to-morrow's thickest fight,
While our green flag floats above us,
Think, boys, 'tis for them we smite.
Down with each mean flag,
None but the green flag
Shall above us be in triumph seen:
Oh! think on its glory,
Long shrined in story,
Charge for Eire and her flag of green!

Think on old Brian,
War's mighty lion,
'Neath that banner 'twas he smote the Dane;
The Northmen and Saxon
Oft turned their backs on
Those who bore it o'er each crimsoned plain.
Beal-an-atha-Buidhe beheld it
Bagenal's fiery onset curb;
Scotch Munroe would fain have felled it—
We, boys, followed him from red Beinburb.
Down with each mean flag,
None but the green flag
Shall above us be in triumph seen:
Oh! think on its glory,
Long shrined in story,
Charge with Eoghan for our flag of green!

And if, at eve, boys,
Comrades shall grieve, boys,
O'er our corses, let it be with pride,
When thinking that each, boys,
On that red beach, boys,
Lies the flood-mark of the battle's tide.

THE GREEN FLAG.—*Continued.*

See! the first faint ray of morning
  Gilds the east with yellow light!
Hark! the bugle note gives warning—
  One full bumper to old friends to-night.
      Down with each mean flag,
      None but the green flag
Shall above us be in triumph seen;
      Oh! think on its glory,
      Long shrined in story,
Fall or conquer for our flag of green!

——o——

MY LAND.

By Thomas Davis.

SHE is a rich and rare land;
Oh! she's a fresh and fair land;
She is a dear and rare land—
  This native land of mine.

No men than hers are braver—
Her women's hearts ne'er waver;
I'd freely die to save her,
  And think my lot divine.

She's not a dull or cold land;
No! she's a warm and bold land;
Oh! she's a true and old land—
  This native land of mine.

Could beauty ever guard her,
And virtue still reward her,
No foe would cross her border—
  No friend within it pine!

Oh! she's a fresh and fair land,
Oh! she's a true and rare land!
Yes, she's a rare and fair land—
  This native land of mine.

THE GREEN ABOVE THE RED.

By Thomas Davis.

Air—"*Irish Molly, O !* "

FULL often, when our fathers saw the Red above the Green,
They rose in rude but fierce array, with sabre. pike, and skian,
And over many a noble town, and many a field of dead,
They proudly set the Irish Green above the English Red.

But in the end, throughout the land, the shameful sight was
     seen—
The English Red in triumph high above the Irish Green :
But well they died in breach and field, who, as their spirits
     fled,
Still saw the Green maintain its place above the English Red.

And they who saw, in after times, the Red above the Green,
Were withered as the grass that dies beneath a forest screen ;
Yet often by this healthy hope their sinking hearts were fed,
That, in some day to come, the Green should flutter o'er the
     Red.

Sure 'twas for this Lord Edward died, and Wolfe Tone sunk
     serene—
Because they could not bear to leave the Red above the
     Green ;
And 'twas for this Owen fought, and Sarsfield nobly bled—
Because their eyes were hot to see the Green above the Red.

So when the strife began again, our darling Irish Green
Was down upon the earth, while high, the English Red was
     seen ;
Yet still we held our fearless course, for something in us said,
"Before the strife is o'er you'll see the Green above the Red."

And 'tis for this we think and toil, and knowledge strive to
     glean,
That we may pull the English Red below the Irish Green,
And leave our sons sweet liberty, and smiling plenty spread
Above the land once dark with blood—*the Green above the Red !*

THE GREEN ABOVE THE RED.—*Continued.*

The jealous English tyrant now has banned the Irish Green,
And forced us to conceal it like a something foul and mean;
But yet, by heavens! he'll sooner raise his victims from the
    dead,
Than force our hearts to leave the Green and cotton to the
    Red!

We'll trust ourselves, for God is good, and blesses those who
    lean
On their brave hearts, and not upon an earthly king or queen;
And, freely as we lift our hands, we vow our blood to shed,
Once and for evermore to raise the Green above the Red!

——o——

KATHLEEN MAVOURNEEN.

By G. Crouch.

Kathleen Mavourneen! the gray dawn is breaking,
The horn of the hunter is heard on the hill,
The lark from her light wing the bright dew is shaking,
Kathleen Mavourneen! what, slumbering still!
Ah! hast thou forgotten soon we must sever?
Oh! hast thou forgotten this day we must part?
It may be for years, and it may be for ever—
Oh! why art thou silent, thou voice of my heart?
It may be for years, and it may be for ever—
Then why art thou silent, Kathleen Mavourneen?

Kathleen Mavourneen! awake from thy slumbers,
The blue mountains glow in the sun's golden light,
Ah! where is the spell that once hung on my numbers?
Arise in thy beauty, thou star of my night,
Arise in thy beauty, thou star of my night!
Mavourneen, Mavourneen, my sad tears are falling
To think that from Erin and thee I must part,
It may be for years, and it may be for ever—
Then why art thou silent, thou voice of my heart?
It may be for years, and it may be for ever,—
Then why art thou silent, Kathleen Mavourneen?

THE GAEL AND THE GREEN.

By M. J. BARRY.

Air.—" *One bumper at parting.*"

COME, fill every glass to o'erflowing,
  With wine, or *potheen* if you will,
Or, if any think these are too glowing,
  Let water replace them—but fill!
Oh! trust me, 'tis churlish and silly
  To ask how the bumper's filled up;
If the tide in the heart be not chilly,
  What matters the tide in the cup?
Oh! ne'er may that heart's tide ascending
  In shame on our foreheads be seen,
While it nobly can ebb in defending
  Our own glorious color—the Green!

In vain did oppression endeavor
  To trample that Green under foot;
The fair stem was broken, but never
  Could tyranny reach to its root.
Then come, and around it let's rally,
  And guard it henceforward like men!
Oh! soon shall each mountain and valley
  Glow bright with its verdure again.
Meanwhile, fill each glass to the brim, boys,
  With water, with wine, or *potheen*,
And on each let the honest wish swim, boys—
  Long flourish the Gael and the Green!

Here, under our host's gay dominion,
  While gathered this table around,
What varying shades of opinion
  In one happy circle are found!
What opposite creeds come together!
  How mingle North, South, East and West!
Yet who minds the diff'rence a feather?—
  Each strives to love Erin the best.
Oh! soon through our beautiful island
  May union as blessed be seen,
While floats o'er each valley and highland
  Our own glorious color—the Green!

THE NEW IRISH EMIGRANT.

FAREWELL dear Erin, I'm going to leave you
  And cross the seas to a foreign land.
Farewell to friends and kind relations,
  And my aged parents I leave behind.
My heart is breaking all for to leave you,
  Where I have spent many happy days,
With lads and lasses and flowing glasses,
  All for to go to America.

Farewell to the green hills and lovely valleys,
  Where with my true love I often roved,
And fondly told her I ne'er would leave her,
  Whilst walking through each sweet silent grove ;
I'm going to leave you, my charming Mary,
  Was fortune kind, love, sure at home I'd stay,
But do not mourn, for I will return,
  And bring you off to America.

" Lovely William, do not leave me !
  I love you dearly, right well you know,
And for to stray to a foreign nation,
  To leave me here, love, in grief and woe.
The crops have failed and the times are changing,
  Which causes thousands to go away,
But if you'll wait, love, until next season,
  We'll both set sail to America."

My love, I'm bound for foreign nations,
  If the Lord be pleased to send me o'er,
To seek for promotion and look for labor,
  Since all things failed on the shamrock shore.
But if you have patience till fortune favors,
  To crown my labor, believe what I say,
I'll come home, love, with golden store,
  And bring you off to America.

" Change your mind and you will find,
  That we'll have good times upon Erin's shore ;
I'll endeavor to work and labor,
  For to maintain you Mavee Lastore.

THE NEW IRISH EMIGRANT.—*Continued.*

I love you dearly, true and sincerely,
  And if you leave me and go away,
My heart will break all for your sake, love,
  While you are placed in America."

When I am rolling on the ocean,
  Sweet Mary, dear, you'll run in my mind.
So do not mourn, for I will return,
  If you prove constant, I will prove.
I must leave you, my blooming Mary,
  Farewell! adieu! I'm going away,
I do intend it, let none prevent it,
  To seek adventures in America.

" Unknown to parents, friends and relations,
  My dearest William with you I'll go,
For I have plenty to take us over,
  Since all things failed on the Shamrock Shore.
He gave consent, straightway they went,
  And they both got married without delay;
For my pound she'd count down twenty,
  The day we sailed to America.

PAT MALLOY.

AT sixteen years of age, I was my mother's fair-hair'd boy :
She kept a little huxter shop, her name it was Malloy.
"I've fourteen children, Pat," says she, "which Heav'n
    to me has sent;
But childer aint like pigs, you know: they can't pay the
    rent!"
She gave me ev'ry shilling there was in the till,
And kiss'd me fifty times or more, as if she'd never get her
    fill.
" Oh! Heav'n bless you! Pat, " says she, "and don't forget,
    my boy,
That ould Ireland is your country, and your name is Pat
    Malloy!

Oh! England is a purty place: of goold there is no lack—
I trudged from York to London wid me scythe upon me
    back.
The English girls are beautiful, their loves I don't decline:
The eating and the drinking, too, is beautiful and fine;
But in the corner of me heart, which nobody can see,
Two eyes of Irish blue are always peeping out at me!
O Molly darlin', never fear: I'm still your own dear boy,
Ould Ireland is me country, and me name is Pat Malloy!

From Ireland to America, across the seas, I roam :
And every shilling that I got, ah! sure I sent it home.
Me mother couldn't write, but oh! there came from Father
    Boyce:
"Oh! Heaven bless you! Pat," says she.... I hear me
    mother's voice !
But, now, I'm going home again, as poor as I began,
To make a happy girl of Moll, and sure I think I can:
Me pockets they are empty, but me heart is fill'd wid joy,
For, ould Ireland is me country, and me name is Pat
    Malloy.

CLARE'S DRAGOONS.

By Thomas Davis.

Air.— " *Viva la.*"

WHEN on Ramillies' bloody field
The baffled French were forced to yield,
The victor Saxon backward reeled
   Before the charge of Clare's Dragoons.
The flags we conquered in that fray
Look lone in Ypres' choir, they say ;
We'll win them company to-day,
   Or bravely die like Clare's Dragoons.

CHORUS.

Viva la for Ireland's wrong !
   Viva la for Ireland's right !
Viva la in battle throng
   For a Spanish steed and sabre bright.

The brave old lord died near the fight,
But, for each drop he lost that night,
A Saxon cavalier shall bite
   The dust before Lord Clare's Dragoons.
For never, when our spurs were set,
And never when our sabres met,
Could we the Saxon soldiers get
   To stand the shock of Clare's Dragoons.

CHORUS.

Viva la the New Brigade !
   Viva la the Old One, too !
Viva la, the Rose shall fade,
   And the Shamrock shine for ever new !

Another Clare is here to lead,
The worthy son of such a breed ;
The French expect some famous deed
   When Clare leads on his bold Dragoons.

CLARE'S DRAGOONS.—*Continued.*

Our colonel comes from Brian's race
His wounds are in his breast and face,
The *bearna baeghail*** is still his place,
   The foremost of his bold Dragoons.

CHORUS.
Viva la the New Brigade!
   Viva la the Old One too!
Viva la, the Rose shall fade,
   And the Shamrock shine for ever new.

There's not a man in squadron here
Was ever known to flinch or fear,
Though first in charge and last in rear
   Have ever been Lord Clare's Dragoons.
But, see! we'll soon have work to do,
To shame our boasts, or prove them true,
For hither comes the English crew
   To sweep away Lord Clare's Dragoons!

CHORUS.
Viva la for Ireland's wrong!
   Viva la for Ireland's right!
Viva la in battle throng
   For a Spanish steed and sabre bright!

O comrades! think how Ireland pines,
Her exiled lords, her rifled shrines,
Her dearest hope the ordered lines
   And bursting charge of Clare's Dragoons.
Then fling your Green Flag to the sky,
Be Limerick your battle-cry,
And charge till blood floats fetlock high
   Around the track of Clare's Dragoons.

CHORUS.
Viva la the New Brigade!
   Viva la the Old One, too!
Viva la, the Rose shall fade,
   And the Shamrock shine for ever new!

* The gap of danger.

THE LAMENT OF *GRAINNE MAOL!**

By Hugh Harkin.

I.

JOHN BULL was a *bodach*, as rich as a Jew ;
As griping, as grinding, as conscienceless too ;
A wheedler, a shuffler, a rogue by wholesale,
And a swindler, moreover, says *Grainne Maol !*

II.

John Bull was a banker, both pursy and fat,
With gold in his pockets, and plenty of that ;
And he tempted his neighbors to sell their entail—
'Tis by scheming he prospers, says *Grainne Maol !*

III.

John Bull was a farmer,with cottiers galore—
Stout "chawbacons" once, that like bullocks could roar ;
Hard work and low wages and Peel's sliding scale
Have bothered their courage, says *Grainne Maol !*

IV.

John Bull was a bruiser, so sturdy and stout,
A boisterous bully—at bottom a clout—
For when you squared up he was apt to turn tail—
Brother Jonathan lashed him, says *Grainne Maol !*

V.

John Bull was a merchant, and many his ships,
His harbors, his dock-yards, and big building slips ;
And the ocean he claimed as his rightful entail—
Monsieur Parley-vouz *bars that*, says *Grainne Maol !*

VI.

John Bull had dependencies, many and great—
Fine, fertile, and fat—every one an estate ;
But he pilfered and plundered wholesale and retail—
There's Canada, sign's on it, says *Grainne Maol !*

VII.

John Bull was a saint in the western clime,
Stood fast for the truths of the Gospel sublime,
Vowed no other faith in the end could avail ;
Is't the Jugghernaut champion ? says *Grainne Maol !*

* Vulgarly written, but rightly pronounced, "Granu Wail."

THE LAMENT OF *GRAINNE MAOL.*—*Continued.*

VIII.

John Bull had a sister, so fair to be seen,
With a blush like a rose, and a mantle of green,
And a soft, swelling bosom !—On hill or in dale,
Oh ! where could you fellow sweet *Grainne Maol ?*

IX.

And John loved his sister, without e'er a flam,
Like the fox and the pullet, the wolf and the lamb ;
So he paid her a visit— but mark her bewail :
My title deed's vanished ! says *Grainne Maol !*

X.

Then he rummaged her commerce and ravaged her plains
Razed her churches and castles—her children in chains,
With pitch-caps, triangles, and gibbets wholesale,
Betokened John's love to poor *Grainne Maol !*

XI.

But one of her children, more *bould* than the rest,
Took it into his head for to make a *request !*
Our rights, Uncle John ! Else our flag on the gale !
Faix, he got an instalment, says *Grainne Maol !*

XII.

And now he is at the *Ould Growler* again,
With his logic, and law, and *—three millions of men !*
And nothing will plaise him, just now, but REPALE,
" *Mo seact n-anam astig tu,*" * says *Grainne Maol !*

XIII.

But should John turn gruff and decline the demand,
What means of success would be at our command,
Although he be humbled, and now getting frail ?
My " NATION " will tell you, says *Grainne Maol !*

XIV.

(" Nation " Loquitur.)
" If, stubborn and wilful, he still should refuse
To hear our just claims, or submit to our views,
And resolve, in his folly, to hold the ' entail,'
We'll ' *Kick his Dumbarton* for *Grainne Maol !* "

* "Seven times as dear as the soul within me."

PADDIES EVERMORE.

Air.—"*Paddies Evermore.*"

THE hour is past to fawn or crouch
　　As suppliants for our right;
Let word and deed unshrinking vouch
　　The banded millions' might:
Let them who scorned the fountain rill
　　Now dread the torrent's roar,
And hear our echoed chorus still,
　　We're Paddies evermore.

What, though they menace? suffering men
　　Their threats and them despise;
Or promise justice once again?
　　We know their words are lies:
We stand resolved those rights to claim
　　They robbed us of before,
Our own dear nation and our name,
　　As Paddies evermore.

Look round—the Frenchman governs France,
　　The Spaniard rules in Spain,
The gallant Pole but waits his chance
　　To break the Russian chain;
The strife for freedom here begun
　　We never will give o'er,
Nor own a land on earth but one—
　　We're Paddies evermore.

That strong and single love to crush
　　The despot ever tried—
A fount it was whose living gush
　　His hated arts defied.
'Tis fresh as when his foot accursed
　　Was planted on our shore,
And now and still, as from the first,
　　We're Paddies evermore.

PADDIES EVERMORE.—*Continued.*

What recked we though six hundred years
  Have o'er our thraldom rolled?
The soul that roused O'Connor's spears
  Still lives as true and bold.
The tide of foreign power to stem
  Our fathers bled of yore;
And we stand here to-day, like them,
  True Paddies evermore.

Where's our allegiance? With the land
  For which they nobly died;
Our duty? By our cause to stand,
  Whatever chance betide;
Our cherished hope? To heal the woes
  That rankle at her core:
Our scorn and hatred? To her foes,
  Like Paddies evermore.

The hour is past to fawn or crouch
  As suppliants for our right;
Let word and deed unshrinking vouch
  The banded millions' might;
Let them who scorned the fountain rill
  Now dread the torrent's roar,
And hear our echoed chorus still,
  We're Paddies evermore.

STAND TOGETHER.

I.

STAND together, brothers all !
  Stand together, stand together !
To live or die, to rise or fall,
  Stand together, stand together !
Old Erin proudly lifts her head—
Of many tears the last is shed ;
Oh ! *for* the living—*by* the dead !
  Stand together, true together !

II.

Stand together, brothers all !
  Close together, close together !
Be Ireland's might a brazen wall—
  Close up together, tight together !
Peace ! no noise !—but, hand in hand,
Let calm resolve pervade your band,
And wait, till nature's God command—
  Then help each other, help each other.

III.

Stand together, brothers all !
  Proud together, bold together !
From Kerry's cliffs to Donegal,
  Bound in heart and soul together !
Unroll the sunburst ! who'll defend
Old Erin's banner, is a friend ;
One foe is ours—oh! blend, boys, blend
  Hands together—hearts together !

IV.

Stand together, brothers all !
  Wait together, watch together !
See, America and Gaul
  Look on together, both together !
Keen impatience in each eye ;
Yet on "ourselves" do we rely—
"Ourselves alone" our rallying cry !
  And "stand together, strike together ! "

BUMPERS, SQUIRE JONES.

YE good fellows all,
Who love to be told where good claret's in store,
Attend to the call
Of one who's ne'er frighted,
But greatly delighted,
With six bottles more :
Be sure you don't pass
The good house Money-glass,
Which the jolly red god so peculiarly owns;
'Twill well suit your humor,
For pray what would you more,
Than mirth, with good claret and bumpers, Squire Jones.

Ye lovers, who pine
For lasses that oft prove as cruel as fair,
Who whimper and whine
For lilies and roses,
With eyes, lips, and noses,
Or tip of an ear,
Come hither, I'll show you
How Phillis and Chloe
No more shall occasion such sighs and such groans;
For what mortal so stupid
As not to quit Cupid,
When called by good claret and bumpers, Squire Jones?

Ye poets, who write,
And brag of your drinking famed Helicon's brook,
Though all you get by't
Is a dinner oft-times,
In reward of your rhymes,
With Humphrey, the duke :
Learn Bacchus to follow,
And quit your Apollo,
Forsake all the Muses, those senseless old crones;
Our jingling of glasses
Your rhyming surpasses,
When crowned with good claret and bumpers, Squire Jones.

BUMPERS, SQUIRE JONES.—*Continued.*

Ye soldiers so stout,
With plenty of oaths, though no plenty of coin,
Who make such a rout
Of all your commanders
Who served us in Flanders,
And eke at the Boyne:
Come leave off your rattling
Of sieging and battling,
And know you'd much better to sleep in whole bones;
Were you sent to Gibraltar
Your notes you'd soon alter,
And wish for good claret, and bumpers, Squire Jones.

Ye clergy so wise,
Who myst'ries profound can demonstrate most clear,
How worthy to rise!
You preach once a week,
But your tithes never seek
Above once in a year:
Come here without failing,
And leave off your railing
'Gainst bishops providing for dull stupid drones;
Says the text so divine,
" What is life without wine? "
Then away with the claret—a bumper, Squire Jones.

Ye lawyers so just,
Be the cause what it will, who so learnedly plead,
How worthy of trust!
You know black from white,
Yet prefer wrong to right
As you chance to be fee'd:
Leave musty reports,
And forsake the king's courts,
Where dulness and discord have set up their thrones;
Burn Salkeld and Ventris,
With all your damned Entries,
And away with the claret—a bumper, Squire Jones.

BUMPERS, SQUIRE JONES.—*Continued.*

Ye physical tribe,
Whose knowledge consists in hard words and grimace,
Whene'er you prescribe,
Have at your devotion
Pills, bolus, or potion,
Be what will the case,
Pray where is the need
To purge, blister, and bleed?
When, ailing yourselves, the whole faculty own
That the forms of old Galen
Are not so prevailing
As mirth with good claret—and bumpers, Squire Jones.

Ye foxhunters eke,
That follow the call of the horn and the hound,
Who your ladies forsake
Before they're awake,
To beat up the brake
Where the vermin is found:
Leave Piper and Blueman,
Shrill Duchess and Trueman:
No music is found in such dissonant tones:
Would you ravish your ears
With the songs of the spheres?
Hark away to the claret—a bumper, Squire Jones.

WHISKEY.

By Joseph O'Leary.

Air.—"*Bobbing Joan.*"

Whiskey, drink divine !
  Why should drivellers bore us
With the praise of wine,
  Whilst we've thee before us?
Were it not a shame,
  Whilst we gaily fling thee
To our lips of flame,
  If we could not sing thee ?
    Whiskey, drink divine !
      Why should drivellers bore us
    With the praise of wine,
      Whilst we've thee before us ?

Greek and Roman sung
  Chian and Falernian—
Shall no harp be strung
  To thy praise, Hibernian?
Yes ! let Erin's sons—
  Generous, brave, and friskey—
Tell the world at once
  They owe it to their whiskey.
    Whiskey, &c.

If Anacreon—who
  Was the grape's best poet—
Drank our *Mountain-dew,*
  How his verse would show it !
As the best then known,
  He to wine was civil ;
Had he *Inishowen,*
  He'd pitch wine to the d—l.
    Whiskey, &c.

Bright as beauty's eye,
  When no sorrow veils it ;
Sweet as beauty's sigh,
  When young love inhales it ;
Come, then, to my lip—
  Come thou rich in blisses !
Every drop I sip
  Seems a shower of kisses.
    Whiskey, &c,

WHISKEY.—*Continued.*

Could my feeble lays
  Half thy virtues number,
A whole *grove* of bays
  Should my brows encumber.
Be his name adored,
  Who summed up thy merits
In one little word,   .
  When he called thee *spirits.*
    Whiskey, &c.

Send it gaily round—
  Life would be no pleasure,
If we had not found
  This enchanting treasure :
And when tyrant death's
  Arrow shall transfix ye,
Let your latest breaths
  Be whiskey ! whiskey ! whiskey !
    Whiskey ! drink divine !
      Why should drivellers bore us
    With the praise of wine,
      Whilst we've thee before us ?

——o——

KATE KEARNEY.

OH ! did you ne'er hear of Kate Kearney ?
She lives on the banks of Killarney :
From the glance of her eye, shun danger and fly
For, fatal's the glance of Kate Kearney.

For, that eye is so modestly beaming,
You'd ne'er think of mischief she's dreaming :
Yet, oh ! I can tell, how fatal's the spell
That lurks in the eye of Kate Kearney.

Oh ! should you e'er meet this Kate Kearney,
Who lives on the banks of Killarney,
Beware of her smile ; for many a wile
Lies hid in the smile of Kate Kearney.

Though she looks so bewitchingly simple,
Yet there's mischief in every dimple,
And who dares inhale her sigh's spicy gale,
Must die by the breath of Kate Kearney.

THE WELCOME.

By Thomas Davis.

Air.—"*An Buachailin Buidhe.*"

Come in the evening or come in the morning,
Come when you're looked for, or come without warning,
Kisses and welcome you'll find here before you,
And the oftener you come here the more I'll adore you.
  Light is my heart since the day we were plighted,
  Red is my cheek that they told me was blighted;
  The green of the trees looks far greener than ever,
  And the linnets are singing, " True lovers! don't sever!

I'll pull you sweet flowers to wear, if you choose them;
Or, after you've kissed them, they'll lie on my bosom.
I'll fetch from the mountain its breeze to inspire you;
I'll fetch from my fancy a tale that won't tire you.
  Oh! your step's like the rain to the summer-vexed farmer,
  Or sabre and shield to a knight without armor,
  I'll sing you sweet songs till the stars rise above me,
  Then, wandering, I'll wish you, in silence, to love me.

We'll look through the trees at the cliff, and the eyrie,
We'll tread round the rath on the track of the fairy,
We'll look on the stars, and we'll list to the river,
Till you ask of your darling what gift you can give her.
  Oh! she'll whisper you, " Love as unchangeably beaming,
  And trust, when in secret, most tunefully streaming
  Till the starlight of heaven above us shall quiver,
  As our souls flow in one down eternity's river."

So come in the evening, or come in the morning,
Come when you're looked for or come without warning,
Kisses and welcome you'll find here before you,
And the oftener you come here the more I'll adore you !
  Light is my heart since the day we were plighted,
  Red is my cheek that they told me was blighted;
  The green of the trees looks far greener than ever,
  And the linnets are singing, " True lovers! don't sever!"

THE SHAMROCK AND THE LILY.

By John Banim.

Air.—" *Fag an Bealach.*"

Sir Shamrock, sitting drinking,
　At close of day, at close of day,
Saw Orange Lily, thinking,
　Come by that way, come by that way;
With can in hand he hailed him,
　And jovial din, and jovial din;
The Lily's drought ne'er failed him—
　So he stept in, so he stept in.

At first they talked together,
　Reserved and flat, reserved and flat,
About the crops, the weather,
　And this and that, and this and that—
But, as the glass moved quicker,
　To make amends, to make amends,
They spoke, though somewhat thicker,
　Yet more like friends, yet more like friends.

" Why not call long before, man,
　To try a glass, to try a glass?"
Quoth Lily—" People told me
　You'd let me pass, you'd let me pass.
Nay, and they whispered, too, man,
　Death in the pot, death in the pot,
Slipt in for me by you, man—
　Though I hope not, though I hope not."

" Oh! foolish, foolish Lily!
　Good drink to miss, good drink to miss,
For gossip all so silly
　And false as this, and false as this;
And 'tis the very way, man,
　With such bald chat, with such bald chat,
You're losing, day by day, man,
　Much more than that, much more than that.

" Here, in this land of mine, man,
　Good friends with me, good friends with me,
A life almost divine, man,
　Your life might be, your life might be.

THE SHAMROCK AND THE LILY.—*Continued.*

But—jars for you ! till in, man,
  My smiling land, my smiling land,
You bilious grow, and thin, man,
  As you can stand, as you can stand.

" Now, if 'tis no affront, man,
  On you I call, on you I call,
To tell me what you want, man,
  At-all-at-all, at-all-at-all :
Come, let us have, in season,
  A word or two, a word or two ;
For there's neither rhyme nor reason
  In your hubbubboo ! your hubbubboo !

"With you I'll give and take, man,
  A foe to cares, a foe to cares,
Just asking, for God's sake, man,
  To say my prayers, to say my prayers,
And, like an honest fellow,
  To take my drop, to take my drop,
In reason, till I'm mellow,
  And then to stop, and then to stop.

"And why should not things *be* so
  Between us both, between us both?
You're so afraid of me ?   Pho !
  All fudge and froth, all fudge and froth !
Or why, for little Willy,
  So much ado, so much ado ?
What is he, silly Lily,
  To me or you, to me or you ?

" Can he, for all you shout, man,
  Back to us come, back to us come,
Our devils to cast out, man,
  And strike them dumb, and strike them dumb?
Or breezes mild make blow, man,
  In summer-peace, in summer-peace,
Until the land o'erflow, man,
  With God's increase, with God's increase?"

THE SHAMROCK AND THE LILY.—*Continued.*

" What you do say, Sir Shamrock,"
   The Lily cried, the Lily cried,
"I 'll think of, my old game-cock!
   And more beside, and more beside.
One thing is certain, brother—
   I 'm free to say, I 'm free to say—
We should be more together
   Just in this way, just in this way."

" Well—top your glass, Sir Lily!
   Our parting one, our parting one—
A bumper and a *tilly* *
   To past and gone, to past and gone—
And to the future day, lad,
   That yet may see, that yet may see
Good humor and fair play, lad,
   'Twixt you and me, 'twixt you and me ! "

———o———

KITTY OF COLERAINE.

As beautiful Kitty one morning was tripping
   With a pitcher of milk from the fair of Coleraine,
When she saw me she stumbled, the pitcher down tumbled,
   And all the sweet butter-milk watered the plain.
Oh! what shall I do now? 'twas looking at you, now ;
   Sure, sure, such a pitcher I'll ne'er meet again ;
'Twas the pride of my dairy ! O Barney M'Cleary,
   You're sent as a plague to the girls of Coleraine !

I sat down beside her, and gently did chide her,
   That such a misfortune should give her such pain ;
A kiss then I gave her, and, ere I did leave her,
   She vowed for such pleasure she'd break it again.
'Twas hay-making season— I can't tell the reason—
   Misfortunes will never come single, tis plain ;
For very soon after poor Kitty's disaster
   The devil a pitcher was whole in Coleraine.

*A little more than good measure.

THE TIE IS BROKE, MY IRISH GIRL.

By Gerald Griffin.

THE tie is broke, my Irish girl,
  That bound thee here to me,
My heart has lost its single pearl,
  And thine at last is free—
Dead as the earth that wraps thy clay,
  Dead as the stone above thee—
Cold as this heart that breaks to say
  It never more can love thee.

I press thee to my aching breast—
  No blush comes o'er thy brow—
Those gentle arms, that once caressed,
  Fall round me deadly now—
The smiles of love no longer part
  Those dead blue lips of thine—
I lay my hand upon thy heart,
  'Tis cold at last to mine.

Were we beneath our native heaven,
  Within our native land,
A fairer grave to thee were given
  Than this wild bed of sand!
But thou wert single in thy faith
  And single in thy worth,
And thou shouldst die a lonely death,
  And lie in lonely earth.

Then lay thee down and take thy rest,
  My last—last look is given!
The earth is smooth above *thy* breast,
  And mine is yet unriven!
No mass—no parting rosary—
  My perished love can have;
But her husband's sighs embalm her corse,
  A husband's tears her grave.

RORY O'MORE.

By Samuel Lover.

Young Rory O'More courted Kathleen bawn,
He was bold as a hawk, and she, soft as the dawn;
He wished in his heart pretty Kathleen to please,
And he thought the best way to do that was to tease;
"Now Rory, be aisy," sweet Kathleen would cry
(Reproof on her lip, but a smile in her eye);
"With your tricks, I don't know, in troth, what I'm about;
Faith, you've teased me till I've put my cloak on inside out!

"Och, jewel," says Rory, "that same is the way
You've thrated my heart for this many a day,
And 'tis pleased that I am, and why not, to be sure?
For 'tis all for good luck," says bold Rory O'More.
"Indeed, then," says Kathleen, "don't think of the like,
For I half gave a promise to soothering Mike;
The ground that I walk on, he loves, I'll be bound."
"Faith," says Rory, "I'd rather love you than the ground."

"Now Rory, I'll cry, if you don't let me go;
Sure I dhrame every night that I'm hating you so."
"Och," says Rory, "that same I'm delighted to hear,
For dhrames always go by contraries, my dear;
So, jewel, keep dhramin' that same till you die,
And bright mornin' will give dirty night the black lie;
For 'tis plased that I am. and why not, to be sure?
Since 'tis all for good luck," says bold Rory O'More.

"Arrah, Kathleen, my darlint, your teased me enough,
And I've thrashed for your sake, Dinny Grimes and James Duff,
And I've made myself, drinkin' your health, quite a baste,
So I think, after that, I may talk to the priest."
Then Rory, the rogue, stole his arm round her neck,
So soft and so white, without freckle or speck,
And he looked in her eyes that were beaming with light,
And he kissed her sweet lips—don't you think he was right?

"Now Rory, leave off, sir; you'll hug me no more;
That's eight times to-day that you've kissed me before."
"Then here goes another," says he, "to make sure,
For there's luck in odd numbers," says Rory O'More.

SONG OF MOINA, THE MANIAC.

Air.—" *County of Monaghan caoine.* "

" I've called my love, but he still sleeps on,
    And his lips are as cold as clay ;
I have kissed them o'er and o'er again—
I have pressed his cheek with my burning brow,
    And I've watched o'er him all the day.
Is it then true that no more thou'lt smile
                                    On Moina.
    Art thou then lost to thy Moina ?

Dear were cottage and garden to me,
    When the hand of the spoiler came;
Bright was the dew on my loved rose tree—
Every leaf looked green as an emerald bright
    Enclosed in a diamond frame.
Withered that tree where my love first wooed
                                    His Moina !
    But more withered the heart of poor Moina.

I once had a lamb my love gave me,
    As the mountain snow 'twas white :
Oh! how I loved it nobody knows !
I decked it each morn with the myrtle and rose—
    With ' forget me not ' at night.
My lover they slew, and they tore my lamb
                                    From Moina.
    They pierced the heart's core of poor Moina !

A linnet sang sweet on a bough hard by,
    Then flew past the hapless maid—
"'Tis my love," she cried, " his voice I know !"
And she followed the bird to the valley below,
    And was lost in the evening shade.
Slowly and heavily home I turned
                                    From Moina—
    And wept o'er the fate of poor Moina.

ONCE I HAD A TRUE LOVE.

BY GERALD GRIFFIN.

ONCE I had a true love,
  I loved him well, I loved him well;
But since he's found a new love,
  Alone I dwell, alone I dwell.
How oft we've wandered lonely,
  Through yon old glen, through yon old glen!
I was his treasure only,
  And true love then, and true love then.
But Mary's singing brought me
  To sigh all day, to sigh all day—
Oh! had my mother taught me
  To sing and play, to sing and play!
                Once I had, &c.

By lone Glenchree at even
  I passed him late, I passed him late;
A glance just sidelong given
  Told all his fate, told all his fate:
His step no longer airy,
  His head it hung, his head it hung—
Ah! well I knew that Mary—
  She had a tongue, she had a tongue.
                Once I had, &c.

The spring is coming early,
  And skies are blue, and skies are blue,
And trees are budding fairly,
  And corn is new, and corn is new;
What clouds the sunny morrow
  Of nature then, of nature then?
And turns young hope to sorrow?
  O fickle men! O fickle men!
Once I had a true love,
  I loved him well, I loved him well;
But since he's found a new love,
  Alone I dwell, alone I dwell.

WHEN THE MOON IS ON THE WATERS.

When the Moon is on the waters,
　　I will hasten, love, to thee;
For, of all earth's fairest daughters,
　　Thou the dearest art to me.
Tho' rude winds disturb the ocean,
　　Still my bark shall tempt the sea,
And, in strains of pure devotion,
　　I will sing love-songs to thee.
When my Star of Hope was waning,
　　There was one, but one heart true—
And which shared, without complaining,
　　All the ills my bosom knew:
It was thine, my gentle Mary:
　　Thou wert all the world to me—
And, however fortune vary,
　　I will still be true to thee!

Thou wert dear to me, in childhood,
　　When the rosebud, on its tree,
As it blossomed in the wild wood,
　　Was an emblem, Love, of thee;
In thy youth, thou wert still dearer:
　　With the dawn of reason, came
Thoughts that brought thee to me nearer,
　　Tho' they bore not yet love's name:
But thy womanhood, unfolding,
　　Won the secret from my heart,
And my life was in thy holding—
　　For, 'twas death from thee to part!
I have loved thee, gentle Mary,
　　I have loved thee, through the past:
And, however fortune vary,
　　I will love thee, to the last!

"WHEN THE MOON IS ON THE WATERS."

WHEN ERIN FIRST ROSE.

By Dr. Drennan.

When Erin first rose from the dark-swelling flood,
God blessed the green island, and saw it was good;
The em'rald of Europe, it sparkled and shone,
In the ring of the world, the most precious stone.
In her sun, in her soil, in her station thrice blest,
With her back towards Britain, her face to the West,
Erin stands proudly insular, on her steep shore,
And strikes her high harp 'mid the ocean's deep roar.

But when its soft tones seem to mourn and to weep,
The dark chain of silence is thrown o'er the deep;
At the thought of the past the tears gush from her eyes,
And the pulse of her heart makes her white bosom rise.
O! sons of green Erin, lament o'er the time
When religion was war, and our country a crime;
When man in God's image inverted His plan,
And moulded his God in the image of man.

When the int'rest of state wrought the general woe,
The stranger a friend, and the native a foe;
While the mother rejoiced o'er her children oppressed,
And clasped the invader more close to her breast;
When, with pale for the body and pale for the soul,
Church and State joined in compact to conquer the whole;
And, as Shannon was stained with Milesian blood,
Eyed each other askance and pronounced it was good.

By the groans that ascend from your forefathers' grave;
For their country thus left to the brute and the slave,
Drive the demon of Bigotry home to his den,
And where Britain made brutes now let Erin make men.
Let my sons, like the leaves of the shamrock, unite,
A partition of sects from one footstalk of right,
Give each his full share of the earth and the sky,
Nor fatten the slave where the serpent would die.

Alas! for poor Erin, that some are still seen
Who would dye the grass red from their hatred to Green;
Yet, oh! when you're up and they're down, let them live,
Then yield them that mercy which they would not give.

WHEN ERIN FIRST ROSE.—*Continued.*

Arm of Erin be strong! but be gentle as brave!
And, uplifted to strike, be still ready to save!
Let no feeling of vengeance presume to defile
The cause of, or men of, the Emerald Isle.

The cause it is good, and the men they are true,
And the Green shall outlive both the orange and blue!
And the trumpets of Erin her daughters shall share,
With the full swelling chest, and the fair flowing hair.
Their bosom heaves high for the worthy and brave,
But no coward shall rest in that soft-swelling wave;
Men of Erin! awake, and make haste to be blest,
Rise—Arch of the Ocean, and Queen of the West!

——o——

THE SONS OF HIBERNIA.

BRAVE sons of Hibernia, your shamrocks display,
For ever made sacred on St. Patrick's day;
'Tis a type of religion, the badge of our saint,
And a plant of that soil which no venom can taint.

Both Venus and Mars to that land lay a claim,
Their title is owned and recorded by fame:
But St. Patrick to friendship has hallowed the ground,
And made hospitality ever abound.

Then with shamrocks and myrtles let's garnish the bowl,
In converse convivial and sweet flow of soul,
To our saint make oblations of generous wine—
What saint would have more?—sure 'tis worship divine!

Though jovial and festive in seeming excess,
We've hearts sympathetic of others' distress.
May our shamrock continue to flourish and prove
An emblem of charity, friendship, and love.

May the blights of disunion no longer remain,
Our shamrock to wither, her glories to stain;
May it flourish forever, we heaven invoke,
Kindly sheltered and fenced by the brave Irish oak.

SONGS OF OUR LAND.

Air.—"*Old Langolee.*"

Songs of our land, ye are with us for ever:
  The power and the splendor of thrones pass away,
But yours is the might of some far flowing river,
  Through summer's bright roses, or autumn's decay.
Ye treasure each voice of the swift-passing ages,
  And truth, which time writeth on leaves or on sand;
Ye bring us the bright thoughts of poets and sages,
  And keep them among us, old songs of our land!

The bards may go down to the place of their slumbers,
  The lyre of the charmer be hushed in the grave,
But far in the future the power of their numbers
  Shall kindle the hearts of our faithful and brave.
It will waken an echo in souls deep and lonely,
  Like voices of reeds by the summer breeze fanned
It will call up a spirit of freedom, when only
  Her breathings are heard in the songs of our land.

For they keep a record of those, the true-hearted,
  Who fell with the cause they had vowed to maintain;
They show us bright shadows of glory departed,
  Of the love that grew cold, and the hope that was vain.
The page may be lost and the pen long forsaken,
  And weeds may grow wild o'er the brave heart and hand;
But ye are still left when all else hath been taken,
  Like streams in the desert, sweet songs of our land!

Songs of our land! ye have followed the stranger
  With power over ocean and desert afar,
Ye have gone with our wand'rers through distance and danger,
  And gladdened their paths like a home-guiding star;
With the breath of our mountains in summers long vanished;
  And visions that passed like a wave from our strand,
With hope for their country and joy from her banished,
  Ye come to us ever, sweet songs of our land!

SONGS OF OUR LAND.—*Continued.*

The spring-time may come with the song of her glory,
　To bid the green heart of the forest rejoice ;
But the pine of the mountain, though blasted and hoary,
　And rock in the desert can send forth a voice.
It is thus in their triumph for deep desolations,
　While ocean waves roll, or the mountains shall stand,
Still hearts that are bravest and best of the nations,
　Shall glory and live in the songs of our land.

——o——

KATE OF GARNAVILLA.

EDWARD LYSAGHT.

HAVE you been at Garnavilla?
　Have you seen at Garnavilla
Beauty's train trip o'er the plain
　With lovely Kate of Garnavilla?
Oh! she's pure as virgin snows
　Ere they light on woodland hill; O
Sweet as dew-drop on wild rose
　Is lovely Kate of Garnavilla!

Philomel, I've listened oft
　To thy lay, nigh weeping willow ;
Oh, the strain's more sweet, more soft,
　That flows from Kate of Garnavilla!
　　　　　Have you been, &c.

As a noble ship I've seen
　Sailing o'er the swelling billow,
So I've marked the graceful mien
　Of lovely Kate of Garnavilla.
　　　　　Have you been, &c.

If poets' prayers can banish cares,
　No cares shall come to Garnavilla :
Joy's bright rays shall gild her days,
And dove-like peace perch on her pillow.
Charming maid of Garnavilla !
Lovely maid of Garnavilla !
Beauty, grace, and virtue wait
On lovely Kate of Garnavilla !

ANNIE DEAR.

By Thomas Davis.

OUR mountain brooks were rushing,
            Annie, dear,
The Autumn eve was flushing,
            Annie, dear;
But brighter was your blushing,
When first, your murmurs hushing,
I told my love outgushing,
            Annie, dear.

Ah ! but our hopes were splendid,
            Annie, dear;
How sadly they have ended,
            Annie, dear;
The ring betwixt us broken,
When our vows of love were spoken,
Of your poor heart was a token,
            Annie, dear.

The primrose flow'rs were shining,
            Annie, dear,
When, on my breast reclining,
            Annie, dear,
Began our *mi-na meala,**
And many a month did follow
Of joy—but life is hollow,
            Annie, dear.

For once, when home returning,
            Annie, dear,
I found our cottage burning,
            Annie, dear,
Around it were the yeomen,
Of every ill an omen,
The country's bitter foemen,
            Annie, dear.

* Honeymoon.

ANNIE DEAR.—*Continued.*

But why arose a morrow,
                          Annie, dear,
Upon that night of sorrow,
                          Annie, dear?
Far better, by thee lying,
Their bayonets defying,
Than live an exile sighing,
                          Annie, dear.

—o—

THE MOUNTAIN DEW.

By Samuel Lover.

By yon mountain tipp'd with cloud,
By the torrent foaming loud,
By the dingle where the purple bells of heather grew,
    Where the Alpine flow'rs are hid,
    And where bounds the nimble kid,
There we wandered both together through the mountain dew!
    With what delight in summer's night we trod the twilight
        gloom,
    The air so full of fragrance from the flowers so full of
        bloom,
    And our hearts so full of joy—for aught else there was
        no room,
As we wandered both together through the mountain dew.

Those sparkling gems that rest
On the mountain's flow'ry breast
Are like the joys we number—they are bright and few,
    For a while to earth are given,
    And are called again to heaven,
When the spirit of the morning steals the mountain dew:
    But memory, angelic, makes a heaven on earth for men,
    Her rosy light recalleth bright the dew-drops back again,
    The warmth of love exhales them from that well-remem-
        bered glen,
Where we wandered both together through the mountain dew.

GARRYOWEN.

Let Bacchus's sons be not dismayed,
But join with me each jovial blade;
Come booze and sing, and lend your aid
  To help me with the chorus ;—
    Instead of Spa we'll drink brown ale,
    And pay the reckoning on the nail,
    No man for debt shall go to gaol
    From Garryowen in glory !

We are the boys that take delight in
Smashing the Limerick lamps when lighting,
Through the streets like sporters fighting,
  And tearing all before us.
    Instead, &c.

We'll break windows, we'll break doors,
The watch knock down by threes and fours;
Then let the doctors work their cures,
  And tinker up our bruises.
    Instead, &c.

We'll beat the bailiffs, out of fun.
We'll make the mayor and sheriffs run :
We are the boys no man dares dun,
  If he regards a whole skin.
    Instead, &c.

Our hearts, so stout, have got us fame,
For soon 'tis known from whence we came;
Where'er we go they dread the name
  Of Garryowen in glory.

Johnny Connell's tall and straight,
And in his limbs he is complete;
He'll pitch a bar of any weight
  From Garryowen to Thomond Gate.
    Instead, &c.

Garryowen is gone to wrack
Since Johnny Connell went to Cork,
Though Darby O'Brien leapt over the dock
  In spite of all the soldiers.
    Instead, &c.

RECRUTING SONG FOR THE IRISH BRIGADE.

By Maurice O'Connell, M.P.

Is there a youthful gallant here
On fire for fame—unknowing fear—
Who in the charge's mad career
On Eire's foes would flesh his spear?
    Come, let him wear the White Cockade,
    And learn the soldier's glorious trade;
    'Tis of such stuff a hero's made;
    Then let him join the bold Brigade.

Who scorns to own a Saxon lord,
And toil to swell a stranger's hoard?
Who for rude blow or gibing word
Would answer with the freeman's sword?
    Come, let him wear the White Cockade, &c.

Does Eire's foully slandered name
Suffuse thy cheek with generous shame?
Wouldst right her wrongs—restore her fame?
Come, then, the soldier's weapon claim—
    Come, then, and wear the White Cockade, &c.

Come, free from bonds your fathers' faith,
Redeem its shrines from scorn and scathe;
The hero's fame, the martyr's wreath,
Will gild your life or crown your death.
    Then come, and wear the White Cockade, &c.

To drain the cup, with girls to toy,
The serf's vile soul with bliss may cloy:
But wouldst thou taste a manly joy?
Oh! it was ours at Fontenoy!
    Come, then, and wear the White Cockade, &c.

To many a fight thy fathers led,
Full many a Saxon's life-blood shed;
From thee, as yet, no foe has fled—
Thou wilt not shame the glorious dead?
    Then come, and wear the White Cockade, &c.

RECRUITING SONG FOR THE IRISH BRIGADE.

Continued.

Oh! come—for slavery, want, and shame,
We offer vengeance, freedom, fame—
With monarchs comrade-rank to claim,
And, nobler still, the patriot's name.
    Oh! come and wear the White Cockade,
    And learn the soldier's glorious trade;
    'Tis of such stuff a hero's made—
    Then come, and join the bold Brigade.

——o——

COME TO GLENGARIFF! COME!

BY GERALD GRIFFIN.

COME to Glengariff! come!
  Close by the sea,
Ours is a happy home,
  Peaceful and free.
There, there, far away,
Happy by our sunny bay,
We live from day to day,
  Blithe as the bee,
For ours is a sunny home,
  Joyous and free!
Come to Glengariff! come!
  Close by the sea.

Thine is a mountain hoar,
  Frowning and wild,
Ours is a lowland shore,
  Fertile and mild.
There, there, loud and strong,
Sudden tempests drive along;
Here, their gentle song
  Scarce moves the tree!
For ours is a lowland home,
  Peaceful and free;
Come from the mountain! come!
  Come to the sea!

FAREWELL! MY GENTLE HARP.

AIR.—" *Ta me dall, aosda, is bacach.*"

FAREWELL! my gentle harp, farewell!
 Thy master's toils are nearly o'er;
These chords, that wont with joy to swell
   Shall thrill no more:
My faithful harp! the wild, the gay
 And plaintive notes were all thy own;
Though now my trembling hands can play
   The sad alone;
And these, alas! must die away
   When I am gone.

And oh! 'tis well that age and pain
 May find a home where Mercy dwells,
For here the wounded heart in vain
   Its sorrow tells.
No more my soul can o'er thee shed
 The light of song that once it knew;
The dreams of hope and joy have fled,
   That fancy drew.
My faithful harp! when I am dead,
   Be silent, too!

———o———

THE IRISH MAIDEN'S SONG.

BY JOHN BANIM.

AIR.—*Domhnall.*

YOU know it, now—it is betrayed
 This moment in mine eye,
And in my young cheek's crimson shade,
 And in my whispered sigh—
You know it, now—yet listen, now—
 Though ne'er was love more true,
My plight and troth and virgin vow
 Still, still I keep from you,
     Ever—

Ever, until a proof you give,
 How oft you've heard me say:
I would not even his empress live
 Who idles life away,

THE IRISH MAIDEN'S SONG.—*Continued.*

Without one effort for the land
  In which my fathers' graves
Were hollowed by a despot hand
  To darkly close on slaves—
                        Never!

See! round yourself the shackles hang,
  Yet come you to love's bowers,
That only he may soothe their pang
  Or hide their links in flowers—
But try all things to snap them, first,
  And, should all fail, when tried,
The fated chain you cannot burst
  My twining arms shall hide—
                        Ever!

———

A SOLDIER—A SOLDIER TO-NIGHT IS OUR GUEST.

BY GERALD GRIFFIN.

FAN, fan the gay hearth and fling back the barred door,
Strew, strew the fresh rushes around on the floor,
And blithe be the welcome in every breast,
For a soldier—a soldier to-night is our guest.

All honor to him who, when danger afar
Had lighted for ruin his ominous star,
Left pleasure and country and kindred behind,
And sped to the shock on the wings of the wind!

If you value the blessings that shine at our hearth—
The wife's smiling welcome, the infant's sweet mirth—
While they charm us at eve, let us think upon those
Who have bought with their blood our domestic repose.

Then share with the soldier your hearth and your home,
And warm be your greeting whene'er he shall come:
Let love light a welcome in every breast,
For a soldier—a soldier to-night is our guest.

LET ERIN REMEMBER THE DAYS OF OLD.

By Thomas Moore.

Let Erin remember the days of old,
  Ere her faithless sons betrayed her;
When Malachi wore the collar of gold
  Which he won from the proud invader;
When her kings, with standard of green unfurled,
  Led the Red-Branch Knights to danger;
Ere the emerald gem of the western world
  Was set in the crown of a stranger.

On Lough Neagh's bank as the fisherman strays,
  When the clear, cold eve's declining,
He sees the round towers of other days,
  In the waves beneath him shining!
Thus shall memory often, in dreams sublime,
  Catch a glimpse of the days that are over;
Thus, sighing, look through the waves of time
  For the long faded glories they cover!

———o———

MARY MACHREE.

The flower of the valley was Mary Machree:
Her smiles, all bewitching, were lovely to see;
The bees, 'round her humming when Summer is gone,
When the roses were dead, might her lips take for one:
Her laugh it was music, her breath it was balm:
Her heart like the lake, was as pure and as calm,
Till love o'er it came—like a breeze o'er the sea—
And made the heart heave of sweet Mary Machree.

She loved and she sighed, for was gladness e'er known
To dwell in the bosom that love makes his own?
His joys are but moments; his griefs are for years;
He comes all in smiles, but he leaves all in tears..
Her lover was gone to a far distant land:
And Mary, in sadness, would pace the lone strand;
And tearfully gaze on the dark rolling sea
That parted her lover from Mary Machree.

MARY MACHREE.—*Continued.*

Oh! pale grew her cheek, when there came, from afar
The tales of the battle, and tidings of war;
Her eyes filled with tears, when the clouds gathered dark:
Her fancy would picture some tempest-tossed bark;
But, when Winter came on and the deep woods were bare,
In the hall was a voice, and a foot on the stair!
Oh! joy to the maiden, for o'er the blue sea,
The soldier returned to his Mary Machree!

———o———

HE SAID THAT HE WAS NOT OUR BROTHER.

By John Banim.

Air.—" *Cailin deas cruite na m-bo.*"

HE said that he was not our brother—
  The mongrel! he said what we knew—
No, ——! our dear island-mother,
  He ne'er had his black blood from you.
And what though the milk of your bosom
  Gave vigor and health to his veins—
He *was* but a foul foreign blossom,
  Blown hither to poison our plains!

He said that the sword had enslaved us—
  That still at its point we must kneel:
The liar!—though often it braved us,
  We crossed it with hardier steel!
This witness his Richard—our vassal!
  His Essex—whose plumes we trod down!
His Willy—whose peerless sword-tassel
  We tarnished at Limerick town!

No! falsehood and feud were our evils,
  While force not a fetter could twine—
Come Northmen,—come Normans,—come devils!
  We gave them our *sparth* to the chine!
And if once again he would try us,
  To the music of trumpet and drum,
And no traitor among us or nigh us—
  Let him come, the brigand! let him come!

THE FEAST OF O'RORKE.

TRANSLATED FROM THE IRISH.

BY DEAN SWIFT, A. D. 1720.

O'RORKE'S noble fare
  Will ne'er be forgot,
By those who were there,
  Or those who were not.

His revels to keep,
  We sup and we dine
On seven score sheep,
  Fat bullocks, and swine.

Usquebaugh to our feast
  In pails is brought up,
A hundred at least,
  And a mether our cup.

'Tis there is the sport!
  We rise with the light,
In disorderly sort,
  From snoring all night.

Oh! how I was tricked;
  My pipe it was broke,
My pocket was picked,
  I lost my new cloak.

"I'm robbed," exclaimed Nell
  "Of mantle and kercher."
Why then fare them well,
  The de'il take the searcher.

"Come harper, strike up,
  But first, by your favor,
Boy, give us a cup—
  Ah! this has some flavor."

O'Rorke's jolly boys
  Ne'er dreamed of the matter,
Till roused by the noise
  And musical clatter.

THE FEAST OF O'RORKE.—*Continued.*

They bounce from their nest,
　No longer will tarry,
They rise ready dressed,
　Without one " Hail Mary."

They dance in a round,
　Cutting capers and romping :
'Tis a mercy the ground
　Didn't burst with their stamping !

The floor is all wet,
　Their leaps and their jumps
Makes the water and sweat
　Splish-splash in their pumps.

Bless you, late and early,
　Laughing O'Henigan :
By my hand, you dance rarely,
　Margery Grinigin.

Bring straw for our bed,
　Shake it down to our feet,
Then over it spread
　The winnowing sheet.

To show I don't flinch,
　Fill the bowl up again,
Then give us a pinch
　Of your sneezing *a bhan.*

Good lord ! what a sight—
　After all their good cheer,
For people to fight
　In the midst of their beer !

They rise from their feast,
　So hot are their brains—
A cubit at least
　The length of their skians.

THE FEAST OF O'RORKE.—*Continued.*

What stabs and what cuts!
  What clattering of sticks!
What strokes on the guts!
  What basting and kicks!

With cudgels of oak,
  Well hardened in flame,
A hundred heads broke—
  A hundred legs lame.

" You churl, I'll maintain
  My father built Lusk,
The castle of Slane,
  And Carrick Drumrusk.

" The Earl of Kildare,
  And Moynalta his brother,
As great as they are,
  I was nursed by their mother.

" Ask that of old madam,
  She'll tell you who's who,
As far up as Adam:
  She knows that 'tis true."

———o———

THE LOST PATH.

By Thomas Davis.

Air—" *Gradh mo Chroidhe.*"

SWEET thoughts, bright dreams, my comfort be
  All comfort else has flown;
For every hope was false to me,
  And here I am alone.
What thoughts were mine in early youth!
  Like some old Irish song,
Brimful of love, and life, and truth,
  My spirit gushed along.

THE LOST PATH.—*Continued.*

I hoped to right my native isle,
  I hoped a soldier's fame,
I hoped to rest in woman's smile,
  And win a minstrel's name:
Oh! little have I served my land,
  No laurels press my brow,
I have no woman's heart or hand,
  Nor minstrel honors now.

But fancy has a magic power,
  It brings me wreath and crown,
And woman's love, the self-same hour
  It smites oppression down.
Sweet thoughts, bright dreams, my comfort be,
  I have no joy beside;
Oh! throng around, and be to me
  Power, country, fame and bride.

——o——

DEAR HARP OF MY COUNTRY.

By Thomas Moore.

Dear harp of my country! in darkness I found thee,
The cold chain of silence had hung o'er thee long,
When, proudly, my own island harp! I unbound thee
And gave all thy chords to light, freedom, and song.
The warm lay of love, and the light note of gladness,
Have wakened thy fondest, thy liveliest thrill;
But so oft has thou echoed the deep sigh of sadness,
That e'en in thy mirth it will steal from thee still.

Dear harp of my country! farewell to thy numbers,
This sweet wreath of song is the last we shall twine;
Go, sleep, with the sunshine of fame on thy slumbers,
Till touched by some hand less unworthy than mine.
If the pulse of the patriot, soldier, or lover,
Have throbbed at our lay, 'tis thy glory alone;
I was *but* as the wind, passing heedlessly over,
And all the wild sweetness I waked was thy own.

A NEW YEAR'S SONG.

BY D. F. M'CARTY,

My countrymen, awake! arise!
  Our work begins anew,
Your mingled voices rend the skies,
  Your hearts are firm and true.
You've bravely marched, and nobly met,
  Our little green isle through;
But, oh! my friends, there's something yet
  For Irishmen to do!

As long as Erin hears the clink
  Of base, ignoble chains—
As long as one detested link
  Of foreign rule remains—
As long as our rightful debt
  One smallest fraction's due,
So long, my friends, there's something yet
  For Irishmen to do!

Too long we've borne the servile yoke,
  Too long the slavish chain,
Too long in feeble accents spoke,
  And ever spoke in vain!
Our wealth has filled the spoiler's net,
  And gorged the Saxon crew;
But, oh! my friends, we'll teach them yet
  What Irishmen can do!

The olive branch is in our hands,
  The white flag floats above;
Peace—peace prevades our myriad bands,
  And proud, forgiving love!
But, oh! let not our foes forget
  We're *men*, as Christians, too,
Prepared to do for Ireland yet
  What Irishmen should do!

A NEW YEAR'S SONG.—*Continued.*

There's not a man of all our land,
  Our country now can spare,
The strong man with his sinewy hand,
  The weak man with his prayer !
No whining tone of mere regret,
  Young Irish bards ! for you ;
But let your songs teach Ireland yet
  What Irishman should do !

And wheresoe'er that duty lead,
  There—there your post should be ;
The coward slave is never freed ;
  The brave alone are free !
O freedom ! firmly fixed are set
  Our longing eyes on you :
And though we die for Ireland yet,
  So Irishmen should do !*

————o————

IT IS NOT THE TEAR AT THIS MOMENT SHED.

BY THOMAS MOORE.

IT is not the tear at this moment shed,
  When the cold turf has just been laid o'er him,
That can tell how beloved is the friend that's fled,
  And how deep in our hearts we deplore him.
'Tis the tear, through many a long day wept,
  Through a life by his loss all shaded ;
'Tis the sad remembrance, fondly kept,
  When all other griefs have faded.

And thus shall we mourn, and his memory's light,
  As it shines through our hearts, shall improve them,
And worth shall seem fairer and truth more bright,
  When we think how he lived but to love them.
And as buried saints the grave perfume,
  Where fadeless they've long been lying,
So our hearts shall borrow a sweetening bloom
  From the image he left there in dying.

* This song first appeared in the *Nation* newspaper.

IF I HAD THOUGHT THOU COULDST HAVE DIED.

Air.—" Gradh mo Chroidhe."

If I had thought thou couldst have died,
　I might not weep for thee ;
But I forgot, when by thy side,
　That thou couldst mortal be ;
It never through my mind had past
　The time would e'er be o'er,
And I on thee should look my last,
　And thou shouldst smile no more.

And still upon that face I look,
　And think 'twill smile again ;
And still the thought I will not brook
　That I must look in vain.
But, when I speak, thou dost not say
　What thou ne'er left'st unsaid ;
And now I feel, as well I may,
　Sweet Mary ! thou art dead.

If thou wouldst stay e'en as thou art,
　All cold, and all serene,
I still might press thy silent heart,
　And where thy smiles have been !
While e'en thy chill, bleak corse I have
　Thou seemest still mine own;
But there I lay thee in thy grave—
　And I am now alone.

I do not think, where'er thou art
　Thou hast forgotten me ;
And I, perhaps, may soothe this heart
　In thinking, too, of thee.
Yet there was round thee such a dawn
　Of light, ne'er seen before,
As fancy never could have drawn,
　And never can restore.

SONG OF AN EXILE.

By James Orr.

In Ireland 'tis evening—from toil my friends hie all,
  And weary, walk home o'er the dew-spangled lea ;
The shepherd in love tunes his grief-soothing viol,
  Or visits the maid that his partner will be;
The blithe milk-maid trips to the herd that stands lowing :
The west richly smiles, and the landscape is glowing ;
The sad-sounding curfew, and torrent fast-flowing,
  Are heard by my fancy, though far, far at sea !

What has my eye seen since I left the green valleys,
  But ships as remote as the prospect could be ?
Unwieldy, huge monsters, as ugly as malice,
  And floats of some wreck, which with sorrow I see?
What's seen but the fowl, that its lonely flight urges,
The lightning, that darts through the sky-meeting surges,
And the sad-scowling sky, that with bitter rain scourges
  This cheek care sits drooping on, far, far at sea ?

How hideous the hold is !—Here, children are screaming—
  There, dames, faint through thirst, with their babes on their
      knee !
Here, down every hatch the big breakers are streaming,
  And there, with a crash, half the fixtures break free !
Some court, some contend, some sit, dull stories telling ;
The mate's mad and drunk, and the tars tasked and yelling ;
What sickness and sorrow pervade my rude dwelling !—
  A huge, floating lazar-house, far, far at sea !

How changed all may be when I seek the sweet village :
  A hedge-row may bloom where its street used to be ;
The floors of my friends may be tortured by tillage,
  And the upstart be served by the fallen grandee ;
The axe may have humbled the grove that I haunted,
And shades be my shield that as yet are unplanted,
Nor one comrade live who repined when he wanted
  The sociable sufferer that's far, far at sea !

SONG OF AN EXILE.—*Continued.*

In Ireland 'tis night—on the flowers of my setting
  A parent may kneel, fondly praying for me ;—
The village is smokeless—the red moon is getting
  That hill for a throne which I hope yet to see.
If innocence thrive, many more have to grieve for;
Success, slow but sure, I'll contentedly live for :
Yes, Sylvia, we'll meet, and your sigh cease to heave for
  The swain your fine image haunts, far, far at sea !

———u———

THE FORSAKEN MAID.

HE is gone ! he is gone !
And my bosom is sore,
For I loved him too well,
And shall ne'er see him more !
Though they said he was false,
Yet I would not believe,
When I gazed in his eyes,
That his heart could deceive.

He is gone ! he is gone !
And I wander alone
By the stream where so oft
He hath called me " his own."
But his vows are forgot,
And my eyes are now dim
With the tears I have wept
For the falsehood of him.

Oh ! the blossoms are fading
And falling away,
For the Summer is gone,
And they haste to decay ;
And this heart, since the sunshine
It bloomed in hath fled,
Must soon, like the flowers,
Lie withered and dead.

NATIVE SWORDS.

A Volunteer Song—1st July, 1792.

By Thomas Davis.

WE'VE bent too long to braggart wrong,
　While force our prayers derided ;
We've fought too long ourselves among,
　By knaves and priests divided ;
United now, no more we'll bow ;
　Foul faction, we discard it ;
And now, thank God ! our native sod
　Has Native Swords to guard it.

Like rivers which, o'er valleys rich,
　Bring ruin in their water,
On native land a native hand
　Flung foreign fraud and slaughter.
From Dermond's crime to Tudor's time
　Our clans were our perdition ;
Religion's name, since then, became
　Our pretext for division.

But, worse than all ! with Limerick's fall
　Our valor seemed to perish ;
Or, o'er the main, in France and Spain,
　For bootless vengeance flourish.
The peasant here grew pale for fear
　He'd suffer for our glory,
While France sang joy for Fontenoy,
　And Europe hymned our story,

But now no clan nor factious plan
　The east and west can sunder—
Why Ulster e'er should Munster fear
　Can only wake our wonder,
Religion's crost when Union's lost,
　And " royal gifts " retard it:
And now, thank God ! our native sod
　Has Native Swords to guard it.

KILLARNEY.

By M. J. Balfe.

By Killarney's lakes and fells,
  Em'rald isles and winding bays,
Mountain paths and woodland dells,
  Mem'ry ever fondly strays.
Bounteous nature loves all lands,
  Beauty wanders ev'ry where
Foot-prints leaves on many strands
  But her home is surely there !
Angels fold their wings and rest
  In that Eden of the west,
Beauty's home, Killarney,
  Ever fair Killarney—

Innisfallen's ruined shrine
  May suggest a passing sigh,
But man's faith can ne'er decline
  Such God's wonders floating by :
Castle Lough and Glenna Bay,
  Mountain's Tore and Eagle's Nest :
Still at Mucross you must pray,
  Though the monks are now at rest,
Angels wonder not that man
  There would fain prolong life's span :
Beauty's home, Killarney,
  Ever fair Killarney—

No place else can charm the eye
  With such bright and varied tints :
Every rock that you pass by
  Verdure broiders or besprints :
Virgin there the green grass grows,
  Every morn Spring's natal day,
Bright-hued berries daff the snows,
  Smiling winter's frown away.
Angels often pausing there,
  Doubt if Eden were more fair :
Beauty's home, Killarney,
  Ever fair Killarney—

KILLARNEY.

KILLARNEY.—*Continued.*

Music there for Echo dwells,
   Makes each sound a harmony,
Many-voiced the chorus swells,
   Till it faints in ecstacy,
With the charmful tints below
   Seems the heaven above to vie:
All rich colors that we know,
   Tinge the cloud wreaths in that sky.
Wings of angels so might shine
   Glancing back soft light divine;
Beauty's home Killarney.
   Ever fair Killarney—

——o——

KATY'S LETTER.

Och! girls dear, did you ever hear I wrote my love a letter?
And altho' he cannot read, sure I thought it all the better;
For, why should he be puzzled with hard spelling in the matter,
When the meaning was so plain, that I love him faithfully?
        I love him faithfully,
And he knows it, oh! he knows it without one word from me

I wrote it, and I folded it, and put a seal upon it—
'Twas a seal almost as big as the crown of my new bonnet;
For, I would have the Postmaster make his remarks upon it,
As I'd said inside the letter, I loved him faithfully,
        I love him faithfully. &c.

My heart was full, but when I wrote, I did not put the half in—
The neighbors know I love him, and they're mighty fond of
        chaffing;
So, I dared not write his name outside, for fear they would be
        laughing;
So, I wrote: "From little Kate to one whom she loves faith-
        fully."   I love him faithfully, &c.

Now, girls, would you believe it? that Postman so consated,
No answer will he bring me, so long as I have waited;
But, may be there mayn't be one for the reason that I stated,
That my love can neither read nor write but he loves me faith-
        fully.   He loves me faithfully
And I know where'er my love is that he is true to me.

OH! THE MARRIAGE

By Thomas Davis.

Air.—" *The Swaggering Jig.*"

Oh! the marriage, the marriage,
  With love and mo buchail for me;
The ladies that ride in a carriage
  Might envy my marriage to me;
For Owen is straight as a tower,
  And tender and loving and true—
He told me more love in an hour
  Than the squires of the county could do.
          Then, oh! the marriage, &c.

His hair is a shower of soft gold,
  His eye is as clear as the day,
His conscience and vote were unsold
  When others were carried away—
His word is as good as an oath
  And freely 'twas given to me—
Oh! sure 'twill be happy for both
  The day of our marriage to see.
          Then, oh! the marriage, &c.

His kinsmen are honest and kind,
  The neighbors think much of his skill,
And Owen's the lad to my mind,
  Though he owns neither castle nor mill.
But he has a tilloch of land,
  A horse, and a stocking of corn,
A foot for the dance, and a hand.
  In the cause of his country to join.
          Then, oh! the marriage, &c.

GLAS-EN-GLORACH.*

'Tis sweet, in midnight solitude,
When the voice of man lies hushed, subdued,
To hear thy mountain voice so rude
  Break silence, *Glas-en-Glorach !*

I love to see thy foaming stream
Dashed sparkling in the bright moonbeam ;
For then of happier days I dream,
  Spent near thee, *Glas-en-Glorach !*

I see the holly and the yew
Still shading thee, as then they grew ;
But there's a form meets not my view,
  As once, near *Glas-en-Glorach !*

Thou gaily, brightly sparklest on,
Wreathing thy dimples round each stone :
But the bright eye that on thee shone
  Lies quenched, wild *Glas-en-Glorach !*

Still rush thee on, thou brawling brook ;
Though on broad rivers I may look
In other lands, thy lonesome nook
  I'll think on, *Glas-en-Glorach !*

When I am low, laid in the grave,
Thou still wilt sparkle, dash, and rave
Seaward, till thou becom'st a wave
  Of ocean, *Glas-en-Glorach !*

Thy course and mine alike have been—
Both restless, rocky, seldom green ;
There rolls for me, beyond the scene,
  An ocean, *Glas-en-Glorach !*

And when my span of life's gone by,
Oh ! if past spirits back can fly,
I'll often ride the night-wind's sigh
  That's breathed o'er *Glas-en-Gorach !*

---

* A mountain torrent, which finds its way into the Atlantic Ocean through Glengariff, in the west of the county of Cork. The name, literally translated, signifies "the noisy green water."

LAMENT OF MORIAN SHEHONE FOR MISS MARY BOURKE.

Translation of an Irish Caoine.

" THERE'S darkness in thy dwelling place, and silence reigns
      above,
And Mary's voice is heard no more, like the soft voice of
      love.
Yes! thou art gone, my Mary dear! and Morian Shehone
Is left to sing his song of woe, and wail for thee alone.
Oh! snow-white were thy virtues—the beautiful the young,
The old with pleasure bent to hear the music of thy tongue:
The young with rapture gazed on thee, and their hearts in
      love were bound,
For thou wast brighter then the sun that sheds its light
      around.
My soul is dark, O Mary dear! thy sun of beauty's set ;
The sorrowful are dumb for thee—grieved their tears forgot ;
And I am left to pour my woe above thy grave alone ;
For dear wert thou to the fond heart of Morian Shehone.

Fast-flowing tears above the grave of the rich man are shed,
But they are dried when the cold stone shuts in his narrow
      bed ;
Not so with my heart's faithful love—the dark grave cannot
      hide
From Morian's eyes thy form of grace, of loveliness and pride.
Thou didst not fall like the sere leaf, when autumn's chill
      winds blow—
'Twas a tempest and a storm-blast that had laid my Mary low.
Hadst thou not friends that love thee well? hadst thou not
      garments rare ?
Wast thou not happy, Mary? wast thou not young and fair ?
Then why should the dread spoiler come, my heart's peace
      to destroy,
Or the grim tyrant tear from me my all of earthly joy ?
Oh ! am I left to pour my woes above thy grave alone !
Thou idol of the faithful heart of Morian Shehone.

* Dirge.

THE MOTHER'S LAMENT.

By Gerald Griffin.

My darling, my darling, while silence is on the moor,
And lone in the sunshine I sit by our cabin door,
When evening falls quiet and calm over land and sea,
My darling, my darling, I think of past times and thee!

Here, while on this cold shore I wear out my lonely hours,
My child in the heavens is spreading my bed with flowers.
All weary my bosom is grown of this friendless clime,
But I long not to leave it—for that were a shame and crime.

They bear to the church-yard the youth in their health away—
I know where a fruit hangs more ripe for the grave than they.
But I wish not for death, for my spirit is all resigned,
And the hope that stays with me gives peace to my aged mind.

My darling, my darling, God gave to my feeble age
A prop for my faint heart, a stay in my pilgrimage;
My darling, my darling, God takes back his gift again—
And my heart may be broken, but ne'er shall my will complain.

—o—

THE EMERALD ISLE.

Alas! border minstrel, the summons is vain,
　For unstrung is the harp, and forgotten the strain
Which Eire once sung in her pride;
　And now, robbed of the glories that circled her reign,
To the heart-rending clang of a conqueror's chain,
　All tuneless she wanders the desolate plain,
With the blood of her patriots dyed!

Gone, gone are the days when the western gale
　Awoke every voice of the lake and the vale,
With the harp, and the lute, and the lyre!
　When justice uplifted her adamant shield,
While valor and freedom illumined the field,
　And thy free-born sons made the foeman to yield,
With a sword and a plumage of fire!

THE EMERALD ISLE.—*Continued.*

And now, border minstrel, the bigot and slave
  Pollute the pure land of the free-born brave,
The land of the sigh and the smile!—
  Then accursed be the recreant heart that could sing,
And withered the hand that would waken a string,
  Till the angel of liberty wave her wild wing
Again o'er the Emerald Isle!

——o——

MOTHER, HE'S GOING AWAY.
By Samuel Lover.

MOTHER.—Now, what are you crying for, Nelly?
  Don't be blubberin' there like a fool—
With the weight of grief, faith, I tell you,
  You'll break down the three-legged stool.
I suppose now you're crying for Barney,
  But don't b'lieve a word that he'd say,
He tells nothin' but big lies and blarney—
  Sure you know how he sarv'd poor Kate Kearney

DAUGHTER.—But, mother—

MOTHER.—Oh, bother!

DAUGHTER.—But, mother, he's going away!
  And I dreamt th' other night
  Of his ghost all in white—
  Oh, mother, he's going away!

MOTHER.—If he's goin' away, all the betther—
  Blessed hour when he's out of your sight,
There's one comfort—you can't get a letther:
  For, yez neither can read or can write.
Sure 'twas only last week you protested,
  Since he coorted fat Jenny M'Cray,
That the sight of the scamp you detested—
  With abuse, sure, your tongue never rested—

DAUGHTER.—But, mother—

MOTHER.—Oh, bother!

DAUGHTER.—But, mother, he's going away,
  And I dream of his ghost
  Walking round my bedpost—
  Oh, mother, he's going away!

SONG OF AN EXILE.

Air--" *Diarmaid O'Dubhda.*"

FAREWELL, and for ever, my loved isle of sorrow,
  Thy green vales and mountains delight me no more;
My bark's on the wave, and the noon of to-morrow
  Will see the poor exile far, far from thy shore.

Again, my loved home, I may never behold thee;
  Thy hope was a meteor—thy glory a dream;
Accurst be the dastards, the slaves that have sold thee,
  And doomed thee, lost *Eire*, to bondage and shame.

The senseless, the cold, from remembrance may ween them,
  Through the world they unloved and unloving may roam:
But the heart of the patriot—though seas roll between them—
  Forgets not the smiles of his once happy home.

Time may roll o'er me its circles uncheering,
  Columbia's proud forests around me shall wave;
But the exile shall never forget thee, loved *Eire*
  Till, unmourned, he sleep in a far, foreign grave.

——o——

BARNEY AVOURNEEN, I WON'T LET YOU IN.

'TWAS a cold winter's night and the tempest was snarlin'
  The snow like a sheet covered cabin and stye,
When Barney flew over the hills to his darlin',
  And tapped at the window where Katty did lie.
" Arrah! jewel, said he, are ye sleepin' or wakin?
  The night's bitter cold, an' my coat it is thin:
Oh! the storm 'tis a brewin', the frost it is bakin'
  Oh! Katty Avourneen, you must let me in."

" Arrah, Barney, cried she, an' she spoke thro' the window:
  Ah! would ye be taken me out of my bed?
To come at this time it's a shame and a sin, too:
  It's whiskey, not love, that's got into your head,
If your heart it was true, of my fame you'd be tender:
  Consider the time, an' there's nobody in,
Oh! what has a poor girl but her name to defend her?
  No, Barney Avourneen, I won't let you in."

BARNEY AVOURNEEN, I WON'T LET YOU IN.
Continued.

" Ah ! cushla," cried he, " it's my heart is a fountain
    That weeps for the wrong I might lay at your door :
Your name is more white than the snow on the mountain,
    And Barney would die to preserve it as pure ;
I'll go to my home, though the winter winds face me,
    I'll whistle them off : for, I'm happy within ;
An' the words of my Kathleen will comfort an' bless me,
    Oh ! Barney Avourneen, I won't let you in."

FOR I AM DESOLATE.

By Gerald Griffin.

The Christmas light is burning bright
    In many a village pane,
And many a cottage rings to-night
    With many a merry strain.
Young boys and girls run laughing by,
    Their hearts and eyes elate;
I can but think on mine, and sigh,
    For I am desolate.

There's none to watch in our old cot,
    Beside the holy light,
No tongue to bless the silent spot
    Against the parting night.
I've closed the door and hither come
    To mourn my lonely fate;
I cannot bear my own old home,
    It is so desolate !

I saw my father's eyes grow dim,
    And clasped my mother's knee;
I saw my mother follow him—
    My husband wept with me.
My husband did not long remain—
    His child was left me yet :
But now my heart's last love is slain,
    And I am desolate !

THE EMERALD ISLE.

Of all the nations under the sun,
  Dear *Erin* does truly excel;
For friendship, for valor, for fun,
  'Tis famed, as the world can tell;
The boys are all hearty, the girls
  Sweet daughters of beauty they prove;
The lads, they ne'er dread any perils
  The lasses are brimful of love.

Then! hurrah! for the Emerald Isle,
  Where shillelahs and shamrocks abound!
May peace and prosperity smile
  O'er the land and its natives around!

Our forefathers tell us Saint Pat
  Drove venom away from our shore,
The shamrock he blessed, and for that
  We steep it in whiskey *galore*;
He told us while time should remain,
  Still happy would be the gay sod,
And bloom in the midst of the main,
  By the footsteps of friendship still trod.
            Then hurrah, &c.

As for heroes, we have them in plenty,
  From gallant old Brian Boroimhe;
In battles, faith! upwards of twenty,
  He leathered the Danes black and blue.
Invasion our sons could not sever,
  Like lions they fought on the strand,
And may their descendants for ever
  Protect their own beautiful land.
            Then success to, &c.

PADDY McSHANE'S SEVEN AGES.

AIR.—*"Sprig of Shillalah."*

IF my own botheration don't alter my plan,
I'll sing seven lines of a tight Irishman,
   Wrote by old Billy Shakspeare, of Ballyporeen.
He said, while a babe I loved whiskey and pap,
That I roared like a bull in my grandmother's lap;
She joulted me hard, just to hush my sweet roar,
When I slipped through her fingers, whack on the floor,
   What a squalling I made, sure, at Ballyporeen!

When I grew up a boy, with a nice, shining face,
With my bag at my back, and a snail-crawling pace,
   Went to school at old Thwackam's, at Ballyporeen:
His wig was so fusty, his birch was my dread;
He larning beat out 'stead of into my head:
"Master McShane, you're a great, dirty dolt;
You've got no more brains than a Monaghan colt;
   You're not fit for our college at Ballyporeen!"

When eighteen years of age, was teazed and perplexed
To know what I should be—so a lover turned next,
   And courted sweet Shelah, of Ballyporeen.
I thought I'd just take her to comfort my life,
Not knowing that she was already a wife;
She asked me just once if to see her I'd come,
When I found her ten children and husband at home—
   A great, big, whacking chairman of Ballyporeen!

I next turned soldier—I did not like that,
So turned servant, and lived with great Justice Pat,
   A big dealer in praties at Ballyporeen.
With turtle and venison he lined his inside—
Ate so many fat capons, that one day he died;
So great was my grief, that, to keep spirits up,
Of some nice whiskey-cordial I took a big sup,
   To my master's safe journey from Ballyporeen!

PADDY McSHANE'S SEVEN AGES.—*Continued.*

Kicked and tossed about, like a weathercock vane,
I packed up my all, and I went back again
  To my grandfather's cottage, at Ballyporeen.
I found him, poor soul! with no legs for his hose,
Could not see through the spectacles put on his nose,
With no teeth in his mouth, so Death locked his chin—
He slipped out of his slippers and 'faith I slipped in,
  And succeeded poor Dennis of Ballyporeen.

——o——

I WOULD NOT DIE.

BY THOMAS FRANCIS MEAGHER.

I WOULD not die in this bright hour,
  While Hope's sweet stream is flowing;
I would not die while Youth's gay flower
  In springtide pride is glowing.
The path I trace in fiery dreams
  For manhood's flight, to-morrow,
Oh, let me tread, 'mid those bright gleams
  Which souls from Fame will borrow.
I would not die! I would not die!
  In Youth's bright hour of pleasure;
I would not leave, without a sigh,
  The dreams, the hopes I treasure!

I set young seeds in earth to-day,
  While yet the sun was gushing,
And shall I pass, ere these, away,
  Nor see the flowerets blushing?
Are these young seeds, when earth looks fair,
  To rise with fragrance teeming,
And shall the hand that placed them there
  Lie cold when they are gleaming?
I would not die! I would not die!
  In Youth's bright hour of pleasure;
I would not leave, without a sigh,
  The dreams, the hopes I treasure!

GO WHERE GLORY WAITS THEE.

By Thomas Moore

Go where glory waits thee,
But while fame elates thee,
  Oh! still remember me,
When the praise thou meetest
To thine ear is sweetest,
  Oh then remember me.
Other arms may press thee,
Dearer friends caress thee,
All the joys that bless thee,
  Sweeter far may be.
But when friends are nearest,
And when joys are dearest,
    Oh! then remember me.

When at eve thou rovest
By the star thou lovest,
  Oh! then remember me,
Think, when home returning,
Bright we've seen it burning,
  Oh! thus remember me.
Oft as summer closes,
When thine eye reposes
On its ling'ring roses,
  Once so loved by thee,
Think of her who wove them,
Her who made thee love them,
  Oh! then remember me.

When around thee dying,
Autumn leaves are lying,
  Oh! then remember me.
And, at night, when gazing
On the gay hearth blazing,
  Oh! then remember me.
Then, should music, stealing
All the soul of feeling,
To thy heart appealing,
  Draw one tear from thee—
Then let memory bring thee
Strains I used to sing thee,
  Oh! then remember me.

MY MARY OF THE CURLING HAIR.

By Gerald Griffin.

Air.—" *Siubhail a Ghradh.*

My Mary of the curling hair
The laughing teeth and bashful air,
Our bridal morn is dawning fair,
   With blushes in the skies.
Shule, shule, shule agra
Shule go socair agus, shule aroon ! *
   My love ! my pearl !
   My own dear girl !
My mountain maid, arise !

Wake, linnet of the osier grove !
Wake, trembling, stainless, virgin dove !
Wake, nestling of a parent's love !
   Let Moran see thine eyes.
     Shule, shule, &c.

I am no stranger, proud and gay,
To win thee from thy home away,
And find thee, for a distant day,
   A theme for wasting sighs,
     Shule, shule, &c.

But we were known from infancy,
Thy father's hearth was home to me ;
No selfish love was mine for thee,
   Unholy and unwise.
     Shule, shule, &c.

And yet, (to see what love can do !)
Though calm my hope has burned, and true,
My cheek is pale and worn for you,
   And sunken are mine eyes !
     Shule, shule, &c.

* This is literally translated —

   Come ! come ! come, my darling --
   Come softly, and come, my love !

MY MARY OF THE CURLING HAIR.—*Continued.*

But soon my love shall be my bride,
And, happy be our own fire-side,
My veins shall feel the rosy tide
    That lingering Hope denies.
        Shule, shule &c.

My Mary of the curling hair,
The laughing teeth and bashful air,
Our bridal morn is dawning fair,
    With blushes in the skies.
Shule, shule, shule agra
Shule go socair agus, shule aroon
    My love! my pearl!
    My own dear girl!
My mountain maid, arise!

———o———

THE NIGHT WAS STILL.

BY J. J. CALLANAN.

AIR.—*"Kitty Scott."*

THE night was still, the air was balm,
    Soft dews around were weeping,
No whisper rose o'er ocean's calm,
    Its waves in light were sleeping;
With Mary on the beach I strayed,
    The stars beamed joy above me;
I pressed her hand and said "Sweet maid,
    Oh! tell me do you love me?"

With modest air she drooped her head,
    Her cheek of beauty veiling;
Her bosom heaved—no word she said;
    I marked her strife of feeling;
" Oh! speak my doom, dear maid," I cried,
    " By yon bright heaven above thee;"
She gently raised her eyes, and sighed,
    "Too well you know I love thee."

THE PRETTY GIRL OF LOCH DAN.

By Samuel Ferguson.

The shades of eve had crossed the glen
  That frowns o'er infant Avonmore,
When, nigh Loch Dan, two weary men,
  We stopped before a cottage door.

'God save all here!" my comrade cries,
  And rattles on the raised latch-pin;
" God save you kindly !" quick replies
  A clear sweet voice, and asks us in.

We enter; from the wheel she starts,
  A rosy girl with soft black eyes;
Her fluttering court'sy takes our hearts,
  Her blushing grace and pleased surprise.

Poor Mary, she was quite alone—
  For, all the way to Glenmalure,
Her mother had that morning gone,
  And left the house in charge with her.

But neither household cares, nor yet
  The shame that startled virgins feel,
Could make the generous girl forget
  Her wonted hospitable zeal.

She brought us, in a beechen bowl,
  Sweet milk that smacked of mountain thyme;
Oat cake, and such a yellow roll
  Of butter—it gilds all my rhyme!

And, while we ate the grateful food
  (With weary limbs on bench reclined),
Considerate and discreet, she stood
  Apart, and listened to the wind.

Kind wishes both our souls engaged,
  From breast to breast spontaneous ran
The mutual thought—we stood and pledged
  THE MODEST ROSE ABOVE LOCH DAN.

THE PRETTY GIRL OF LOCH DAN.—*Continued.*

"The milk we drink is not more pure,
  Sweet Mary—bless those budding charms!
Than your own generous heart, I'm sure,
  Nor whiter than the breast it warms!

She turned and gazed, unused to hear
  Such language in that homely glen;
But, Mary, you have nought to fear,
  Though smiled on by two stranger men.

Not for a crown would I alarm
  Your virgin pride by word or sign,
Nor need a painful blush disarm
  My friend of thoughts as pure as mine.

Her simple heart could not but feel
  The words we spoke were free from guile,
She stooped, she blushed—she fixed her wheel—
  'Tis all in vain—she can't but smile!

Just like sweet April's dawn appears
  Her modest face—I see it yet—
And though I lived a hundred years,
  Methinks I could never forget

The pleasure that, despite her heart,
  Fills all her downcast eyes with light—
The lips reluctantly apart,
  The white teeth struggling into sight;

The dimples eddying o'er her cheek.—
  The rosy cheek that won't be still!
Oh! who could blame what flatterers speak,
  Did smiles like this reward their skill!

For such another smile, I vow,
  Though loudly beats the midnight rain,
I'd take the mountain-side e'en now,
  And walk to Luggelaw again!

THE CONVICT OF CLONMELL.

TRANSLATED FROM THE IRISH.

BY JEREMIAH JOSEPH CALLANAN.

How hard is my fortune,
 And vain my repining !
The strong rope of fate
 For his young neck is twining.
My strength is departed;
 My cheek sunk and sallow !
While I languish in chains,
 In the gaol of Clonmala.*

No boy in the village
 Was ever yet milder,
I'd play with a child,
 And my sport would be wilder.
I'd dance without tiring
 From morning till even,
And the goal-ball I'd strike
 To the lightning of Heaven.

At my bed-foot decaying,
 My hurlbat is lying,
Through the boys in the village
 My goal-ball is flying;
My horse 'mong the neighbors
 Neglected may fallow,—
While I pine in my chains,
 In the gaol of Clonmala.

Next Sunday the patron
 At home will be keeping.
And the young active hurlers
 The field will be sweeping.
With the dance of fair maidens
 The evening they'll hallow,
While this heart, once so gay,
 Shall be cold in Clonmala.

* *Clonmala*,—Recess, or field of honey.— Irish of Clonmell.

EIBHLIN, A RUIN.*

BY GERALD GRIFFIN.

WHEN, like the early rose,
     Eibhlin, a Ruin!
Beauty in childhood blows,
     Eibhlin, a Ruin!
When, like a diadem,
Buds blush around the stem,
Which is the fairest gem?
     Eibhlin, a Ruin!

Is it the laughing eye,
     Eibhlin, a Ruin!
Is it the timid sigh,
     Eibhlin, a Ruin!
Is it the tender tone,
Soft as the stringed harp's moan?
Oh! it is truth alone,
     Eibhlin, a Ruin!

When, like the rising day,
     Eibhlin, a Ruin!
Love sends his early ray,
     Eibhlin, a Ruin!
What makes his dawning glow
Changeless through joy or woe?
Only the constant know—
     Eibhlin, a Ruin!

I know a valley fair,
     Eibhlin, a Ruin!
I knew a cottage there,
     Eibhlin, a Ruin!
Far in that valley's shade
I knew a gentle maid,
Flower of a hazel glade,
     Eibhlin, a Ruin!

Who in the song so sweet?
     Eibhlin, a Ruin!
Who in the dance so fleet?
     Eibhlin, a Ruin!

*Pronounced Eileen aroon

EIBHLIN A RUIN.—*Continued.*

Dear were her charms to me,
Dearer her laughter free,
Dearest her constancy,
   Eibhlin, a Ruin!

Were she no longer true,
   Eibhlin, a Ruin!
What should her lover do?
   Eibhlin, a Ruin!
Fly with his broken chain
Far o'er the sounding main,
Never to love again,
   Eibhlin, a Ruin!

Youth must with time decay,
   Eibhlin, a Ruin!
Beauty must fade away,
   Eibhlin, a Ruin!
Castles are sacked in war,
Chieftains are scattered far,
Truth is a fixed star,
   Eibhlin, a Ruin!

LAMENT FOR THE MILESIANS.

By Thomas Davis.

Oh! proud were the chieftains of proud Innis-Fail,
      As strue gon na air na farragh!
The stars of our sky and the salt of our soil,
      As strue gon na air na farragh :
Their hearts were as soft as a child in the lap,
Yet they were " the men in the gap"—
And now that the cold clay their limbs doth enwrap,
      *As strue gon na air na farragh !**

'Gainst England long battling, at length they went down,
      As strue gon na air na farragh!
But they've left their deep tracks on the road of renown,
      As strue gon na air na farragh!
We are heirs of their fame, if we're not of their race,
And deadly and deep our disgrace,
If we live o'er their sepulchres, abject and base,
      As strue gon na air na farragh !

Oh ! sweet were the minstrels of kind Innis-Fail!
      As strue gon na air na farragh !
Whose music, nor ages nor sorrow can spoil,
      As strue gon na air na farragh !
But their sad, stifled tones are like streams flowing hid,
Their *caoine* and their pibroch were chid,
And their language, "that melts into music," forbid,
      As strue gon na air na farragh !

How fair were the maidens of fair Innis-Fail!
      As strue gon na air na farragh !
As fresh and as free as the sea-breeze from soil,
      As strue gon na air na farragh !
Oh ! are not our maidens as fair and as pure?
Can our music no longer allure ?
And can we but sob, as such wrongs we endure,
      As strue gon na air na farragh !

Their famous, their holy, their dear Innis-Fail,
      As strue gon na air na farragh !
Shall it still be a prey for the stranger to spoil?
      As strue gon na air na farragh !

    * It is a pity there are none now like them.

LAMENT FOR THE MILESIANS.—*Continued.*

Sure, brave men would labor by night and by day
To banish that stranger away,
Or, dying for Ireland, the future would say,
As strue gon na air na farragh !

Oh, shame !—for unchanged is the face of our isle,
As strue gon na air na farragh !
That taught them to battle, to sing, and to smile,
As strue gon na air na farragh !
We are heirs of their rivers, their sea, and their land
Our sky and our mountains as grand—
We are heirs—oh! we're not!—of their heart and their hand,
As strue gon na air na farragh!

———o———

THE LEAVES SO GREEN.

WHEN life hath left this senseless clay
    By all but thee forgot,
Oh! bear me, dearest, far away,
    To some green lonely spot,
Where none with careless step may tread
    The grass upon my grave,
But gently o'er my narrow bed
    " The leaves so green" may wave.

The wild flowers, too, I loved so well,
    Shall breathe their sweetness there,
While thrush and blackbird's songs shall swell
    Amid the fragrant air.
No noisy burst of joy or woe
    Will there disturb my rest,
But silent tears in secret flow
    From those who loved me best.

The crowded town and haunts of men
    I never loved to tread ;
To sheltered vale or lonely glen
    My weary spirit fled.
Then lay me, dearest, far away,
    By other eyes unseen,
Where gleams of sunshine rarely stray
    Beneath " the leaves so green."

THE WOMAN OF THREE COWS.

TRANSLATED FROM THE IRISH.

BY JAMES CLARENCE MANGAN.

O, WOMAN of Three Cows, agragh! don't let your tongue
    thus rattle!
O, don't be saucy, don't be stiff, because you may have cattle.
I have seen—and, here's my hand to you, I only say what's
    true—
A many a one with twice your stock not half so proud as you.

Good luck to you, don't scorn the poor, and don't be their
    despiser;
For worldly wealth soon melts away, and cheats the very
    miser:
And death soon strips the proudest wreath from haughty
    human brows.
Then don't be stiff, and don't be proud, good Woman of
    Three Cows!

See where Momonia's heroes lie, proud Owen More's de-
    scendants,
'Tis they that won the glorious name, and had the grand at-
    tendants!
If *they* were forced to bow to Fate, as every mortal bows,
Can *you* be proud, can *you* be stiff my Woman of Three
    Cows?

The brave sons of the Lord of Clare, they left the land to
    mourning;
Mavrone*! for they were banish'd, with no hope of their re-
    turning—
Who knows in what abodes of want those youths were driven
    to house?
Yet *you* can give yourself these airs, O Woman of Three
    Cows!

O, think of Donnell of the ships, the Chief whom nothing
    daunted—
See how he fell in distant Spain, unchronicled, unchanted!

*My grief.

THE WOMAN OF THREE COWS.—*Continued.*

He sleeps, the great O'Sullivan, where thunder cannot
    rouse—
Then ask yourself, should *you* be proud, good Woman of
    Three Cows!

O'Ruark, Maguire, those souls of fire, whose names are
    shrin'd in story—
Think how their high achievements once made Erin's great-
    est glory—
Yet now their bones lie mouldering under weeds and cypress
    boughs,
And so, for all your pride, will yours, O Woman of Three
    Cows!

Th' O'Carrolls, also famed, when the fame was only for the
    boldest,
Rest in forgotten sepulchres with Erin's best and oldest;
Yet who so great as they of yore in battle or carouse?
Just think of that, and hide your head, good Woman of
    Three Cows!

Your neighbor's poor, and you, it seems, are big with vain
    ideas,
Because *inagh !* you've got three cows, one more, I see, than
    she has ;
That tongue of yours wags more at times than charity al-
    lows—
But, if you're strong, be merciful, great Woman of Three
    Cows!

THE SUMMING-UP.

Now, there you go! You still, of course, keep up your scorn-
    ful bearing,
And I'm too poor to hinder you; but, by the cloak I'm wear-
    ing,
If I had but *four* cows myself, even though you were my
    spouse,
I'd thwack you well to cure your pride, my Woman of Three
    Cows!

THE GRAVE OF MACCAURA.

By Mrs. Downing.

And this is thy grave MacCaura,
  Here by the pathway lone ;
When the thorn blossoms are bending
Over thy mouldered stone.
Alas! for the sons of glory :
  Oh ! thou of the darkened brow,
And the eagle plume, and the belted clans,
  Is it here thou art sleeping now?

Oh ! wild is the spot, MacCaura,
  In which they have laid thee low—
The field where thy people triumphed
  Over a slaughtered foe :
And loud was the banshee's wailing,
  And deep was the clansmen's sorrow,
When with bloody hands and burning tears
  They buried thee here, MacCaura.

And now thy dwelling is lonely—
  King of the rushing horde :
And now thy battles are over—
  Chief of the shining sword.
And the rolling thunder echoes
  O'er torrent and mountain free,
But alas ! and alas ! MacCaura,
  It will not awaken thee.

Farewell to thy grave, MacCaura,
  Where the slanting sunbeams shine,
And the brier and waving fern
  Over thy slumbers twine ;
Thou whose gathering summons
  Could waken the sleeping glen ;
MacCaura ! alas for thee and thine,
  'Twill **never** be heard again !

THE FAIRY CHILD.

By Dr. Anster.

The summer sun was sinking
  With a mild light, calm and mellow—
It shone on my little boy's bonny cheeks,
  And his loose locks of yellow.

The robin was singing sweetly,
  And his song was sad and tender:
And my little boy's eyes, while he heard the song,
  Smiled with a sweet, soft splendor.

My little boy lay on my bosom,
  While his soul the song was quaffing;
The joy of his soul had ting'd his cheek,
  And his heart and his eyes were laughing.

I sate alone in my cottage,
  The midnight needle plying;
I feared for my child, for the rush's light
  In the socket now was dying!

There came a hand to my lonely latch,
  Like the wind at midnight moaning;
I knelt to pray, but rose again,
  For I heard my little boy groaning.

I crossed my brow and I crossed my breast,
  But that night my child departed—
They left a weakling in his stead,
  And I am broken-hearted!

Oh! it cannot be my own sweet boy,
  For his eyes are dim and hollow;
My little boy is gone—is gone,
  And his mother soon will follow!

The dirge for the dead will be sung for me
  And the mass be chanted meetly,
And I shall sleep with my little boy,
  In the moonlit churchyard sweetly.

THE IRISH REAPER'S HARVEST HYMN.

By John Keegan.

ALL hail! Holy Mary, our hope and our joy!
Smile down, blessed Queen! on the poor Irish boy,
Who wanders away from his dear belov'd home;
Oh, Mary! be with me wherever I roam.
   Be with me, Oh! Mary,
   Forsake me not, Mary,
But guide me, and guard me, wherever I roam.

From the home of my fathers in anguish I go,
To toil for the dark-livered, cold-hearted foe,
Who mocks me, and hates me, and calls me a slave,
An alien, a savage, all names but a knave;
   But, blessed be Mary,
   My sweet, Holy Mary,
The *bodagh** he never dare call me a knave.

From my mother's mud sheeling, an outcast I fly,
With a cloud on my heart and a tear in my eye;
Oh! I burn as I think as if *Some One* would say,
"Revenge on your tyrants"—but Mary, I pray
   From my soul's depth, Oh! Mary,
   And hear me, sweet Mary,
For Union and Peace to old Ireland I pray.

The land that I fly from is fertile and fair.
And more than I ask for or wish for is there—
But I must not taste the good things that I see,
" There's nothing but rags and green rushes for me."†
   Oh! mild Virgin Mary,
   Oh! sweet Mother Mary,
Who keeps my rough hand from red murder but thee?

* *Bodagh*, a clown, a churl.

† Taken literally from a conversation with a young peasant on his way to reap the harvest in England.

THE IRISH REAPER'S HARVEST HYMN.—*Continued.*

But sure in the end our dear freedom we'll gain,
And wipe from the Green Flag each Sassanach stain,
And oh! Holy Mary, your blessing we crave,
Give hearts to the timid, and hands to the brave;
  And then, Mother Mary,
   Our own blessed Mary,
Light liberty's flame in the hut of the slave.

——o——

SERENADE.

By J. J. Callanan.

The blue waves are sleeping,
 The breezes are still,
The light dews are weeping
 Soft tears on the hill.
The moon in mild beauty
 Shines brightly above;
Then come to the casement,
 Oh! Mary, my love.

No form from the lattice
 Did ever recline
Over Italy's waters
 More lovely than thine.
Then come to the window,
 And shed from above
One glance of thy bright eye—
 One smile of thy love.

From the storms of this world
 How gladly I'd fly
To the calm of that breast—
 To the heaven of that eye.
How deeply I love thee
 'Twere useless to tell;
Farewell, then, my dear one,
 My Mary, farewell!

THE MI NA MEALA* NOW IS PAST.

By Gerald Griffin.

Air.—" *A Mhuire s' Truagh.*"

The *mi na meala* now is past,
A wirra stru, a wirra stru,†
And I must leave my home at last,
A wirra stru, a wirra stru,
I look into my father's eyes,
I hear my mother's parting sighs—
Ah! fool to pine for other ties—
A wirra stru, a wirra stru!

This evening they must sit alone,
A wirra stru, a wirra stru,
They'll talk of me when I am gone,
A wirra stru, a wirra stru,
Who now will cheer my weary sire,
When toil and care his heart shall tire?
My chair is empty by the fire;
A wirra stru, a wirra stru!

How sunny looks my pleasant home,
A wirra stru, a wirra stru,
Those flowers for me shall never bloom—
A wirra stru, a wirra stru!
I seek new friends, and I am told
That they are rich in lands and gold;
Ah! will they love me like the old?
A wirra stru, a wirra stru!

Farewell! dear friends, we meet no more—
A wirra stru, a wirra stru!
My husband's horse is at the door,
A wirra stru, a wirra stru!
Ah, love! ah, love! be kind to me:
For by this breaking heart you see
How dearly I have purchased thee!
A wirra stru, a wirra stru!

* *Mi na Meala*—Honeymoon.
† Vulgo, " *Wirrasthrue*," " Oh! Mary who art merciful!"

INIS-EOGHAIN

By Charles Gavan Duffy.

GOD bless the grey mountains of dark *Donegal*
God bless royal *Ailene* the pride of them all!
For she sits evermore like a queen on her throne,
And smiles on the valleys of green *Inis-Eoghain*
   And fair are the valleys of green *Inis-Eoghain*
   And hardy the fishers that call them their own—
   A race that nor traitor nor coward has known
   Enjoys the fair valleys of green *Inis-Eoghain*

Oh! simple and bold are the bosoms they bear,
Like the hills that with silence and nature they share:
For our God, who hath planted their home near His own,
Breath'd His spirit abroad upon fair *Inis-Eoghain*
   Then praise to our Father for wild *Inis-Eoghain*
   Where fiercely for ever the surges are thrown—
   Nor weather nor fortune a tempest hath blown
   Could shake the strong bosoms of brave *Inis-Eoghain*

See the bountiful *Couldah** careering along—
A type of their manhood so stately and strong—
On the weary for ever its tide is bestown,
So they share with the stranger in fair *Inis-Eoghain*
   God guard the kind homesteads of fair *Inis-Eoghain*
   Which manhood and virtue have chos'n for their own;
   Not long shall the nation in slavery groan
   That rears the tall peasants of fair *Inis-Eoghain*

Like the oak of St. Bride, which nor devil, nor Dane,
Nor Saxon, nor Dutchman, could rend from her fane,
They have clung by the creed and the cause of their own,
Through the midnight of danger in true *Inis-Eoghain*
   Then shout for the glories of old *Inis-Eoghain*
   The stronghold that foeman has never o'erthrown—
   The soul and the spirit, the blood and the bone,
   That guard the green valleys of true *Inis-Eoghain*

* The Couldah, or Culdaff, is a chief river in the Innishowen mountains

INIS-EOGHAIN.—*Continued.*

Nor purer of old was the tongue of the Gael,
When the charging *Abu* made the foreigner quail,
Than it gladdens the stranger in welcome's soft tone,
In the home-loving cabins of kind *Inis-Eoghain*
   Oh! flourish, ye homesteads of kind *Inis-Eoghain*
   Where seeds of a people's redemption are sown ;
   Right soon shall the fruit of that sowing have grown,
   To bless the kind homesteads of green *Inis-Eoghain.*

When they tell us the tale of a spell-stricken band,
All entranced, with their bridles and broad swords in hand,
Who await but the word to give *Eire* her own,
They can read you that riddle in proud *Inis-Eoghain*
   Hurra for the spæmen of proud *Inis-Eoghain*
   Long live the wild seërs of stout *Inis-Eoghain*
   May Mary, our mother, be deaf to their moan
   Who love not the promise of proud *Inis-Eoghain,*

———o———

GO! FORGET ME.

By Rev. Charles Wolfe.

Air—" *Open the Window.*"

Go! forget me, why should sorrow
   O'er that brow a shadow fling?
Go! forget me—and to-morrow
   Brightly smile, and sweetly sing.
Smile—though I shall not be near thee,
Sing—though I shall never hear thee,
   May thy soul with pleasure shine,
   Lasting as the gloom of mine.

Like the sun, thy presence glowing
   Clothes the meanest things in light;
And when thou, like him, art going,
   Loveliest objects fade in night.
All things looked so bright about thee,
That they nothing seem without thee.
   By that pure and lucid mind
   Earthly things were too refined.

GO ! FORGET ME.—*Continued.*

Go ! thou vision, wildly gleaming,
  Softly on my soul that fell,
Go ! for me no longer beaming,
  Hope and beauty, fare ye well !
Go ! and all that once delighted
Take—and leave me, all benighted,
  Glory's burning gen'rous swell,
  Fancy and the poet's shell.

———o———

ROISIN DUBH.*

BY THOMAS FURLONG.

OH ! my sweet little rose, cease to pine for the past,
For the friends that came eastward shall see thee at last ;
They bring blessings and favors the past never knew,
To pour forth in gladness on my Róisín Dubh.

Long, long, with my dearest, through strange scenes I've gone,
O'er mountains and broad valleys I still have toiled on ;
O'er the Erne I have sailed as the rough gales blew,
While the harp poured its music for my Róisín Dubh.

Though wearied, oh ! my fair one ! do not slight my song,
For my heart dearly loves thee, and hath loved thee long ;
In sadness and in sorrow I still shall be true,
And cling with wild fondness round my Róisín Dubh.

There's no flower that e'er bloomed can my rose excel,
There's no tongue that e'er moved half my love can tell,
Had I strength, had I skill the wide world to subdue,
Oh ! the queen of that wide world should be Róisín Dubh.

Had I power, oh ! my loved one, but to plead thy right,
I should speak out in boldness for my heart's delight ;
I would tell to all round me how my fondness grew,
And bid them bless the beauty of my Róisín Dubh.

The mountains, high and misty, through the moors must go,
The rivers shall run backward, and the lakes overflow,
And the wild waves of old ocean wear a crimson hue,
Ere the world sees the ruin of my Róisín Dubh.

* Little Black Rose.

MITCHELLSTOWN CASTLE.

THE DESMOND.

By Thomas Moore.

By the Feal's wave benighted,
  No star in the skies,
To thy door by love lighted,
  I first saw those eyes.
Some voice whispered o'er me,
  As the threshold I crost,
There was ruin before me—
  If I lov'd I was lost.

Love came and brought sorrow
  Too soon in his train :
Yet so sweet, that to-morrow
  'Twere welcome again.
Though misery's full measure
  My portion should be,
I would drain it with pleasure,
  If pour'd out by thee.

You, who call it dishonor
  To bow to this flame,
If you've eyes look but on her,
  And blush while you blame.
Hath the pearl less whiteness
  Because of its birth?
Hath the violet less brightness
  For growing near earth?

No—man for his glory
  To ancestry flies;
But women's bright story
  Is told in her eyes.
While the monarch thus traces
  Through mortals his line,
Beauty, born of the Graces,
  Ranks next to divine !

O'BRIEN OF ARA.

By Thomas Davis.

Air.—"*The Piper of Blessington.*"

TALL are the towers of O'Kennedy—
  Broad are the lands of MacCarha—
Desmond feeds five hundred men a-day;
  Yet, here's to O'Brien of Ara!
      Up from the Castle of Drumineer,
        Down from the top of Camailte,
      Clansman and kinsman are coming here
        To give him the CEAD MILE FAILTE.

See you the mountains look huge at eve—
  So is our chieftain in battle—
Welcome he has for the fugitive,
  Usquebaugh, fighting, and cattle!
      Up from the Castle of Drumineer,
        Down from the top of Camailte,
      Gossip and ally are coming here
        To give him the CEAD MILE FAILTE.

Horses the valleys are tramping on,
  Sleek from the Sasanach manger—
Creaghts the hills are encamping on,
  Empty the bawns of the stranger!
      Up from the Castle of Drumineer,
        Down from the top of Camailte,
      Kern and bonaght are coming here
        To give him the CEAD MILE FAILTE.

He has black silver from Killaloe—
  Ryan and Carroll are neighbors—
Nenagh submits with a pillileu—
  Butler is meat for our sabres!
      Up from the Castle of Drumineer,
        Down from the top of Camailte,
      Ryan and Carroll are coming here
        To give him the CEAD MILE FAILTE.

O'BRIEN OF ARA.—*Continued.*

'Tis scarce a week since through Ossory
  Chased he the Baron of Durrow—
Forced him five rivers to cross, or he
    Had died from the sword of Red Murrough,
      Up from the Castle of Drumineer,
        Down from the top of Camailte,
      All the O'Briens are coming here
        To give him the CEAD MILE FAILTE.

Tall are the towers of O'Kennedy—
  Broad are the lands of MacCarha—
Desmond feeds five hundred men a day;
  Yet, here's to O'Brien of Ara!
      Up from the Castle of Drumineer,
        Down from the top of Camailte,
      Clansman and kinsman are coming here
        To give him the CEAD MILE FAILTE.

---o---

THE FAREWELL TO MY HARP.

By Thomas Moore.

DEAR Harp of my country! in darkness I found thee,
The cold chain of silence had hung o'er thee long,
When proudly, my own island Harp! I unbound thee,
And gave all thy chords to light, freedom, and song!
The warm lay of love, and the light note of gladness,
Have waken'd thy fondest, thy liveliest thrill;
But so oft hast thou echoed the deep sigh of sadness,
That e'en in thy mirth it will steal from thee still.

Dear Harp of my country! farewell to thy numbers,
This sweet wreath of song is the last we shall twine,
Go—sleep with the sunshine of fame on thy slumbers,
Till touch'd by some hand less unworthy than mine.
If the pulse of the patriot, soldier, or lover,
Have throbb'd at our lay, 'tis thy glory alone;
I was but as the wind, passing heedlessly over,
And all thy wild sweetness I wak'd was thy own!

NORA CREINA.

By Thomas Moore.

Lesbia hath a beaming eye,
But no one knows for whom it beameth,
Right and left its arrows fly,
But what they aim at no one dreameth!
Sweeter 'tis to gaze upon
My Nora's lid that seldom rises;
Few its looks, but every one
Like unexpected light, surprises!
Oh! my Nora Creina, dear!
My gentle, bashful Nora Creina!
Beauty lies in many eyes,
But love in yours, my Nora Creina!

Lesbia wears a robe of gold,
But all so close the nymph hath lac'd it.
Not a charm of beauty's mould
Presumes to stay where Nature plac'd it.
Oh! my Nora's gown for me,
That floats as wild as mountain breezes,
Leaving every beauty free
To sink or swell as Heav'n pleases!
Yes, my Nora Creina, dear!
My simple, graceful Nora Creina!
Nature's dress is loveliness—
The dress *you* wear, my Nora Creina!

Lesbia hath a wit refin'd,
But, when its points are gleaming round us,
Who can tell, if they're design'd
To dazzle merely or to wound us!
Pillow'd on my Nora's heart,
In safer slumber Love reposes—
Bed of peace! whose roughest part
Is but the crumpling of the roses.
Oh! my Nora Creina, dear!
My mild, my artless, Nora Creina!
Wit, tho' bright, hath not the light
That warms your eyes, my Nora Creina!

THE MINSTREL BOY.

By Thomas Moore.

THE minstrel boy to the war is gone,
  In the ranks of death you'll find him;
His father's sword he has girded on,
  And his wild harp slung behind him.
" Land of song!" said the warrior bard,
  " Tho' all the world betray thee;
One sword, at least, thy right shall guard—
  One faithful harp shall praise thee!"

The minstrel fell—but the foeman's chain
  Could not bring his proud soul under;
The harp he loved ne'er spoke again,
  For he tore its cords asunder;
And said, " No chain shall sully thee,
  Thou soul of love and bravery!
Thy songs were made for the pure and free,
  They shall never sound in slavery!"

———o———

AND MUST WE PART?

By J. J. Callanan.

Air.—" Ni mheall far me aris."*

AND must we part? then fare thee well!
But he that wails it—he can tell
How dear thou wert, how dear thou art,
And ever must be, to this heart;
But now 'tis vain—it cannot be:
Farewell! and think no more on me.

Oh! yes—this heart would sooner break
Than one unholy thought awake;
I'd sooner slumber into clay
Than cloud thy spirit's beauteous ray;
Go, free as air—as angel free,
And, lady, think no more on me.

*" I will not be deceived again."

AND MUST WE PART.—*Continued.*

Oh! did we meet when brighter star
Sent its fair promise from afar,
I then might hope to call thee mine—
The minstrel's heart and harp were thine;
But now 'tis past—it cannot be;
Farewell! and think no more on me.

Or do!—but let it be the hour
When mercy's all-atoning pow'r
From His high throne of glory hears
Of souls like thine, the prayers, the tears;
Then, whilst you bend the suppliant knee,
Then—then, O lady! think on me.

———o———

THE MEETING OF THE WATERS.

By Thomas Moore.

THERE is not in the wide world a valley so sweet
As that vale in whose bosom the bright waters meet;
Oh! the last rays of feeling and life must depart
Ere the bloom of that valley shall fade from my heart.

Yet it was not that nature had shed o'er the scene
Her purest of crystal and brightest of green:
'Twas not the soft magic or streamlet or hill,
Oh! no,—it was something more exquisite still.

Twas that friends, the belov'd of my bosom, were near,
Who made each dear scene of enchantment more dear,
And who felt how the blest charms of nature improve
When we see them reflected from looks that we love.

Sweet vale of Avoca! how calm could I rest
In thy bosom of shade with the friends I love best,
Where the storms which we feel in this cold world should
    cease,
And our hearts, like thy waters, be mingled in peace!

SHE IS FAR FROM THE LAND.

By Thomas Moore.

SHE is far from the land where her young hero sleeps,
  And lovers are round her sighing;
But coldly she turns from their gaze, and weeps
  For her heart in his grave is lying!

She sings the wild song of her dear native plains,
  Every note which he lov'd awaking—
Ah! little they think, who delight in her strains,
  How the heart of the minstrel is breaking!

He had liv'd for his love, for his country he died,
  They were all that to life had entwin'd him;
Nor soon shall the tears of his country be dried,
  Nor long will his love stay behind him!

Oh! make her a grave where the sunbeams rest,
  When they promise a glorious morrow;
They'll shine o'er her sleep, like a smile from the west,
  From her own lov'd island of sorrow!

——o——

THE HARP THAT ONCE THROUGH TARA'S HALLS.

By Thomas Moore.

THE harp that once through Tara's halls
  The soul of music shed,
Now hangs as mute on Tara's walls
  As if that soul were fled.
So sleeps the pride of former days,
  So glory's thrill is o'er,
And hearts that once beat high for praise,
  Now feel that pulse no more.

No more to chiefs and ladies bright
  The harp of Tara swells;
The chord alone that breaks at night,
  Its tale of ruin tells.
Thus freedom now so seldom wakes,
  The only throb she gives;
Is when some heart indignant breaks
  To show that still she lives.

THE COUNTY OF MAYO.

TRANSLATED FROM THE IRISH.

BY GEORGE FOX.

[This specimen of our ancient Irish literature is one of the most popular songs of the peasantry of the counties of Mayo and Galway, and is evidently a composition of the seventeenth century. The original Irish, which is the composition of one Thomas Lavelle, has been published, without a translation, by Mr. Hardiman, in his "Irish Minstrelsy."

ON the deck of Patrick Lynch's boat I sat in woful plight,
Through my sighing all the weary day, and weeping all the
   night,
Were it not that full of sorrow from my people forth I go,
By the blessed sun! 'tis royally I'd sing thy praise, Mayo!

When I dwelt at home in plenty, and my gold did much
   abound,
In the company of fair young maids the Spanish ale went
   round—
'Tis a bitter change from those gay days that now I'm
   forced to go,
And must leave my bones in Santa Cruz, far from my own
   Mayo.

They are all altered girls in Irrul now; 'tis proud they're
   grown and high,
With their hair-bags and their top-knots, for I pass their buckles
   by—
But it's little now I heed their airs, for God will have it so,
That I must depart for foreign lands, and leave my sweet
   Mayo.

'Tis my grief that Patrick Loughlin is not Earl of Irrul still,
And that Brian Duff no longer rules as Lord upon the hill:
And that Colonel Hugh MacGrady should be lying dead and
   low,
And I sailing, sailing swiftly from the county of Mayo.

THE PATRIOT MOTHER.

A BALLAD OF '98.

COME tell us the name of the rebelly crew,
Who lifted the pike on the Curragh with you, ·
Come, tell us the treason, and then you'll be free,
Or right quickly you'll swing from the high gallows tree.

Alanna! alanna! the shadow of shame
Has never yet fallen upon one of your name,
And oh! may the food from my bosom you drew,
In your veins turn to poison, if *you* turn untrue.

The foul words—oh! let them not blacken your tongue,
That would prove to your friends and your country a wrong,
Or the curse of a mother, so bitter and dread,
With the wrath of the Lord—may they fall on your head!

I have no one but you in the whole world wide,
Yet false to your pledge, you'd ne'er stand at my side:
If a traitor you liv'd you'd be farther away
From my heart than, if true, you were wrapp'd in the clay.

Oh! deeper and darker the mourning would be,
For your falsehood   so base, than your death proud and free,
Dearer, far dearer than ever to me,
My darling you'll be on the brave gallows tree.

'Tis holy, agra, from the bravest and best—
Go! go! from my heart, and be join'd with the rest,
Alanna, machree! O alanna, machree!
Sure a "*stag*"* and a traitor you never will be.

There's no look of a traitor upon the young brow
That's raised to the tempters so haughtily now;
No traitor e'er held up the firm head so high—
No traitor e'er show'd such a proud flashing eye.

On the high gallows tree! on the brave gallows tree!
Where smil'd leaves and blossoms, his sad doom met he!
But it never bore blossom so pure or so fair,
As the heart of the martyr that hangs from it there.

* "Stag" an informer.

THE MAN WHO LED THE VAN OF IRISH VOLUNTEERS.

By Edward Lysaght.

THE gen'rous sons of Erin, in manly virtue bold,
With hearts and hands preparing our country to uphold,
Though cruel knaves and bigot slaves disturbed our isle some
        years,
Now hail the man who led the van of Irish Volunteers.

Just thirty years are ending, since first his glorious aid,
Our sacred rights defending, struck shackles from our trade;
To serve us still, with might and skill, the vet'ran now appears,
That gallant man who led the van of Irish Volunteers,

He sows no vile dissensions; good will to all he bears;
He knows no vain pretensions, no paltry fears or cares;
To Erin's and to Britain's sons his worth his name endears;
They love the man who led the van of Irish Volunteers.

Opposed by hirelings sordid, he broke oppression's chain;
On statute-books recorded his patriot acts remain;
The equipoise his mind employs of Commons, King, and Peers,
The upright man who led the van of Irish Volunteers.

A British constitution (to Erin ever true),
In spite of state pollution, he gained in "*Eighty-two;*"
"*He watched it in its cradle, and bedewed its hearse with tears,*" *
This gallant man who led the van of Irish Volunteers.

While other nations tremble, by proud oppressors galled,
On hustings we'll assemble, by Erin's welfare called;
Our Grattan, there we'll meet him, and greet him with three
        cheers;
The gallant man who led the van of Irish Volunteers,

---

* Mr. Grattan's feeling and impressive words were these : "I watched by the cradle of Irish Independence, and I followed its hearse."

HENRY GRATTAN.

THOUGH THE LAST GLIMPSE OF ERIN WITH SOR-
ROW I SEE.

By Thomas Moore

Though the last glimpse of Erin with sorrow I see,
Yet wherever thou art shall seem Erin to me;
In exile thy bosom shall still be my home,
And thine eyes make my climate wherever we roam.

To the gloom of some desert or cold rocky shore,
Where the eye of the stranger can haunt us no more,
I will fly with my Coulin, and think the rough wind
Less rude than the foes we leave frowning behind

And I'll gaze on thy gold hair, as graceful it wreathes,
And hang o'er thy soft harp, as wildly it breathes;
Nor dread that the cold-hearted Saxon will tear
One chord from that harp, or one lock from that hair.

———o———

FAREWELL, BUT WHENEVER, &c.

By Thomas Moore.

Farewell! but whenever you welcome the hour
That awakens the night-song of mirth in your bower,
Then think of the friend who once welcom'd it too,
And forgot his own griefs to be happy with you.
His griefs may return—not a hope may remain
Of the few friends that brighten'd his pathway of pain—
But he ne'er will forget the short vision that threw
Its enchantment around him while lingering with you.

And still on that evening when pleasure fills up
To the highest top sparkle each heart and each cup;
Where'er my path lies, be it gloomy or bright
My soul, happy friends, shall be with you that night—
Shall join in your revels, your sports, and your wiles,
And return, too, beaming all o'er with your smiles
Too blest if it tell me that, 'mid the gay cheer,
Some kind voice had murmur'd " I wish he were here. "

FAREWELL, BUT WHENEVER.—*Continued.*

Let fate do her worst, there are relics of joy,
Bright beams of the past, which she cannot destroy—
Which come in the night-time of sorrow and care,
And bring back the features which joy us'd to wear.
Long, long be my heart with such memories fill'd !
Like the vase in which roses have once been distill'd
You may break, you may ruin the vase if you will,
But the scent of the roses will hang round it still.

————o————

THE POOR MAN'S LABOR'S NEVER DONE.

I MARRIED a wife for to sit by me, which makes me sorely to
    repent :
Matches, they say, are made in heaven, but mine was for a
    penance sent.
I soon became a servant to her, to milk her cows and black
    her shoes,
For woman's ways, they must have pleasure, and the poor
    man's labor's never done.

The very first year that we were married, she gave to me a
    pretty babe ;
She sat me down to rock its cradle, and give it cordial when
    it waked ;
If it cried she would bitterly scold me, and if it bawled I
    should run away ;
For woman's ways, they must have pleasure, and the poor
    man's labor's never done.

So all ye young men that are inclined to marry, be sure and
    marry a loving wife,
And do not marry my wife's sister, or she will plague you
    all your life ;
Do not marry her mother's daughter, or she will grieve your
    heart full sore ;
Take from me my wife, and welcome ; and then my care and
    trouble is o'er

MOLLY ASTORE.*

From the Irish.　Translated by S. FERGUSON, M.R.I.A.

OH, Mary dear—oh, Mary fair,
　Oh, branch of generous stem,
White blossom of the banks of Nair,
　Though lilies grow on them ;
You've left me sick at heart for love,
　So faint I cannot see ;
The candle swims the board above,
　I'm drunk for love of thee !
Oh, stately stem of maiden pride,
　My woe it is and pain,
That I, thus severed from thy side,
　The long night must remain.

Through all the towns of Innisfail
　I've wandered far and wide,
But, from Downpatrick to Kinsale,
　From Carlow to Kilbride,
'Mong lords and dames of high degree,
　Where'er my feet have gone,
My Mary, one to equal thee
　I never looked upon :
I live in darkness and in doubt
　Whene'er my love's away—
But were the gracious sun put out,
　Her shadow would make day.

'Tis she, indeed, young bud of bliss,
　And gentle as she's fair—
Though lily-white her bosom is,
　And sunny bright her hair,
And dewy azure, her blue eye,
　And rosy red, her cheek,
Yet brighter she in modesty,
　More beautifully meek !
The world's wise men, from north to south
　Can never ease my pain—
But one kiss from her honey mouth
　Would make me well again.

* Molly my treasure.

WHEN FIRST I MET THEE.

By Thomas Moore.

WHEN first I met thee, warm and young,
  There shone such truth about thee,
And on thy lip such promise hung,
  I did not dare to doubt thee.
I saw thee change, yet still relied,
  Still clung with hope the fonder,
And thought, though false to all beside,
  From me thou couldst not wander.
    But go, deceiver! go,—
      The heart whose hopes could make it
    Trust one so false, so low,
      Deserves that thou shouldst break it!

When every tongue thy follies nam'd,
  I fled th' unwelcome story;
Or found, in even the faults they blam'd,
  Some gleams of future glory.
I still was true, when nearer friends
  Conspired to wrong, to slight thee;
The heart that now thy falsehood rends,
  Would then have bled to right thee.
    But go, deceiver! go,—
      Some day, perhaps, thou'lt waken
    From pleasure's dream, to know
      The grief of hearts forsaken.

Even now, though youth its bloom hath shed,
  No lights of age adorn thee:
The few who lov'd thee once have fled,
  And they who flatter scorn thee.
Thy midnight cup is pledg'd to slaves,
  No genial ties enwreath it;
The smiling there, like light on graves,
  Has rank, cold hearts beneath it;
    Go—go—though worlds were thine,
      I would not now surrender
    One taintless tear of mine
      For all thy guilty splendor!

NO, NOT MORE WELCOME.

By Thomas Moore.

No, not more welcome the fairy numbers
  Of music fall on the sleeper's ear,
When half awaking from fearful slumbers,
  He thinks the full choir of Heaven is near,
Then came that voice, when, all forsaken,
  This heart long had sleeping lain,
Nor thought its cold pulse would ever waken
  To such benign, blessed sounds again.

Sweet voice of comfort! 'twas like the stealing
  Of summer wind thro' some wreathed shell
Each secret winding, each inmost feeling
  Of all my soul echoed to its spell!
'Twas whisper'd balm—'twas sunshine spoken!—
  I'd live years of grief and pain,
To have my long sleep of sorrow broken
  By such benign blessed sounds again!

———o———

AVENGING AND BRIGHT.

By Thomas Moore.

Avenging and bright fell the swift sword of Erin,
  On him who the brave sons of Usna betray'd!
For ev'ry fond eye which he waken'd a tear in,
  A drop from his heart-wounds shall weep o'er her blade.

By the red cloud that hung o'er Connor's dark dwelling,
  When Ulad's three champions lay sleeping in gore—
By the billows of war which, so often high swelling,
  Have wafted these heroes to victory's shore!—

We swear to revenge them! no joy shall be tasted,
  The harp shall be silent, the maiden unwed;
Our halls shall be mute, and our fields shall lie wasted,
  Till vengeance is wreak'd on the murderer's head!

Yes, monarch! though sweet are our home recollections,
  Though sweet are the tears that from tenderness fall;
Though sweet are our friendships, our hopes, our affections,
  Revenge on a tyrant is sweetest of all!

BOUCHELLEEN-BAWN.

By John Banim.

Air.—" *Lough Sheeling.* "

[This ballad refers to the abortive scheme of proselytism, commonly known as the "New Reformation."]

AND where are you going, *ma bouchelleen-bawn,**
From father and mother so early at dawn?
Och! rather run idle from evening till dawn,
Than darken *their* threshold, *ma bouchelleen-bawn* !

For there they would tell you, *ma bouchelleen-bawn,*
That the mother whose milk to your heart you have drawn,
And the father who prays for you, evening and dawn,
Can never be heard for you, *bouchelleen-bawn.*

That the faith we have bled for, from father to son,
Since first by a lie our fair valleys were won,
And which oft in the desert, our knees to the sod,
We kept from them all, for our sons and our God—

That this was idolatry, heartless and cold,
And now grown more heartless because it is old;
And for something that's newer they'd ask you to pawn
The creed of your fathers, *ma bouchelleen-bawn* !

And now *will* you go to them, *bouchelleen-bawn,*
From father and mother, so early at dawn?
Och! the cloud from your mind let it never be drawn,
But cross not *their* threshold, *ma bouchelleen-bawn* !

——o——

WAR SONG OF O'DRISCOL.

By Gerald Griffin.

FROM the shieling that stands by the lone mountain river,
Hurry, hurry down, with the axe and the quiver;
From the deep-seated Coom, from the storm beaten highland.
Hurry, hurry down. to the shores of your island.
    Hurry down, hurry down!
    Hurry, hurry, &c.

* My little fair boy.

WAR SONG OF O'DRISCOL.—*Continued.*

Galloglach and kern, hurry down to the sea—
There the hungry Raven's beak is gaping for a prey;
Farrah! to the onset! farrah! to the shore!
Neast him with the pirate's flesh, the bird of gloom and gore!
    Hurry down, hurry down!
    Hurry, hurry, &c.

Hurry, for the slaves of Bel are mustering to meet ye:
Hurry by the beaten cliff, the Nordman longs to greet ye;
Hurry from the mountain! hurry, hurry from the plain!
Welcome him and never let him leave our land again!
    Hurry down, hurry down!
    Hurry, hurry, &c.

On the land a sulky wolf, and in the sea a shark,
Hew the ruffian spoiler down, and burn his gory bark!
Slayer of the unresisting! ravager profane!
Leave the white sea-tyrant's limbs to moulder on the plain.
    Hurry down, hurry down!
    Hurry, hurry, &c,

———o———

COME, REST IN THIS BOSOM.

By Thomas Moore.

Come, rest in this bosom, my own stricken dear!
Tho' the herd have fled from thee, thy home is still here;
Here still is the smile that no cloud can o'ercast,
And the heart and the hand all my own to the last!

Oh! what was love made for, if 'tis not the same
Through joy and through torments, through glory and
    shame?
I know not, I ask not, if guilt's in that heart,
I but know that I lov'd thee, whatever thou art!

Thou hast call'd me thy Angel in moments of bliss,
And thy Angel I'll be, 'mid the horrors of this,—
Through the furnace unshrinking, thy steps to pursue,
And shield thee, and save thee, or—perish there, too.

OH! BLAME NOT THE BARD.

By Thomas Moore.

Oh! blame not the bard, if he fly to the bowers
   Where pleasure lies carelessly smiling at Fame;
He was born for much more, and, in happier hours,
   His soul might have burn'd with a holier flame.
The string that now languishes loose o'er the lyre,
   Might have bent a proud bow to the warrior's dart,
And the lip which now breathes but the song of desire,
   Might have pour'd the full tide of the patriot's heart.

But, alas for his country! her pride is gone by,
   And that spirit is broken which never would bend;
O'er the ruin her children in secret must sigh,
   For 'tis treason to love her, and death to defend.
Unpriz'd are her sons till they've learn'd to betray;
   Undistinguish'd they live, if they shame not their sires:
And the torch, that would light them through dignity's way,
   Must be caught from the pile where their country expires!

Then blame not the bard, if, in pleasure's soft dream,
   He should try to forget what he never can heal;
Oh! give but a hope—let a vista but gleam
   Through the gloom of his country, and mark how he'll feel.
That instant his heart at her shrine would lay down
   Ev'ry passion it nurs'd, ev'ry bliss it ador'd,
While the myrtle, now idly entwin'd with his crown,
   Like the wreath of Harmodius, should cover his sword.

But, though glory be gone, and though hope fade away,
   Thy name, loved Erin, shall live in his songs;
Not ev'n in the hour when his heart is most gay
   Will he lose the remembrance of thee and thy wrongs!
The stranger shall hear thy lament on his plains:
   The sigh of thy heart shall be sent o'er the deep,
Till thy masters themselves, as they rivet thy chains,
   Shall pause at the song of their captive, and weep.

FLY NOT YET.

By Thomas Moore.

FLY not yet, 'tis just the hour
When pleasure, like the midnight flow'r,
That scorns the eye of vulgar light,
Begins to bloom for sons of night,
　And maids who love the moon!
'Twas but to bless these hours of shade
That beauty and the moon were made;
'Tis then their soft attractions glowing
Set the tides and goblets flowing.
　Oh! stay,—oh! stay,—
Joy so seldom weaves a chain
Like this to-night, that, oh! 'tis pain
　To break its links so soon.

Fly not yet; the fount that play'd,
In times of old, through Ammon's shade,
Though icy cold by day it ran,
Yet still, like souls of mirth, began
　To burn when night was near;
And thus should woman's heart and looks
At noon be cold as winter brooks,
Nor kindle till the night, returning,
Brings their genial hour for burning,
Oh! stay,—oh! stay,—
When did morning ever break,
And find such beaming eyes awake
As those that sparkle here.

———o———

HOW DEAR TO ME THE HOUR.

By Thomas Moore.

How dear to me the hour when daylight dies,
　And sunbeams melt along the silent sea;
For then sweet dreams of other days arise,
　And mem'ry breathes her vesper sigh to thee.

And, as I watch the line of light that plays
　Along the smooth wave tow'rd the burning west,
I long to tread that golden path of rays,
　And think 'twould lead to some bright isle of rest.

BY THAT LAKE, WHOSE GLOOMY SHORE.

By Thomas Moore.

By that lake, whose gloomy shore
Skylark never warbles o'er,
Where the cliff hangs high and steep,
Young Saint Kevin stole to sleep.
" Here at least," he calmly said,
" Woman ne'er shall find my bed."
Ah! the good saint little knew
What that wily sex can do.

'Twas from Kathleen's eyes he flew—
Eyes of most unholy blue!
She had lov'd him well and long,
Wish'd him her's, nor thought it wrong.
Wheresoe'er the saint would fly,
Still he heard her light foot nigh;
East or west, where'er he turn'd,
Still her eyes before him burn'd.

On the bold cliff's bosom cast,
Tranquil now he sleeps at last;
Dreams of Heaven, nor thinks that e'er
Woman's smile can haunt him there.
But nor earth nor Heaven is free
From her power, if fond she be:
Even now, while calm he sleeps,
Kathleen o'er him leans and weeps.

Fearless she had track'd his feet
To this rocky wild retreat:
And when morning met his view,
Her mild glances met it too.
Ah! your saints have cruel hearts!
Sternly from his bed he starts,
And, with rude repulsive shock,
Hurls her from the beetling rock.

BY THAT LAKE, WHOSE GLOOMY SHORE.

Continued.

Glendalough ! thy gloomy wave
Soon was gentle Kathleen's grave ;
Soon the saint (yet, ah ! too late)
Felt her love, and mourn'd her fate.
When he said, " Heaven rest her soul ! "
Round the lake light music stole ;
And her ghost was seen to glide,
Smiling, o'er the fatal tide !

——o——

LOVE AND THE NOVICE.

By Thomas Moore.

Here we dwell in holiest bowers,
  Where angels of light o'er our orisons bend ;
Where sighs of devotion and breathings of flowers
  To Heaven in mingled odor ascend !
    Do not disturb our calm, oh Love !
    So like is thy form to the cherubs above,
It well might deceive such hearts as ours.

Love stood near the Novice and listen'd,
  And Love is no novice in taking a hint ;
His laughing blue eyes now with piety glisten'd ;
  His rosy wing turn'd to Heaven's own tint.
    " Who would have thought," the urchin cries,
    "That Love could so well, so gravely disguise
His wandering wings and wounding eyes !"

Love now warms thee, waking and sleeping,
  Young Novice ; to him all thy orisons rise ;
He tinges the heavenly fount with his weeping,
  He brightens the censer's flame with his sighs,
    Love is the saint enshrin'd in thy breast,
    And angels themselves would admit such a guest,
If he came to them cloth'd in Piety's vest.

I LOVE BUT THEE.

By Thomas Moore.

If, after all, you still will doubt and fear me,
  And think this heart to other loves will stray ;
If I must swear, then, lovely doubter, hear me :
  By ev'ry dream I have, when thou'rt away,
By ev'ry throb I feel, when thou art near me,
  I love but thee! I love but thee !

By those dark eyes, where light is ever playing,—
  Where Love, in depth of shadow, holds his throne,—
And by those lips, which give whate'er thou'rt saying,
  Or grave, or gay, a music of its own,
A music far beyond all minstrel's playing,
  I love but thee ! I love but thee !

By that fair brow, where innocence reposes,
  As pure as moonlight sleeping upon snow,
And by that cheek, whose fleeting blush discloses
  A hue too bright to bless this world below,
And only fit to dwell on Eden's roses,
  I love but thee ! I love but thee !

——o——

COME O'ER THE SEA.

By Thomas Moore.

Come o'er the sea,
  Maiden, with me,
Mine through sunshine, storm, and snows !
  Seasons may roll,
  But the true soul
Burns the same, where'er it goes.
Let Fate frown on, so we love and part not ;
'Tis life where thou art, 'tis death where thou art not !
  Then come o'er the sea,
  Maiden, with me,
Come wherever the wild wind blows ;
  Seasons may roll,
  But the true soul
Burns the same where'er it goes.

COME O'ER THE SEA.—*Continued.*

Is not the sea
Made for the free,
Land for courts and chains alone?
Here we are slaves,
But, on the waves,
Love and Liberty's all our own!
No eye to watch, and no tongue to wound us,
All earth forgot, and all Heaven around us!—
Then come o'er the sea,
Maiden, with me,
Mine through sunshine, storm, and snows!
Seasons may roll,
But the true soul
Burns the same where'er it goes.

——o——

THERE'S NOT A WORD

By Thomas Moore.

THERE'S not a word, a look, of thine,
My soul hath e'er forgot;
Thou ne'er hast bid a ringlet shine,
Nor giv'n thy locks one graceful twine
Which I remember not.
There never yet a murmur fell
From that beguiling tongue,
Which did not, with a ling'ring spell,
Upon my charmed senses dwell,
Like something Heav'n had sung

Ah! that I could at once forget
All, all that haunts me so!
And yet, thou witching girl! and yet
To die were sweeter than to let
The lov'd remembrance go.
No, if this slighted heart must see
Its faithful pulse decay,
Oh! let it die rememb'ring thee,
And, like the burnt aroma, be
Consum'd in sweets away!

YOU REMEMBER ELLEN.

By Thomas Moore.

You remember Ellen, our hamlet's pride,
   How meekly she bless'd her humble lot,
When the stranger, William, made her his bride,
   And Love was the light of their lowly cot.
Together they toil'd through winds and rains,
   Till William at length, in sadness, said,
" We must seek our fortune on other plains ;"—
   Then, sighing, she left her lowly shed.

They roam'd a long and a weary way,
   Nor much was the maiden's heart at ease,
When now, at the close of one stormy day,
   They see a proud castle among the trees.
" To-night," said the youth " we'll shelter there ;
   The wind blows cold, the hour is late ;"—
So he blew the horn with a chieftain's air,
   And the porter bow'd as they pass'd the gate.

" Now, welcome, Lady !" exclaim'd the youth, —
   " This castle is thine, and these dark woods all.
She belive'd him wild, but his words were truth,
   For Ellen is Lady of Rosna Hall !—
And dearly the Lord of Rosna loves
   What William the stranger woo'd and wed ;
And the light of bliss, in these lordly groves,
   Is as pure as it shone in the lowly shed.

——o——

WHEN DAYLIGHT WAS YET SLEEPING.

By Thomas Moore.

When daylight was yet sleeping under the billow,
   And stars in the heavens still lingering shone,
Young Kitty, all blushing, rose up from her pillow,
   The last time she e'er was to press it alone.
For the youth that she treasur'd her heart and her soul in,
   Had promis'd to link the last tie before noon,
And when once the young heart of a maiden is stolen,
   The maiden herself will steal after it soon.

WHEN DAYLIGHT WAS YET SLEEPING.—*Continued.*

As she look'd in the glass, which a woman ne'er misses,
   Nor ever wants time for a sly glance or two,
A butterfly, fresh from the night-flower's kisses,
   Flew over the mirror, and shaded her view.
Enrag'd with the insect for hiding her graces,
   She brush'd him—he fell, alas! never to rise—
" Ah! such " said the girl, " is the pride of our faces
   For which the soul's innocence too often dies."

While she stole thro' the garden, where heart's-ease was
        growing,
   She cull'd some, and kiss'd off its night-fallen dew;
And a rose, farther on, look'd so tempting and glowing,
   That, spite of her haste, she must gather it too.
But while o'er the roses too carelessly leaning,
   Her zone flew in two, and the heart's-ease was lost—
" Ah! this means," said the girl (and she sighed at its mean-
        ing),
   " That love is scarce worth the repose it will cost."

——o——

ERIN! THE TEAR AND THE SMILE.

By Thomas Moore.

Erin! the tear and the smile in thine eyes
Blend like the rainbow that hangs in thy skies!
   Shining through sorrow's stream,
   Sadd'ning through pleasure's beam,
   Thy suns, with doubtful gleam,
      Weep while they rise!

Erin! thy silent tear never shall cease,
Erin! thy languid smile ne'er shall increase,
   Till, like the rainbow's light,
   Thy various tints unite,
   And form, in Heaven's sight,
      One arch of peace!

ONE BUMPER AT PARTING.

By Thomas Moore.

ONE bumper at parting !—though many
　　Have circled the board since we met,
The fullest, the saddest of any
　　Remains to be crowned by us yet.
The sweetness that pleasure has in it 　.
　　Is always so slow to come forth,
That seldom, alas! till the minute
　　It dies, do we know half its worth !
But, fill! may our life's happy measure
　　Be all of such moments made up;
They're born on the bosom of pleasure,
　　They die 'midst the tears of the cup.

As onward we journey, how pleasant
　　To pause and inhabit awhile
Those few sunny spots, like the present,
　　That 'mid the dull wilderness smile!
But Time like a pitiless master,
　　Cries, "Onward !" and spurs the gay hours;
And never does Time travel faster
　　Than when his way lies among flowers.
But, come—may our life's happy measure
　　Be all of such moments made up;
They're born on the bosom of pleasure,
　　They die 'midst the tears of the cup.

This evening we saw the sun sinking,
　　In waters his glory made bright—
Oh! trust me, our farewell of drinking
　　Should be like that farewell of light.
You saw how he finish'd by darting
　　His beam o'er a deep billow's brim—
So fill up !—let's shine, at our parting,
　　In full liquid glory, like him.
And oh! may our life's happy measure
　　Of moments like this be made up;
'Twas born on the bosom of pleasure,
　　It dies 'mid the tears of the cup !

I SAW THY FORM.

By Thomas Moore.

I saw thy form in youthful prime,
  Nor thought that pale decay
Would steal before the steps of time,
  And waste its blood away, Mary!
Yet still thy features wore that light
  Which fleets not with the breath;
And life ne'er look'd more truly bright
  Than in thy smile of death, Mary!

As streams that run o'er golden mines,
  Yet humbly, calmly glide,
Nor seem to know the wealth that shines
  Within their gentle tide, Mary!
So, veil'd beneath the simplest guise,
  Thy radiant genius shone,
And that which charm'd all other eyes
  Seem'd worthless in thy own, Mary!

If souls could always dwell above,
  Thou ne'er hadst left that sphere;
Or, could we keep the souls we love,
  We ne'er had lost thee here, Mary!
Though many a gifted mind we meet,
  Though fairest forms we see,
To live with them is far less sweet
  Than to remember thee. Mary!

—— o ——

DRINK TO HER.

By Thomas Moore.

Drink to her who long
  Hath wak'd the poet's sigh,
The girl who gave to song
  What gold could never buy!
Oh! woman's heart was made
  For minstrel-hands alone;
By other fingers play'd,
  It yields not half the tone.
    Then here's to her, &c.

I SAW THY FORM IN YOUTHFUL PRIME.

DRINK TO HER.—*Continued.*

At Beauty's door of glass
  When Wealth and Wit once stood,
They ask'd her " *Which* might pass?"
  She answer'd, " He who could."
With golden key Wealth thought
  To pass—but 'twould not do:
While Wit a diamond brought,
  Which cut his bright way through!
    So here's to her, &c.

The love that seeks a home
  Where wealth or grandeur shines,
Is like the gloomy gnome
  That dwells in dark gold mines.
But oh! the poet's love
  Can boast a brighter sphere;
Its native home's above,
  Though woman keeps it here!
    Then drink to her, &c.

——o——

'TIS THE LAST ROSE OF SUMMER.

BY THOMAS MOORE.

Tis the last rose of summer, left blooming alone;
All her lovely companions are faded and gone;
No flow'r of her kindred, no rosebud is nigh,
To reflect back her blushes, or give sigh for sigh!

I'll not leave thee, thou lone one, to pine on the stem;
Since the lovely are sleeping, go, sleep thou with them;
Thus kindly I scatter thy leaves o'er thy bed,
Where thy mates of the garden lie scentless and dead.

So soon may I follow, when friendships decay,
And from Love's shining circle the gems drop away!
When true hearts lie wither'd, and fond ones are flown,
Oh! who would inhabit this bleak world alone?

THE ROCKY ROAD TO DUBLIN.

Air : Irish Jig.

In the merry month of June, when first from home I started,
And left the girls alone, sad and broken-hearted,
Shook hands with Father dear, kissed my darling Mother,
Drank a pint of beer my tears and grief to smother :
Then off to reap the corn and leave where I was born,
I cut a stout black-thorn, to banish ghost or goblin :
With a pair of bran new brogues I rattle o'er the bogs :
Sure I frightened all the dogs on the rocky road to Dublin.

CHORUS.

For, it is the rocky road, here's the road to Dublin ;
Here's the rocky road, now fire away to Dublin !

The steam-coach was at hand, the driver said he'd cheap ones,
But sure the luggage van was too much for my ha'pence.
For England I was bound, it would never do to balk it :
For every step of the road, be dad ! says I, I'll walk it.
I did not sigh nor moan until I saw Athlone—
A pain in my shin bone, it set my heart a bubbling ;
And fearing the big cannon, looking o'er the Shannon,
I very quickly ran on the rocky road to Dublin.
　　　　　　For, it is the rocky road, &c.

In Mullingar that night I rested limbs so weary—
Started by daylight, with spirits light and airy :
Took a drop of pure, to keep my spirits from sinking.
That's always an Irishman's cure, whenever he's troubled with
　　　　thinking.
To see the lasses smile, laughing all the while
At my comical style, set my heart a bubbling ;
They axed if I was hired, the wages I required,
Until I was almost tired of the rocky road to Dublin.
　　　　　　For, it is the rocky road, &c.

In Dublin next arrived—I thought it was a pity
To be so soon deprived of a view of that fine city.
'Twas then I took a stroll all among the quality—
My bundle then was stole in a neat locality.

THE ROCKY ROAD TO DUBLIN.—*Continued.*

Something crossed my mind—thinks I, I'll look behind—
No bundle could I find upon my stick a wobbling.
Inquiring for the rogue, they said my Connaught brogue
It wasn't much in vogue on the rocky road to Dublin.
   For, it is the rocky road, &c.

A coachman raised his hand, as if myself was wanting—
I went up to a stand full of cars for jaunting.
Step up, my boy, says he, ah, ah! that I will with pleasure—
And to the strawberry beds I'll drive you at your leisure.
A strawberry bed says I, faith that would be too high.
On one of straw I'll lie, and the berries won't be troubling.
He drove me out as far, upon an outside car—
Faith such a jolting never were on the rocky road to Dublin.
   For, it was the rocky road, &c.

I soon got out of that my spirits never failing—
I landed on the quay just as the ship was sailing.
The Captain at me roared, swore that no room had he,
But when I leaped on board, they a cabin found for Paddy.
Down among the pigs I played such rummy rigs,
Danced some hearty jigs, with the water round me bubbling.
But when off Holyhead, I wished that I was dead,
Or safely put in bed, on the rocky road to Dublin.
   For, it is the rocky road, &c.

The boys in Liverpool, when in the dock I landed,
Called myself a fool—I could no longer stand it ;
My blood began to boil, my temper I was losing,
And poor Old Erin's Isle they all began abusing.
Hurrah! my boys, says I, my Shillelah I let fly :
Some Galway boys were by, they saw I was a hobble in :
Then, with a loud Hurrah, they joined me in the fray ;
Faugh-a-ballagh ! clear the way for the rocky road to Dublin.
   For, it is the rocky road, &c.

THE LAND OF THE WEST.

By Samuel Lover.

Oh! come to the West, love; oh! come there with me,
'Tis a sweet land of verdure that springs from the sea,
Where fair plenty smiles from her emerald throne;
Oh! come to the West, and I'll make thee my own;
I'll guard thee, I'll tend thee, I'll love thee the best,
And you'll say there's no land like the land of the West.

The south has its roses, and bright skies of blue;
But ours are more sweet with love's own changeful hue,
Half sunshine, half tears, like the girl I love best—
Oh! what is the south to the Beautiful West?
Then come there with me, and the rose on thy mouth
Will be sweeter to me than the flowers of the south.

The north has its snow-tow'rs of dazzling array,
All sparkling with gems in the ne'er-setting day,
There the storm-king may dwell in the halls he loves best,
But the soft-breathing zephyr he plays in the West;
Then come to the West, where no cold wind doth blow,
And thy neck will seem fairer to me than the snow.

The sun in the gorgeous east chaseth the night,
When he riseth refreshed in his glory and might,
But where doth he go when he seeks his sweet rest?
Oh! doth he not haste to the beautiful West!
Then come there with me, 'tis the land I love best,
'Tis the land of my sires! 'tis my own darling West!

———o———

THE WHITE COCKADE.

By J. J. Callanan.

[This is a translation of one of the Irish Jacobite songs.]

King Charles he is King James's son
And from a royal line is sprung;
Then up with shout, and out with blade,
And we'll raise once more the white cockade.
Oh! my dear, my fair-haired youth,
Thou yet hast hearts of fire and truth;
Then up with shout, and out with blade—
We'll raise once more the white cockade.

THE WHITE COCKADE.—*Continued.*

My young men's hearts are dark with woe;
On my virgins' cheeks the grief-drops flow;
The sun scarce lights the sorrowing day
Since our rightful prince went far away.
He's gone, the stranger holds his throne;
The royal bird far off is flown
But up with shout, and out with blade—
We'll stand or fall with the white cockade.

No more the cuckoo hails the spring;
The woods no more with the staunch-hounds ring;
The song from the glen, so sweet before,
Is hushed since Charles has left our shore.
The prince is gone; but he soon will come,
With trumpet sound and with beat of drum
Then up with shout and out with blade—
Huzza for the right and the white cockade!

———o———

THE IRISH MOTHER IN THE PENAL DAYS.

By John Banim.

Now welcome, welcome, baby boy, unto a mother's fears,
The pleasure of her sufferings, the rainbow of her tears.
The object of your father's hope, in all the hopes to do,
A future man of his own land, to live him o'er anew!

How fondly on thy little brow a mother's eye would trace,
And in thy little limbs, and in each feature of thy face,
His beauty, worth, and manliness, and everything that's his,
Except, my boy, the answering mark of where the fetter is!

Oh! many a weary hundred years his sires that fetter wore,
And he has worn it since the day that him his mother bore;
And now, my son, it waits on you, the moment you are born,
The old hereditary badge of suffering and scorn!

Alas, my boy so beautiful!—alas, my love so brave!
And must your gallant Irish limbs still drag it to the grave?
And you, my son, yet have a son, freedom'd a slave to be,
Whose mother still must weep o'er him the tears I weep o'er
      thee!

RICH AND RARE WERE THE GEMS SHE WORE.

By Thomas Moore.

Rich and rare were the gems she wore,
And a bright gold ring on her wand she bore;
But oh! her beauty was far beyond
Her sparkling gems or snow-white wand.

" Lady ! dost thou not fear to stray,
So lone and lovely, through this bleak way?
Are Erin's sons so good or so cold,
As not to be tempted by woman or gold?"

" Sir knight ! I feel not the least alarm,
No son of Erin will offer me harm :
For though they love women and golden store,
Sir knight! they love honor and virtue more !"

On she went and her maiden smile
In safety lighted her round the green isle;
And blest for ever is she who relied
Upon Erin's honor, and Erin's pride.

―――o―――

BELIEVE ME, IF ALL THOSE ENDEARING YOUNG CHARMS.

By Thomas Moore.

Believe me, if all those endearing young charms,
    Which I gaze on so fondly to-day,
Were to change by to-morrow, and fleet in my arms,
    Like fairy gifts fading away ;
Thou would'st still be ador'd, as this moment thou art,
    Let thy loveliness fade as it will,
And around the dear ruin each wish of my heart
    Would entwine itself verdantly still.

It is not while beauty and youth are thine own,
    And thy cheeks unprofan'd by a tear,
That the fervor and faith of a soul can be known,
    To which time will but make thee more dear.
Oh, the heart that has truly lov'd never forgets,
    But as truly loves on to the close,
As the sun-flower turns on her god when he sets,
    The same look which she gave when he rose.

MARY LE MORE.

The Maniac of 1798.

GEORGE NUGENT REYNOLDS.   Air,— "Savourneen Deelish."

As I stray'd o'er the common on Cork's rugged border,
    While the dew-drops of morn the sweet primrose array'd,
I saw a poor maiden whose mental disorder
    Her quick-glancing eye and wild aspect betray'd.
On the sward she reclin'd, by the green fern surrounded,
At her side speckled daisies and wild flow'rs abounded;
To its inmost recesses her heart had been wounded;
    Her sighs were unceasing—'twas Mary le More.

Her charms by the keen blasts of sorrow were faded,
    Yet the soft tinge of beauty still play'd on her cheek;
Her tresses a wreath of pale primroses braided,
    And strings of fresh daises hung loose on her neck.
While with pity I gaz'd, she exclaim'd, "O my Mother!
See the blood on that lash, 'tis the blood of my brother;
They have torn his poor flesh, and they now strip another—
    'Tis Connor, the friend of poor Mary le More.

"Though his locks were as white as the foam of the ocean,
    Those wretches shall find that my father is brave;
My father!" she cried, with the wildest emotion,
    "Ah! no, my poor father now sleeps in the grave!
They have tolled his death-bell, they've laid the turf o'er him;
His white locks were bloody! no aid could restore him;
He is gone! he is gone! and the good will deplore him,
    When the blue waves of Erin hide Mary le More."

————o————

THERE'S NOTHING TRUE BUT HEAVEN.

BY THOMAS MOORE.

This world is all a fleeting show,
    For man's illusion given.
The smiles of joy, the tears of woe,
Deceitful shine, deceitful flow,
    There's nothing true but heaven.

THERE'S NOTHING TRUE BUT HEAVEN.—*Continued.*

Poor wand'rers of a stormy day,
  From wave to wave we're driv'n ;
And Fancy's flash, and Reason's ray,
Serve but to light the troubled way.
  The smiles of joy, &c.

And false the light on glory's plume,
  As fading hues of even ;
And love and hope, and beauty's bloom,
Are blossoms gather'd for the tomb.
  The smiles of joy, &c.

———()———

O, LADY FAIR !

Glee for three Voices.

By Thomas Moore.

1st Voice. O, Lady fair! where art thou roaming ?
      The sun is sunk the night is coming.
  2d. Stranger, I go o'er moor and mountain,
      To tell my beads at Agnes' fountain.
  1st. And who is the man with his white locks flowing,
      O, lady fair ! where is he going ?
  3d. A wandering pilgrim, weak I falter,
      To tell my beads at Agnes' altar.
Tutti. Chill falls the rain, night winds are blowing,
      Dreary and dark's the way we're going.
        Chill falls the rain, &c.

  1st. Fair lady, rest till morning blushes,
      I'll strew for thee a bed of rushes.
  2d. Ah ! stranger, when my beads I'm counting,
      I'll bless thy name at Agnes' fountain.
  1st. Thou pilgrim, turn, and rest thy sorrow,
      Thou'lt go to Agnes' shrine to-morrow.
  3d. Good stranger, when my beads I'm telling,
      My saint shall bless thy leafy dwelling.
Tutti. Strew then, O strew our bed of rushes !
      Here we shall rest till morning blushes.
        Strew then, O strew, &c.

ROBERT EMMET.

WHEN HE WHO ADORES THEE.

Sarah Curran's address to Robert Emmet.

BY THOMAS MOORE.

WHEN he who adores thee has left but the name
  Of his fault and his sorrow behind,
O say, wilt thou weep, when they darken the fame
  Of a life that for thee was resign'd?
Yes, weep, and however my foes may condemn,
  Thy tears shall efface their decree ;
For heav'n can witness, though guilty to them,
  I have been but too faithful to thee !

With thee were the dreams of my earliest love ;
  Every thought of my reason was thine :—
In my last humble prayer to the Spirit above,
  Thy name shall be mingled with mine!
Oh ! blest are the lovers and friends who shall live,
  The days of thy glory to see ;
But the next dearest blessing that heaven can give,
  Is the pride of thus dying for thee !

———o———

IT'S LITTLE FOR GLORY I CARE

CHARLES LEVER. Air.—"The Grinder."

IT'S little for glory I care ;
  Sure ambition is only a fable ;
I'd as soon be myself as Lord Mayor,
  With lashins of drink on the table.
I like to lie down in the sun,
  And drame when my faytures is scorchin',
That when I'm too ould for more fun,
  Why, I'll marry a wife with a fortune.

And in winter, with bacon and eggs,
  And a place at the turf fire basking,
Sip my punch as I roasted my legs,
  Oh ! the devil a more I'd be asking.
For I haven't a jaynius for work,—
  It was never the gift of the Bradies,—
But I'd make a most illigant Turk,
  For I'm fond of tobacco and ladies.

I'D MOURN THE HOPES THAT LEAVE ME.

BY THOMAS MOORE.

I'd mourn the hopes that leave me,
   If thy smiles had left me too ;
I'd weep when friends deceive me,
   Hadst thou been like them untrue.
But while I've thee before me,
   With heart so warm, and eyes so bright,
No clouds can linger o'er me,
   That smile turns them all to light.

'Tis not in fate to harm me,
   While fate leaves thy love to me ;
'Tis not in joy to charm me,
   Unless joy be shar'd with thee.
One minute's dream about thee
   Were worth a long and endless year
Of waking bliss without thee,
   My own love, my only dear !

And, though the hope be gone, love,
   That long sparkled o'er our way,
Oh ! we shall journey on, love,
   More safely without its ray.
Far better lights shall win me,
   Along the path I've yet to roam ;
The mind, that burns within me,
   And pure smiles from thee at home.

Thus, when the lamp that lighted
   The traveller, at first goes out,
He feels awhile benighted,
   And looks around in fear and doubt.
But soon, the prospect clearing,
   By cloudless star-light on he treads,
And thinks no lamp so cheering
   As that light which heaven sheds !

FILL THE BUMPER FAIR.

By Thomas Moore.

FILL the bumper fair !
  Ev'ry drop we sprinkle
O'er the brow of Care
  Smooths away a wrinkle.
Wit's electric flame
  Ne'er so swiftly passes,
As when through the frame
  It shoots from brimming glasses.
Fill the bumper fair !
  Ev'ry drop we sprinkle
O'er the brow of Care
  Smooths away a wrinkle.

Sages can, they say,
  Grasp the lightning's pinions,
And bring down its ray
  From the starr'd dominions :—
So we sages sit,
  And, 'mid bumpers bright'ning,
From the heaven of wit
  Draw down all its lightning !
            Fill the bumper, &c.

Wouldst thou know what first
  Made our souls inherit
This ennobling thirst
  For wine's celestial spirit ?
It chanced upon that day,
  When, as bards inform us,
Prometheus stole away
  The living fires that warm us.
            Fill the bumper, &c.

The careless youth, when up
  To Glory's fount aspiring,
Took nor urn nor cup
  To hide the pilfer'd fire in—:

FILL THE BUMPER FAIR.—*Continued.*

But oh, his joy ! when, round
   The walls of Heaven spying,
Amongst the stars he found
   A bowl of Bacchus lying.
        Fill the bumper, &c.

Some drops were in that bowl,
   Remains of last night's pleasure,
With which the sparks of soul
   Mix'd their burning treasure ;
Hence the goblet's shower
   Hath such a spell to win us—
Hence its mighty power
   O'er that flame within us.
        Fill the bumper, &c,

———o———

WHAT THE BEE IS TO THE FLOW'RET.

By Thomas Moore.

He.—What the bee is to the flow'ret,
   When he looks for honey-dew
Through the leaves that close embower it,
   That, my love, I'll be to you !

She.—What the bank, with verdure glowing,
   Is to waves that wander near,
Whispering kisses, while they're going,
   That I'll be to you, my dear !
    Duet.—What the bank, &c.

She.—But, they say, the bee's a rover,
   That he'll fly when sweets are gone ;
And, when once the kiss is over,
   Faithless brooks will wander on !

He.— Nay, if flowers *will* lose their looks,
   If sunny banks *will* wear away.
'Tis but right that bees and brooks
   Should sip and kiss them while they may.

OH! THINK NOT MY SPIRITS.

By Thomas Moore.

Oh! think not my spirits are always as light
  And as free from a pang, as they seem to you now;
Nor expect that the heart-beaming smile of to-night
  Will return with to-morrow to brighten my brow;
No, life is a waste of wearisome hours,
  Which seldom the rose of enjoyment adorns;
And the heart that is soonest awake to the flow'rs
  Is always the first to be touch'd by the thorns!
But send round the bowl, and be happy awhile;
  May we never meet worse, in our pilgrimage here,
Than the tear that enjoyment can gild with a smile,
  And the smile that compassion can turn to a tear!

The thread of our life would be dark, Heaven knows!
  If it were not with friendship and love intertwin'd;
And I care not how soon I may sink to repose,
  When these blessings shall cease to be dear to my mind
But they who have lov'd the fondest, the purest,
  Too often have wept o'er the dream they believ'd;
And the heart that has slumber'd in friendship securest,
  Is happy indeed if 'twas never deceived;
But send round the bowl; while a relic of truth
  Is in man or in woman, this pray'r shall be mine—
That the sunshine of Love may illumine our youth,
  And the moonlight of Friendship console our decline.

——o——

MARY, I BELIEVED THEE TRUE.

By Thomas Moore.

Mary, I believed thee true,
  And I was bless'd in thus believing;
But now I mourn that e'er I knew
  A girl so fair and so deceiving!

Few have ever lov'd like me,—
  O! I have lov'd thee too sincerely;
And few have e'er deceiv'd like thee,—
  Alas! deceiv'd me too severely!

MARY, I BELIEVED THEE TRUE.—*Continued.*

Fare-thee-well! yet think awhile
  On one whose bosom bleeds to doubt thee;
Who now would rather trust that smile,
  And die with thee than live without thee!

Fare-thee-well! I'll think of thee—
  Thou leav'st me many a bitter token;
For see, distracting woman! see,
  My peace is gone, my heart is broken.
      Fare-thee-well!

——— ——

OH! 'TIS SWEET TO THINK.

By Thomas Moore.

Oh! tis sweet to think that, where 'er we rove,
  We are sure to find something blissful and dear;
And that, when we're far from the lips we love,
  We have but to make love to the lips we are near!
The heart, like a tendril, accustom'd to cling,
  Let it grow where it will, cannot flourish alone,
But will lean to the nearest and loveliest thing
  It can twine with itself, and make closely its own.
Then oh! what pleasure, where'er we rove,
  To be doom'd to find something still that is dear;
And to know, when far from the lips we love,
  We have but to make love to the lips we are near.

'Twere a shame, when flowers around us rise,
  To make light of the rest if the rose is not there;
And the world's so rich in resplendent eyes,
  'Twere a pity to limit one's love to a pair.
Love's wing and the peacock's are nearly alike;
  They are both of them bright, but they're changeable too;
And wherever a new beam of beauty can strike,
  It will tincture Love's plume with a different hue.
      Then oh! what pleasure, &c.

I'LL NEVER FORGET THAT, MA'AM!

By. Samuel Lover.

THEY say the men are faithless all,
   And never will prove thrue, dear,
But of all in all, both great and small,
   I'll never forget *you*, dear.
For 'tis you that took the *hoighth* o'care
 . To keep my memory thrue, dear ;
My memory's not very good—but I'll never forget *you*, dear.
  Oh, Kitty, dear, you need not fear
That I will e'er forget you,
   I remember all your tindherness
From the hour that first I met you.

'Twas at the fair your coaxin' air
   First made me be your suithor,
Where I spent my wealth to dhrink your health,
   And toss'd the costly pewther;
A lock o' your hair you promised me—
   With joy my heart was big, ma'am !
But in the bottom o' the quart
   I found the fiddler's wig, ma'am !
Oh, indeed, Miss Kit, the dickins a bit
   You'll wheedle me now with your chat, ma'am
My memory's not very good
   But I'll never forget that, ma'am.

When you bid me step up to the house,
   To spake to your mother and father,
And said, of all the boys you knew
   'Twas myself that you would rather ;
" Won't you take a sate," says you," my dear ? "
   With a most seducin' air, ma'am :
But, oh ! what a thunderin' lump of a pin
   You stuck in the sate of the chair, ma'am !
Indeed, Miss Kit, the dickins a bit
   You'll wheedle me now with your chat, ma'am,
My memory's not very good—
   But I'll never forget that, ma'am.

I'LL NEVER FORGET THAT, MA'AM.—*Continued.*

When I said 'twas you could raise the flame,
   My love, you did not mock it,
For didn't you put a coal o' fire
   Into my new coat pocket?
And when I blazed, 'twas you did shout
   With laughter, to be sure, ma'am,
"Oh," says you, "my dear, I'll *put you out*,"
   But, faix, 'twas *out o' the door*, ma'am.
Indeed, Miss Kit, the dickins a bit
   You'll wheedle me now with your chat, ma'am.
My memory's not very good—
   But I'll never forget that, ma'am.

Then didn't I see black Darby Keogh
   To the little back window pass, ma'am?
His ugly face he there did squeeze
   Till he flattened his nose on the glass, ma'am.
Then the sash was riz—I heer'd it squeal—
   There was nothing then between you:
'Faith, *I know how he flatten'd his nose after that!*
   Tho' you thought there was nobody seen you.
Oh, indeed, Miss Kit, the dickins a bit
   You'll wheedle me now with your chat, ma'am:
My memory's not very good,—but I'll never forget that,
   ma'am!

——o——

THE FISHERMAN'S DAUGHTER.

By Samuel Lover.

"Why art thou wand'ring alone by the shore?
The wind whistles loud and the white breakers roar."
"Oh! I am wand'ring alone by the sea,
To watch if my father's returning to me;
For the wind it blew hard in the depth of the night,
And I'm watching here since the dawning of light,
Looking thro' tears o'er the wild raging sea,
To watch if my father's returning to me.

THE FISHERMAN'S DAUGHTER.—*Continued.*

" Last night when my father put forth on the deep,
To our cottage returning, I lay down to sleep,
But while the calm of sweet sleep came to me,
The voice of the tempest was waking the sea !
Methought, in a dream, 'twas my father that spoke—
But, oh !—to the voice of the tempest I woke,
While the father I dreamt of was far on the sea,
Ah—why, in my dream, cried my father to me?

" Vainly I look thro' the fast-driving gale—
Hopeless, I see what hope *fancies* a sail,
But 'tis only the wing of the sea gull flits by,
And my heart it sinks low at the bird's wailing cry :
For the storm must blow hard when the gull comes on shore—
Oh ! that the fisherman's gift were no more
Than the gift of the wild bird to soar o'er the sea—
Good angels ! *thy* wings bear my father to me"

———o———

TAKE BACK THE SIGH.

By Thomas Moore.

TAKE back the sigh, thy lips of art
   In passion's moment breath'd to me ;
Yet, no—it must not, will not part,
'Tis now the life-breath of my heart,
   And has become too pure for thee !

Take back the kiss, that faithless sigh
   With all the warmth of truth imprest ;
Yet, no—the fatal kiss may lie,
Upon *thy* lip its sweets would die,
   Or bloom to make a rival blest !

Take back the vows that, night and day,
   My heart receiv'd, I thought, from thine ;
Yet, no—allow them still to stay,
They might some other heart betray,
   As sweetly as they've ruin'd mine !

AFTER DEATH.

By Fanny Parnell.

[This beautiful and prophetic poem was written by Miss Fanny Parnell
August 27th 1881.—]

SHALL mine eyes behold thy glory, O my country?
   Shall mine eyes behold thy glory?
Or shall the darkness close around them, ere the sun-blaze
   Break at last upon thy story?

When the nations ope for thee their queenly circle,
   As a sweet, new sister hail thee,
Shall these lips be sealed in callous death and silence,
   That have known but to bewail thee?

Shall the ear be deaf that only loved thy praises,
   When all men their tribute bring thee?
Shall the mouth be clay that sang thee in thy squalor,
   When all poets' mouths shall sing thee?

Ah! the harpings and the salvos and the shoutings
   Of thy exiled sons returning!
I should hear, though dead and mouldered, and the grave-
      damps
   Should not chill my bosom's burning.

Ah! the tramp of feet victorious! I should hear them
   'Mid the shamrocks and the mosses,
And my heart should toss within the shroud, and quiver
   As a captive dreamer tosses.

I should turn and rend the cere-clothes round me.
   Giant sinews I should borrow,
Crying, " O, my brothers, I have also loved her,
   In her lowliness and sorrow,

" Let me join with you the jubilant procession,
   Let me chant with you her story;
Then contented I shall go back to the shamrocks,
   Now mine eyes have seen her glory."

MISS FANNY PARNELL.

Financial Secretary of the "Ladies' Land League."

BURNING OF AN EMIGRANT SHIP.

STREET BALLAD.

COME all ye Irish people,
  And hear my mournful theme:
While I relate our hardships great
  Upon the watery main:
The fourth day of September,
  For New York did we set sail,
On board the ship the " Austria,"
  With a sweet and pleasant gale.

Six hundred souls we had on board,
  Both passengers and crew;
For nine long days we ploughed the seas,
  Right well the wind it blew,
Until this dreadful fire took place,
  With flames that raged all round—
Four hundred souls were burned
  Or in the cold sea drown'd!

Our captain, when the fire burst forth,
  " O, Lord, we're lost! " he cried,
And to escape the raging flames
  Plunged wildly in the tide!
O, God, the cries of children dear!
  The blazing, pitchy seams:
The mother's bitter tears could not
  Subdue the cruel flames!

The most of these were emigrants
  From Galway's pleasant strand;
From racking tyrant landlords,
  They quit their native land;
In hope to live more happily
  'Mong strangers far away,
They bent their course to New York,
  All on this woful day.

BURNING OF AN EMIGRANT SHIP.—*Continued.*

The cries of these poor passengers
  Would pierce your heart with grief ;
All shrieking on the burning deck
  So vainly for relief ;
The mothers to their children clung,
  " O, we may rue the day
We left our poor old Ireland,
  For countries far away !"

Their bitter groans and sufferings,
  Would pierce your very heart,
Without a spot to shun the flames
  Or bid their fate depart ;
They lost their lives and property,
  In flames and in the waves ;
And not a mass was offer'd up
  Above their lonely graves !

O, neighbors dear, O, Irishmen,
  Let every Christian pray,
That God will rid our native land
  Of racking landlord sway ;
And as these banish'd people did,
  In awful sufferings, die,—
God grant them sweet salvation
  With his dear Son on high !

PADDY O'RAFTHER.

By Samuel Lover.

Paddy, in want of a dinner one day,
Credit all gone, and no money to pay,
Stole from a priest a fat pullet, they say,
   And went to confession just afther;
" Your riv'rince," says Paddy, " I stole this fat hen."
" What, what !" says the priest, "at your owld thricks again?
Faith, you'd rather be staalin' than sayin' *amen*,
                Paddy O'Rafther !"

" Sure you wouldn't be angry," says Pat, " if you knew
That the best of intintions I had in my view,
For I stole it to make it a present to you,
   And you can absolve me afther."
" Do you think," says the priest, " I'd partake of your theft ?
Of your seven small senses you must be bereft—
You're the biggest blackguard that I know, right or left,
                Paddy O'Rafther !"

" Then what shall I do with the pullet," says Pat,
" If your riv'rince won't take it ?—By this and by that
I don't know no more than a dog or a cat
   What your riv'rince would have me be afther."
" Why then ' says his rev'rence " you sin-blinded owl,
Give back to the man that you stole from, his fowl,
For if you do not, 'twill be worse for your sowl,
                Paddy O'Rafther."

Says Paddy, " I ask'd him to take it—'tis thrue
As this minit I'm talkin', your riv'rince, to you ;
But he would'nt resaive it—so what can I do ?"
   Says Paddy, nigh chokin' with laughter.
" By my throth," says the priest, " but the case is absthruse ;
If he won't take his hen, why the man is a goose—
'Tis not the first time my advice was no use,
                Paddy O'Rafther.

" But, for the sake of your sowl, I would sthrongly advise
To some one in want you would give your supplies,
Some widow, or orphan, with tears in their eyes ;
   And *then* you may come to *me* afther."

PADDY O'RAFTHER.—*Continued.*

So Paddy went off to the brisk Widow Hoy,
And the pullet, between them, was eaten with joy,
And, says she, "'pon my word you're the cleverest boy,
                    Paddy O'Rafther!"

Then Paddy went back to the priest the next day,
And told him the fowl he had given away
To a poor lonely widow, in want and dismay,
    The loss of her spouse weeping afther.
"Well, now," says the priest, "I'll absolve you, my lad,
For repentantly making the best of the bad,
In feeding the hungry and cheering the sad,
                    Paddy O'Rafther!'

—o—

I SAW FROM THE BEACH.

By Thomas Moore.

I saw from the beach, when the morning was shining,
    A bark o'er the waters move gloriously on ;
I came; when that sun o'er the beach was declining,—
    the bark was still there, but the waters were gone !

Ah ! such is the fate of our life's early promise,
    So passing the spring-tide of joy we have known :
Each wave, that we danc'd on at morning, ebbs from us,
    And leaves us, at eve, on the bleak shore alone !

Ne'er tell me of glories serenely adorning
    The close of our day, the calm eve of our night :—
Give me back, give me back the wild freshness of morning,
    Her clouds and her tears are worth evening's best light.

Oh ! who would not welcome that moment's returning,
    When passion first waked a new life through his frame,
And his soul—like the wood that grows precious in burning—
    Gave out all its sweets to Love's exquisite flame ?

THE TIME I'VE LOST IN WOOING.

By Thomas Moore.

THE time I've lost in wooing,
In watching and pursuing
    The light that lies
    In woman's eyes,
Has been my heart's undoing.
Though Wisdom oft has sought me,
I scorn'd the lore she brought me ;
    My only books
    Were woman's looks,
And folly's all they've taught me.

Her smile, when Beauty granted,
I hung with gaze enchanted,
    Like him, the sprite
    Whom maids by night
Oft meet in glen that's haunted.
Like him, too, Beauty won me,
But while her eyes were on me—
    If once their ray
    Was turn'd away,
Oh ! winds could not outrun me.

And are those follies going ?
And is my proud heart growing
    Too cold or wise
    For brilliant eyes
Again to set it glowing ?
No—vain, alas ! the endeavor
From bonds so sweet to sever ;—
    Poor Wisdom's chance
    Against a glance
Is now as weak as ever !

WE MAY ROAM THROUGH THIS WORLD.

By Thomas Moore.

WE may roam through this world like a child at a feast,
 Who but sips of a sweet, and then flies to the rest;
And when pleasure begins to grow dull in the east,
 We may order our wings, and be off to the west;
But if hearts that feel, and eyes that smile,
 Are the dearest gifts that Heav'n supplies,
We never need leave our own green isle
 For sensitive hearts and for sunbright eyes.
Then remember, wherever your goblet is crown'd,
 Through this world whether eastward or westward you
   roam,
When a cup to the smile of dear woman goes round,
 Oh! remember the smile which adorns her at home.

In England, the garden of beauty is kept
 By a dragon of prudery placed within call;
But so oft this unamiable dragon has slept,
 That the garden's but carelessly watch'd after all.
Oh! they want the wild sweet briery fence,
 Which round the flowers of Erin dwells,
Which warms the touch, while winning the sense,
 Nor charms us least when it most repels.
    Then remember, &c.

In France, when the heart of a woman sets sail,
 On the ocean of wedlock its fortune to try,
Love seldom goes far in a vessel so frail,
 But just pilots her off, and then bids her good bye!
While the daughters of Erin keep the boy
 Ever smiling beside his faithful oar,
Through billows of woe and beams of joy
 The same as he look'd when he left the shore.
    Then remember, &c.

DRIMIN DONN DILIS.

By John Walsh.

Oh! Drimin donn dilis! the landlord has come,
Like a foul blast of death has he swept o'er our home.
He has withered our rooftree—beneath the cold sky,
Poor, houseless and homeless, to-night must we lie.

My heart it is cold as the white winter's snow;
My brain is on fire, and my blood's in a glow.
Oh! Drimin donn dilis, 'tis hard to forgive
When a robber denies us the right we should live.

With my health and my strength, with hard labor and toil,
I dried the wet marsh and I tilled the harsh soil—
I toiled the long day through, from morn till even,
And I thought in my heart I'd a foretaste of heaven.

The summer shone round us, above and below,
The beautiful summer that makes the flowers blow.
Oh! 'tis hard to forget it, and think I must bear
That strangers shall reap the reward of my care.

Your limbs they were plump then, your coat it was silk,
And never was wanted the mether of milk,
For freely it came in the calm summer's noon,
While you munched to the time of the old milking croon.

How often you left the green side of the hill,
To stretch in the shade and to drink of the rill;
And often I freed you before the gray dawn,
From your snug little pen at the edge of the bawn.

But they racked and they ground me with tax and with rent,
'Till my heart it was sore and my life-blood was spent;
To-day they have finished; and on the wide world,
With the mocking of friends from my home was I hurled.

I knelt down three times for to utter a prayer,
But my heart it was seared, and the words were not there;
Oh! wild were the thoughts through my dizzy head came,
Like the rushing of wind through a forest of flame.

I bid you, old comrade, a long, last farewell,
For the gaunt hand of famine has clutched us too well;
It severed the master and you, my good cow,
With a blight on his life, and a brand on his brow.

BY MEMORY INSPIRED.

STREET BALLAD.

Air.—"Cruiskeen Lawn."

By Memory inspired
And love of country fired,
The deeds of MEN I love to dwell upon;
And the patriotic glow
Of my spirit must bestow
A tribute to O'Connell that is gone, boys, gone!
Here's a memory to the friends that are gone!

In October 'Ninety-Seven—
May his soul find rest in heaven—
William Orr to execution was led on:
The jury, drunk, agreed
That IRISH was his creed:
For perjury and threats drove them on, boys, on·
Here's the memory of John Mitchel, that is gone!

In 'Ninety-Eight—the month July—
The informer's pay was high;
When Reynolds gave the gallows brave MacCann;
But MacCann was Reynolds' first—
One could not allay his thirst—
So he brought up Bond and Byrne that are gone, boys, gone
Here's the memory of the friends that are gone!

We saw a nation's tears
Shed for John and Henry Shears:
Betrayed by Judas, Captain Armstrong;
We may forgive, but yet
We never can forget
The poisoning of Maguire that is gone, boys, gone:
Our high Star and true Apostle that is gone!

How did Lord Edward die?
Like a man, without a sigh;
But he left his handiwork on Major Swan!
But Sirr, with steel-clad breast,
And coward heart at best,
Left us cause to mourn Lord Edward that is gone, boys, gone·
Here's the memory of our friends that are gone!

BY MEMORY INSPIRED.—*Continued.*

September, Eighteen-three,
Closed this cruel history,
When Emmet's blood the scaffold flowed upon :
O, had their spirits been wise,
They might then realize
Their freedom—but we drink to Mitchel that is gone, boys
gone :
Here's the memory of the friends that are gone !

———o———

'TIS GONE AND FOR EVER.

By Thomas Moore.

'Tis gone, and for ever, the light we saw breaking,
  Like Heaven's first dawn o'er the sleep of the dead,
When man, from the slumber of ages, awaking,
  Look'd upward, and bless'd the pure ray ere it fled !
'Tis gone, and the gleams it has left of its burning
But deepen the long night of bondage and mourning,
That dark o'er the kingdoms of earth is returning,
  And darkest of all, hapless Erin ! o'er thee.

For high was thy hope, when those glories were darting
  Around thee, through all the gross clouds of the world;
When Truth, from her fetters indignantly starting,
  At once, like a sun-burst, her banner unfurl'd.
Oh, never shall earth see a moment so splendid !
Then, then—had one hymn of deliverance blended
The tongues of all nations—how sweet had ascended
  The first note of Liberty, Erin, from thee.

But shame on those tyrants who envied the blessing ;
  And shame on the light race unworthy its good,
Who, at Death's reeking altar, like furies caressing
  The young hope of Freedom, baptiz'd it in blood !
Then vanish'd for ever that fair sunny vision,
Which, spite of the slavish, the cold heart's derision,
Shall long be remember'd, pure, bright, and elysian,
  As first it arose, my lost Erin ! to thee !

O, MOLLY, I CAN'T SAY YOU'RE HONEST.

By Samuel Lover.

O, MOLLY, I can't say you're honest,
    You've stolen my heart from my breast ;
I feel like a bird that's astonish'd
    When young *vagabones* rob its nest.
My brightest of sunshine at night is,
    'Tis just between midnight and dawn ;
For then, Molly dear, my delight is
    To sing you my little *cronawn*—
        Weira sthru !
        Phillilew !
        But I'm kilt—
        May the quilt
Lie light on your beautiful form
    When the weather is hot.
    But, my love, when 'tis not,
May it rowl you up cozey and warm !

Now, if you are sleepin,' dear Molly,
    O, don't let me waken you, dear ;
Some tindher memorial I'll lave you,
    To just let you know I was here.
So I'll throw a big stone at the *windy*,
    And if any glass I should brake,
'Tis for love all the *panes* I am takin'—
    What wouldn't I smash for your sake ?
        Weira sthru !
        Phillilew ! &c., &c.

I know that your father is stingy,
    And likewise your mother the same ;
'Tis very small change that you'll bring me
    Exceptin' the change o' your name :
So be quick with the change, dearest Molly,
    Be the same more or less as it may,
And my own name, my darlin', I'll give you,
    The minnit that you name the day !
        Weira sthru !
        Phillilew ! &c., &c.

MARY O'MARA.

BY SAMUEL LOVER.

MARY O'MARA, I think that I see thee,
  Still blooming and young,
Crown'd with a beauty as dazzlingly beaming
  As poet e'er sung :
    Lovers deep-sighing,
    All emulous vying,
      Thy love to secure ;
    While 'twas mine to adore,
    And my lot to deplore—
      For thy minstrel was poor,
          Mary O'Mara.

Mary O'Mara, the lordly O'Hara,
  Might make thee his own,
For his lineage was high, while the light of thine eye
  Might have challeng'd a throne !
    If his love rise
    To the worth of the prize,
      He hath captur'd in thee,
    Then a homage is thine
    That a saint in her shrine
      Scarcely deeper may see,
          Mary O'Mara !

Mary O'Mara, I think that I hear thee,
  With voice like a bell,
So silver-sweet ringing, the minstrelsy singing
  Of him who lov'd well ;
    Of him who, still loving,
    And hopelessly roving
      In regions afar,
    Still thinks of the time
    That he wove the sweet rhyme
      To his heart's brightest star—
          Mary O'Mara.

THE BOATMAN OF KINSALE.

By Thomas Davis.

Air.—"*The Owl Cula.*"

His kiss is sweet, his word is kind,
  His love is rich to me;
I could not in a palace find
  A truer heart than he.
The eagle shelters not his nest
  From hurricane and hail,
More bravely than he guards my breast—
  The Boatman of Kinsale.

The wind that round the Fastnet sweeps
  Is not a whit more pure—
The goat that down Cnoc Sheehy leaps
  Has not a foot more sure.
No firmer hand nor freer eye
  E'er faced an Autumn gale—
De Courcy's heart is not so high—
  The Boatman of Kinsale.

The brawling squires may heed him not,
  The dainty stranger sneer—
But who will dare to hurt our cot,
  When Myles O'Hea is here?
The scarlet soldiers pass along,
  They'd like, but fear to rail—
His blood is hot, his blow is strong—
  The Boatman of Kinsale.

His hooker's in the Scilly van,
  When seines are in the foam;
But money never made the man,
  Nor wealth a happy home.
So, blest with love and liberty,
  While he can trim a sail,
He'll trust in God and cling to
  The Boatman of Kinsale.

SLOPERTON COTTAGE.

WHILE GAZING ON THE MOON'S LIGHT.

By Thomas Moore.

While gazing on the moon's light,
　A moment from her smile I turn'd,
To look at orbs that, more bright,
　In lone and distant glory burn'd:
　　　But too far
　　　Each proud star,
　For me to feel its warming flame ;
　　　Much more dear
　　　That mild sphere,
　Which near our planet smiling came ;
Thus, Mary, dear ! be thou mine own,
　While brighter eyes unheeded play,
I'll love those moonlight looks alone,
　Which bless my home, and guide my way !

The day had sunk in dim showers,
　But midnight now, with lustre meek,
Illumin'd all the pale flowers,
　Like hope, that lights a mourner's cheek.
　　　I said (while
　　　The moon's smile
　Play'd o'er a stream in dimpling bliss,)
　　　"The moon looks
　　　On many brooks,
　The brook can see no moon but this ;"
And thus, I thought, our fortunes run,
　For many a lover looks to thee ;
While oh ! I feel there is but *one*,
One Mary in the world for me !

———o———

THRO' GRIEF AND THRO' DANGER.

By Thomas Moore.

Thro' grief and thro' danger thy smile hath cheer'd my way,
Till hope seem'd to bud from each thorn that round me lay ;
The darker our fortune, the brighter our pure love burn'd,
Till shame into glory, till fear into zeal was turn'd :
Oh ! slave as I was, in thy arms my spirit felt free,
And bless'd e'en the sorrows that made me more dear to thee.

THRO' GRIEF AND THRO' DANGER.—*Continued.*

Thy rival was honor'd, while thou wert wrong'd and scorn'd ;
Thy crown was of briers, while gold her brows adorn'd ;
She woo'd me to temples, whilst thou lay'st hid in caves :
Her friends were all masters, while thine, alas ! were slaves.
Yet cold in the earth at thy feet I would rather be,
Than wed what I lov'd not, nor turn one thought from thee !

They slander thee sorely who say thy vows are frail :
Hadst thou been a false one, thy cheek had look'd less pale !
They say, too, so long thou hast worn those lingering chains,
That deep in thy heart they have printed their servile stains ;
Oh ! do not believe them—no chain could that soul subdue :
Where shineth thy spirit, there liberty shineth too.

———o———

SLEEP MY BABE, SLEEP.

By Samuel Lover.

Sleep, my babe, sleep, while my tears wet thy pillow,
  Sleep without rocking, this night with me,
To-morrow we'll rock on the deep-rolling billow,
  The wind for thy lullaby then shall be ;
But when across the wide wave, yonder,
In freedom thro' distant lands we wander,
This heart, with a holier feeling, and fonder
  Will turn, dearest Erin, back to thee.

To the land of the stranger, my boy, we are going,
  Where flowers and birds and their songs are new ;
We'll miss in the spring our own wild flowers growing,
  And listen, in vain, for the sweet cuckoo :
But, in our dreams, still sweetly ringing,
We'll fancy we hear the spring-bird singing,
And gather the flow'rs in our own valley springing—
  And weep, when we wake, that the dream is untrue.

THE FLOWER OF FINAE.

A BRIGADE BALLAD.

By Thomas Davis.

Bright red is the sun on the waves of Lough Sheelin,
A cool gentle breeze from the mountain is stealing,
While fair round its islets the small ripples play,
But fairer than all is the Flower of Finae.

Her hair is like night, and her eyes like gray morning,
She trips on the heather as if its touch scorning,
Yet her heart and her lips are as mild as May day,
Sweet Eily MacMahon, the Flower of Finae.

But who down the hill-side than red deer runs fleeter?
And who on the lake side is hastening to greet her?
Who but Fergus O'Farrell, the fiery and gay,
The darling and pride of the Flower of Finae.

One kiss and one clasp, and one wild look of gladness;
Ah! why do they change on a sudden to sadness—
He has told his hard fortune, nor more he can stay,
He must leave his poor Eily to pine at Finae.

For Fergus O'Farrell was true to his sire-land,
And the dark hand of tyranny drove him from Ireland;
He joins the Brigade, in the wars far away,
But he vows he'll come back to the Flower of Finae.

He fought at Cremona—she hears of his story:
He fought at Cassano—she's proud of his glory,
Yet sadly she sings "Shule Aroon" all the day,
"Oh, come, come, my darling, come home to Finae."

Eight long years have pass'd, till she's nigh broken-hearted,
Her "reel," and her "rock," and her "flax," she has parted;
She sails with the "Wild geese" to Flanders away,
And leaves her sad parents alone in Finae.

Lord Clare on the field of Ramilies is charging—
Before him the Sasanach squadrons enlarging—
Behind him the Cravats their sections display—
Behind him rides Fergus and shouts for Finae.

THE FLOWER OF FINAE.—*Continued.*

On the slopes of La Judoigne the Frenchmen are flying,
Lord Clare and his squadrons the foe still defying,
Outnumbered, and wounded, retreat in array ;
And bleeding rides Fergus and thinks of Finae.

In the cloisters of Ypres a banner is swaying,
And by it a pale weeping maiden is praying ;
That flag's the sole trophy of Ramilies' fray,
This nun is poor Eily, the Flower of Finae.

——o——

OH ! WHERE'S THE SLAVE.

By Thomas Moore.

Oh ! where's the slave, so lowly,
Condemn'd to chains unholy,
 Who, could he burst
 His bonds at first,
Would pine beneath them slowly ?
What soul whose wrongs degrade it,
Would wait till time decay'd it,
 When thus its wing
 At once may spring
To the throne of Him who made it ?
Farewell Erin ! farewell, all
Who live to weep our fall !

Less dear the laurel growing,
Alive, untouched and blowing,
 Than that whose braid
 Is pluck'd to shade
The brows with victory glowing !
We tread the land that bore us,
Her green flag glitters o'er us,
 The friends we've tried
 Are by our side,
And the foe we hate, before us ;
Farewell, Erin !—farewell, all
Who live to weep our fall !

SUBLIME WAS THE WARNING.

By Thomas Moore.

SUBLIME was the warning which liberty spoke,
And grand was the moment when Spaniards awoke
  Into life and revenge from the conqueror's chain!
Oh, Liberty! Let not this spirit have rest,
Till it move, like a breeze, o'er the waves of the West—
Give the light of your looks to each sorrowing spot,
Nor oh! be the Shamrock of Erin forgot,
  While you add to your garland the Olive of Spain!

If the fame of our fathers bequeath'd with their rights,
Give to country its charm and to home its delights,
  If deceit be a wound and suspicion a stain—
Then, ye men of Iberia! our cause is the same;
  And oh! may his tomb want a tear and a name,
Who would ask for a nobler, a holier death,
Than to turn his last sigh into victory's breath
  For the Shamrock of Erin, and Olive of Spain!

Ye Blakes and O'Donnels, whose fathers resign'd
The green hills of their youth, among strangers to find
  That repose which at home they had sigh'd for in vain,
Join, join in our hope that the flame which you light,
May be felt yet in Erin, as calm and as bright;
And forgive even Albion while blushing she draws,
Like a truant, her sword, in the long slighted cause
  Of the Shamrock of Erin and Olive of Spain!

God prosper the cause!—on! it cannot but thrive,
While the pulse of one patriot heart is alive,
  Its devotion to feel, and its rights to maintain.
Then how sainted by sorrow its martyrs will die!
The finger of Glory shall point where they lie,
While far from the footstep of coward or slave,
The young Spirit of Freedom shall shelter their grave,
  Beneath Shamrocks of Erin and Olives of Spain!

KITTY MACLURE.

By Samuel Lover.

Of the beauties of old
Heathen poets have told,
But I, on the faith of a Christian, more pure,
Abjure all the lays
Of their classical days,
For my own Irish beauty—sweet Kitty Maclure !
Cleopatra, the gipsy—
Ariadne, the tipsy—
Tho' bumper'd by Bacchus in nectar so pure,
Were less worthy a toast
Than the beauty I boast,
So, in bright mountain-dew here's to Kitty Maclure !

Fair Helen of Greece
And the Roman Lucrece,
Compared with my swan were but geese, I am sure :
What poet could speak
Of a beauty antique,
Compared with my young one—sweet Kitty Maclure ?
Oh, sweet Kitty,
So pretty, so witty,
To melt you to pity what flames I endure ;
While I sigh forth your name,
It increases my flame,
Till I'm turn'd into cinders for Kitty Maclure !

This world below here
Is but darksome and drear,
So I set about finding for darkness a cure,
And I got the sweet knowledge
From Cupid's own college—
'Twas light from the eyes of sweet Kitty Maclure.
If all the dark pages
Of all the dark ages
Were bound in one volume, you might be secure
To illumine them quite,
With the mirth-giving light
That beams from the eyes of sweet Kitty Maclure !

KITTY MACLURE.—*Continued.*

As Cupid, one day,
Hide-and-seek went to play,
He knew where to hide himself, sly and secure ;
So, away the rogue dashes
To hide 'mid the lashes
That fringe the bright eyes of sweet Kitty Maclure.
She thought 'twas a fly
That got into her eye,
So she wink'd—for the tickling she could not endure ;
But love would not fly
At her winking so sly,
And still lurks in the eye of sweet Kitty Maclure !

———o———

THE FAIRY ISLE.

By Samuel Lover.

O, waft me back to that fairy isle
    Where the skies are ever blue,
Where faithful ever is friendship's smile,
    And hearts are ne'er untrue ;
Where thoughts are fresh and bright and pure
    As flowers in early spring,
Where vows for ever will endure,
    And time no change can bring !

O, where is that sunny isle so blest,
    And where is that fairy sea ?
O, who would not wish in that isle to rest,
    And who would not sail with me !
But I may seek that isle no more,
    Alas ! I have lost the way :—
When youth is o'er, in vain that shore
    Is sought by a pilot gray !
Yet still I *dream* of that fairy isle
    Where the skies are ever blue,
And faithful ever is friendship's smile,
    And hearts are ne'er untrue.

O'BYRNE'S BARD TO THE CLANS OF WICKLOW.

BY SAMUEL FERGUSON.

GOD be with the Irish host,
Never be their battle lost!
For in battle, never yet
Have they basely earned defeat.

Host of armor, red and bright,
May ye fight a valiant fight!
For the green spot of the earth,
For the land that gave you birth.

Who in Erin's cause would stand
Brother of the avenging band,
He must wed immortal quarrel,
Pain, and sweat, and bloody peril.

On the mountain bare and steep,
Snatching short but pleasant sleep,
Then, ere sunrise, from his eyrie,
Swooping on the Saxon quarry.

What, although you've failed to keep
Liffey's plain or Tara's steep,
Cashel's pleasant streams to save,
Or the meads of Cruachan Macv.

Want of conduct lost the town,
Broke the white-walled castle down,
Moira lost, and old Taltin,
And let the conquering stranger in,

'Twas the want of right command,
Not the lack of heart or hand,
Left your hills and plains to-day
'Neath the strong Clan Saxon's sway.

Ah! had heaven never sent
Discord for our punishment,
Triumphs few o'er Erin's host
Had Clan London now to boast.

O'BYRNE'S BARD TO THE CLANS OF WICKLOW.
Continued.

Woe is me, 'tis God's decree
Strangers have the victory :
Irishmen may now be found
Outlaws upon Irish ground.

Like a wild beast in his den
Lies the chief by hill and glen,
While the strangers, proud and savage,
Creevan's * richest valleys ravage.

Woe is me, the foul offence,
Treachery and violence,
Done against my people's rights—
Well may mine be restless nights !

When old Leinster's sons of fame,
Heads of many a warlike name,
Redden their victorious hilts
On the Gaul, my soul exults.

When the grim Gauls, who have come
Hither o'er the ocean foam,
From the fight victorious go,
Then my heart sinks deadly low.

———o———

LARRY O'GAFF.

BY SAMUEL LOVER.

LARRY O'GAFF was a brave boy for marching,
  His instep was large—but his income was small ;
So he set up, one day, as a soldier of fortune—
  The meaning of which is—no fortune at all.
In battles, bombardments, and sieges he grew up,
Till he did'nt much care if towns flourish'd or blew up,
And his maxims in life—for he picked one or two up—
  Were short, sweet and simple for Larry O'Gaff.

* A king of ancient Erin.

LARRY O'GAFF.—*Continued.*

"If your purse it is slender" says Larry, "'tis better
　To owe a small trifle than want a great deal;
If, soliciting cash, a solicitor's letter,
　Or your mercer, maliciously make an appeal—
Look sad, and say ' Sir, your account shall be paid
Now my uncle is dead and my fortune is made; '
Then order some mourning—proceedings are stay'd,
　And black's genteel wearing," says Larry O'Gaff.

Says Larry, " Love all men—except an attorney :
　The ladies without an exception at all;
But beware of a widow on love's mazy journey—
　For, mostly, they've seven small *childre* that squall:
And then, from those eyes that love's glances have darted,
They sometimes rain showers—and sham broken-hearted,
Deploring the loss of ' *the dear man departed;* '
　Oh ! them widows are sarpints !" says Larry O'Gaff.

" But if with some charming young creature you'd run away,
　Court her fat mother—a middle-aged dame,
While her daughter, up stairs, is then packing, like fun away,
　A small change of clothes, before changing her name ;
Mamma smiles resistance—but yields in amaze,
You rush for a license to save all delays;
But go—round the corner with Miss, in a chaise,
　And then, ' heigh for Gretna ! ' " says Larry O'Gaff.

"Your wife is cut off with a shilling," says Larry,
　" But Providence spares her an old maiden aunt,
Who hates all the brazen young women who marry,
　Tho' she. all her life, has been grieving she can't.
Round *her* you must flatter and wheedle and twist,
Let her snub you in company—cheat you at whist—
But you'll win the odd trick when the Legacy list,
　Shows her will all in favor of Larry O'Gaff.

A TRUE STORY.—CALLED MOLLY BAWN.

A Street Ballad.

A STORY, a sad story, to you I will relate,
Of a beautiful young maiden, who met a woful fate ;
As she walked out one evening, at the setting of the sun,
And rested in a bower, a passing shower to shun.

Young Jemmy with his gun, had been fowling all the day ;
And down beside the lake he came at close of twilight gray :
Her apron being about her, he took her for a fawn,
But alas, to his grief, 'twas his own Molly Bawn !

Now all ye brave young men, who go sporting with the gun,
Beware of shooting late, and gray mists about the sun—
Her apron being about her—he took her for a fawn,
But, alas, to his grief, 'twas his own Molly Bawn !

When he came to the bower, and found that it was she,
His limbs they grew feeble, his eyes they could not see ;
He took her in his arms, across her uncle's lawn,
And his tears flowed like fountains on his own Molly Bawn.

Young Jemmy he went home, with his gun beneath his hand,
Sick and broken-hearted, like a felon in the land ;
Crying,—" Father, O, my father—by the lake—a fair white
　　　　　fawn—
I levelled and I shot her dead—my own Molly Bawn ! "

That night to her uncle her spirit did appear,
Saying, " uncle—dearest uncle—my truelove—he is clear—
My apron being about me—he took me for a fawn—
But, alas, to his grief, 'twas his own Molly Bawn ! "

O, Molly was his jewel, his sweetheart and his pride !
If she had lived another year she would have been his bride
The flower of all the valley, the pride of hut and hall—
Oh, Jemmy soon will follow his own Molly Bawn.

SILENT, O MOYLE.

By Thomas Moore.

Silent, O Moyle! be the roar of thy water,
　Break not, ye breezes ! your chain of repose,
While murmuring mournfully, Lir's lonely daughter
　Tells to the night-star her tale of woes.
When shall the swan, her death-note singing,
　Sleep with wings in darkness furl'd ?
When will Heaven, its sweet bell ringing,
　Call my spirit from this stormy world ?

SILENT O'MOYLE.—*Continued.*

Sadly, O Moyle, to thy winter-wave weeping,
 Fate bids me languish long ages away ;
Yet still in her darkness doth Erin lie sleeping,
 Still doth the pure light its dawning delay !
When will that day-star, mildly springing,
 Warm our isle with peace and love ?
When will Heaven, its sweet bell ringing,
 Call my spirit to the fields above ?

———o———

WEEP ON, WEEP ON.

By Thomas Moore.

Weep on, weep on, your hour is past,
 Your dreams of pride are o'er ;
The fatal chain is round you cast,
 And you are men no more !
In vain the hero's heart hath bled ;
 The sage's tongue hath warn'd in vain ;—
Oh, Freedom ! once thy flame hath fled,
 It never lights again !

Weep on ! perhaps in after days
 They'll learn to love your name :
When many a deed shall wake in praise
 That now must sleep in blame !
And, when they tread the ruin'd isle,
 Where rest, at length, the lord and slave,
They'll wondering ask, how hands so vile
 Could conquer hearts so brave ?

" 'Twas fate," they'll say, " a wayward fate
 Your web of discord wove ;
And, while your tyrants join'd in hate,
 You never join'd in love !
But hearts fell off that ought to twine,
 And man profan'd what God hath giv'n,
Till some were heard to curse the shrine
 Where others knelt to Heaven !"

I'M NOT MYSELF AT ALL.

By Samuel Lover.

Oh, I'm not myself at all,
    Molly dear, Molly dear,
I'm not myself at all!
  Nothin' carin', nothin' knowin',
  'Tis afther, you I'm goin',
  Faith your shadow 'tis I'm growin',
    Molly dear,
  And I'm not myself at all!
  Th' other day I went confessin',
  And I ask'd the father's blessin';
"But," says I, "don't give me one intirely,
  For I fretted so last year
  But the half o' me is here,
So give the other half to Molly Brierly:"
  Oh, I'm not myself at all!

Oh, I'm not myself at all,
    Molly dear, Molly dear,
My appetite's so small.
  I once could pick a goose,
  But my buttons is no use,
  Faith my tightest coat is loose,
    Molly dear,
And I'm not myself at all!
  If thus it is I waste,
  You'd betther, dear, make haste,
Before your lover's gone away intirely;
  If you don't soon change your mind,
  Not a bit of me you'll find—
And what 'ud you think o' that, Molly Brierly?
  Oh, I'm not myself at all!

Oh, my shadow on the wall,
    Molly dear, Molly dear,
Isn't like myself at all.
  For I've got so very thin,
  Myself says 'tisn't him,
  But that purty girl so slim,
    Molly dear,
  And I'm not myself at all!

I'M NOT MYSELF AT ALL.—*Continued.*

If thus I smaller grew,
All fretting, dear, for you,
'Tis you should make me up the deficiency;
So just let Father Taaffe,
Make you my betther half,
And you will not the worse of the addition be—
Oh, I'm not myself at all!

I'll be not myself at all,
Molly dear, Molly dear,
Till you my own I call!
Since a change o'er me there came,
Sure you might change your name—
And 'twould just come to the same,
Molly dear,
'Twould just come to the same:
For, if you and I were one,
All confusion would be gone,
And 'twould simplify the matther intirely;
And 'twould save us so much bother,
When we'd both be one another—
So listen now to rayson, Molly Brierly;
Oh, I'm not myself at all!

———o———

LOVE'S YOUNG DREAM.

By Thomas Moore.

Oh! the days are gone, when beauty bright
My heart's chain wove;
When my dream of life, from morn till night,
Was love, still love!
New hopes may bloom, and days may come,
Of milder, calmer beam,
But there's nothing half so sweet in life
As love's young dream!

LOVE'S YOUNG DREAM.—*Continued.*

Though the bard to a purer fame may soar,
    When wild youth's past ;
Though he win the wise, who frown'd before,
    To smile at last ;
He'll never meet a joy so sweet,
    In all his noon of fame,
As when first he sung to woman's ear
    His soul-felt flame,
And, at every close, she blush'd to hear
    The one lov'd name !

Oh ! that hallow'd form is ne'er forgot,
    Which first love trac'd ;
Still it lingering haunts the greenest spot
    On memory's waste !
'Twas odor fled as soon as shed,
    'Twas morning's winged dream !
'Twas a light that ne'er can shine again
    On life's dull stream.
Oh ! 'twas light that ne'er can shine again
    On life's dull stream.

———o———

AS A BEAM O'ER THE FACE OF THE WATERS.

By Thomas Moore.

As a beam o'er the face of the waters may glow,
While the tide runs in darkness and coldness below,
So the cheek may be ting'd with a warm sunny smile,
Though the cold heart to ruin runs darkly the while,

One fatal remembrance, one sorrow that throws
Its bleak shade alike o'er our joys and our woes,
To which life nothing darker or brighter can bring,
For which joy has no balm and affliction no sting !

Oh! this thought in the midst of enjoyment will stay,
Like a dead, leafless branch in the summer's bright ray ;
The beams of the warm sun play round it in vain,
It may smile in his light, but it blooms not again.

HONOR THE BRAVE.

[Reprinted for the Philadelphia Convention.]

HONOR the brave who battle still
  For Irish right in English lands;
No rule except their quenchless will,
  No power save in their naked hands;
Who waged by day and waged by night,
  In groups of three or bands of ten,
Our savage, undespairing fight
  Against two hundred thousand men.

No pomp of war their eyes to blind,
  No blare of music as they go,
With just such weapons as they find,
  In desperate onset on the foe.
They seize the pike, the torch, the scythe—
  Unequal contest—but what then?
With steadfast eyes and spirits blithe
  They face two hundred thousand men.

The jails are yawning through the land,
  The scaffold's fatal click is heard,
But still moves on the scanty band,
  By jail and scaffold undeterred.
A moment's pause to wail the last
  Who fell in freedom's fight, and then,
With teeth firm set, and breathing fast,
  They face two hundred thousand men.

Obscure, unmarked, with none to praise
  Their fealty to a trampled land;
Yet never knight in Arthur's days
  For desperate cause made firmer stand.
They wage no public war, 'tis true;
  They strike and fly, and strike—what then?
'Tis only thus these faithful few
  Can front two hundred thousand men.

You call them ignorant, rash and wild;
  But who can tell how patriots feel
With centuries of torment piled
  Above the land to which they kneel?

HONOR THE BRAVE.—*Continued.*

And who has made them what we find—
  Like tigers lurking in their den,
And breaking forth with fury blind -
  To beard two hundred thousand men ?

Who made their lives so hard to bear
  They care not how their lives are lost?
Their land a symbol of despair—
  A wreck on ruin's ocean tossed.
We, happier here, may carp and sneer,
  And judge them harshly—but what then?
No gloves for those who have as foes
  To face two hundred thousand men.

Honor the brave ! Let England rave
  Against them as a savage band ;
We know their foes, we know their woes,
  And hail them as a hero band.
With iron will they battle still,
  In groups of three or files of ten,
Nor care we by what savage skill
  They fight two hundred thousand men.

———o———

WHEN FIRST I OVER THE MOUNTAIN TROD.
By Samuel Lover.

When first I over the mountain trod,
How bright the flowers, how green the sod,
The breeze was whisp'ring of soft delight,
And the fountains sparkled like diamonds bright.

But now I wander o'er the mountain lone,
The flow'rs are drooping, their fragrance gone,
The breeze of morn like a wail appears,
And the dripping fountain seems weeping tears.

And are ye changed, oh, ye lovely hills ?
Less sparkling are ye, bright mountain rills ?
Does the fragrant bloom from the flow'r depart?—
No—there's nothing changed but this breaking heart.

MY CONNOR.

OH! weary's on money—and weary's on wealth,
And sure we don't want them while we have our health;
'Twas they tempted Connor over the sea,
And I lost my lover, my *cushla machree*. *
  Smiling—beguiling—cheering—endearing—
  Oh! dearly I lov'd him, and he loved me.
  By each other delighted—and fondly united—
  My heart's in the grave with my *cushla machree*.

My Connor was handsome, good-humored, and tall,
At hurling and dancing the best of them all;
But when he came courting beneath our old tree,
His voice was like music—my *cushla machree*.
  Smiling, &c.

So true was his heart and so artless his mind,
He could not think ill of the worst of mankind,
He went bail for his cousin who ran beyond sea,
And all his debts fell on my *cushla machree*.
  Smiling, &c.

Yet still I told Connor that I'd be his bride,—
In sorrow or death not to stir from his side.
He said he could ne'er bring misfortune on me,
But sure I'd be rich with my *cushla machree*.
  Smiling, &c.

The morning he left us I ne'er will forget,
Not an eye in our village but with crying was wet,
" Don't cry any more, *mavourneen*," said he,
" For I will return to my *cushla machree*."
  Smiling, &c.

Sad as I felt then, hope mixed with my care,
Alas! I have nothing left now but despair.
His ship—it went down in the midst of the sea,
And its wild waves roll over my *cushla machree*.
  Smiling—beguiling—cheering—endearing—
  Oh! dearly I lov'd him and he loved me.
  By each other delighted—and fondly united—
  My heart's in the grave with my *cushla machree*.

* " Vein of my heart."

OH! THE SHAMROCK!

BY THOMAS MOORE.

THROUGH Erin's Isle,
To sport awhile,
As Love and Valor wander'd,
With Wit, the sprite,
Whose quiver bright
A thousand arrows squander'd;
Where'er they pass,
A triple grass
Shoots up, with dewdrops streaming,
As softly green
As em'ralds, seen
Through purest crystal gleaming!
Oh, the Shamrock, the green, immortal Shamrock!
Chosen leaf
Of bard and chief,
Old Erin's native Shamrock!

Says Valor, " See,
They spring for me,
Those leafy gems of morning !"
Says Love, " No, no,
For me they grow,
My fragrant path adorning !"
But Wit perceives
The triple leaves
And cries, " Oh ! do not sever
A type that blends
Three god-like friends,
Love, Valor, Wit, for ever !"
Oh ! the Shamrock, &c.

So, firmly fond
May last the bond
They wove that morn together,
And ne'er may fall
One drop of gall
On Wit's celestial feather !

OH ! THE SHAMROCK.—*Continued.*

May Love, as shoot
His flowers and fruit,
Of thorny falsehood weed 'em !
May Valor ne'er
His standard rear
Against the cause of Freedom !
Oh! the Shamrock, &c.

————o————

SONG OF THE GALLOPING O'HOGAN. *

By Robert Dwyer Joyce.

Air.—*"He thought of the Charmer,"* &c.

Hurra! boys, hurra! for the sword by my side,
The spur and the gallop o'er bogs deep and wide ;
Hurra! for the helmet an' shining steel jack,
The sight of the spoil, an' good men at my back !
  An' we'll sack and burn for King and sireland,
  An' chase the black foe from ould Ireland !

At the wave of my sword start a thousand good men,
And we ride like the blast over moorland and glen ;
Like dead leaves of winter in ruin an' wrath,
We sweep the cowed Saxon away from our path,
  An' we'll sack and burn for King and sireland,
  An' chase the black foe from ould Ireland !

The herds of the foe graze at noon by the rills ;
We have them at night in our camp 'mid the hills—
Their towns lie in peace at the eve of the night,
But they're sacked an' in flames ere the next mornin' light !
  An' we'll sack and burn for King and sireland,
  An' chase the black foe from ould Ireland !

And we go ridin' by night and by day,
An' fight for our country an' all the rich prey ;
The roar of the battle sweet music we feel,
An' the light of our hearts is the flashin' of steel !
  An' we'll sack and burn for King and sireland,
  An' chase the black foe from ould Ireland !

* One of the Rapparee chiefs in the time of King James the Second.

GERALD GRIFFIN.

THE SISTER OF CHARITY.

By Gerald Griffin.

SHE once was a lady of honor and wealth,
Bright glowed on her features the roses of health;
Her vesture was blended of silk and of gold,
And her motion shook perfume from every fold;
Joy revell'd around her—love shone at her side,
And gay was her smile as the glance of a bride,
And light was her step in the mirth-sounding hall,
When she heard of the daughters of Vincent de Paul.

She felt in her spirit the summons of grace,
That caused her to live for the suffering race;
And heedless of pleasure, of comfort, of home,
Rose quickly, like Mary, and answer'd " I come."
She put from her person the trappings of pride,
And pass'd from her home with the joy of a bride,
Nor wept at the threshold, as onwards she moved,—
For her heart was on fire in the cause it approved.

Lost ever to fashion—to vanity lost,
That beauty that once was the song and the toast—
No more in the ball-room that figure we meet,
But gliding at dusk to the wretch's retreat.
Forgot in the halls is that high-sounding name,
For the Sister of Charity blushes at fame;
Forgot are the claims of her riches and birth,
For she barters for heaven the glory of earth.

Those feet, that to music could gracefully move,
Now bear her alone on the mission of love;
Those hands that once dangled the perfume and gem
Are tending the helpless, or lifted for them:
That voice that once echoed the song of the vain,
Now whispers relief to the bosom of pain;
And the hair that was shining with diamond and pearl
Is wet with the tears of the penitent girl.

THE SISTER OF CHARITY.—*Continued.*

Her down bed a pallet—her trinkets a bead,
Her lustre—one taper that serves her to read;
Her sculpture—the crucifix nailed by her bed,
Her paintings, one print of the thorn-crowned head;
Her cushion the pavement that wearies her knees,
Her music the psalm, or the sigh of disease;
The delicate lady lives mortified there,
And the feast is forsaken for fasting and prayer.

Yet not to the service of heart and of mind,
Are the cares of that heaven-minded virgin confined,
Like Him whom she loves, to the mansions of grief
She hastes with the tidings of joy and relief.
She strengthens the weary, she comforts the weak,
And soft is her voice in the ear of the sick;
Where want and affliction on mortals attend,
The Sister of Charity *there* is a friend.

Unshrinking where pestilence scatters his breath,
Like an angel she moves in the vapor of death;
Where rings the loud musket, and flashes the sword,
Unfearing she walks, for she follows the Lord.
How sweetly she bends o'er each plague-tainted face,
With looks that are lighted with holiest grace;
How kindly she dresses each suffering limb,
For she sees in the wounded the image of Him.

Behold her, ye worldly! behold her, ye vain!
Who shrink from the pathway of virtue and pain!
Who yield up to pleasure your nights and your days,
Forgetful of service, forgetful of praise.
Ye lazy philosophers—self-seeking men,
Ye fireside philanthropists, great at the pen,
How stands in the balance your eloquence, weighed
With the life and the deeds of that high-born maid?

THE EMIGRANT MOTHER.

YOUR eyes have the twin stars' light, *ma croidhe*
  Mo cuisle Inghean ban ; *
And your swan-like neck is dear to me,
  Mo caillin og alain :
And dear is your fairy foot so light,
  And dazzling milk-white hand,
And your hair ! it's a thread of the golden light
  That was spun in the rainbow's band.

Oh! green be the fields of my native shore.
  Where you bloom like a young rose-tree;
Mo varia astore—we meet no more !
  But the pulse of my heart's with thee.
No more may your voice with it's silver sound,
  Come like music in a dream !
Or your heart's sweet laugh ring merrily round,
  Like the gush of the summer's stream.

Oh ! *mo varia*, the stately halls are high
  Where Erin's splendors shine !
Yet their hearts shall swell to the wailing cry
  That my heart sends forth to thine.
For an exile's heart is fountain deep,
  Far hid from the gladsome sun—
Where the bosom's yearning ne'er may sleep;
  Mo thruaidh ! mo chreach ! och on !

———o———

ERIN! O ERIN!

BY THOMAS MOORE.

LIKE the bright lamp that shone in Kildare's holy fane,
  And burn'd through long ages of darkness and storm,
Is the heart that sorrows have frown'd on in vain.
  Whose spirit outlives them unfading and warm :
Erin ! O Erin ! thus bright through the tears
Of a long night of bondage thy spirit appears.

* My pulse, my white daughter.

ERIN! O ERIN!—*Continued.*

The nations have fall'n, and thou still art young,
  Thy sun is but rising when others are set;
And though slavery's cloud o'er thy morning hath hung,
  The full noon of freedom shall beam round thee yet.
Erin! O Erin! though long in the shade,
Thy star shall shine out when the proudest shall fade.

Unchill'd by the rain, and unwak'd by the wind,
  The lily lies sleeping through winter's cold hour,
Till the hand of spring her dark chain unbind,
  And daylight and liberty bless the young flower.
Erin! O Erin! *thy* winter is past,
And the hope that liv'd through it shall blossom at last.

——o——

COME, SEND ROUND THE WINE.

By Thomas Moore.

Come, send round the wine, and leave points of belief
  To simpleton sages and reasoning fools;
This moment's a flow'r too fair and brief
  To be wither'd and stain'd by the dust of the schools.
Your glass may be purple, and mine may be blue;
  But while they're both fill'd from the same bright bowl,
The fool that would quarrel for diff'rence of hue,
  Deserves not the comfort they shed o'er the soul.

Shall I ask the brave soldier who fights by my side
  In the cause of mankind, if our creeds agree?
Shall I give up the friend I have valued and tried,
  If he kneel not before the same altar with me?
From the heretic girl of my soul shall I fly,
  To seek somewhere else a more orthodox kiss?
No! perish the hearts and the laws that try
  Truth, valor, or love by a standard like this!

THE BRIDAL OF MALAHIDE.

BY GERALD GRIFFIN.

THE joy-bells are ringing
  In gay Malahide,
The fresh wind is singing
  Along the sea-side :
The maids are assembling
  With garlands of flowers,
And the harpstrings are trembling
  In all the glad bowers.

Swell, swell the gay measure !
  Roll trumpet and drum !
'Mid greetings of pleasure
  In splendor they come !
The chancel is ready,
  The portal stands wide
For the lord and the lady,
  The bridegroom and bride.

What years, ere the latter,
  Of earthly delight,
The future shall scatter
  O'er them in its flight !
What blissful caresses
  Shall fortune bestow,
Ere those dark-flowing tresses
  Fall white as the snow !

Before the high altar
  Young Maud stands array'd,
With accents that falter
  Her promise is made—
From father and mother
  For ever to part,
For him and no other
  To treasure her heart.

THE BRIDAL OF MALAHIDE.—*Continued.*

The words are repeated,
  The bridal is done,
The rite is completed—
  The two, they are one;
The vow, it is spoken
  All pure from the heart,
That must not be broken
  Till life shall depart.

Hark! 'mid the gay clangor
  That compass'd their car,
Loud accents in anger
  Come mingling afar!
The foe's on the border,
  His weapons resound
Where the lines in disorder
  Unguarded are found.

As wakes the good shepherd
  The watchful and bold,
When the ounce or the leopard
  Is seen in the fold,
So rises already
  The chief in his mail,
While the new-married lady
  Looks fainting and pale.

" Son, husband, and brother,
  Arise to the strife,
For the sister and mother,
  For children and wife!
O'er hill and o'er hollow,
  O'er mountain and plain,
Up, true men, and follow!
  Let dastards remain ! "

TO LADIES' EYES.

By Thomas Moore.

To ladies' eyes around, boys,
  We can't refuse, we can't refuse,
Though bright eyes so abound, boys,
  'Tis hard to choose, 'tis hard to choose.
For thick as stars that lighten
  Yon airy bowers, yon airy bowers,
The countless eyes that brighten
  This earth of ours, this earth of ours.
But fill the cup—where'er, boys,
  Our choice may fall, our choice may fall,
We're sure to find love there, boys,
  So drink them all! so drink them all!

Some looks there are so holy,
  They seem but given, they seem but given,
As splendid beacons, solely,
  To light to heaven, to light to heaven.
While some—oh! ne'er believe them—
  With tempting ray, with tempting ray
Would lead us (God forgive them!)
  The other way, the other way.
      But fill the cup, &c.

In some, as in a mirror,
  Love seems portray'd, love seems portray'd;
But shun the flattering error,
  'Tis but his shade, 'tis but his shade.
Himself has fix'd his dwelling
  In eyes we know, in eyes we know,
In lips—but this is telling;
  So here they go! so here they go!
      Fill up, fill up where'er, boys, &c.

I'M VERY HAPPY WHERE I AM.

A Peasant Woman's Song.   1864.

Dion Boucicault.

I'M very happy where I am,
  Far across the say,
I'm very happy far from home,
  In North Amerikay.

It's only in the night, when Pat
  Is sleeping by my side,
I lie awake, and no one knows
  The big tears that I've cried ;

For a little voice still calls me back
  To my far, far counthrie,
And nobody can hear it spake,
  Oh ! nobody but me.

There is a little spot of ground
  Behind the chapel wall,
It's nothing but a tiny mound,
  Without a stone at all ;

It rises like my heart just now
  It makes a dawny hill ;
It's from below the voice comes out,
  I cannot keep it still.

Oh ! little voice ; ye call me back
  To my far, far counthrie,
And nobody can hear ye spake,
  Oh ! nobody but me.

THE JAUNTING CAR.

By Samuel Lover.

A FULL and a faithful account I'll sing
   Of the wonderful things that in Ireland are;
And first I would fain to your notice bring
   That magic contrivance, a Jaunting Car.
For its magic is great, as I'll soon impart,
   And naught can compare to it near or far;
Would you find the soft side of a lady's heart,
   Just sit by her side on a Jaunting Car:
The lordly brougham, the ducal coach,
   My lady's chariot, less speedy are
To make their way to the church, they say,
   Than a nice little drive on a Jaunting Car.

The Greeks and the Romans fine cars display'd,
   If to history you'll let me go back so far;
But, the wretches, in these it was war they made,
   While 'tis love that is made on a Jaunting Car.
But in love, as in war, you may kill your man,
   And if you're inclined to proceed so far,
Just call him out, and go ride about
   A mile and a half on a Jaunting Car.

THE JAUNTING CAR.—*Continued.*

Let lovers praise the moon's soft rays,
  The falling dew or the rising star,
The streamlet's side at the even tide,
  But give *me* the side of a Jaunting Car.

Ere Cupid was taught to take steps with art
  (Little staggering bob as most babies are,)
His mother she bought him a little go-cart,—
  'Twas the earliest form of the Jaunting Car.
And the walking gift it can soon impart
  To all who to Cupid inclined are,
If you would walk off with a lady's heart,
  Just take her a drive on a Jaunting Car.
The cushions, soft as the tale that's told,
  The shafts, as certain as Cupid's are,
The springs go bump—and your heart goes jump,
  At the thumping vows on a Jaunting Car,

——o——

THE YOUNG MAY MOON.

By Thomas Moore.

THE young May moon is beaming, love,
The glow-worm's lamp is gleaming love,
How sweet to rove through Morna's grove,
While the drowsy world is dreaming, love.
Then awake, the heavens look bright, my dear.
'Tis never too late for delight my dear;
And the best of all ways to lengthen our days,
Is to steal a few hours from the night, my dear.

Now all the world is sleeping, love,
But the sage, his star-watch keeping, love,
And I whose star, more glorious far,
Is the eye from that casement peeping, love,
Then awake till rise of sun, my dear,
The sage his glass will shun, my dear,
Or, in watching the flight of the bodies of light
He might happen to take thee for one, my dear.

FINEEN THE ROVER.

Robert Dwyer Joyce.

Air.—"You'd think, if you heard their pipes squealing."

An old castle towers o'er the billow
  That thunders by Cleena's green land,
And there dwelt as gallant a rover
  As ever grasped hilt by the hand—
Eight stately towers of the waters
  Lie anchored in Baltimore Bay,
And over their twenty score sailors,
  Oh, who but the Rover holds sway?
      Then ho! for Fineen the rover!
        Fineen O'Driscoll the free!
      Straight as the mast of his galley,
        And wild as the wave of the sea!

The Saxons of Cork and Moyallo,
  They harried his lands with their powers;
He gave them a taste of his cannon,
  And drove them like wolves from his towers.
The men of Clan London brought over
  Their strong fleet to make him a slave;
They met him by Mizen's wild highland
  And the sharks crunched their bones 'neath the wave!
      Then ho! for Fineen the Rover,
        Fineen O'Driscoll the free,
      With step like the red stag of Beara,
        And voice like the bold sounding sea.

Long time in that old battered castle,
  Or out on the waves with his clan
He feasted, and ventured, and conquered,
  But ne'er struck his colors to man.
In a fight 'gainst the foes of his country,
  He died as a brave man should die,
And he sleeps 'neath the waters of Cleena,
  Where the waves sing his *caoine* to the sky!
      Then ho! for Fineen the Rover,
        Fineen O'Driscoll the free,
      With eye like the osprey's at morning,
        And smile like the sun on the sea.

THE LETTER.

By Samuel Lover.

A small spark, attached to the wick of a candle, is considered to indicate the arrival of a letter to the one before whom it burns.

Fare thee well, Love, now thou art going
   Over the wild and trackless sea ;
Smooth be its waves, and fair the wind blowing
   Tho' 'tis to bear thee far from me.
But when on the waste of ocean,
   Some happy home-bound bark you see,
Swear by the truth of thy heart's devotion,
   To send a letter back to me.

Think of the shore thou'st left behind thee,
   Even when reaching a brighter strand ;
Let not the golden glories blind thee
   Of that gorgeous Indian land ;
Send me not its diamond treasures,
   Nor pearls from the depth of its sunny sea,
But tell me of all thy woes and pleasures,
   In a long letter back to me.

And while dwelling in lands of pleasure,
   Think, as you bask in their bright sunshine,
That while the ling'ring time I measure,
   Sad and wintry hours are mine
Lonely by my taper weeping,
   And watching, the spark of promise to see ;
All for that bright spark, my night watch keeping,
   For oh ! 'tis a letter, Love, from thee !
To say that soon thy sail will be flowing,
   Homeward to bear thee over the sea ;
Calm be the waves and swift the wind blowing,
   For oh ! thou *art* coming back to me !

LANTY LEARY.

By Samuel Lover.

Lanty was in love, you see,
　With lovely, lively Rosie Carey,
But her father can't agree
　To give the girl to Lanty Leary.
" Up to fun, away we'll run,"
　Says she, " my father's so conthrairy,
Won't you follow me ? won't you follow me ? "
　" Faith I will," says Lanty Leary !

But her father died one day
　(I hear 'twas not by dhrinkin' wather) ;
House and land and cash, they say,
　He left by will to Rose his daughter ;
House and land and cash to seize,
　Away she cut so light and airy,
" Won't you follow me ? won't you follow me ? "
　" Faith I will ! " says Lanty Leary !

Rose, herself, was taken bad,
　The fayver worse each day was growin',
" Lanty dear," says she, " 'tis sad,
　To th' other world I'm surely goin',
You can't survive my loss I know,
　Nor long remain in Tipperary,
Won't you follow me ? won't you follow me ? "
　" Faith I won't," says Lanty Leary !

———o———

MY DARK-HAIR'D GIRL.

By Samuel Lover.

My dark-hair'd girl, thy ringlets deck,
In silken curl, thy graceful neck ;
Thy neck is like the swan, and fair as the pearl,
And light as air the step is of my dark-hair'd girl !

My dark-hair'd girl, upon thy lip
The dainty bee might wish to sip,
For thy lip it is the rose, and thy teeth they are pearl,
And diamond is the eye of my dark-hair'd girl !

MY DARK-HAIR'D GIRL.—*Continued.*

My dark-hair'd girl, I've promised thee,
And thou thy faith hast given to me,
And oh! I would not change for the crown of an earl,
The pride of being loved by my dark-hair'd girl!

———o———

SECRETS WERE NOT MEANT FOR THREE.

By Samuel Lover.

Come with me where violets lie
   Like thine eye—hidden deep,
When their lurking glances blue
   Thro' long lashes peep;
There, amid the perfume sweet,
   Wafted on the balmy breeze,
Shelter'd by the secret shade
   Beneath the whisp'ring trees,
Whisp'ring there would I be too—
I've a secret, meant for you,
Sweeter than the wild bee's hum—
Will you come?

Come not when the day is bright,
   But at night, when the moon
Lights the grove where nightingales
   Sing the lover's tune :—
But sweeter than the silver song
   That fair Philomel doth sing—
Sweeter than the fragrance fresh
   The flowers round us fling—
Sweeter than the poet's dream
By Castalia's gifted stream,
Is the tale I'll tell to thee—
Come with me!

AFTER THE BATTLE.

By Thomas Moore.

NIGHT clos'd around the conqueror's way,
  And lightning show'd the distant hill,
Where those that lost that dreadful day
  Stood few and faint, but fearless still.
The soldier's hope, the patriot's zeal,
  For ever dimm'd for ever cross'd ;
Oh ! who shall say what heroes feel,
  When all but life and honor's lost !

The last sad hour of freedom's dream,
  And valor's task mov'd slowly by,
While mute they watch'd, till morning's beam
  Should rise, and give them light to die.
There is a world where souls are free,
  Where tyrants taint not nature's bliss ;
If death that world's bright opening be,
  Oh ! who would live a slave in this ?

———o———

NORAH'S LAMENT.

By Samuel Lover.

OH, I think I must follow my *Cushla-ma-chree*,
For I can't break the spell of his words so enthralling :
  Closer the tendrils around my heart creep—
  I dream all the day, and at night I can't sleep,
For I hear a sad voice that is calling me—calling—
" Oh Norah, my darling, come over the sea ! "

For my brave and my fond one is over the sea,
  He fought for " the cause " and the troubles came o'er him ;
  He fled for his life when the King lost the day,
  He fled for his life—and he took mine away ;
For 'tis death here without him : I, dying, deplore him,
Oh ! life of my bosom !—my *Cushla-ma-chree !*

THE MINSTREL'S WALK.

By Rev. James Wills.

(To the old Irish air of " *Bidh mid a gol sa poga namban.* ")

Green hills of the West, where I carolled along,
In the May-day of life, with my harp and my song,
Though the winter of time o'er my spirit hath roll'd,
And the steps of the minstrel are weary and old ;
Though no more by those famous old haunts shall I stray—
Once the themes of my song, and the guides of my way,
That each had its story, and true-hearted friend—
Before I forget ye, life's journey shall end.

Oh! 'twas joy in the prime of life's morning to go
On the path where Clan Connell once followed Hugh Roe,
O'er the hill of Ceiscorran, renowned Ballymote,
By the Boyle, or by Newport, all passes of note,
Where the foe their vain armaments haughtily kept ;
But the foot of th' avenger went by while they slept—
The hills told no tale—but the night-cloud was red,
And the friends of the Sasanach quaked at their tread.

By the plains of Rath Croghan, fields famous of yore,
Though stronghold and seat of the kingly no more ;
By Tulsk and Tomona, hill, valley, and plain,
To gray Ballintubber, O'Connor's domain ;
Then ages rolled backward in lengthened array,
In song and old story, the long summer day ;
And cloud-like, the glories of Connaught rolled by,
Till they sank in the horrors of grim Athenry !

Through the heaths of Kiltullagh, kind, simple, though rude,
To Acluin's bright waters, where Willsborough stood,
Ballinlough then spoke welcome from many a door,
Where smiles lit kind faces that now smile no more :
Then away to the Moyne, o'er the Moors of Mayo,
Still onward, still welcomed by high and by low—
Blake, Burke, and O'Malley, Lynch, Kirwan and Browne ;
By forest, lake, mountain, through village and town.

THE MINSTREL'S WALK.—*Continued.*

And kind were the voices that greeted my way—
Twas *cead mile failte* at closing of day,
When young hearts beat lightly, and labor was done,
For joy tracked my steps as light follows the sun ;
Then tales pleased the hamlet, and news cheered the hall,
And the tune of old times was still welcome to all ;
The praise of thy glory, dear Land of the West—
But thy praises are still, and thy kind bosoms rest.

My blessing rest with you, dear friends, though no more
Shall the poor and the weary rejoice at your door ;
Though like stars to your homes I have seen you depart,
Still ye live, O ye live in each vein of my heart !
Still the light of your looks on my darkness is thrown ;
Still your voices breathe round me when weary and lone ;
Like shades ye come back with each feeling old strain—
But the world shall ne'er look on your equals again.

——o——

UNDER THE ROSE.

By Samuel Lover.

If a secret you'd keep there is one I could tell,
Though I think, from my eyes, you might guess it as well,
But as it might ruffle another's repose,
Like a thorn let it be ;—that is—under the rose.

As Love, in the garden of Venus, one day,
Was sporting where he was forbidden to play,
He feared that some Sylph might his mischief disclose.
So he slily concealed himself—under a rose.

Where the likeness is found to thy breath and thy lips,
Where honey the sweetest the summer bee sips,
Where Love, timid Love, found the safest repose,
There our secret we'll keep, dearest,—under the rose.

The maid of the East a fresh garland may wreathe,
To tell of the passion she dares not to breathe :
Thus, in *many* bright flowers she her flame may disclose,
But in *one* she finds secrecy ;—under the rose.

OH! GIVE ME THY HAND FAIR LADY.

By Samuel Lover

Oh! give me thy hand, fair lady,
  That snowy-white hand, so small,
Thy bow'r shall be dainty, sweet lady,
  In a bold baron's ancient hall;
There, beauties of noble line, lady,
  Shine forth from the pictur'd wall,
But if thou wilt be bride of mine, lady,
  Then mine will outshine them all!

OH! GIVE ME THY HAND, FAIR LADY.—*Continued.*

I see thou wilt not give thy hand, lady,
  I see, by that clear cold eye—
If thou to my suit didst incline, lady,
  The rose from thy cheek would fly;
Thy lip is all ruby-red, lady,
  But mine is so pale the while—
Nay, frown not, I ask not thy hand, lady,
  But ah !—let me see thee smile.

I only did ask for thy smile, lady,
  Yet scorn to thy lip doth cling—
That ruby bow will not bend, lady,
  Till Cupid hath touch'd the string ;
But if thoul't not smile, fair lady,
  A humbler suit I'll try,—
For the heart thou hast broken, fair lady,
  Oh ! give me, at least, thy sigh !

——o——

WHEN AND WHERE.

By Samuel Lover.

" Oh tell me when and tell me where
Am I to meet with thee, my fair?"
  " I'll meet thee in the secret night,
  When stars are beaming gentle light,
  Enough for love, but not too bright
To tell who blushes there."

" You've told me *when*, now tell me *where*,
Am I to meet with thee, my fair?"
  " I'll meet thee in that lovely place,
  Where flow'rets dwell in sweet embrace,
  And zephyr comes to steal a grace
To shed on the midnight air."

" You've told me *when*, and told me *where*,
But tell me *how* I'll know thou'rt there ?"
  " Thou'lt know it when I sing the lay
  That wandering boys on organs play,
  No lover, sure, can miss his way,
When led by this signal air."

HAS SORROW THY YOUNG DAYS SHADED?

By Thomas Moore.

Has sorrow thy young days shaded,
  As clouds o'er the morning fleet?
Too fast have those young days faded,
  That even in sorrow were sweet?
Does time with his cold wing wither
  Each feeling that once was dear?—
Then, child of misfortune! come hither,
  I'll weep with thee tear for tear.

Has love, to that soul so tender,
  Been like our Lagenian mine,
Where sparkles of golden splendor
  All over the surface shine—
But, if in pursuit you go deeper,
  Allured by the gleam that shone,
Ah! false as the dream of the sleeper,
  Like Love, the bright ore is gone.

Has Hope, like the bird in the story,
  That flitted from tree to tree
With the talisman's glittering glory—
  Has Hope been that bird to thee?
On branch after branch alighting,
  The gem did she still display,
And, when nearest and most inviting,
  Then waft the fair gem away?

If thus the sweet hours have fleeted,
  When Sorrow herself look'd bright:
If thus the fond hope has cheated,
  That led thee along so light.
If thus too, the cold world wither
  Each feeling that once was dear;—
Come, child of misfortune! come hither,
  I'll weep with thee, tear for tear.

EVELEEN'S BOWER.

By Thomas Moore.

Oh! weep for the hour,
When to Eveleen's bower
The lord of the valley with false vows came;
The moon hid her light
From the heavens that night,
And wept behind the clouds o'er the maiden's shame.
The clouds pass'd soon
From the chaste cool moon,
And Heav'n smil'd again with her vestal flame;
But none will see the day
When the clouds shall pass away,
Which that dark hour left upon Eveleen's fame.

The white snow lay
On the narrow pathway,
Where the lord of the valley cross'd over the moor;
And many a deep print
On the white snow's tint
Show'd the track of his footstep to Eveleen's door.
The next sun's ray
Soon melted away
Ev'ry trace on the path where the false lord came:
But there's a light above
Which alone can remove
That stain upon the snow of fair Eveleen's fame.

————o————

AT THE MID HOUR OF NIGHT.

By Thomas Moore.

At the mid hour of night, when stars are weeping, I fly
To the lone vale we lov'd when life was warm in thine eye;
  And I think that if spirits can steal from the regions of air,
  To revisit past scenes of delight thou wilt come to me there,
And tell me our love is remember'd e'en in the sky!

Then I sing the wild song it once was rapture to hear,
When our voices, commingling, breath'd like one on the ear;
  And, as Echo far off through the vale my sad orison rolls,
  I think, oh, my love! 'tis thy voice from the kingdom of souls,
Faintly answering still the notes that once were so dear.

MARY OF TIPPERARY.

By Samuel Lover.

FROM sweet Tipperary,
   See light-hearted Mary,
Her step, like a fairy, scarce ruffles the dew,
   As she joyously springs
   And as joyously sings,
Disdaining such things as a stocking or shoe!
   For she goes bare-footed,
   Like Venus or Cupid,
And who'd be so stupid to put her in silk,
   When her sweet foot and ankle,
   The dew-drops bespangle,
   As she trips o,er the lawn,
   At the blush of the dawn,
As she trips o'er the lawn with her full pail of milk.

   For the dance when arrayed,
   See this bright mountain maid,
If her hair she would braid with young beauty's fond lure
   O'er some clear fountain stooping,
   Her dark tresses looping :—
Diana herself ne'er had mirror more pure !
   How lovely that toilet ;—
   Would Fashion dare soil it
With paint or with patches—when Nature bestows
   A beauty more simple,
   In mirth's artless dimple,
   Heaven's light in her eye —
   (The soft blue of the sky)
Heaven's light in her eye and a blush like the rose.

——o——

COME BACK TO ME.

By Samuel Lover.

WHY, dearest, dost thou linger
   Far away from me ?
While pensive mem'ry's finger
   Ever points to thee ;

COME BACK TO ME.—*Continued.*

Over what mountains bounding,
  Over what silent sea,
With dangers dark surrounding ?—
  Oh, come back to me !

But darker than the danger
  That dwells upon the sea,
The thought, that some fair stranger
  May cast her love on thee ;
Perchance she's now bestowing
  Some fatal glance on thee,
Love-spells around thee throwing—
  Oh, come back to me !

————o————

SOFT ON THE EAR.

By Samuel Lover.

Soft on the ear falls the serenade,
  When the calm evening is closing ;
Sweet are the echoes by music made,
  When the lake is in moonlight reposing :
      Hark, how the sound
      Circles around,—
As if each note of the measure
      Was caught, as it fell,
      In some water-sprite's shell,
Who floated away with the treasure,
                Soft on the ear, &c.

Soft on the ear falls the serenade
  When we guess who the soft strain is breathing ;
The spirit of song is more melting made,
  With the spirit of tenderness wreathing.
      Oh, such the delight,
      In the calm summer's night,
When thro' casements, half open, is stealing
      The soft serenade
      To the half-waking maid,
Who sighs at each tender appealing
                Soft on the ear, &c.

O'DONOVAN'S DAUGHTER.

By Edward Walsh.

Air.—"*The Juice of the Barley.*"

One midsummer's eve, when the Bel-fires were lighted,
And the bagpiper's tone call'd the maidens delighted,
I join'd a gay group by the Araglin's water,
And danced till the dawn with O'Donovan's Daughter.

Have you seen the ripe monadan glisten in Kerry,
Have you mark'd on the Galteys the black whortle-berry,
Or ceanabhan wave by the wells of Blackwater?
They're the cheek, eye, and neck of O'Donovan's Daughter.

Have you seen a gay kidling on Claragh's round mountain,
The swans arching glory on Sheeling's blue fountain,
Heard a weird woman chant what the fairy choir taught her?
They've the step, grace, and tone of O'Donovan's Daughter!

Have you marked in its flight the black wing of the raven,
The rosebuds that breathe in the summer breeze waven,
The pearls that lie hid under Lene's magic water?
They're the teeth, lip, and hair of O'Donovan's Daughter!

Ere the Bel-fire was dimmed or the dancers departed,
I taught her a song of some maid broken-hearted:
And that group, and that dance, and that love-song I taught
        her
Haunt my slumbers at night with O'Donovan's Daughter!

God grant, 'tis no fay from Cnoc-Firinn that wooes me,
God grant, 'tis not Cliodhna the queen that pursues me,
That my soul lost and lone has no witchery wrought her,
While I dream of dark groves and O'Donovan's Daughter.

If, spell-bound, I pine with an airy disorder,
Saint Gobnate has sway over Musgry's wide border;
She'll scare from my couch, when with prayer I've besought
        her,
That bright airy sprite like O'Donovan's Daughter.

THE FAIR HILLS OF IRELAND.

TRANSLATED FROM THE IRISH.

BY SAMUEL FERGUSON.

A PLENTEOUS place is Ireland for hospitable cheer,
   Uileacan dubh O !
Where the wholesome fruit is bursting from the yellow bar-
  ley ear ;
   Uileacan dubh O !
There is honey in the trees where her misty vales expand,
And her forest paths in summer are by falling waters fanned ;
There is dew at high noontide there, and springs i' the yellow
  sand,
 On the fair hills of holy Ireland.

Curled he is and ringleted, and plaited to the knee,
   Uileacan dubh O !
Each captain who comes sailing across the Irish sea :
   Uileacan dubh O !
And I will make my journey, if life and health but stand,
Unto that pleasant country, that fresh and fragrant strand,
And leave your boasted braveries, your wealth and high
  command,
 For the fair hills of holy Ireland.

Large and profitable are the stacks upon the ground ;
   Uileacan dubh O !
The butter and the cream do wondrously abound,
   Uileacan dubh O !
The cresses on the water and the sorrels are at hand,
And the cuckoo's calling daily his note of music bland,
And the bold thrush sings so bravely his song i' the forests
  grand
 On the fair hills of holy Ireland.

THE GIRL I LEFT BEHIND ME.

By Samuel Lover.

The hour was sad I left the maid,
  A lingering farewell taking,
Her sighs and tears my steps delay'd—
  I thought her heart was breaking;
In hurried words her name I bless'd,
  I breathed the vows that bind me,
And to my heart, in anguish, press'd
  The girl I left behind me.

Then to the East we bore away
  To win a name in story;
And there, where dawns the sun of day,
  There dawn'd our sun of glory!
Both blaz'd in noon on Alma's height,
  Where, in the post assign'd me,
I shar'd the glory of that fight,
  Sweet girl I left behind me.

Full many a name our banners bore
  Of former deeds of daring,
But they were of the days of yore,
  In which we had no sharing;
But now, *our* laurels, freshly won,
  With the old ones shall entwined be,
Still worthy of our sires, each son,
  Sweet girl I left behind me.

The hope of final victory
  Within my bosom burning,
Is mingling with sweet thoughts of thee
  And of my fond returning:
But should I ne'er return again,
  Still worth thy love thou'lt find me,
Dishonor's breath shall never stain
  The name I'll leave behind me!

A LAMENTATION.

By J. Clarence Mangan.

[This lamentation is not an Irish ballad, but an imitation of Irish ballad poetry. It is translated from the German of Goethe : a strange and suggestive fact, that the greatest intellect of this age should have been devoted to the study and illustration of our native poetry, while it was neglected at home.]

O! RAISE the woful *Phillalu*,
   And let your tears in streams be shed ;
Och, orro, orro, ollalu !
   The Master's eldest hope is dead !

Ere broke the morning dim and pale,
   The owlet flapp'd his heavy wing,
We heard the winds at evening wail,
And now our dirge of death we sing.
     Och, orro, orro, ollalu !

Why wouldst thou go ? How couldst thou die?
   Why hast thou left thy parents dear—
Thy friends, thy kindred far and nigh,
   Whose cries, *movrone !* thou dost not hear?
     Och, orro, orro, ollalu !

Thy mother, too !—how could she part
   From thee, her darling, fair and sweet—
The heart that throbb'd within her heart,
   The pulse, the blood that made it beat?
     Och, orro, orro, ollalu !

Oh ! lost to her and all thy race,
   Thou sleepest in the House of Death,
She sees no more thy cherub face,
   She drinks no more thy violet breath :
     Och, orro, orro, ollalu !

By strand and road, by field and fen,
   The sorrowing clans come thronging all;
From camp and dun, from hill and glen,
   They crowd around the castle wall.
     Och, orro, orro, ollalu !

A LAMENTATION.—*Continued.*

From East and West, from South and North
  To join the funeral train they hie,
And now the mourners issue forth,
  And far they spread the *keening* cry.
    Och, orro, orro, ollalu !

Then raise the woful *Phillalu,*
  And let your tears in streams be shed,
Och, orro, orro, ollalu !
  The Chieftain's pride, his heir, is dead.

------o------

THE NEW MOON.

By Samuel Lover.

When our attention is directed to the New Moon by one of the opposite sex. it
is considered lucky.

Oh, don't you remember the lucky new moon,
Which I show'd you as soon as it peep'd forth at eve?
When I spoke of omens, and you spoke of love,
And in both, the fond heart will for ever believe!
And while you whisper'd soul-melting words in my ear
I trembled—for love is related to fear;
And before that same moon had declined in its wane,
I held you my own, in a mystical chain;
Oh, bright was the omen, for love follow'd soon,
And I bless'd as I gazed on the lovely new Moon.

And don't you remember those two trembling stars?
That rose up, like gems, from the depths of the sea!
Or like two young lovers, who stole forth at eve
To meet one another, like you, love, and me.
And we thought them a type of our meeting on earth,
Which show'd that our love had in heaven its birth.
The Moon's waning crescent soon faded away,
But the love she gave birth to, will never decay!
Oh, bright was the omen, for love follow'd soon,
And I bless when I gaze on the lovely new Moon.

THE VALLEY LAY SMILING BEFORE ME.

By Thomas Moore.

THE valley lay smiling before me,
  Where lately I left her behind ;
Yet I trembled, and something hung o'er me,
  That sadden'd the joy of my mind.
I look'd for the lamp which she told me
  Should shine when her Pilgrim return'd ;
But though darkness began to enfold me,
  No lamp from the battlements burn'd.

I flew to her chamber—'twas lonely
  As if the lov'd tenant lay dead !—
Ah ! would it were death, and death only !
  But no—the young false one had fled.
And there hung the lute that could soften
  My very worst pains into bliss,
While the hand that had wak'd it so often
  Now throbb'd to a proud rival's kiss.

There was a time, falsest of women !
  When Breffni's good sword would have sought
That man, through a million of foemen,
  Who dar'd but to doubt thee *in thought !*
While now—oh, degenerate daughter
  Of Erin—now fall'n is thy fame !
And, through ages of bondage and slaughter,
  Our country shall bleed for thy shame.

Already the curse is upon her,
  And strangers her valleys profane ;
They come to divide—to dishonor,
  And tyrants they long will remain.
But, onward !—the green banner rearing,
  Go, flesh ev'ry sword to the hilt ;
On *our* side is Virtue and Erin !
  On *theirs* is the Saxon and Guilt.

IT MAY BE YET.

By Samuel Lover.

"It may be yet, it may be yet :"
   How oft that dreamy thought hath charm'd!
"It may be yet, it may be yet,"
   Hath oft despair disarm'd.
The Sun, tho' clouded all the day,
   In glory bright may set ;
So may we watch for Love's bright ray,
And, hopeful thro' the darkness, say,
   "It may be yet, it may be yet,
   My own dear love, it may be yet !"

The sailor, by some dangerous shore,
   Impatient on a breezeless tide,
Within the breakers' warning roar
   That tells where dangers bide,
Undaunted still, with hopeful care
   His steadfast eye is set
To watch the coming breeze so fair—
That breath from Heaven—that whispers there,
   "It may be yet, it may be yet,
   Oh! sailor bold, it may be yet !"

The weeping maid, in sunlit bow'r,
   Whose sparkling dew-drops mock her tears,
Waking her harp's pathetic pow'r
   Some strain of gladness hears :
As if some pitying angel's wing
   O'er chords with tear-drops wet,
Had gently swept the wailing string,
And bade one tone of promise ring
   "It may be yet, it may be yet,
   Oh ! weeping maid, it may be yet !"

MO CRAOIBHIN CNO.*

By Edward Walsh.

My heart is far from Liffey's tide
    And Dublin town;
It strays beyond the Southern side
    Of Cnoc-Maol-Donn,†
Where Capa-chuinn‡ hath woodlands green,
  Where Amhan-Mhor's § waters flow,
Where dwells unsung, unsought, unseen,
    Mo craoibhin cno !
Low clustering in her leafy screen,
    Mo craoibhin cno!

The high-bred dames of Dublin town
    Are rich and fair,
With wavy plume and silken gown,
    And stately air;
Can plumes compare thy dark brown hair?
  Can silks thy neck of snow?
Or measur'd pace thine artless grace,
    Mo craoibhin cno ?
When harebells scarcely show thy trace,
    Mo craoibhin cno ?

I've heard the songs by Liffey's wave
    That maidens sung—
They sung their land the Saxon's slave,
    In Saxon tongue—
Oh ! bring me here that Gaelic dear
  Which cursed the Saxon foe,
When thou didst charm my raptured ear,
    Mo craoibhin cno !
And none but God's good angels near,
    Mo craoibhin cno !

---

* *Mocraoibhin cno* literally means *my cluster of nuts;* but it figuratively signifies *my nut-brown maid.*

† *Cnoc-maol-Donn—The Brown bare hill.* A lofty mountain between the county of Tipperary and that of Waterford, commanding a glorious prospect of unrivalled scenery.

‡ Cappoquin. A romantically situated town on the Blackwater, in the county of Waterford. The Irish name denotes the *head of the tribe of Conn.*

§ *Amhon-mhor—The Great River.* The Blackwater, which flows into the sea at Youghal. The Irish name is uttered in two sounds, *Oan Vore.*

MO CRAOIBHIN CNO.—*Continued.*

I've wandered by the rolling Lee!
    And Lene's green bowers—
I've seen the Shannon's wide-spread sea,
    And Limerick's towers—
And Liffey's tide, where halls of pride
  Frown o'er the flood below ;
My wild heart strays to Amhan-mhor's side
    Mo craoibhin cno!
With love and thee for aye to bide,
    Mo craoibhin cno!

———o———

THE FAIRY TEMPTER.

By Samuel Lover.

A FAIR girl was sitting in the green-wood shade,
List'ning to the music the spring birds made,
When, sweeter by far than the birds on the tree,
A voice murmur'd near her, " Oh come, love, with me.
        In earth or air,
        A thing so fair
      I have not seen as thee !
  Then come, love, with me."

" With a Star for thy home, in a palace of light,
Thou wilt add a fresh grace to the beauty of night ;
Or, if wealth be thy wish, thine are treasures untold,—
I will show thee the birthplace of jewels and gold.
        And pearly caves,
        Beneath the waves,
      All these, all these are thine,
  If thou wilt be mine."

Thus whisper'd a Fairy to tempt the fair girl,
But vain was his promise of gold and of pearl ;
For she said. " Tho' thy gifts to a poor girl were dear,
My Father, my Mother, my Sisters are here.
        Oh! what would be
        Thy gifts to me
      Of Earth, and Sea, and Air,
  If my heart were not there ?"

THE LUPRACAUN: OR FAIRY SHOEMAKER.

(A rhyme for children.)

By William Allingham.

LITTLE cowboy, what have you heard,
  Up on the lonely rath's green mound?
Only the plaintive yellow bird
  Singing in sultry fields around,
Charry, charry, charry, chee-e!
Only the grasshopper and the bee?
    " Tip-tap, rip-rap,
    Tick-a-tack-too!
  Scarlet leather sewn together,
    This will make a shoe.
  Left, right, pull it tight:
    Summer days are warm;
  Underground, in winter,
    Laughing at the storm!"
Lay your ear close to the hill,
Do you not catch the tiny clamor;
Busy click of an elfin hammer,
Voice of the Lupracaun sinking shrill
  As he merrily plies his trade?
    He's a span
    And a quarter in height.
Get him in sight, hold him fast,
    And you're a made
      Man!

You watch your cattle the summer day,
Sup on potatoes sleep in the hay;
  How should you like to roll in your carriage,
  And look for a duchess's daughter in marriage?
Seize the Shoemaker—so you may!
    " Big boots a hunting,
    Sandals in the hall,
  White for a wedding feast,
    And pink for a ball.
  This way, that way,
    So we make a shoe,
  Getting rich every stich,
    Tick-tack-too!

THE LUPRACAUN: OR FAIRY SHOEMAKER.
Continued.

Nine and ninety treasure-crocks
This keen miser-fairy hath,
Hid in mountain, wood, and rocks,
Ruin and round-tower, cave and rath,
  And where the cormorants build;
      From times of old
      Guarded by him;
      Each of them filled
      Full to the brim
        With gold!

I caught him at work one day myself,
  In the castle-ditch where the foxglove grows;
A wrinkled, wizened, and bearded elf,
  Spectacles stuck on the point of his nose,
  Silver buckles to his hose,
  Leather apron—shoe in his lap—
    " Rip-rap, tip-tap,
    Tick-tack-too!
  A grig skipped upon my cap,
    Away the moth flew.
  Buskins for a fairy prince,
    Brogues for his son,—
  Pay me well, pay me well,
    When the job is done!"
The rogue was mine, beyond a doubt,
I stared at him; he stared at me;
" Servant, sir!" " Humph!" says he,
  And pulled a snuffbox out.
He took a long pinch, looked better pleased,
  The queer little Lupracaun;
Offered the box with a whimsical grace,—
Pouf! he flung the dust in my face,
  And, while I sneezed,
    Was gone!

THIS LIFE IS ALL CHEQUERED.

By Thomas Moore.

This life is all chequer'd with pleasures and woes,
  That chase one another like waves of the deep,
Each billow, as brightly or darkly it flows,
  Reflecting our eyes as they sparkle or weep.
So closely our whims on our miseries tread,
  That the laugh is awak'd ere the tear can be dried;
And, as fast as the rain-drop of Pity is shed,
  The goose-feathers of Folly can turn it aside,

But pledge me the cup—if existence would cloy,
  With hearts ever happy, and heads ever wise;
Be ours the light grief that is sister to joy,
  And the short brilliant folly that flashes and dies.
When Hylas was sent with his urn to the fount,
  Thro' fields full of sunshine, with heart full of play,
Light rambled the boy over meadow and mount,
  And neglected his task for the flow'rs on the way.

Thus, some who like me, should have drawn and have tasted
  The fountain that runs by philosophy's shrine,
Their time with the flow'rs on the margin have wasted,
  And left their light urns as empty as mine!
But pledge me the goblet—while idleness weaves
  Her flow'rets together, if wisdom can see
One bright drop or two, that had fall'n on the leaves
  From her fountain divine, 'tis sufficient for me.

——o——

OH! HAD WE SOME BRIGHT LITTLE ISLE.

By Thomas Moore.

Oh! had we some bright little isle of our own,
In a blue summer ocean far off and alone;
Where a leaf never dies in the still blooming bow'rs,
And the bee banquets on through a whole year of flow'rs;
Where the sun loves to pause with so fond a delay,
That the night only draws a thin veil o'er the day.
Where simply to feel that we breathe, that we live,
Is worth the best joys that life else can give!

OH ! HAD WE SOME BRIGHT LITTLE ISLE.—*Continued.*

There with soul ever ardent and pure as the clime,
We should love as they lov'd in the first golden time ;
The glow of the sunshine, the balm of the air,
Would steal to our hearts, and make all summer there !
With affection, as free from decline as the bowers,
And with hope, like the bee, living always on flowers,
Our life should resemble a long day of light,
And our death come on holy and calm as the night !

——o——

REMEMBER THE GLORIES OF BRIEN THE BRAVE.

By Thomas Moore.

REMEMBER the glories of Brien the Brave,
  Though the days of the hero are o'er
Though lost to Mononia, and cold in the grave,
  He returns to Kinkora no more !
That star of the field, which so often has pour'd
  Its beam on the battle, is set ;
But enough of its glory remains on each sword
  To light us to victory yet !

Mononia ! when nature embellish'd the tint
  Of thy fields and thy mountains so fair,
Did she ever intend that a tyrant should print
  The footstep of Slavery there !
No, Freedom ! whose smile we shall never resign,
  Go, tell our invaders, the Danes,
That 'tis sweeter to bleed for an age at thy shrine,
  Than to sleep but a moment in chains !

Forget not our wounded companions who stood
  In the day of distress by our side ;
While the moss of the valley grew red with their blood,
  They stirr'd not but conquer'd and died !
The sun that now blesses our arms with his light
  Saw them fall upon Ossory's plain !
Oh ! let him not blush, when he leaves us to-night,
  To find that they fell there in vain !

YES AND NO.

By Samuel Lover.

There are two little words that we use,
  Without thinking from whence they both came,
But if you will list to my muse,
  The birth-place of each I will name:
The one came from Heaven, to bless,
  The other was sent from below:
What a sweet little angel is " Yes!"
  What a demon-like dwarf is that "No!"

And "No" has a friend he can bid
  To aid all his doings as well,
In the delicate arch it lies hid
  That adorns the bright eye of the belle;
Beware of the shadowy Frown
  Which darkens her bright brow of snow,
As, bent like a bow to strike down,
  Her lip gives you death with a "No."

But "Yes" has a twin-sister sprite,—
  'Tis a Smile you will easily guess,—
That sheds a more heavenly light
  On the doings of dear little "Yes;"
Increasing the charm of the lip
  That is going some lover to bless,
Oh sweet is the exquisite smile
  That dimples and plays around "Yes."

————o————

NEVER DESPAIR.

By Samuel Lover.

Oh never despair, for our hopes oftentime
Spring swiftly as flow'rs in some tropical clime,
Where the spot that was barren and scentless at night
Is blooming and fragrant at morning's first light;
The mariner marks where the tempest sings loud
That the rainbow is brighter the darker the cloud,
    Then up! up! Never despair!

NEVER DESPAIR.—*Continued.*

The leaves which the Sybil presented of old,
Tho' lessen'd in number were not worth less gold;
And tho' Fate steal our joys, do not think they're the best,
The few she has spared may be worth all the rest;
Good-fortune oft comes in Adversity's form,
And the rainbow is brightest when darkest the storm,
  Then up! up! Never despair!

And when all creation was sunk in the flood,
Sublime o'er the deluge the Patriarch stood;
Tho destruction around him in thunder was hurl'd,
Undaunted he looked on the wreck of the world;
For high o'er the ruin hung Hope's blessed form,
The rainbow beamed bright thro' the gloom of the storm,
  Then up! up! Never despair!

————o————

NATIVE MUSIC.

By Samuel Lover.

Air.—"A Sailor Courted a Farmer's Daughter."

Oh, native music! beyond comparing
The sweetest far on the ear that falls,
Thy gentle numbers the heart remembers,
Thy strains enchain us in tender thralls.
  Thy tones endearing,
  Or sad or cheering,
The absent soothe on a foreign strand:
  Oh! who can tell
  What a holy spell
Is in the song of our native land?

The proud and lowly, the pilgrim holy,
The lover, kneeling at beauty's shrine,
The bard who dreams by the haunted streams,—
All, all are touch'd by thy power divine!
  The captive cheerless,
  The soldier fearless,
The mother,—taught by Nature's hand,
  Her child when weeping,
  Will lull to sleeping,
With some sweet song of her native land!

THE WILD GEESE.*

A BRIGADE BALLAD.

By Dr. Drennan.

How solemn sad by Shannon's flood
  The blush of morning sun appears!
To men who gave for us their blood,
  Ah! what can woman give but tears?
How still the field of battle lies!
  No shouts upon the breeze are blown!
We heard our dying country's cries,
  We sit deserted and alone.
    Ogh hone, ogh hone, ogh hone, ogh hone,
    Ogh hone, &c.
Ah! what can woman give but tears!

Why thus collected on the strand
  Whom yet the God of mercy saves,
Will ye forsake your native land?
  Will you desert your brothers' graves?
Their graves give forth a fearful groan—
  Oh! guard your orphans and your wives;
Like us, make Erin's cause your own,
  Like us, for her yield up your lives.
    Ogh hone, ogh hone, ogh hone, ogh hone,
    Ogh hone, &c.
Like us, for her yield up your lives.

———o———

THE BLARNEY.

By Samuel Lover.

There is a certain coign-stone on the summit of Blarney Castle, in the county of Cork, the kissing of which is said to impart the gift of persuasion. Hence the phrase, applied to those who make a flattering speech,—"you've kissed the Blarney Stone."

Oh! did you ne'er hear of the "Blarney"
That's found near the banks of Killarney?
    Believe it from me,
    No girl's heart is free,
Once she hears the sweet sound of the Blarney.

* "The Wild Geese' was the popular name for the recruits of the Irish Brigade.

THE BLARNEY.—*Continued.*

For the Blarney's so great a deceiver,
That a girl thinks you're there, though you leave her;
    And never finds out
    All the tricks you're about,
Till she's quite gone herself,—with your Blarney.

Oh! say, would you find this same " Blarney? "
There's a castle, not far from Killarney,
    On the top of it's wall—
    (But take care you don't fall),
There's a stone that contains all this Blarney.
Like a magnet, its influence such is,
That attraction it gives all it touches;
    If you kiss it, they say,
    From that blessed day
You may kiss whom you please with your Blarney.

———o———

LIVE IN MY HEART AND PAY NO RENT.*

By Samuel Lover.

VOURNEEN, when your days were bright,
  Never an eye did I dare to lift to you,
But, now, in your fortune's blight,
  False ones are flying, in sunshine that knew you,
But still on one welcome true rely,
Tho' the crops may fail, and the cow go dry,
And the cabin be burn'd—and all be spent,
Come live in my heart and pay no rent!
    Live in my heart, *Ma Vourneen!*

Vourneen, dry up those tears;—
  The sensible people will tell you to wait, dear;
But, ah, in the wasting of love's young years,
  On our innocent hearts we're committing a cheat, dear:—
For hearts, when they're young, should pledge the vow,
For when they grow old sure they don't know how,
So, marry at once—and you'll ne'er repent, †
When you live in my heart and pay no rent.
    Come! live in my heart, *Ma Vourneen.*

*One of many affectionate Irish sayings.
† An allusion to another old Irish saying, " Marry in haste, and repent at leisure."

SALLY.

By Samuel Lover.

" SALLY, Sally, shilly, shally,
    Sally, why not name the day ? "
" Harry, Harry, I will tarry
    Longer in love's flow'ry way !"
" Can't you make your mind up, Sally?
    Why embitter thus my cup?"
" Harry, I've so great a mind,
    It takes a long time making up."

" Sally, Sally, in the valley,
    You have promised many a time,
On the sunny Sunday morning,
    As we've heard the matin chime ;
Heark'ning to those sweet bells ringing,
    Calling grateful hearts to pray,
I have whispered—' Oh ! how sweetly
    They'll proclaim our wedding day!' "

" Harry, Harry, I'll not marry,
    Till I see your eyes don't stray ;
At Kate Riley, you, so shly,
    Stole a wink the other day."
" Sure Kate Riley, she's my cousin:"
    " Harry, I've a cousin too ;
If *you* like such close relations,
    I'll have cousins close as you."

" Sally, Sally, do not rally,
    Do not mock my tender woe ;
Play me not thus shilly shally.
    Sally, do not tease me so !
While you're smiling, hearts beguiling,
    Doing all a woman can ;
Think—though you're almost an angel,
    I am but a mortal man !"

MY MOUNTAIN HOME.

By Samuel Lover.

My mountain home! My mountain home!
  Dear are thy hills to me!
Where first my childhood lov'd to roam—
  Wild, as the summer bee:
The summer bee may gather sweet
  From flow'rs in sunny prime;
And mem'ry brings, with wing as fleet,
  Sweet thoughts of early time:
Still fancy bears me to the hills,
  Where childhood lov'd to roam—
I hear—I see your sparkling rills,
  My own, my mountain home!

I've seen their noble forests wide,
  I've seen their smiling vale;
Where proudly rolls the silver tide
  That bears their glorious sail:—
But these are of the earth below;
  Our home is in the sky!
The eagle's flight is not more bright
  Than paths that we may try!
While all around sweet echoes ring,
  Beneath heaven's azure dome;—
Then, well the mountaineer may sing,
  " My own, my mountain home!"

——o——

MY MOTHER DEAR.

By Samuel Lover.

There was a place in childhood that I remember well,
And there a voice of sweetest tone bright fairy tales did tell,
And gentle words and fond embrace were giv'n with joy to me,
When I was in that happy place,—upon my mother's knee.

When fairy tales were ended, " Good-night," she softly said,
And kiss'd and laid me down to sleep within my tiny bed:
And holy words she taught me there—methinks I yet can see
Her angel eyes, as close I knelt beside my mother's knee.

MY MOTHER DEAR.—*Continued.*

In the sickness of my childhood; the perils of my prime:
The sorrows of my riper years; the cares of ev'ry time;
When doubt and danger weighed me down—then pleading
    all for me,
It was a fervent pray'r to Heaven that bent my mother's knee.

———o———

BEFORE THE BATTLE.

By Thomas Moore.

By the hope within us springing,
  Herald of to-morrow's strife,
And by that sun, whose light is bringing
  Chains or freedom, death or life—
Oh! remember life can be
No charm for him who lives not free.
  Sinks the hero to his grave,
  Like the day-star in the wave,
Midst the dew-fall of a nation's tears.
  Blessed is he o'er whose decline
  The smiles of home may soothing shine,
And light him down the steep of years,
  But oh! how grand they sink to rest,
  Who close their eyes in vict'ry's breast.

O'er his watch-fire's fading embers,
  Now the foeman's cheek turns white,
While his heart that field remembers,
  Where we dimm'd his glory's light.
Never let him bind again
A chain like that we broke from then.
  Hark! the horn of combat calls—
  Oh! before the evening falls,
May we pledge that horn in triumph round.
  Many a heart that now beats high,
  In slumber cold at night shall lie,
Nor waken even at victory's sound;—
  But oh! how blest that hero's sleep,
  O'er whom a wondering world shall weep!

THE SORROWFUL LAMENTATION OF CALLAGHAN
GREALLY AND MULLEN,
KILLED AT THE FAIR OF TURLOUGHMORE.

" Come tell me, dearest mother, what makes my father stay,
Or what can be the reason that he's so long away?"
" Oh I hold your tongue, my darling son, your tears do grieve
   me sore,
I fear he has been murdered at the fair of Turloughmore."

Come, all you tender Christians, I hope you will draw near,
It's of this dreadful murder I mean to let you hear,
Concerning those poor people whose loss we do deplore—
(The Lord have mercy on their souls) that died at Turlough-
   more.

It was on the First of August, the truth I will declare,
Those people they assembled that day all at the fair;
But little was their notion what evil was in store,
All by the bloody Peelers at the fair of Turloughmore.

Were you to see that dreadful sight it would grieve your
   heart I know,
To see the comely women and the men all lying low;
God help their tender parents, they will never see them more,
For cruel was their murder at the fair of Turloughmore.

It's for that base blood-thirsty crew, remark the word I say,
The Lord he will reward them against the judgment-day,
The blood they have taken innocent for it they'll suffer sore,
And the treatment that they gave to us that day at Turlough-
   more.

The morning of their trial as they stood up in the dock,
The words they spoke were feeling, the people round them
   flock,
"I tell you, Judge and Jury, the truth I will declare,
It was Brew that ordered us to fire that evening at the fair."

THE SORROWFUL LAMENTATION OF CALLAGHAN,
GREALLY AND MULLEN.—*Continued.*

Now to conclude and finish this sad and doleful fray,
I hope their souls are happy against the judgment-day;
It was little time they got, we know, when they fell like new-
mowed hay,
May the Lord have mercy on their souls against the judg-
ment-day.

THE SNOW.

By Samuel Lover.

An old man sadly said,
 Where's the snow
That fell the year that's fled—
 Where's the snow ?
As fruitless were the task
Of many a joy to ask,
 As the snow !

The hope of airy birth,
 Like the snow,
Is stained on reaching earth,
 Like the snow :
While 'tis sparkling in the ray
'Tis melting fast away,
 Like the snow.

A cold deceitful thing
 Is the snow,
Though it come on dove-like wing—
 The false snow !
'Tis but rain disguis'd appears;
And our hopes are frozen tears—
 Like the snow.

——o——

BETWEEN MY SLEEVE AND ME.

By Samuel Lover.

My Katty, sweet enslaver,
'Twas loth I was to lave her,
I made my best endeavor to keep my courage high;
 But when she softly spoke me
 I thought the grief would choke me,
For pride it would revoke the tear was rising to my eye;
 But, as the grief grew stronger,
 I dared not linger longer,

BETWEEN MY SLEEVE AND ME.—*Continued.*

One kiss!—sure 'twas not wrong before I rush'd away to sea,
    No one could then discover
    The weakness of the lover,
And, if my grief ran over—'twas between my sleeve and me.

    Oh! 'twould be hard believing
    How fond hearts may be grieving
When taking or when giving merry jokes with comrades
    gay,
    While deeper thoughts are straying,
    Some distant land away in,
Like wand'ring pilgrims praying at some shrine that's far
    away,
    When merry cups are ringing,
    I join the round of singing,
To help the joyous winging of the sportive evening's glee;
    But when the mirth is over,
    My sadness none discover,
For if my grief runs over—'tis between my sleeve and me.

——o——

FATHER LAND AND MOTHER TONGUE.

By Samuel Lover.

Our Father land! and would'st thou know
    Why we should call it Father land?
It is, that Adam here below,
    Was made of earth by Nature's hand;
And he, our father, made of earth,
    Hath peopled earth on ev'ry hand,
And we, in memory of his birth,
    Do call our country, " Father land."

At first, in Eden's bowers, they say,
    No sound of speech had Adam caught,
But whistled like a bird all day—
    And may be, 'twas for want of thought:
But Nature, with resistless laws,
    Made Adam soon surpass the birds,
She gave him lovely Eve—because
    If he'd a wife—they must *have words.*

FATHER LAND AND MOTHER TONGUE.—*Continued.*

And so, the NATIVE LAND I hold,
  By male descent is proudly mine ;
The LANGUAGE, as the tale hath told,
  Was given in the female line.
And thus, we see, on either hand,
  We name our blessings whence they've sprung,
We call our country FATHER *land,*
  We call our language MOTHER *tongue.*

———o———

KATHLEEN AND THE SWALLOWS.

BY SAMUEL LOVER.

SWEET Kathleen, bewitching young charmer,
  Look'd cautiously round thro' the vale,
Not a sight nor a sound did alarm her,
  As she set down her full milking-pail ;
Then, quick o'er a letter she bended
  With eager intent her dark eye,
Do you think that young Kate was offended ?—
  Let her smile of contentment reply.

"Oh Kate," said the letter," believe me,
  While wand'ring o'er land and o'er sea,
No time of my love can bereave thee,
  Thou ever art present to me.
As the hills, o'er the lake softly swelling,
  In the waters reflected are seen,
So softly, so deeply is dwelling
  In my heart thy sweet image, Kathleen !"

Now, as there is no one to hear me,
  Says Kathleen, "I'll speak out what's true :
I wish, Dermot dear, you were near me,
  Or at least, dear, that I was near you !
O'er the water is sporting the swallow,"
  Sigh'd Kathleen—a tear in her eye,
" Oh ! 'tis o'er the wide world I would follow
  My Dermot *astore*, could I fly ! "

DERMOT O'DOWD.

By Samuel Lover.

WHEN Dermot O'Dowd coorted Molly M'Can,
　They were sweet as the honey and soft as the down,
But when they were wed they began to find out
　That Dermot could storm and that Molly could frown;
They would neither give in—so the neighbors gave out—
　Both were hot, till a coldness came over the two,
And Molly would flusther, and Dermot would blusther,
　Stamp holes in the flure, and cry out " wirrasthru!
　　　　Oh murther! I'm married,
　　　　I wish I had tarried;
　　I'm sleepless and speechless—no word can I say,
　　　　My bed is no use,
　　　　I'll give back to the goose
　　The feathers I plucked on last Michaelmas day."

" Ah!" says Molly, " you once used to call me a bird."
　" Faix, you're ready enough still to fly out," says he.
" You said then my eyes were as bright as the skies,
　And my lips like the rose—now no longer like me."
Says Dermot, " your eyes are as bright as the morn,
　But your brow is as black as a big thunder cloud,
If your lip is a rose—sure your tongue is a thorn
　That sticks in the heart of poor Dermot O'Dowd."

Says Molly, " you once said my voice was a thrush,
　But now it's a rusty ould hinge with a creak;"
Says Dermot, " you call'd me a duck when I coorted,
　But now I'm a goose every day in the week.
But all husbands are geese, though our pride it may shock,
　From the first 'twas ordained so by Nature, I fear,
Ould Adam himself was the first o' the flock,
　And Eve, with her apple sauce, cooked him, my dear."

THE HOUR BEFORE DAY.

BY SAMUEL LOVER.

There is a beautiful saying amongst the Irish peasantry to inspire hope under adverse circumstances.—" Remember," they say, " that the darkest hour of all, is the hour before day."

BEREFT of his love, and bereaved of his fame,
A knight to the cell of the old hermit came;
" My foes they have slander'd and forced me to fly,
Oh, tell me, good father, what's left but to die ? "
" Despair not, my son ;—thou'lt be righted ere long—
For heaven is above us to right all the wrong !
Remember the words the old hermit doth say,—
'Tis always the darkest, the hour before day !'

" Then back to the tourney and back to the court,
And join thee, the bravest, in chivalry's sport ;
Thy foes will be there—and thy lady-love too,
And show *both*, thou'rt a knight that is gallant and true ! "
He rode in the lists—all his foes he o'erthrew,
And a sweet glance he caught from a soft eye of blue.
And he thought of the words the old hermit did say,
For her glance was as bright as the dawning of day.

The feast it was late in the castle that night,
And the banquet was beaming with beauty and light ;
But brightest of all is the lady who glides
To the porch where a knight with a fleet courser bides.
She paused 'neath the arch, at the fierce ban dog's bark,
She trembled to look on the night—'twas so dark ;
But her lover, he whisper'd—and thus did he say,
" Sweet love, it is darkest, the hour before day."

THE PILGRIM HARPER.

By Samuel Lover.

THE night was cold and dreary—no star was in the sky,
When, travel-tired and weary, the harper raised his cry;
He raised his cry without the gate, his night's repose to win,
And plaintive was the voice that cried, "Ah, won't you
     let me in?"

The portal soon was open'd, for in the land of song,
The minstrel at the outer gate yet never linger'd long;
And inner doors were seldom closed 'gainst wand'rers
     such as he
For locks or hearts to open soon, sweet music is the key.

But if gates are oped by melody, so grief can close them fast,
And sorrow o'er that once bright hall its silent spell had cast;
All undisturb'd the spider there, his web might safely spin,
For many a day no festive lay—no harper was let in.

But when this harper enter'd, and said he came from far,
And bore with him from Palestine the tidings of the war,
And he could tell of all who fell, or glory there did win,
The warder knew his noble dame would let *that* harper in.

———o———

I LEAVE YOU TO GUESS.

By Samuel Lover.

THERE'S a lad that I know; and I know that he
     Speaks softly to me
     The *cushla-ma-chree.*
He's the pride of my heart, and he loves me well,
But who the lad is,—I'm not going to tell.

He's as straight as a rush, and as bright as the stream
     That around it doth gleam,
     Oh! of him how I dream;
I'm as high as his shoulder—the way that I know
Is, he caught me one day, just my measure to show.

I LEAVE YOU TO GUESS.—*Continued.*

He whisper'd a question one day in my ear;
When he breathed it,—oh dear!
How I trembled with fear!
What the question he ask'd was, I need not confess,
But the answer I gave to the question was—" Yes."

His eyes they are bright, and they looked so kind
When I was inclined
To speak my mind.
And his breath is so sweet—oh, the rose's is less,
And how I found it out,—why, I leave you to guess.

————o————

THE MAY-DEW.

By Samuel Lover.

To gather the dew from the flowers on May-morning, before the sun has risen is reckoned a bond of peculiar power between lovers.

Come with me, love, I'm seeking
A spell in the young year's flowers;
The magical May-dew is weeping
Its charm o'er the summer bow'rs;
Its pearls are more precious than those they find
In jewell'd India's sea;
For the dew-drops, love, might serve to bind
Thy heart, for ever, to me!
Oh come with me, love, I'm seeking
A spell in the young year's flowers;
The magical May-dew is weeping
Its charm o'er the summer bow'rs.

Haste, or the spell will be missing,
We seek in the May-dew now;
For soon the warm sun will be kissing
The bright drops from blossom and bough:

THE MAY-DEW.—*Continued.*

And the charm is so tender the May-dew sheds
   O'er the wild flowers' delicate dyes,
That e'en at the touch of the sunbeam, 'tis said,
   The mystical influence flies.
      Oh come with me, love, I'm seeking
         A spell in the young year's flowers;
      The magical May-dew is weeping
         Its charm o'er the summer bow'rs.

———o———

THE MEETING OF FOES AND THE MEETING OF FRIENDS.

BY SAMUEL LOVER.

FILL the cup! fill it high! Let us drink to the might
Of the manhood that joyously rushes to fight;
And, true to the death, all unflinching will stand,
For our home, and our hearth, and our own native land!
'Tis the bright sun of June, that is gilding the crest
Of the warriors that fight for their isles of the West;
The breeze that at morning but plays with the plume,
At evening may wave the red grass o'er the tomb;
The corn that has ripen'd in summer's soft breath,
In an hour may be reap'd in the harvest of death:
Then drink to their glory—the glory of those
Who triumph'd or fell in that meeting of foes.

But fill the cup higher to drink to the friends
Bound fast in affection that life only ends;
Whose hearths, when defended from foes that have dared,
Are prized all the more when with friends they are shared!
Far better the wine-cup with ruby may flow,
To the health of a friend than the fall of a foe;
Tho' bright are the laurels that glory may twine,
Far softer the shade of the ivy and vine:—
Then fill the cup higher! The battle is won—
Our perils are over—our feast has begun!—
On the meeting of foemen, pale sorrow attends:—
Rosy joy crowns *our* meeting—the meeting of friends!

PADDY'S ISLAND OF GREEN.

AIR.—*"In Ireland so frisky."*

AH, pooh, botheration, dear Ireland's the nation
  Which all other nations together excels;
Where worth, hospitality, conviviality,
  Friendship, and open sincerity dwells.
Sure I've roamed the world over, from Dublin to Dover,
  But, in all the strange countries wherever I've been,
I ne'er saw an island, on sea or on dry land,
  Like Paddy's own sweet little island of green.

In England, your roses make beautiful posies;
  Provoke Scotia's thistle, you'll meet your reward;
But sure for its beauty, an Irishman's duty
  Will teach him his own native plant to regard:
Saint Patrick first set it, with tear-drops he wet it,
  And often to cherish and bless it was seen;
Its virtues are rare, too—it's fresh and it's fair, too—
  And flowers but in Paddy's own island of green.

Oh, long life to old Ireland, its bogs and its moorland,
  For there's not such a universe under the sun
For honor, for spirit, fidelity, merit,
  For wit and good fellowship, frolic and fun!
With wine and with whiskey, when once it gets frisky
  An Irishman's heart in true colors is seen;
With mirth overflowing, with love it is glowing—
  With love for its own native island of green.

——o——

BARNEY O'HEA.

By SAMUEL LOVER.

Now let me alone!—tho' I know you won't,
  Impudent Barney O'Hea!
    It makes me outrageous,
    When you're so contagious,
  And you'd better look out for the stout Corny Creagh,
    For he is the boy
    That believes I'm his joy,
So you'd better behave yourself, Barney O'Hea!

BARNEY O'HEA.—*Continued.*

Impudent Barney!
None of your blarney!
Impudent Barney O'Hea!

I hope you're not going to Bandon fair,
For indeed I'm not wanting to meet you there!
Impudent Barney O'Hea!
For Corny's at Cork,
And my brother's at work,
And my mother sits spinning at home all the day.
So as none will be there
Of poor me to take care,
I hope you wont follow me, Barney O'Hea!
Impudent Barney!
None of your blarney!
Impudent Barney O'Hea!

But as I was walking up Bandon street,
Just who do you think 'twas myself should meet,
But that impudent Barney O'Hea!
He said I look'd killin',
I call'd him a villain,
And bid him, that minute, get out of my way.
He said I was jokin'—
And look'd so provokin'—
I could not help laughing with Barney O'Hea!
Impudent Barney!
'Tis he has the blarney!
That impudent Barney O'Hea!

He knew 'twas all right when he saw me smile,
For he is the rogue up to every wile,
That impudent Barney O'Hea!
He coax'd me to choose him,
For, if I'd refuse him,
He swore he'd kill Corny the very next day;
So, for fear 'twould go further,
And—just to save murther,
I think I must marry that madcap O'Hea.
Bothering Barney!
'Tis he has the blarney!
To make a girl Misthress O'Hea!

WHAT WILL YOU DO, LOVE?

By Samuel Lover.

" WHAT will you do, love, when I am going
With white sail flowing,
     The seas beyond—
What will you do, love, when waves divide us
And friends may chide us
     For being fond ? "
" Tho' waves divide us—and friends be chiding,
In faith abiding,
     I'll still be true !
And I'll pray for thee on the stormy ocean,
In deep devotion—
     That's what I'll do ! "

' What would you do, love, if distant tidings
Thy fond confidings
     Should undermine ?—
And I, abiding 'neath sultry skies,
Should think other eyes
     Were as bright as thine ? "—
" Oh, name it not !—Tho' guilt and shame
Were on thy name
     I'd still be true :
But that heart of thine—should another share it—
I could not bear it !
     What would I do ? "

"What would you do, love, when home returning
With hopes high burning,
     With wealth for you,
If my bark, which bounded o'er foreign foam
Should be lost near home—
     Ah ! what would you do ? "—
" So thou wert spared—I'd bless the morrow,
In want and sorrow,
     That left me you :
And I'd welcome thee from the wasting billow,
This heart thy pillow—
     That's what I'd do ! "

PADDY'S PASTORAL RHAPSODY.

By Samuel Lover.

WHEN Molly, th' other day, sir,
Was makin' of the hay, sir,
I ask'd her for to be my bride,
And Molly she began to chide ;
Says she, " you are too young, dear Pat,"
Says I, "my jew'l, I'll mend o' that."
" You are too poor," says she beside,
And to convince her then I tried,
That wealth is an invintion
Which the wise should never mintion,
And that flesh is grass, and flowers will fade,
And it's better be wed than die an owld maid.

The purty little sparrows
Have neither ploughs nor harrows,
Yet they live at aise and are contint,
Bekase, you see, they pay no rint.
They have no care nor flustherin',
About diggin' or *industherin'*,
No foolish pride their comfort hurts—
For they *eat* the flax and wear no shirts—
For wealth is an invintion, &c., &c.

Sure Nature clothes the hills, dear,
Without any tailors' bills, dear,
And the bees they sip their sweets, my sowl,
Though they never had a sugar bowl,
The dew it feeds the rose of June—
But 'tis not from a silver spoon :
Then let us patthern take from those,
The birds, and bees, and lovely rose,
For wealth is an invintion, &c., &c.

Here's a cup to you, my darlin',
Tho' I'm not worth a farthin',
I'll pledge my coat to drink your health,
And then I'll envy no man's wealth ;
For when I'm drunk, I think I'm rich,
I've a feather bed in every ditch,
I dhrame o' you, my heart's delight,
And how could I pass a pleasanter night?
For wealth is an invintion, &c., &c.

THERE'S NO SUCH GIRL AS MINE.

By Samuel Lover.

OH, there's no such girl as mine
  In all the wide world round;
With her hair of golden twine,
  And her voice of silver sound.
Her eyes are as black as the sloes,
  And quick is her ear so fine,
And her breath is as sweet as the rose,
  There's no such girl as mine!

Her spirit so sweetly flows,
  Unconscious winner of hearts,
There's a smile wherever she goes,
  There's a sigh whenever she parts;
A blessing she wins from the poor,
  To court her the rich all incline,
She's welcome at every door—
  O there's no such girl as mine!

She's light to the banquet hall,
  She's balm to the couch of care,
In sorrow—in mirth—in all—
  She takes her own sweet share.
Enchanting the many abroad,
  At home doth she brightest shine,
'Twere endless her worth to laud—
  There's no such girl as mine!

———o———

THE FAIRY BOY.

By Samuel Lover.

When a beautiful child pines and dies, the Irish peasant believes the healthy infant has been stolen by the fairies, and a sickly elf left in its place.

A MOTHER came, when stars were paling,
  Wailing round a lonely spring,
Thus she cried while tears were falling,
  Calling on the Fairy King:
" Why, with spells my child caressing,
  Courting him with fairy joy,
Why destroy a mother's blessing
  Wherefore steal my baby boy?

THE FAIRY BOY.—*Continued.*

"O'er the mountain, thro' the wild wood,
  Where his childhood loved to play,
Where the flow'rs are freshly springing
  There I wander, day by day;
There I wander, growing fonder
  Of the child that made my joy,
On the echoes wildly calling
  To restore my fairy boy.

"But in vain my plaintive calling,
  Tears are falling all in vain,
He now sports with fairy pleasure,
  He's the treasure of their train!
Fare thee well! my child, for ever,
  In this world I've lost my joy,
But in the *next* we ne'er shall sever,
  There I'll find my angel boy."

BAD LUCK TO THIS MARCHING.

Air.—*Paddy O'Carroll.*

Bad luck to this marching,
Pipeclaying and starching;
How neat one must be to be killed by the French!
I'm sick of parading,
Through wet and cowld wading,
Or standing all night to be shot in the trench.
To the tune o' the fife,
They dispose of your life,
You surrender your soul to some illigant lilt,
Now I like Garryowen,
When I hear it at home,
But it's not half so sweet when you're going to be kilt.

Then though up late and early,
Our pay comes so rarely,
The devil a farthing we've ever to spare;
They say some disaster,
Befel the paymaster;
On my conscience, I think that the money's not there.
And, just think, what a blunder;
They won't let us plunder,
While the people invite us to rob them, 'tis clear,
Though there isn't a village,
But cries, "Come and pillage."
Yet we leave all the mutton behind for Mounseer.

Like a sailor that's nigh land,
I long for that island
Where even the kisses we steal if we please;
Where it is no disgrace,
If you don't wash your face,
And you've nothing to do but stand at your ease.
With no sergeant t' abuse us,
We fight to amuse us,
Sure it's better beat Christian than kick a baboon,
How I'd dance like a fairy,
To see ould Dunleary,
And think twice ere I'd leave it to be a dragoon.

BRYAN O'LYNN.

BRYAN O'LYNN was a gentleman born,
He lived at a time when no clothes they were worn,
But as fashions walked out, of course Bryan walked in,
Whoo! I'll soon lead the fashions, says Bryan O'Lynn.

Bryan O'Lynn had no breeches to wear,
He got a sheep skin for to make him a pair;
With the fleshy side out and the woolly side in,
Whoo! they're pleasant and cool, says Bryan O'Lynn.

Bryan O'Lynn had no shirt to his back,
He went to a neighbor's and borrowed a sack,
Then he puckered the meal bag up under his chin,
Whoo! they'll take them for ruffles, says Bryan O'Lynn.

Bryan O'Lynn had no hat to his head,
He stuck on the pot being up to the dead,
Then he murdered a cod for the sake of its fin,
Whoo! 'twill pass for a feather, says Bryan O'Lynn.

Bryan O'Lynn was hard up for a coat,
He borrowed a skin of a neighboring goat,
With the horns sticking out from his oxters, and then,
Whoo! they'll take them for pistols, says Bryan O'Lynn.

Bryan O'Lynn had no stockings to wear,
He bought a rat's skin for to make him a pair,
He then drew them over his manly skin,
Whoo! they're illegant wear, says Bryan O'Lynn.

Bryan O'Lynn had no brogue to his toes,
He hopped in two crab shells to serve him for those,
Then he split up two oysters that matched like twins,
Whoo! they'll shine out like buckles, says Bryan O'Lynn.

Bryan O'Lynn had no watch to put on,
He scooped out a turnip to make him a one,
Then he planted a cricket right under the skin,
Whoo! they'll think it's a ticking, says Bryan O'Lynn.

Bryan O'Lynn to his house had no door,
He'd the sky for a roof, and the bog for a floor;
He'd a way to jump out, and a way to swim in,
Whoo! it's very convaynient, says Bryan O'Lynn.

BRYAN O'LYNN.—*Continued.*

Bryan O'Lynn, his wife and wife's mother,
They all went home o'er the bridge together,
The bridge it broke down, and they all tumbled in,
Whoo! we'll go home by water, says Bryan O'Lynn.

——o——

THE AVENGER.

A Jacobite Relic.

By Jeremiah Joseph Callanan

OH! heavens, if that long-wished-for morning I spied
As high as three kings I'd leap up in my pride;
With transport I'd laugh, and my shout should arise,
As the fire from each mountain blazed bright to the skies.

The Avenger shall lead us right on to the foe;
Our horns should sound out, and our trumpets should blow;
Ten thousand huzzas should ascend to high heaven,
When onr prince was restored, and our fetters were riven.

Oh! Chieftains of Ulster, when will you come forth,
And send your strong cry to the winds of the North?
The wrongs of a king call aloud for your steel—
Red stars of the battle—O'Donnell, O'Néill!

Bright house of O'Connor, high offspring of kings,
Up, up, like the eagle, when heavenward he springs!
Oh! break you once more from the Saxon's strong rule,
Lost race of MacMurchad, O'Bryne, and O'Toole.

Mononia of Druids—green dwelling of song!—
Where, where are thy minstrels—why sleep they thus long?
Does no bard live to wake, as they oft did before,
MacCarthy—O'Brien—O'Sullivan More?

O come from your hills, like the waves to the shore,
When the storm girded-headlands are mad with the roar!
Ten thousand huzzas shall ascend to high heaven,
When our Prince is restored, and our fetters are riven.

THE LAMENTATION OF HUGH REYNOLDS.

A Street Ballad.

My name it is Hugh Reynolds, I come of honest parents,
  Near Cavan I was born, as plainly you may see ;
By loving of a maid, one Catherine MacCabe,
  My life has been betrayed ; she's a dear maid to me.

The country were bewailing my doleful situation,
  But still I'd expectation this maid would set me free ;
But oh! she was ungrateful, her parents proved deceitful,
  And though I loved her faithful, she's a dear maid to me.

Young men and tender maidens, throughout this Irish
        nation,
  Who hear my lamentation, I hope you'll pray for me ;
The truth I will unfold, that my precious blood she sold,
  In the grave I must lie cold, she's a dear maid to me.

For now my glass is run, and the hour it is come,
  And must die for love and the height of loyalty :
I thought it was no harm to embrace her in my arms,
  Or take her from her parents ; but she's a dear maid to me.

Adieu, my loving father, and you, my tender mother,
  Farewell, my dearest brother, who has suffered sore for
        me ;
With irons I'm surrounded, in grief I lie confounded,
  By perjury unbounded ! she's a dear maid to me.

Now, I can say no more, to the Law-board* I must go,
  There to take the last farewell of my friends and coun-
        terie ;
May the angels, shining bright, receive my soul this night,
  And convey me into heaven to the blessed Trinity.

* Gallows.

THE BURIAL OF SIR JOHN MOORE.

By The Rev. Charles Wolfe.

Not a drum was heard, not a funeral note,
  As his corse to the rampart we hurried:
Not a soldier discharged his farewell shot
  O'er the grave where our hero we buried.

We buried him darkly at dead of night,
  The sods with our bayonets turning,
By the struggling moonbeam's misty light,
  And the lantern dimly burning.

No useless coffin enclosed his breast,
  Not in sheet or in shroud we wound him ;
But he lay like a warrior taking his rest,
  With his martial cloak around him.

Few and short were the prayers we said,
  And we spoke not a word of sorrow ;
But we steadfastly gazed on the face that was dead,
  And we bitterly thought of the morrow.

We thought as we hollow'd his narrow bed,
  And smooth'd down his lonely pillow,
That the foe and the stranger would tread o'er his head
  And we far away on the billow !

Lightly they'll talk of the spirit that's gone,
  And o'er his cold ashes upbraid him,—
But little he'll reck, if they let him sleep on
  In the grave where a Briton has laid him.

But half of our heavy task was done,
  When the clock struck the hour for retiring ;
And we heard the distant and random gun
  That the foe was sullenly firing.

Slowly and sadly we laid him down,
  From the field of his fame fresh and gory ;
We carved not a line, we raised not a stone—
  But we left him alone in his glory !

THE GERALDINE'S DAUGHTER.

SPEAK low !—speak low—the Banshee is crying ;
Hark ! hark to the echo !—she's dying ! " she's dying."
What shadow flits dark'ning the face of the water?
'Tis the swan of the lake—'Tis *the Geraldine's Daughter.*

Hush, hush ! have you heard what the Banshee said ?
Oh ! list to the echo l she's dead ! " she's dead !'"
No shadow now dims the face of the water ;
Gone, gone is the wraith of *the Geraldine's Daughter.*

The step of yon train is heavy and slow,
There's wringing of hands, there's breathing of woe
What melody rolls over mountain and water ?
'Tis the funeral chant for *the Geraldine's Daughter.*

The requiem sounds like the plaintive moan
Which the wind makes over the sepulchre's stone ;
" Oh, why did she die? our heart's blood had bought her !
Oh, why did she die, *the Geraldine's Daughter ?*"

The thistle-beard floats—the wild roses wave
With the blast that sweeps over the newly-made grave
The stars dimly twinkle, and hoarse falls the water,
While night-birds are wailing *the Geraldines Daughter.*

———o———

PEGGY BROWNE.

CAÑOLAN. Translated by THOMAS FURLONG.

OH, dark, sweetest girl, are my days doomed to be,
While my heart bleeds in silence and sorrow for thee :
In the green spring of life, to the grave I go down,
Oh ! shield me, and save me, my lov'd Peggy Browne.

I dreamt that at evening my footsteps were bound
To yon deep spreading wood where the shades fall around,
I sought, midst new scenes, all my sorrows to drown,
But the cure of my grief rests with thee, Peggy Browne.

PEGGY BROWNE.—*Continued.*

'Tis soothing, sweet maiden, thy accents to hear,
For, like wild, fairy music, they melt on the ear,
Thy breast is as fair as the swan's clothed in down;
Oh, peerless, and perfect's my own Peggy Browne.

Dear, dear is the bark to its own cherished tree,
But dearer, far dearer, is my lov'd one to me:
In my dreams I draw near her, uncheck'd by a frown,
But my arms spread in vain to embrace Peggy Browne.

————o————

LADY MINE!

By Samuel Lover.

Lady mine! lady mine!
Take the rosy wreath I twine;
All its sweets are less than thine,
    Lady, lady mine!
The blush that on thy cheek is found
Bloometh fresh the *whole* year round;
Thy sweet *breath* as sweet gives *sound*,
    Lady, lady mine!

Lady mine! lady mine!
How I love the graceful vine,
Whose tendrils mock thy ringlets' twine,
    Lady, lady mine!
How I love that gen'rous tree,
Whose ripe clusters promise me
Bumpers bright,—to pledge to *thee,*
    Lady, lady mine!

Lady mine! lady mine!
Like the stars that nightly shine,
Thy sweet eyes shed light divine,
    Lady, lady mine!
And as sages wise, of old,
From the stars could fate unfold,
Thy bright eyes *my* fortune told,
    Lady, lady mine!

TRUE LOVE CAN NE'ER FORGET.

By Samuel Lover.

It is related of Carolan, the Irish bard, that when deprived of sight, and after the lapse of twenty years, he recognized his first love by the touch of her hand. Tho lady's name was Bridget Cruise; and though not a pretty name, it deserves to be recorded, as belonging to the woman who could inspire such a passion.

" True love can ne'er forget :
Fondly as when we met,
Dearest, I love thee yet,
  My darling one !"
Thus sung a minstrel grey
His sweet impassion'd lay,
Down by the ocean's spray,
  At set of sun.
But wither'd was the minstrel's sight,
Morn to him was dark as night,
Yet his heart was full of light,
  As he this lay begun ;
" True love can ne'er forget,
Fondly as when we met,
Dearest, I love thee yet,
  My darling one !

" Long years are past and o'er,
Since from this fatal shore,
Cold hearts and cold winds bore
  My love from me."
Scarcely the minstrel spoke,
When quick, with flashing stroke,
A boat's light oar the silence broke
  Over the sea ;
Soon upon her native strand
Doth a lovely lady land,
While the minstrel's love-taught hand
  Did o'er his wild harp run ;
" True love can ne'er forget,
Fondly as when we met,
Dearest, I love thee yet,
  My darling one !"

TRUE LOVE CAN NE'ER FORGET.—*Continued.*

Where the minstrel sat alone,
There, that lady fair hath gone,
Within his hand she placed her own,
   The bard dropp'd on his knee ;
From his lip soft blessings came,
He kiss'd her hand with truest flame,
In trembling tones he named—*her* name,
   Though her he could not see ;
But oh !—the touch the bard could tell
Of that dear hand, remember'd well,
Ah !—by many a secret spell
   Can true love find his own !
For true love can ne'er forget,
Fondly as when they met ;
He loved his lady yet,
   His darling one.

——o——

THE NIGHTCAP.

JOLLY PHŒBUS his car to the coach-house had driven,
   And unharnessed his high-mettled horses of light ;
He gave them a feed from the manger of heaven,
   And rubbed them, and littered them down for the night.

Then off to the kitchen he leisurely strode,
   Where Thetis, the housemaid, was sipping her tea ;
He swore he was tired with that rough up-hill road,
   He'd have none of her slops nor hot water, not he.

So she took from the corner a little cruiskeen
   Well filled with the nectar Apollo loves best—
From the neat Bog of Allen, some pretty poteen—
   And he tippled his quantum and staggered to rest.

His many-caped box-coat around him he threw,
   For his bed, faith, 'twas dampish, and none of the best ;
All above him the clouds their bright fringed curtains drew,
   And the tuft of his nightcap lay red in the west.

SHEMUS O'BRIEN.

A TALE OF NINETY-EIGHT,

As related by an Irish Peasant.

BY R. B. S. LEFANU.

JIST after the war, in the year 'Ninety-Eight,
As soon as the Boys wor all scattered and bate,
'Twas the custom, whenever a peasant was got,
To hang him by trial—barrin' such as was shot.

'There was trial by jury goin' on by day-light,
And the martial law hangin' the lavings by night.
It's them was hard times for an honest gossoon;
If he missed in the judges he'd meet a dragoon;

An' whether the sojers or judges gave sentence,
The devil a much time they allowed for repentance;
An' the many a fine Boy was then on his keepin',
With small share of restin' or sittin' or sleepin'.

An' because they loved Erin, and scorned to sell it,
A prey for the bloodhound, a mark for the bullet—
Unsheltered by night and unrested by day,
With the heath for their barrack, revenge for their pay.

An' the bravest an' honestest Boy of thim all
Was Shemus O'Brien, from the town of Glingall;
His limbs wor well set, an' his body was light,
An' the keen-fanged hound had not teeth half as white.

But his face was as pale as the face of the dead,
An' his cheek never warm'd with the blush of the red;
An' for all that he wasn't an ugly young Boy,
For the devil himself couldn't blaze with his eye.

So droll an' so wicked, so dark an' so bright,
Like a fire-flash that crosses the depth of the night;
An' he was the best mower that ever has been,
An' the elegantest hurler that ever was seen.

SHEMUS O'BRIEN.—*Continued.*

In fencin' he gave Patrick Mooney a cut,
An' in jumpin' he bate Tom Malony a foot ;
For lightness of foot there was not his peer,
For, by Heavens! he almost outrun the red deer ;

An' his dancin' was such that the men used to stare,
An' the women turn crazy, he did it so quare ;
An' sure the whole world gave in to him there!

An' it's he was the Boy that was hard to be caught,
An' it's often he ran, an' it's often he fought,
An' it's many the one can remember quite well
The quare things he did, and it's oft I heerd tell.

How he frightened the magistrates in Cahirbally,
An' escaped through the sojers in Aherloe valley,
An' leather'd the yeoman, himself agen four,
An' stretched the four strongest on old Galtimore.

But the fox must sleep sometimes, the wild deer must rest,
And treachery prey on the blood of the best ;

An' many an action of power an' of pride,
An' many a night on the mountain's bleak side,
An' a thousand great dangers an' toils overpast,
In darkness of night he was taken at last.

Now Shemus, look back on the beautiful moon,
For the door of the prison must close on you soon ;
An' take your last look at her dim, misty light,
That falls on the mountain and valley to-night.

One look at the village, one look at the flood,
An' one at the sheltering far-distant wood ;
Farewell to the forest, farewell to the hill,
An' farewell to the friends that will think of you still.

Farewell to the patthern, the hurlin' an' wake,
An' farewell to the girl that would die for your sake !
An' twelve sojers brought him to Maryborough jail,
An' with irons secured him, refusin' all bail.

SHEMUS O'BRIEN.—*Continued.*

The fleet limbs wor chained and the strong hands wor bound,
And he lay down his lenth on the cold preson ground,
And the dhrames of his childhood kem over him there
As gentle and soft as the sweet summer air ;

An' happy rimimbrances crowdin' an' ever,
As fast as the foam flakes dhrift down on the river,
Bringin' fresh to his heart merry days long gone by,
Till the tears gathered heavy an' thick in his eye.

But the tears didn't fall, for the pride iv his heart
Wouldn't suffer one dhrop down his pale cheek to start ;
An' he sprang to his feet in the dark preson cave,
An' he swore with a fierceness, that misery gave,
By the hopes iv the good an' the cause iv the brave,
That when he was mouldering in the cowld grave,
His inimies never should have it to boast
His scorn iv their vengeance one moment was lost.
His bosom might bleed, but his cheek should be dhry,
For undaunted he lived, and undaunted he'd die.

PART SECOND.

Well, as soon as a few weeks were over an' gone,
The terrible day of the trial came on ;
There was such a crowd there was scarce room to stand,
An' sojers on guard, an' dragoons sword in hand.

An' the court-house so full that the people were bothered :
An' attorneys an' criers on the point of being smothered,
An' counsellors almost gave over for dead,
An' the jury sittin' up in the box overhead.

An' the judge settled out so determined an' big,
An' the gown on his back, an' an elegant wig,
An' silence was call'd, an' the minute 't was said,
The court was as still as the heart of the dead.

An' they heard but the opening of one prison-lock,
An' Shemus O'Brien kem into the dock—
For one minute he turned his eyes round on the throng,
An' then looked on the bars, so firm and so strong.

SHEMUS O'BRIEN.—*Continued.*

An' he saw that he had not a hope nor a friend,
A chance to escape, nor a word to defend ;
An' he folded his arms as he stood there alone,
As calm an' as cold as a statue of stone.

An' they read a big writin', a yard long at least,
An' Shemus didn't see it, nor mind it a taste,
An' the judge took a big pinch of snuff, an' he says :
" Are you guilty or not, Jim O'Brien, if you please ?"

An' all held their breath in silence of dread,
An' Shemus O'Brien made answer an' said :—
" My Lord, if you ask me if in my life-time
I thought any treason, or did any crime,

That should call to my cheek, as I stand alone here,
The hot blush of shame or the coldness of fear,
Though I stood by the grave to receive my death blow,
Before God an' the world I would answer you, No !

But if you would ask me, as I think it like,
If in the rebellion I carried a pike,
An' fought for Ould Ireland, from the first to the close,
An' shed the heart's blood of her bitterest foes—

I answer you, YES ; an' I tell you again,
Though I stand here to perish, it's my glory that then
In her cause I was willin' my veins should run dry,
An' that now for her sake I am ready to die."

Then the silence was great, and the jury smiled bright,
An' the judge wasn't sorry the job was made light ;
By my soul it's himself was the crabbled ould chap !
In a twinkling he pulled on his ugly black cap.

Then Shemus's mother, in the crowd standin' by,
Called out to the judge with a pitiful cry,
" Oh ! judge, darlin', don't—oh ! don't say the word !
The crathur is young—have mercy, my lord !

" You don't know him, my lord : oh ! don't give him to ruin
He was foolish—he didn't know what he was doin',
He's the kindliest crathur, the tinderest hearted ;—
Don't part us forever, we that's so long parted !

SHEMUS O'BRIEN.—*Continued.*

" Judge, mavourneen, forgive him—forgive him, my lord!
An' God will forgive you—oh! don't say the word!—
That was the first minute O'Brien was shaken,
When he saw that he was not quite forgot or forsaken!

An' down his pale cheek, at the words of his mother,
The big tears were running, one after the other,
An' two or three times he endeavored to spake,
But the strong manly voice used to falter an' break.

But at last, by the strength of his high-mounting pride,
He conquer'd an' master'd his grief's swelling tide;
An' says he, " Mother, don't—don't break your poor heart,
Sure, sooner or later, the dearest must part.

" An' God knows it's better than wand'ring in fear
On the bleak trackless mountain among the wild deer,
To be in the grave, where the heart, head, an' breast
From labor an' sorrow for ever shall rest.

" Then mother, my darlin', don't cry any more—
Don't make me seem broken in this my last hour;
For I wish, when my heart's lyin' under the raven,
No true man can say that I died like a craven."

Then towards the judge Shemus bent down his head,
An' that minute the solemn death-sentence was said.

PART THIRD.

The mornin' was bright, an' the mists rose on high,
An' the lark whistled merrily in the clear sky,—
But why are the men standing idle so late?
An' why do the crowd gather fast in the street?

What come they to talk of? what come they to see?
An' why does the long rope hang from the cross tree?
Oh! Shemus O'Brien pray fervent an' fast,
May the Saints take your soul, for this day is your last.

SHEMUS O'BRIEN.—*Continued.*

Pray fast an' pray strong, for the moment is nigh,
When strong, proud, an' great as you are, you must die!
At last they drew open the big prison gate,
An' out came the Sheriffs an' sojers in state.

An' a cart in the middle, an' Shemus was in it—
Not paler, but prouder than ever, that minit ;
An' soon as the people saw Shemus O'Brien,
Wid prayin' an' blessin', an' all the girls cryin',

A wild wailin' sound kem on all by degrees,
Like the sound of the lonesome wind blowin' through trees!
On, on to the gallows the Sheriffs are gone,
An' the car an' the sojers go steadily on.

An at every side swellin' around of the cart,
A wild, sorrowful sound that would open your heart,—
Now under the gallows the cart takes its stand,
An' the hangman gets up with a rope in his hand.

An' the priest havin' blest him, gets down on the ground,
An' Shemus O'Brien throws one look around.
Then the hangman drew near, and the people grew still,
Young faces turn sickly, an' warm hearts turn chill ;

An' the rope bein' ready, his neck was made bare,
For the gripe of the life-strangling cords to prepare ;
An' the good priest has left him havin' said his last prayer.

But the good priest did more—for his hands he unbound,
An' with one daring spring Jim has leap'd on the ground !
Bang ! Bang ! go the carbines, an' clash go the sabres :
He's not down ! he's alive ! now attend to him neighbors

By one shout from the people the heavens are shaken,—
One shout that the dead of the world might awaken ;
Your swords they may glitter, your carbines go bang,
But if you want hangin' 'tis yourselves you must hang.

To-night he'll be sleepin' in Aherloe glin,
An' the devil in the dice if you catch him again ;
The sojers run this way, and the Sheriffs run that,
An' Father Malone lost his new Sunday-hat,

SHEMUS O'BRIEN.

SHEMUS O'BRIEN.—*Continued.*

An' the Sheriffs were, both of them, punished sevarely,
An' fined like the devil, because Jim done them fairly.

A week after this time, without firin' a cannon,
A sharp Yankee schooner sailed out of the Shannon:
An' the captain left word he was goin' to Cork,
But the devil a bit—he was bound for New York.

The very next spring—a bright mornin' in May,—
An' just six months after the great hangin' day,—
A letter was brought to the town of Kildare,
An' on the outside was written out fair :—
" To ould Mrs. O'Brien, in Ireland, or elsewhere."

An' the inside began :—" My dear good ould Mother,
I'm safe, and I'm happy—an' not wishin' to bother
You in the radin'—with the help of the priest—
I send you enclosed in this letter, at least,
Enough to pay him an' fetch you away
To the land of the free and the brave—Amerikay !
Here you'll be happy an' never made cryin'
As long as you're mother of Shemus O'Brien.

Give my love to sweet Biddy, an' tell her beware
Of that spalpeen who calls himself " Lord of Kildare ;"
An just say to the judge, I don't now care a rap
For him, or his wig, or his dirty black cap.

An' as for the dragoons—them paid men of slaughter
Say I love them as well as the devil loves holy water.
An' now, my good mother, one word of advice—
Fill your bag with potatoes, an' bacon, an' rice.

An' tell my sweet Biddy, the best way of all
Is now, an' forever to leave ould Glengall,
An' come with you, takin' a snug cabin berth,
An' bring us a sod of the ould Shamrock earth.

An' when you start from ould Ireland, take passage at Cork,
An' come straight across to the town of New York ;
An' there ask the Mayor the best way to go
To the town of Cincinnati—the State Ohio ;
An' there you will find me, without much tryin',
At the " Harp an' the Eagle," kept by Shemus O'Brien."

KITTY CREAGH.

By Samuel Lover.

" Oh ! tell me where are you going,
 Sweet Kitty Creagh?"
" To the glen where the hazels are growing,
 I'm taking my way."
" The nuts are not ripe yet, sweet Kitty,
 As yet we're but making the hay.
An autumn excuse
Is in summer no use,
 Sweet Kitty Creagh."

" What is it to you where I'm going,
 Misther Maguire?
The twigs in the hazel glen growing
 Make a good fire."
" The turf in the bog's nearer, Kitty,
 And fitter for firing, they say ;
Don't think me a goose,
Faith I *twig* your excuse,
 Sly Kitty Creagh."

"We're saving our turf for the winther,
 Misther Maguire ;
And your gibes and your jokes shall not hindher
 What I require. "
" Ah, I know why you're going there, Kitty,
 Not *fire*, but a *flame* you should say
You seek in the shade
Of the hazel wood glade—
 Sly Kitty Creagh!

" There's a stream through that hazel wood flowing,
 Sweet Kitty Creagh ;
Where I see, with his fishing rod going,
 Phelim O'Shea ;
'Tis not for the nuts *you* are seeking,
 Nor gath'ring of fuel in May,
And 'tis not catching trout
That young Phelim's about—
 Sweet Kitty Creagh !"

MILD MABLE KELLY.

By Carolan. Born 1670. Died 1738. Translated by Samuel Ferguson.

Whoever the youth who, by heaven's decree,
 Has his happy right hand 'neath that bright head of thine,
  'Tis certain that he
  From all sorrow is free,
 Till the day of his death :—if a life so divine
Should not raise him in bliss above mortal degree.
Mild Mable Ni Kelly, bright *coolun** of curls!
 All stately and pure as the swan on the lake,
Her mouth of white teeth is a palace of pearls,
 And the youth of the land are love-sick for her sake.

No strain of the sweetest e'er heard in the land
 That she knows not to sing in a voice so enchanting,
  That the cranes on the sand
  Fall asleep where they stand ;
 Oh, for her blooms the rose, and the lily ne'er wanting
To shed its mild lustre on bosom or hand.
The dewy blue blossom that hangs on the spray,
 More blue than her eyes human eye never saw ;
Deceit never lurked in its beautiful ray—
 Dear lady, I drink to you, *slainte go bragh !*†

To gaze on her beauty the young hunter lies
 'Mong the branches that shadow her path in the grove ;
  But, alas ! if her eyes
  The rash gazer surprise,
 All eyesight departs from the victim of love,
And the blind youth steals home with his heart full of sighs.
Oh, pride of the Gael, of the lily-white palm,
 Oh, coolun of curls to the grass at your feet ;
At the goal of delight and of honor I am,
 To boast such a theme for a song so unmeet.

---

* *Coolun, or cuilin*—head of hair.
† Pronounced softly, *Slawn-tha' go bra,* meaning "Save you, or health to you for ever."

O, JUDITH, MY DEAR!

Translated from the Irish by EDWARD WALSH.

O, JUDITH, my dear, 'tis thou that hast left me for dead ;
O, Judith, my dear, thou'st stolen all the brain in my head :
O, Judith, my dear, thou'st cross'd between Heaven and me,
And 'twere better be blind than ever thy beauty to see !

Thy person is peerless—a jewel full fashioned with care,
Thou art the mild maiden so modest at market and fair ;
With cheek like the rose, and kiss like the store o' the bee,
And musical tones that call'd me from death unto thee !

————o————

HOW OFT, LOUISA.

BY R. B. SHERIDAN.

How oft, Louisa, hast thou said—
  Nor wilt thou the fond boast disown—
Thou wouldst not lose Antonio's love
  To reign the partner of a throne !
And by those lips that spoke so kind,
  And by this hand I press'd to mine,
To gain a subject nation's love
  I swear I would not part with thine.

Then how, my soul, can we be poor,
  Who own what kingdoms could not buy ?
Of this true heart thou shalt be queen,
  And, serving thee—a monarch I.
And thus control'd in mutual bliss,
  And rich in love's exhaustless mine—
Do thou snatch treasures from my lip,
  And I'll take kingdoms back from thine !

A MUNSTER KEEN.*

By Edward Walsh.

On Monday morning, the flowers were gaily springing,
The skylark's hymn in middle air was singing,
When, grief of griefs, my wedded husband left me,
And since that hour of hope and health bereft me.
    Ulla gulla, gulla g'one ! &c., &c. †

Above the board, where thou art low reclining.
Have parish priests and horsemen high been dining,
And wine and usquebaugh, while they were able,
They quaffed with thee—the soul of all the table.
    Ulla gulla, gulla g'one ! &c., &c.

Why didst thou die?   Could wedded wife adore thee
With purer love than that my bosom bore thee?
Thy children's cheeks were peaches ripe and mellow,
And threads of gold their tresses long and yellow.
    Ulla gulla, gulla g'one ! &c., &c.

In vain for me are pregnant heifers lowing ;
In vain for me are yellow harvests growing ;
Or thy nine gifts of love in beauty blooming—
Tears blind my eyes, and grief my heart's consuming !
    Ulla gulla, gulla g'one ! &c., &c.

Pity her plaints whose wailing voice is broken,
Whose finger holds our early wedding token,
The torrents of whose tears have drain'd their fountain,
Whose piled-up grief on grief is past recounting.
    Ulla gulla, gulla g'one ! &c., &c.

I still might hope, did I not thus behold thee,
That high Knockferin's airy peak might hold thee,
Or Crohan's fairy halls, or Corrin's towers,
Or Lene's bright caves, or Cleana's magic bowers.‡
    Ulla gulla, gulla g'one ! &c., &c.

* Properly *Gnione.*
† The keener alone sings the extempore death-song; the burden of the ullagone, or chorus, is taken up by all the females present.
‡ Places celebrated in fairy topography.

A MUNSTER KEEN.—*Continued.*

But Oh! my black despair! when thou wert dying
O'er thee no tear was wept, no heart was sighing—
No breath of prayer did waft thy soul to glory;
But lonely thou didst lie, all maim'd and gory!
    Ulla gulla, gulla g'one! &c., &c.

Oh! may your dove-like soul on whitest pinions
Pursue her upward flight to God's dominions,
Where saints and martyrs' hands shall gifts provide thee-
And Oh! my grief that I am not beside thee!
    Ulla gulla, gulla g'one! &c., &c.

——o——

FAREWELL, BESSY.

By Thomas Moore.

Sweetest love, I'll ne'er forget thee,
 Time shall only teach my heart,
Fonder, warmer, to regret thee,
 Lovely, gentle, as thou art!
  Farewell, Bessy!
We may meet again.

Yes, oh! yes, again we'll meet, love,
 And repose our hearts at last:
Oh! sure 'twill then be sweet, love
 Calm to think on sorrow past.
  Farewell, Bessy!
We may meet again.

Yet I feel my heart is breaking,
 When I think I stray from thee,
Round the world that quiet seeking
 Which I fear is not for me!
  Farewell, Bessy!
We may meet again.

Calm to peace thy lover's bosom—
 Can it, dearest, must it be,
Thou within an hour wilt lose him,—
 He for ever loses thee?
  Farewell, Bessy!
Yet, oh! not for ever.

DARLING OLD STICK.

My name is Morgan McCarthy, from Trim!
My relations are all dead except one, brother Jim—
  And he's now gone sojering to Cabul,
  And I expect he's laid low with a nick in his skull!

CHORUS.

    Let him be dead or be livin',
    A prayer for his soul shall be given,
    That he shall be sent home or to heaven,
  For he left me this Darling Old Stick!

If this stick it could spake, it would tell you some tales,
How it battered the countenances of the O'Nales!
  It has caused bits o' skull to fly up in the air;
  It was the promotion of fun at every fair.
The last time I used it 'twas on Patrick's Day,
Larry Fagan and I jumped into a shay;
  We went to a fair at the side of Athloy,
  Where we danced, and when done, kissed Kate McAlvoy!
  And her sweetheart went out for her cousin;
  By the powers! he brought in a dozen.
  What a doldrum they'd have knocked us in,
If I hadn't have had this Darling Old Stick!

War! was the word when a faction came in,
For they pummelled me well—they stripped off to the skin!
Like a rector I stood, watching the attack,
And the first one came up I knocked on his back!
  Then I poked out the eye of Pat Glancy,
  For he once humbugged my sister Nancy!
  In the meantime Miss Kate took a fancy
To me and my innocent Stick!

I smathered her sweetheart until he was black,
Kate tipped me the wink, we were off in a thwack!
  We went to a house at the end of the town,
  Where we kept up our spirits by pouring some down.
  When the whiskey began to warm her,
  I got her snug up in a corner;
  She said her sweetheart would inform on her!
'Twas there I said praise to my Stick!

DARLING OLD STICK.—*Continued.*

Kate she drank whiskey to such a degree
That for her support she had to lean upon me ;
  I said I would see her safe to her abode,
  'Twas there we fell in the middle of the road ;
  Until roused by the magistrate's orders,
  Devil a toe could we go farther,
  Surrounded by police for murder,
Was myself and my innocent Stick.

When I was acquitted I jumped from the dock,
An' all the gay fellows around me did flock,
  They gave me a sore arm they shook my hand so often,
  It was only for fear of seeing my own coffin !
  I went and I bought a gold ring, sirs,
  Miss Kate to the Priest I did bring, sirs—
  That night we did joyfully sing, sirs,
The adventures of myself and my Stick !

——o——

WHEN YOUR BEAUTY APPEARS.

By The Rev. Dr. Parnell.

Born, 1679. Died, 1717.

When your beauty appears,
  In its graces and airs,
All bright as an angel new dropt from the sky ;
At a distance I gaze, and am awed by my fears,
  So strangely you dazzle my eye !

  But when without art,
  Your kind thoughts you impart,
When your love runs in blushes through every vein ;
When it darts from your eyes, when it pants in your heart,
  Then I know you're a woman again.

  " There's a passion and pride
  In our sex," she replied,
"And, thus (might I gratify both) I would do :
Still an angel appear to each lover beside,
  And still be a woman, to you."

THE WOODS OF CAILLINO.

THE WOODS OF CAILLINO.

Song of the Irish Emigrant in North America.

By Mrs. Ellen Fitzsimon, (O'Connell's Daughter.)

My heart is heavy in my breast—my eyes are full of tears,
My memory is wandering back to long departed years—
To those bright days, long, long ago,
When nought I dreamed of sordid care, of worldly woe—
But roved, a gay, light-hearted boy, the woods of Caillino

There, in the spring time of my life, and spring time of the
           year,
I've watched the snow-drop start from earth, the first young
           buds appear;
The sparkling stream o'er pebbles flow,
The modest violet, and the golden primrose blow,
Within thy deep and mossy dells, beloved Caillino!

'Twas there I wooed my Mary Dhuv, and won her for my
           bride,
Who bore me three fair daughters, and four sons, my age's
           pride;
Though cruel fortune was our foe,
And steeped us to the lips in bitter want and woe,
Yet cling our hearts to those sad days we passed near Caillino!

At length by misery bowed to earth, we left our native
           strand—
And crossed the wide Atlantic to this free and happy land;
Though toils we had to undergo,
Yet soon content—and happy peace 'twas ours to know,
And plenty, such as never blessed our hearth near Caillino!

And heaven a blessing has bestowed, more precious far than
           wealth,
Has spared us to each other, full of years, yet strong in health;
Across the threshold when we go,
We see our children's children round us grow,
Like sapling oaks within thy woods, far distant Caillino!

THE WOODS OF CAILLINO.—*Continued.*

Yet sadness clouds our hearts to think that when we are no
    more,
Our bones must find a resting-place, far, far from Erin's shore
For us—no funeral sad and slow—
Within the ancient abbey's burial ground shall go—
No, we must slumber far from home, far, far from Caillino!

Yet, oh! if spirits e'er can leave the appointed place of rest.
Once more will I revisit thee, dear Isle that I love best,
O'er thy green will hover slow,
And many a tearful parting blessing will bestow
On all—but most of all on *thee,* my native Caillino!

————o————

INSPIRING FOUNT OF CHEERING WINE.

A close translation from the Irish.

Air.—"*Tiagharna* "*Mhaighe-eo* " (Lord Mayo).

INSPIRING fount of cheering wine!
    Once more I see thee flow ;
Help me to raise the lay divine—
    Propitiate thy Mayo !
Mayo, whose valor sweeps the field
    And swells the trump of fame.
May Heaven's high power the champion shield,
    And deathless be his name !
Of glory's sons, oh, thou the heir—
    Thou branch of honor's root !
Desert me not, but bend thine ear
    Propitious to my suit.

Oh ! bid thy exiled bard return,—
    Too long from safety fled ;
No more in absence let him mourn,
    Till earth shall hide his head !
Shield of defence and princely sway,
    May he who rules the sky
Prolong on earth thy glorious day,
    And every good supply !
Thy death his days would quickly close
    Who lives but in thy grace ;
And ne'er on earth can taste repose
    'Till thou shalt seal his peace !

HY-BRASAIL—THE ISLE OF THE BLEST.

By Gerald Griffin.

On the ocean that hollows the rocks where ye dwell,
A shadowy land has appeared, as they tell;
Men thought it a region of sunshine and rest,
And they call it *Hy-Brasail*, the Isle of the Blest.
From year unto year, on the ocean's blue rim,
The beautiful spectre showed lovely and dim;
The golden clouds curtained the deep where it lay,
And it looked like an Eden,—away, far away!
A peasant who heard of the wonderful tale,
In the breeze of the Orient loosened his sail;
From Ara, the holy, he turned to the west,
For though Ara was holy, *Hy-Brasail* was blest.
He heard not the voices that called from the shore—
He heard not the rising wind's menacing roar;
Home, kindred, and safety he left on that day,
And he sped to *Hy-Brasail*, away, far away!

Morn rose on the deep, and that shadowy isle,
O'er the faint rim of distance, reflected its smile;
Noon burned on the wave, and that shadowy shore
Seemed lovelily distant, and faint as before;
Lone evening came down on the wanderer's track,
And to Ara again he looked timidly back;
Oh! far on the verge of the ocean it lay,
Yet the Isle of the Blest was away, far away!
Rash dreamer, return! O, ye winds of the main,
Bear him back to his own peaceful Ara again.
Rash fool! for a vision of fanciful bliss
To barter thy calm life of labor and peace.
The warning of reason was spoken in vain;
He never revisited Ara again!
Night fell on the deep, amidst tempest and spray,
And he died on the waters, away, far away!

DIGGING FOR GOOLD.

DARBY KELLY below in Kilkenny did live,
A sketch of whose character I'm going to give;
He was thought by the people a green polished rogue,
He could wastle the whiskey, or wastle the old brogue;
All kinds of diseases with herbs he could cure,
He'd interpret your dreams to be certain and sure,
By the boys of the village he was often fool'd;
For aslape or awake, he was dreaming of goold.
Fol de dol, &c.

He had a fine open house, but the windows were broke,
The gables were down to let out the smoke;
Some beautiful pigs, through the wide world to range,
Though they were thin, they were thick with the mange.
He was so neglectful of domestic affairs,
The rats eat the bottoms all out of the chairs,
And the wife by the husband was so overruled,
When she asked him for coppers, he was talking of goold.
Fol de dol, &c.

The house thus neglected, sure nothing went right;
When a youth of the village came to him one night.
A nice boy he was, his name was Dan Mac,
And ready to fly with the duds on his back;
All the clothes that he had wasn't enough
To make him a bolster to stick on a crutch,
And his juvenile days in a lime-kiln were schooled,
But he used to cod Darby about finding goold.
Fol de dol, &c.

Says Dan: " Ere last night I had a beautiful dream;
But bad luck to the doubt! last night I'd the same;
And to-day, as I dozed, after slacking some lime,
I dreamt it again for the third and last time."
" Och, murder! " says Darby, " come tell us your dream,"
Same time his two eyes like rockets did gleam,
Says Dan : " I dreamt at the castle Kilcool
I found a jar that was crammed full of goold."
Fol de dol, &c.

DIGGING FOR GOOLD.—*Continued.*

Poor Darby a big mouth opened like a dead hake,
Saying : " You'll be a hero, just like your name-sake ·
You'll ride in your coach, you fortunate elf,
While I may be in one, going down to the hulks.
No matter," said Darby, "we must emigrate,
So, come down at mid-night, and don't be too late ;
Bring some boys whose courage won't easy be cooled,
And we'll dig till daylight to find all the goold."
Fol de dol, &c.

They arrived at the castle, at about one o'clock,
Where Dan dreamt he found all the goold in a crock,
They all set to work with picks, shovels and spades.
And a hole, that would swallow a house, soon was made,
Says Darby : "Bad luck to the curse we must give,
Or we'll be beggars as long as we live ! "
Says Dan : " May a load on my back be stooled,
For, I have bursted my breeches in digging for goold!"
Fol de dol, &c.

The prayers availed nothing, the crock was soon found,
Tim Rooney he lifted it over the ground ;
With joy Darby leaped on the back of Ned Fail,
Like a fish from the stream with a hook in his tail,
Says Darby : " My wife won't abuse me to-night,
When I take home the shiners so yellow and bright !
I'll buy house and land about Kilcool.
And we'll all bless the night we went digging for goold ! "
Fol de dol, &c.

The crock was then placed on Darby's own back
To carry home and each man have his whack,
They arrived at the door with the goold in a sack
When Mac with a spade knocked the crock into smash.
Poor Darby, near smothered, ran in with affright ;
His wife jumps up to get him a light :
When she heard Darby mourning, her passion was cooled,
She knew by the smell he was covered with goold !
Fol de dol, &c.

MAIRGRÉAD NI CHEALLEADH.

(MARGARET KELLY.)

By Edward Walsh.

At the dance in the village
Thy white foot was fleetest;
Thy voice 'mid the concert
Of maidens was sweetest;
The swell of thy white breast
Made rich lovers follow;
And thy raven hair bound them,
Young Mairgréad ni Chealleadh.

Thy neck was, lost maid,
Than the ceanabhan whiter,
And the glow of thy cheek
Than the monadan brighter;
But death's chain hath bound thee
Thine eye's glazed and hollow,
That shone like a sunburst,
Young Mairgréad ni Chealleadh.

No more shall mine ear drink
Thy melody swelling;
Nor thy beamy eye brighten
The outlaw's dark dwelling;
Or thy soft heaving bosom
My destiny hallow,
When thine arms twine around me,
Young Mairgréad ni Chealleadh.

The moss couch I brought thee
To-day from the mountain,
Has drank the last drop
Of thy young heart's red fountain—
For this good *skian** beside me
Struck deep and rung hollow
In thy bosom of treason,
Young Mairgréad ni Chealleadh.

* A knife, pronounced as if written skeen.

MAIRGRÉAD NI CHEALLEADH.—*Continued.*

With strings of rich pearls
Thy white neck was laden,
And thy fingers with spoils
Of the Sassanach maiden;
Such rich silks enrob'd not
The proud dames of Mallow—
Such pure gold they wore not
As Mairgréad ni Chealleadh.

Alas! that my loved one
Her outlaw would injure—
Alas! that he e'er proved
Her treason's avenger!
That this right hand should make thee
A bed cold and hollow,
When in Death's sleep it laid thee,
Young Mairgréad ni Chealleadh!

And while to this lone cave
My deep grief I'm venting,
The Saxon's keen bandog
My footsteps is scenting;
But true men await me
Afar in Duhallow.
Farewell, cave of slaughter,
And Mairgréad ni Chealleadh.

———o———

SWEET SEDUCER.

By Thomas Moore.

Sweet seducer, ever smiling!
  Charming still and still beguiling!
Oft I swore to love thee never—
  But I love thee more than ever.

Oh! be less, be less enchanting,
  Let some little grace be wanting;
Let my eyes, when I'm expiring,
  Gaze awhile without admiring!

THE BRIGADE AT FONTENOY.

By Bartholomew Dowling.

May 11, 1745.

By our camp-fires rose a murmur,
  At the dawning of the day,
And the tread of many footsteps
  Spoke the advent of the fray;
And, as we took our places,
  Few, and stern were our words,
While some were tightening horse-girths,
  And some were girding swords.

The trumpet blast has sounded
  Our footmen to array—
The willing steed has bounded,
  Impatient for the fray—
The green flag is unfolded,
  While rose the cry of joy—
" Heaven speed dear Ireland's banner
  To-day at Fontenoy !"

We looked upon that banner,
  And the memory arose
Of our homes and perished kindred
  Where the Lee or Shannon flows:
We looked upon that banner,
  And we swore to God on high
To smite to-day the Saxon's might—
  To conquer or to die.

Loud swells the charging trumpet—
  'Tis a voice from our own land—
God of battles ! God of vengeance !
  Guide to-day the patriot's brand !
There are stains to wash away,
  There are memories to destroy,
In the best blood of the Briton
  To-day at Fontenoy.

Plunge deep the fiery rowels
  In a thousand reeking flanks—
Down, chivalry of Ireland,
  Down on the British ranks !

THE BRIGADE AT FONTENOY.—*Continued.*

Now shall their serried columns
   Beneath our sabres reel—
Through their ranks, then, with the war-horse—
   Through their bosoms with the steel.

With one shout for good King Louis
   And the fair land of the vine,
Like the wrathful Alpine tempest
   We swept upon their line—
Then rang along the battle-field
   Triumphant our hurrah,
And we smote them down, still cheering,
   " *Erin, slanthagal go bragh !* " *

As prized as is the blessing
   From an aged father's lip—
As welcome as the haven
   To the tempest-driven ship—
As dear as to the lover
   The smile of gentle maid—
Is this day of long-sought vengeance
   To the swords of the Brigade.

See their shattered forces flying,
   A broken, routed line—
See, England, what brave laurels
   For your brow to-day we twine.
Oh, thrice blest the hour that witnessed
   The Briton turn to flee
From the chivalry of Erin,
   And France's *fleur-de-lis.*

As we lay beside our camp fires
   When the sun had passed away,
And thought upon our brethren
   That had perished in the fray—
We prayed to God to grant us,
   And then we'd die with joy,
One day upon our own dear land
   Like this of Fontenoy.

* Erin, your bright health for ever.

THE IRISH DRAGOON.

By Charles Lever.

Air.— "*Sprig of Shillelah.*"

Oh, love is the soul of an Irish dragoon,
In battle, in bivouac, or in saloon—
  From the tip of his spur to his bright sabertasche.
With his soldierly gait and his bearing so high,
His gay laughing look and his light speaking eye,
He frowns at his rival, he ogles his wench,
He springs on his saddle and *chasses* the French—
  With his jingling spur and his bright sabertasche.

His spirits are high and he little knows care,
Whether sipping his claret or charging a square—
  With his jingling spur and his bright sabertasche.
As ready to sing or to skirmish he's found,
To take off his wine or to take up his ground;
When the bugle may call him how little he fears
To charge forth in column and beat the Mounseers—
  With his jingling spur and his bright sabertasche.

When the battle is over he gaily rides back
To cheer every soul in the night bivouac—
  With his jingling spur and his bright sabertasche.
Oh! there you may see him in full glory crown'd,
And he sits 'mid his friends on the hardly-won ground,
And hear with what feeling the toast he will give,
As he drinks to the land where all Irishmen live—
  With his jingling spur and his bright sabertasche.

DEAR OLD IRELAND.

By T. D. Sullivan.

DEEP in Canadian woods we've met,
  From our bright island flown ;
Great is the land we tread, but yet
  Our hearts are with our own ;
And ere we leave this shanty small,
  While fades the Autumn day,
    We'll toast old Ireland !
    Dear old Ireland !
    Ireland ! boys,
      Hurrah !

We've heard her faults a hundred times,
  The new ones and the old,
In songs and sermons, rants and rhymes
  Enlarged some fifty-fold.
But take them all, the great and small
  And this we've got to say :—
    Here's dear old Ireland !
    Good old Ireland !
    Ireland ! boys,
      Hurrah !

We know that brave and good men tried
  To snap her rusty chain,
That patriots suffered, martyrs died,
  And all, 'tis said, in vain ;
But no, boys, no : a glance will show
  How far they've won their way,
    Here's good old Ireland !
    Lov'd old Ireland !
    Ireland ! boys,
      Hurrah!

We've seen the wedding and the wake,
  The pattern and the fair;
The stuff they take, the fun they make
  And the heads they break down there,

DEAR OLD IRELAND.—*Continued.*

With a loud " hurroo" and a " phillalu "
  And a thundering " clear the way, "
    Here's gay old Ireland !
    Dear old Ireland !
    Ireland ! boys,
      Hurrah !

And well we know, in the cool grey eves
  When the hard day's work is o'er,
How soft and sweet are the words that greet
  The friends who meet once more :
With " Mary Machree!" and " My Pat, 'tis he ! "
  And " My own heart night and day ! "
    Ah, fond old Ireland !
    Dear old Ireland !
    Ireland ! boys,
      Hurrah !

And happy and bright are the groups that pass
  From their peaceful homes for miles,
O'er fields and roads and hills to mass,
  When Sunday morning smile ;
And deep the zeal their true hearts feel,
  When low they kneel and pray ;
    Oh, dear old Ireland !
    Blest old Ireland !
    Ireland! boys,
      Hurrah !

But deep in Canadian woods we've met,
  And never may see again
The dear old isle where our hearts are set,
  And our first fond hopes remain !
But come, fill up another cup ;
  And with every sup let's say——
    Here's lov'd old Ireland !
    Good old reland !
    Ireland ! boys
      Hurrah !

MARY DRAPER.

By Charles Lever.

Don't talk to me of London dames,
Nor rave about your foreign flames,
That never lived,—except in drames
  Nor shone, except on paper;
I'll sing you 'bout a girl I knew,
Who lived in Ballywhackmacrew,
And, let me tell you, mighty few—
  Could equal Mary Draper.

Her cheeks were red, her eyes were blue,
Her hair was brown of deepest hue,
Her foot was small, and neat to view,
  Her waist was slight and taper;
Her voice was music to your ear,
A lovely brogue, so rich and clear,
Oh, the like I ne'er again shall hear
  As from sweet Mary Draper.

She'd ride a wall, she'd drive a team,
Or with a fly she'd whip a stream,
Or may be sing you " Rousseau's dream."
  For nothing could escape her;
I've seen her, too—upon my word—
At sixty yards bring down her bird—
Oh! she charmed all the Forty-third!
  Did lovely Mary Draper.

And, at the spring assizes ball,
The junior bar would, one and all,
For all her fav'rite dances call,
  And Harry Deane would caper;
Lord Clare would then forget his lore;
King's counsel voting law a bore,
Were proud to figure on the floor
  For love of Mary Draper.

The parson, judge, sub-sheriff too,
Were all her slaves, and so would you,
If you had only but one view
  Of such a face or shape, or
Her pretty ankles—but, alone,
It's only west of old Athlone
Such girls were found—and now they're gone—
  So, here's to Mary Draper!

HOURS LIKE THOSE.

By J. J. Callanan.

Hours like those I spent with you,
So bright, so passing, and so few,
May never bless me more—farewell!
My heart can feel, but dare not tell,
The rapture of those hours of light
Thus snatched from sorrow's cheerless night.

'Tis not thy cheek's soft blended hue;
'Tis not thine eye of heavenly blue;
'Tis not the radiance of thy brow,
That thus would win or charm me now;
It is thy heart's warm light, that glows
Like sunbeams on December snows.

It is thy wit, that flashes bright
As lightning on a stormy night,
Illuming e'en the clouds that roll
Along the darkness of my soul,
And bidding, with an angel's voice,
The heart, that knew no joy—rejoice.

Too late we met—too soon we part;
Yet dearer to my soul thou art
Than some whose love has grown with years,
Smiled with my smile, and wept my tears.
Farewell! but, absent, thou shalt seem
The vision of some heavenly dream,
Too bright on child of earth to dwell:
It must be so—my friend, farewell!

———o———

'TIS A BIT OF A THING THAT A BODY MAY SING.

Air.—"*The Bunch of Green Rushes.*"

Och, is that what you mean, now—a bit of a song?
Faith, I'll not keep you waiting, or bother you long;
I don't need no teasing, no pressing, nor stuff,
By my soul if you're ready I'm willing enough;
But to give you an end I must make a beginning,
In troth tho' the music is not mighty fine,
    'Tis a bit of a thing
    That a body may sing,
Just to set you agoing, and season the wine.

TIS A BIT OF A THING THAT A BODY MAY SING.

Continued.

I once was a lover, like some of you here,
And could feed a whole day on a sigh or a tear;
No sunshine I knew but in Katty's black eye,
And the world was a desert when she was not by:
But, the devil knows how, I grew fond of Miss Betsy,
Which placed in my heart quite another design—
     'Tis a bit of a thing
     That a body may sing,
Just to set you agoing, and season the wine.

Then Lucy came next, with a languishing eye,
Like the azures of heaven we see in the sky;
The beauties of Betsy she threw in the shade,
And I vowed that for ever I'd love the dear maid;
But the beautiful Fanny one day came before me,
Which placed in my heart quite another design—
     'Tis a bit of a thing
     That a body may sing,
Just to set you agoing, and season the wine.

Now Fanny was stately, majestic, and tall,
In shape and in size what a goddess you'd call,
I vowed if she cruelly slighted my hope,
I'd give up the world, and die by a rope;
But, before I did that, sure I saw her fat sister,
Which placed in my heart quite another design
     'Tis a bit of a thing
     That a body might sing,
Just to set you agoing, and season the wine.

'Tis thus I go on, ever constant and blest,
For I find I've a great store of love in my breast,
And it never grows cool, for whenever I try
To get one in my heart—I get two in my eye;
Thus to all kinds of beauties I pay my devotions,
And all sorts of liquors by turns I make mine:
     So I'll finish the thing,
     Now you see that I sing,
With a bumper to woman, to season our wine.

THE WINTER IT IS PAST.

Air.—" *Cruiskin Lawn*".

THE winter it is past,
And the summer's come at last,
And the small birds sing on every tree;
The hearts of those are glad,
Whilst mine is very sad;
Whilst my true love is absent from me.

I'll put on my cap of black,
And fringe about my neck,
And rings on my fingers I'll wear;
All this I'll undertake,
For true lover's sake,
For he rides at the Curragh of *Kildare*.

A livery I'll wear,
And I'll comb down my hair,
And I'll dress in the velvet so green;
Straightways I will repair
To the Curragh of *Kildare*.
And 'tis there I will get tidings of him.

With patience she did wait,
Till they ran for the plate
In thinking young Johnston to see;
But Fortune prov'd unkind,
To that sweetheart of mine
For he's gone to *Lurgan* for me.

I should not think it strange,
The wide world for to range.
If I could obtain my heart's delight:
But here in Cupid's chains
I'm obliged to remain,
Whilst in tears do I spend the whole night.

My love is like the sun,
That in the firmament doth run,
Which is always constant and true:
But yours is like the moon,
That doth wander up and down
And in every month it's new.

THE WINTER IT IS PAST.—*Continued.*

All you that are in love,
And cannot it remove,
For you pittied are by me:
Experience makes me know
That your heart is full of woe,
Since my true love is absent from me.

Farewell my joy and heart,
Since you and I must part,
You are the fairest that I e'er did see;
And I never do design,
For to alter my mind
Although you are below my degree.

————o————

HAD I A HEART FOR FALSEHOOD FRAMED.

By Richard Brinsley Sheridan.

Air.—"*Molly Astore.*"

Had I a heart for falsehood framed,
  I ne'er could injure you,
For, tho' your tongue no promise claim'd,
  Your charms would make me true:
Then, lady, dread not here deceit,
  Nor fear to suffer wrong,
For friends in all the aged you'll meet,
  And lovers in the young.

But when they find that you have bless'd
  Another with your heart,
They'll bid aspiring passion rest,
  And act a brother's part.
Then, lady, dread not here deceit
  Nor fear to suffer wrong,
For friends in all the aged you'll meet
  And brothers in the young.

GREEN WERE THE FIELDS.

By George Nugent Reynolds.

Air.—"*Savourneen Deelish.*"

Green were the fields where my forefathers dwelt, O ;
 Erin, *ma vourneen ! slan leat go brah !* *
Tho' our farm it was small, yet comforts we felt, O.
 Erin, &c.
At length came the day when our lease did expire,
Fain would I live where before lived my sire :
But, ah ! well-a-day ! I was forced to retire.
 Erin, &c.

Tho' the laws I obey'd, no protection I found, O,
 Erin, &c.
With what grief I beheld my cot burn'd to the ground, O !
 Erin, &c.
Forc'd from my home ; yea, from where I was born,
To range the wide world—poor, helpless, forlorn ;
I look back with regret—and my heart-strings are torn.
 Erin, &c.

With principles pure, patriotic, and firm,
 Erin, &c.
To my country attached, and a friend to reform,
 Erin, &c.
I supported old Ireland—was ready to die for it ;
If her foes e'er prevail'd I was well known to sigh for it ;
But my faith I preserv'd, and am now forced to fly for it.
 Erin, &c.

But hark ! I hear sounds, and my heart is strong beating,
 Erin, &c.
Loud cries for redress, and avaunt on retreating,
 Erin, &c.
We have numbers and numbers do constitute power,
Let us will to be free—and we're free from that hour ;
Of Hibernia's brave sons, oh ! we feel we're the flower.
 Erin, &c.

* Ireland, my darling ! for ever adieu !

PHELIM O'NEILE.

By Carolan.

Translated by Thomas Furlong.

At length thy bard is steering,
  To find thy gay hearth again:
Thy hand, thy voice so cheering
  Still soothes him in grief or pain:
Thy sires have shone in story,
  Their fame with friendly pride we hail:
But a milder, gentler glory
  Is thine, my belov'd O'Neile!

Still cheerful have I found thee,
  All changeless in word or tone;
Still free when friends were round thee
  And free with thy bard alone;
Fill up the bowls—be drinking—
  'Tis cheering still, in woe or weal;
Come pledge with lips unshrinking,
  The dear, the belov'd O'Neile!

Of blameless joy the centre,
  Thy home thro' each night hath been,
There might the wanderer enter,
  And there the blind bard was seen:
There wit and sport came blended
  In careless song or merry tale;
But let thy praise be ended—
  Who loves not my lov'd O'Neile?

———o———

BRIDGET CRUISE.

By Carolan. Translated by Thomas Furlong.

Oh! turn thee to me, my only love,
  Let not despair confound me;
Turn, and may blessings from above
  In life and death surround thee,
This fond heart throbs for thee alone—
  Oh! leave me not to languish,
Look on these eyes, whence sleep hath flown,
  Bethink thee of my anguish:
My hopes, my thoughts, my destiny—
  All dwell, all rest, sweet girl, on thee.

BRIDGET CRUISE.—*Continued.*

Young bud of beauty, for ever bright,
  The proudest must bow before thee;
Source of my sorrow and my delight—
  Oh! must I in vain adore thee?
Where, where, through earth's extended round,
Where may such loveliness be found?
  Talk not of fair ones known of yore;
Speak not of Deirdre the renowned—
    She whose gay glance each minstrel hail'd;
  Nor she whom the daring Dardan bore
From her fond husband's longing arms;
Name not the dame whose fatal charms,
    When weighed against a world, prevail'd;
To each might blooming beauty fall,
  Lovely, thrice lovely, might they be;
But the gifts and graces of each and all
  Are mingled, sweet maid, in thee!

How the entranc'd ear fondly lingers
  On the turns of thy thrilling song;
How brightens each eye as thy fair white fingers
  O'er the chords fly gently along;
The noble, the learn'd, the ag'd, the vain,
  Gaze on the songstress and bless the strain.
How winning, dear girl, is thine air,
  How glossy thy golden hair;
Oh! lov'd one, come back again.
  With thy train of adorers about thee—
Oh! come, for in grief and in gloom we remain—
  Life is not life without thee.

My memory wanders—my thoughts have stray'd—
  My gathering sorrows oppress me—
Oh! look on thy victim, bright peerless maid,
  Say one kind word to bless me.
Why, why on thy beauty must I dwell
  When each tortur'd heart knows its power too well?
Or why need I say that favor'd and bless'd
  Must be the proud land that bore thee?
Oh! dull is the eye and cold the breast
  That remains unmov'd before thee.

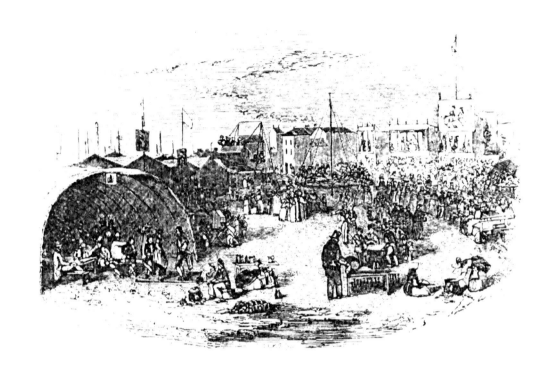

THE DONNYBROOK JIG

Oh! 'twas Dermot O'Nolan M'Figg,
That could properly handle a twig:
 He went to the fair,
 And kicked up a dust there,
In dancing the Donnybrook jig,
    With his wig,
Oh! my blessing to Dermot M'Figg.

When he came to the midst of the fair
He was all in a *paugh* of fresh air,
 For the fair very soon,
 Was as full as the moon,
Such mobs upon mobs were there.
    Oh, rare!
So more luck to sweet Donnybrook fair.

THE DONNYBROOK JIG.—*Continued.*

The souls they came pouring in fast,
To dance while the leather would last,
    For the Thomas-street brogue
    Was there in much vogue,
And oft with a brogue a joke passed,
              Quite fast,
While the cash and the whiskey did last.

But Dermot, his mind on love bent,
In search of his sweetheart he went,
    Peeped in here and there,
    As he walked through the fair,
And took a small drop in each tent
              As he went,
Och! on whiskey'd love he was bent.

And who should he spy in a jig,
With a meal man, so tall and so big,
    But his own darling Kate,
    So gay and so nate—
Faith, her partner he hit him a dig,
              The pig,
He beat the meal out of his wig.

Then Dermot, with conquest elate,
Drew a stool near beautiful Kate:
    "Arrah, Katty!" says he,
    " My own cushlamachree!
Sure, the world for beauty, you beat,
              Complete,
So we'll just take a dance while we wait."

The piper to keep him tune,
Struck up a gay lilt very soon,
    Until an arch wag
    Cut a hole in his bag,
And at once put an end to the tune,
              Too soon,
Och! the music flew up to the moon.

THE DONNYBROOK JIG.— *Continued.*

To the fiddler says Dermot M'Figg,
" If you'll please to play, ' Shelah na gig,
   We'll shake a loose toe,
   While you humor the bow,
To be sure you won't warm the wig,
            Of M'Figg,
While he's dancing a tight Irish jig."

The meal man he looked very shy,
While a great big tear stood in his eye.
   He cried, " Oh, dear, how I'm kilt,
   All alone for that jilt,
With her may the birds fly high
           In the sky,
For I'm murder'd and don't know for why.'

" Oh !" says Dermot, and he in the dance,
Whilst a step towards his foe did advance,
   " By the Father of men,
   Say but that word again,
And I'll soon knock you back in a trance
          To your dance,
For with me you'd have but a small chance."

" But," says Katty, the darlint, says she,
" If you'll only just listen to me,
   It's myself that will show,
   That he can't be your foe,
Though he fought for his cousin,that'sme,"
         Says she,
For, sure, Billy's related to me.

" For my own cousin-jarmin, Anne Wild
Stood for Biddy Mulrooney's first child,
   And Biddy's step son,
   Sure he married Bess Dunn,
Who was gossip to Jenny, as mild
         A child,
As ever at mother's breast smiled.

THE DONNYBROOK JIG.—*Continued.*

" And may be you don't know Jane Brown,
Who served goats' whey in sweet Dundrum town.
    'Twas her uncle's half-brother
    That married my mother,
And bought me this new yellow gown,
               To go down,
Where the marriage was held in Milltown."

Oh then how the girls did look,
When the clergyman opened his book,
    Till young Nelly Shine,
    Tipt Dermot a sign,
Faith, he soon popped her into a nook
             Near the brook,
And there he linked arms with the cook.

" By the powers!" then says Dermot, " 'tis plain,
Like the son of that rapscallion Cain,
    My best friend I've kilt,
    Though no blood there is spilt,
And the never a harm did I mean,
            That's plain,
But by me he'll ne'er be kilt again."

Then the mealman forgave him the blow,
That laid him a-sprawling so low,
    And being quite gay,
    Asked them both to the play,
But Katty, being bashful, said " No,
            No, no."
Yet he treated them all to the show.

MAURYEEN.

THE cottage is here as of old I remember,
  The pathway is worn as it always hath been ;
On the turf-piled hearth there still lives a bright ember,
  But where is Mauryeen ?

The same pleasant prospect still lieth before me,—
  The river—the mountain—the valley of green ;
And heaven itself (a bright blessing !) is o'er me :—
  But where is Mauryeen ?

Lost ! lost ! like a dream that hath come and departed
  (Ah, why are the loved and the lost ever seen ?)
She has fallen—hath flown with a lover false-hearted—
  So mourn for Mauryeen !

And she who so loved her is slain—(the poor mother !)
  Struck dead in a day by a shadow unseen ;
And the home we once loved is the home of another—
  And lost is Mauryeen !

Sweet Shannon, a moment by thee let me ponder—
  A moment look back to the things that have been ;
Then away to the world, where the ruin'd ones wander,
  To seek for Mauryeen !

Pale peasant, perhaps, 'neath the frown of high heaven,
  She roams the dark deserts of sorrow unseen,
Unpitied—unknown ; but I—*I* shall know even
  The *ghost* of Mauryeen !

——o——

THE HAUNTED SPRING.

By Samuel Lover.

It is said Fays have the power to assume various shapes for the purpose of lur-
ing mortals into Fairyland : hunters seem to have been particularly the objects
of the lady-fairies' fancies.

GAILY through the mountain glen
  The hunter's horn did ring,
    As the milk-white doe
    Escaped his bow,
  Down by the haunted spring ;

THE HAUNTED SPRING.—*Continued.*

In vain his silver horn he wound,—
  'Twas echo answer'd back;
For neither groom nor baying hound
  Was on the hunter's track;
In vain he sought the milk-white doe
That made him stray, and 'scaped his bow,
For, save himself, no living thing
Was by the silent haunted spring.

The purple heath-bells, blooming fair,
  Their fragrance round did fling,
    As the hunter lay,
    At close of day,
  Down by the haunted spring;
A lady fair, in robe of white,
  To greet the hunter came;
She kiss'd a cup with jewels bright,
  And pledged him by his name;
"Oh, lady fair," the hunter cried,
"Be thou my love, my blooming bride,
A bride that well might grace a king!
Fair lady of the haunted spring."

In the fountain clear she stoop'd,
  And forth she drew a ring;
    And that loved knight
    His faith did plight
  Down by the haunted spring:—
But since that day his chase did stray,
  The hunter ne'er was seen,
And legends tell, he now doth dwell
  Within the hills so green;*
But still the milk-white doe appears,
And wakes the peasants' evening fears,
While distant bugles faintly ring
Around the lonely haunted spring.

* In Ireland, the fairies are said to abide in the "green hills."

SAVOURNEEN DEELISH EILEEN OGE.

Ah! the moment was sad, when my Love and I parted-
  Savourneen deelish Eileen oge!
As I kiss'd off her tears, I was nigh broken-hearted—
  Savourneen deelish Eileen oge!

Wan was her cheek which hung on my shoulder;
  Damp was her hand, no marble was colder;
I felt that again I should never behold her,
  Savourneen deelish Eileen oge!

SAVOURNEEN DEELISH EILEEN OGE.—*Continued.*

When the word of command put our men into motion,
  Savourneen deelish Eileen oge!
I buckled up my knapsack to cross the wide Ocean,
  Savourneen deelish Eileen oge!

SAVOURNEEN DEELISH EILEEN OGE.—*Continued.*

Brisk were our troops, all roaring like thunder,
  Pleased with their voyage, impatient for plunder ;
My bosom with grief was almost torn asunder,
  Savourneen deelish Eileen oge!

SAVOURNEEN DEELISH EILEEN OGE.—*Continued.*

Long I fought for my Country, far, far from my true love,
  Savourneen deelish Eileen oge!
All my pay and my bounty I hoarded for you, Love,
  Savourneen deelish Eileen oge!

SAVOURNEEN DEELISH EILEEN OGE.—*Continued.*

But peace was proclaim'd, I escap'd from the slaughter,
  Landed at home, my sweet girl I sought her:
But sorrow, alas! to a cold grave had brought her,
  Savourneen deelish Eileen oge!

MY NATIVE TOWN.

By Samuel Lover.

WE have heard of Charybdis and Scylla of old ;
Of Maelstrom the modern enough has been told ;
Of Vesuvius's blazes all travellers bold
    Have established the bright renown :
But spite of what ancients or moderns have said
Of whirlpools so deep, or volcanoes so red,
The place of all others on earth that I dread
    Is my beautiful native town.

Where they sneer if you're poor, and they snarl if you're rich
They know every cut that you make in your flitch ;
If your hose should be darn'd, they can tell every stitch ;
    And they know when your wife got a gown.
The *old* one, they say, was made *new*—for the brat ;
And they're sure you love mice—for you can't keep a cat ;
In the hot flame of scandal how blazes the fat,
    When it falls in your native town !

If a good stream of blood chance to run in your veins,
They think to remember it not worth the pains,
For *losses* of caste are to them all the *gains*,
    So they treasure each base renown.
If your mother sold apples—your father his oath,
And was cropp'd of his ears—yet you'll hear of them both ;
For loathing all low things they never are loath,
    In your virtuous native town.

If the dangerous heights of renown you should try,
And give all the laggards below the go-by,
For fear you'd be hurt with your climbing so high,
    They're the first to pull you down.
Should Fame give you wings, and you mount in despite,
They swear Fame is wrong, and that they're in the right,
And reckon you *there*—though you're far out of sight,
    Of the owls of your native town.

Then give me the world, boys ! that's open and wide,
Where honest in purpose, and honest in pride,
You are taken for *just what you're worth* when you're *tried*
    And have paid your reckoning down.
Your coin's not mistrusted—the critical scale
Does not weigh ev'ry piece, like a huxter at sale ;
The mint-mark is on it—although it might fail
    To pass in your native town.

NOW CAN'T YOU BE AISY?

By Charles Lever.

Air. *"Arrah, Katty, now can't you be aisy?"*

Oh! what stories I'll tell when my sodgering's o'er,
  And the gallant fourteenth is disbandĕd;
Not a drill nor parade will I hear of no more,
  When safely in Ireland landed.
With the blood that I spilt—the Frenchmen I kilt,
  I'll drive all the girls half crazy;
And some 'cute one will cry, with a wink of her eye,
  " Mr. Free, now—why can't you be aisy?"

I'll tell how we routed the squadrons in fight,
  And destroyed them all at " Talavera,"
And then I'll just add how we finished the night
  In learning to dance the " Bolera;"
How by the moonshine we drank real wine,
  And rose next day fresh as a daisy;
Then some one will cry, with a look mighty sly
  " Arrah, Mickey—now can't you be aisy?"

I'll tell how the nights with Sir Arthur we spent,
  Around a big fire in the air too,
Or may be enjoying ourselves in a tent,
  Exactly like Donnybrook fair too;
How he'd call out to me—" pass the wine, Mr. Free,
  For you're a man never is lazy!"
Then some one will cry, with a wink of her eye,
  " Arrah, Mickey dear—can't you be aisy?"

I'll tell, too, the long years in fighting we passed,
  Till Mounseer asked Bony to lead him;
And Sir Arthur, grown tired of glory at last,
  Begged of one Mickey Free to succeed him.
But, " acushla," says I, " the truth is, I'm shy!
  There's a lady in Ballynacrazy!
And I swore on the book—" she gave me a look,
  And cried, " Mickey, now can't you be aisy?"

OH! ONCE WE WERE ILLIGANT PEOPLE.

By Charles Lever.

Oh! once we were illigant people,
  Though we now live in cabins of mud ;
And the land that ye see from the steeple
  Belonged to us all from the flood.
My father was then king of Connaught,
  My grandaunt viceroy of Tralee ;
But the Sassenach came, and, signs on it !
  The divil an acre have we.

The least of us then were all earls,
  And jewels we wore without name ;
We drank punch out of rubies and pearls—
  Mr. Petrie can tell you the same.
But, except some turf mould and potatoes,
  There's nothing our own we can call :
And the English—bad luck to them !—hate us,
  Because we've more fun than them all !

My grandaunt was niece to St. Kevin,
  That's the reason my name's Mickey Free !
Priest's nieces—but sure he's in Heaven,
  And his failins is nothin' to me.
And we still might get on without doctors,
  If they'd let the ould island alone ;
And if purplemen, priests, and tithe-proctors
  Were crammed down the great gun of Athlone.

---o---

KATHALEEN NY-HOULAHAN.*

A Jacobite relic—translated from the Irish.

By James Clarence Mangan.

Long they pine in weary woe, the nobles of our land,
Long they wander to and fro, proscribed, alas ! and banned ;
Feastless, houseless, altarless, they bear the exile's brand ;
  But their hope is in the coming-to of Kathaleen Ny-
    Houlahan !

* One of the many names by which Ireland was typified

KATHALEEN NY-HOULAHAN.—*Continued.*

Think her not a ghastly hag, too hideous to be seen,
Call her not unseemly names, our matchless Kathaleen;
Young she is, and fair she is, and would be crowned a queen,
   Were the king's son at home here with Kathaleen Ny-
    Houlahan!

Sweet and mild would look her face, O none so sweet and
    mild,
Could she crush the foes by whom her beauty is reviled;
Woollen plaids would grace herself and robes of silk her child,
   If the king's son were living here with Kathaleen Ny-
    Houlahan!

Sore disgrace it is to see the arbitress of thrones,
Vassal to a *Saxoneen* of cold and sapless bones!
Bitter anguish wrings our souls—with heavy sighs and groans
   We wait the Young Deliverer of Kathaleen Ny-Houla-
    han!

Let us pray to Him who holds life's issues in His hands—
Him who formed the mighty globe, with all its thousand
    lands;
Girdling them with seas and mountains, rivers deep, and
    strands,
   To cast a look of pity upon Kathaleen Ny-Houlahan!

He who over sands and waves led Israel along—
He who fed, with heavenly bread, that chosen tribe and
    throng—
He who stood by Moses when his foes were fierce and strong—
   May He show forth His might in saving Kathaleen Ny-
    Houlahan!

THE MOTHER TO HER SON.

By Mrs. Downing.

Speed thee boy! the battle cry
   Already echoes through the glen;
And freemen's swords are flashing high
   In Erin's sacred cause again;
From rocky dale, from sunny vale,
   From rugged mountain's craggy brow,
Her warrior sons, in gleaming mail,
   Are rushing at the signal now.

Speed thee boy! thy hand is weak,
   'Twas never yet in battle tried;
The down of youth is on thy cheek,
   But think on how thy father died.
Away—the clans are rushing by;
   The Saxon thunders on the plains:
O'Nial's fire is in thine eye:
   McCaura's blood is in thy veins.

Nay, check not, boy, those manly tears!
   The heart that often fiercest proves—
That braves the death-field without fear—
   May weep to part from those it loves.
And heed not mine, they've fall'n before,
   When from my side thy father fled;
Remember 'mid the battle's roar
   The sacred cause for which he bled.

Away, boy! be thy bosom strong;
   Again is pealed the signal word,
And, now, the foeman pours along—
   And, now, the clash of war is heard!
Away!—amid the battle wild,
   O'Nial's glittering steel will tell,
When brandished by McCaura's child—
   Speed thee, my boy!—farewell!—farewell!

A SPINNING-WHEEL SONG.

By J. F. Waller, LL. D.

Mellow the moonlight to shine is beginning:
Close by the window young Eileen is spinning;
Bent o'er the fire her blind grandmother, sitting,
Is croning, and moaning, and drowsily knitting—
" Eileen, achora, I hear some one tapping."—
" 'Tis the ivy, dear mother, against the glass flapping."
" Eileen, I surely hear somebody sighing."—
" 'Tis the sound, mother dear, of the summer wind dying."
    Merrily, cheerily, noisily whirring,
    Swings the wheel, spins the reel, while the foot's stirring,
    Sprightly, and lightly, and airily ringing,
    Thrills the sweet voice of the young maiden singing.

" What's that noise that I hear at the window, I wonder?"—
" 'Tis the little birds chirping the holly-bush under."
" What makes you be shoving and moving your stool on,
And singing all wrong that old song of 'The Coolun'?"—
There's a form at the casement—the form of her true-love—
And he whispers, with face bent, "I'm waiting for you, love;
Get up on the stool, through the lattice step lightly,
We'll rove in the grove while the moon's shining brightly."
    Merrily, cheerily, noisily whirring
    Swings the wheel, spins the reel, while the foot's stirring;
    Sprightly, and lightly, and airily ringing,
    Thrills the sweet voice of the young maiden singing.

The maid shakes her head, on her lips lays her fingers,
Steals up from the seat—longs to go, and yet lingers;
A frightened glance turns to her drowsy grandmother;
Puts one foot on the stool, spins the wheel with the other.
Lazily, easily, swings now the wheel round;
Slowly and lowly is heard now the reel's sound;
Noiseless and light to the lattice above her
The maid steps—then leaps to the arms of her lover.
    Slower—and slower—and slower the wheel swings;
    Lower—and lower—and lower the reel rings;
    Ere the reel and the wheel stopped their ringing and mov-
        ing,
    Thro' the grove the young lovers by moonlight are roving.

THE TWIG OF THE SHANNON.

ON the beautiful banks of the Shannon,
  There grows such an illagant tree,
And the fruit that it bears is shillalah,
  I've a sprig of it here you may see.
'Tis the remnant of all my large fortune,
  It's the friend that ne'er played me a trick,
And I'd rather lose half my supportin'
  Than part with this illagant stick.

THE TWIG OF THE SHANNON.—*Continued.*

CHORUS.

T'was a delicate sprig in the summer,
  When I first cut it from the tree,
And I've kept it through all the cold weather,
  Faix, the sprig of shillalah for me.

It's the porter that carried my luggage,
  For I've shouldered for many a mile,
And from thieves it will safely protect me,
  In a beautiful delicate style.
It is useful for rows in the summer,
  And when winter comes on with a storm,
If you're short of a fire in the cabin,
  You can burn it to keep yourself warm.
          'Twas a delicate sprig, &c.

It's a friend both so true and so constant,
  It's constancy pen cannot paint,
For it always is there when it's wanted,
  And sometimes it's there when it aint.
It beats all your guns and your rifles,
  For it goes off when'er you desire,
And it's shure to hit whate'er it's aimed at,
  For shillalahs they never miss fire.
          'Twas a delicate sprig, &c.

It's a talisman so upright and honest,
  Twenty shillings it pays to the pound;
So if ever it gets you in debt, sir.
  You are sure to be paid, I'll be bound.
It never runs up a long score, sir,
  In trade it's not given to fail,
There's no danger of it's being insolvent,
  For it always pays down on the nail.
          'Twas a delicate sprig, &c.

And faith, at an Irish election,
  An argument striking it's there;
For with brickbats and sprigs of the Shannon
  We see things go all right and square.

THE TWIG OF THE SHANNON.—*Continued*.

It's then there's no bribery at all, sir,
   They vote as they like, every soul,
But it's no use opposing the shillalah.
   Or it's sure to come down on the poll.
               'Twas a delicate sprig, &c.

———o———

I WAS THE BOY FOR BEWITCHING THEM.

I WAS the boy for bewitching them,
   Whether good humor'd or coy ;
All cried, when I was beseeching them,
   " Do what you will with me, joy."
" Daughters be cautious and steady,"
   Mothers would cry out for fear—
" Won't you take care now of Teddy.
   Oh ! he's the divil, my dear."
     For I was the boy for bewitching them,
       Whether good humor'd or coy ;
     All cried when I was beseeching them,
       " Do what you will with me, joy.

From every quarter I gather'd them,
   Very few rivals had I ;
If I found any I leather'd them,
   And that made them look mighty shy.
Pat Mooney, my Shelah once meeting,
   I twigg'd him beginning his clack—
Says he, " at my heart I've a beating."
   Says I, " then have one at your back."
         For I was the boy, &c.

Many a lass that would fly away
   When other wooers but spoke,
Once if I looked her a die-away
   There was an end of the joke.
Beauties, no matter how cruel,
   Hundreds of lads though they'd crost,
When I came nigh to them, jewel,
   They melted like mud in the frost.
         For I was the boy. &c.

DANCE LIGHT, FOR MY HEART IT LIES UNDER YOUR FEET, LOVE.

Air.—" Huish the cat from under the table."

By John F. Waller, LL. D.

" Ah, sweet Kitty Neil, rise up from that wheel—
Your neat little foot will be weary from spinning;
Come trip down with me to the sycamore tree,
Half the parish is there, and the dance is beginning.
The sun is gone down, but the full harvest moon
Shines sweetly and cool on the dew-whitened valley;
While all the air rings with the soft, loving things,
Each little bird sings in the green shaded alley."

With a blush and a smile, Kitty rose up the while,
Her eye in the glass, as she bound her hair, glancing;
'Tis hard to refuse when a young lover sues—
So she couldn't but choose to go off to the dancing.
And now on the green, the glad groups are seen—
Each gay-hearted lad with the lass of his choosing;
And Pat, without fail, leads our sweet Kitty Neil—
Somehow when he asked, she ne'er thought of refusing.

Now, Felix Magee puts his pipes to his knee,
And, with flourish so free, sets each couple in motion;
With a cheer and a bound, the lads patter the ground—
The maids move around just like swans on the ocean.
Cheeks bright as the rose—feet light as the doe's
Now coyly retiring, now boldly advancing—
Search the world all round, from the sky to the ground,
No such sight can be found as an Irish lass dancing!

Sweet Kate! who could view your bright eyes of deep blue
Beeming humidly through their dark lashes so mildly,
Your fair-turned arm, heaving breast, rounded form,
Nor feel his heart warm, and his pulses throb wildly?
Young Pat feels his heart, as he gazes, depart,
Subdued by the smart of such painful yet sweet love;
The sight leaves his eye, as he cries with a sigh,
" *Dance light, for my heart it lies under your feet, love!*

A SIGH FOR KNOCKMANY.

By William Carleton.

Take, proud ambition, take thy fill
  Of pleasures won through toil or crime;
Go, learning, climb thy rugged hill,
  And give thy name to future time:
Philosophy, be keen to see
  Whate'er is just, or false, or vain,
Take each thy meed, but, oh! give me
  To range my mountain glens again.

Pure was the breeze that fann'd my cheek,
  As o'er Knockmany's brow I went;
When every lonely dell could speak
  In airy music, vision sent:
False world, I hate thy cares and thee,
  I hate the treacherous haunts of men;
Give back my early heart to me,
  Give back to me my mountain glen.

How light my youthful visions shone,
  When spann'd by Fancy's radiant form;
But now her glittering bow is gone,
  And leaves me but the cloud and storm.
With wasted form, and cheek all pale—
  With heart long seared by grief and pain;
Dunroe, I'll seek thy native gale,
  I'll tread my mountain glens again.

Thy breeze once more may fan my blood,
  Thy valleys all are lovely still;
And I may stand, where oft I stood,
  In lonely musings on thy hill.
But, ah! the spell is gone;—no art
  In crowded town, or native plain,
Can teach a crush'd and breaking heart
  To pipe the song of youth again.

THE BOYNE WATER.

The following song, on which all members of the Orange Society waste so much enthusiasm, would be considered a very common-place production but for the false estimate set on it. It is inserted purely as a curious evidence of the fanaticism of the class who use it as a hymn of praise of one class of Irishmen over another, in favor of the foreigners.

The whole number of casualties of the Irish party was about 1,500, and of the foreigners 500.—Less than in many of the skirmishes in our late civil war.

JULY the first, in Oldbridge-town
   There was a grievous battle,
Where many a man lay on the ground
   By cannons that did rattle.
King James he pitched his tents between
   The lines for to retire;
But King William threw his bomb-balls in,
   And set them all on fire.

Thereat enraged, they vowed revenge
   Upon King William's forces,
And oft did vehemently cry
   That they would stop their courses.
A bullet from the Irish came,
   And grazed King William's arm,
They thought his Majesty was slain,
   Yet it did him little harm.

Duke Schomberg then, in friendly care,
   His King would often caution
To shun the spot where bullets hot
   Retained their rapid motion;
But William said, " He don't deserve
   The name of Faith's Defender,
Who would not venture life and limb
   To make a foe surrender."

When we the Boyne began to cross,
   The enemy they descended;
But few of our brave men were lost,
   So stoutly we defended;
The horse was the first that marched o'er
   The foot soon followed after;
But brave Duke Schomberg was no more,
   By venturing over the water.

THE BOYNE WATER.—*Continued.*

When valiant Schomberg he was slain,
    King William he accosted
His warlike men for to march on,
    And he would be the foremost;
" Brave boys," he said, " be not dismayed
    For the loss of one commander,
For God will be our King this day,
    And I'll be General under."

Then stoutly we the Boyne did cross,
    To give the enemies battle;
Our cannon, to our foes 'great cost,
    Like thund'ring claps did rattle.
In majestic mien our prince rode o'er;
    His men soon followed after,
With blows and shout put our foes to the rout
    The day we crossed the water.

The Protestants of Drogheda
    Have reason to be thankful,
That they were not to bondage brought,
    They being but a handful.
First to the Tholsel they were brought,
    And tied at Millmount after;
But brave King William set them free,
    By venturing over the water.

The cunning French near to Duleek
    Had taken up their quarters,
And fenced themselves on every side,
    Still waiting for new orders;
But in the dead time of the night
    They set the fields on fire,
And long before the morning light
    To Dublin they did retire.

THE BOYNE WATER.—*Continued.*

Then said King William to his men,
　After the French departed,
"I'm glad," said he, "that none of ye
　Seem to be faint-hearted;
So sheathe your swords and rest awhile,
　In time we'll follow after."
Those words he uttered with a smile
　The day he crossed the water.

Come, let us all with heart and voice
　Applaud our lives' defender,
Who at the Boyne his valor showed,
　And made his foe surrender.
To God above the praise we'll give
　Both now and ever after;
'And bless the glorious memory
　Of King William that crossed the water.

CŒLIA'S MY FOE.

'SINCE Cœlia's my foe,
To a Desert I'll go,
 Where some river
 For ever
Shall Echo my woe:

The Trees shall appear
More relenting than her,
 In the morning
 Adorning
Each leaf with a tear.

When I make my sad moan
To the Rocks all alone,
 From each hollow
 Will follow
Some pitiful groan.

But with silent disdain
She requites all my pain,
 To my mourning
 Returning
No answer again.

Ah Cœlia adieu,
When I cease to pursue,
 You'll discover
 No Lover
Was ever so true.

Your sad Shepherd flies
From those dear cruel eyes
 Which not seeing
 His being
Decays, and he dies.

WAITING FOR THE MAY.

By D. F. McCarthy.

Ah! my heart is weary waiting,
 Waiting for the May—
Waiting for the pleasant rambles,
Where the fragrant hawthorn-brambles,
 With the woodbine alternating,
  Scent the dewy way.
 Ah! my heart is weary waiting,
  Waiting for the May.

Ah! my heart is sick with longing,
 Longing for the May—
Longing to escape from study
To the fair young face and ruddy,
 And the thousand charms belonging
  To the summer's day.
 Ah! my heart is sick with longing,
  Longing for the May.

Ah! my heart is sore with sighing,
 Sighing for the May—
Sighing for their sure returning
When the summer-beams are burning,
 Hopes and flowers that dead or dying
  All the winter lay.
 Ah! my heart is sore with sighing,
  Sighing for the May.

Ah! my heart is pained with throbbing,
 Throbbing for the May—
Throbbing for the seaside billows,
Or the water-wooing willows,
 Where in laughing and in sobbing
  Glide the streams away.
 Ah! my heart is pained with throbbing,
  Throbbing for the May.

WAITING FOR THE MAY.—*Continued.*

Waiting, sad, dejected, weary,
Waiting for the May.
Spring goes by with wasted warnings—
Moonlit evenings, sunbright mornings—
Summer comes, yet dark and dreary
Life still ebbs away—
Man is ever weary, weary,
Waiting for the May!

LIMERICK IS BEAUTIFUL.

LIMERICK is beautiful,
  As everybody knows,
The river Shannon, full of fish,
  Through that city flows;
But 'tis not the river or the fish,
  That weighs upon my mind,
Nor with the town of Limerick
  I've any fault to find.
                    Ochone, ochone.

The girl I love is beautiful,
  And soft-eyed as the fawn,
She lives in Garryowen,
  And is called the Colleen Bawn.
And proudly as that river flows
  Through that famed city,
As proudly and without a word
  That colleen goes by me.
                    Ochone, ochone.

If I was made the Emperor
  Of Russia to command,
Or Julius Cæsar, or the
  Lord Lieutenant of the land,
I'd give my plate and golden store,
  I'd give up my army,
The horses, the rifles, and the foot,
  And the Royal Artillery.
                    Ochone, ochone,

I'd give the crown from off my head,
  My people on their knees,
I'd give the fleet of sailing ships
  Upon the briny seas;
A beggar I would go to bed,
  And happy rise at dawn,—
If by my side for my sweet bride
  I had found my Colleen Bawn.
                    Ochone, ochone.

OH YIELD, FAIR LIDS.

By R. B. Sheridan.

Oh yield, fair lids, the treasures of my heart,
   Release those beams, that make this mansion bright;
From her sweet sense, Slumber! though sweet thou art,
   Begone, and give the air she breathes in light.

Or while, oh, Sleep, thou dost those glances hide,
   Let rosy slumbers still around her play,
Sweet as the cherub Innocence enjoy'd,
   When in thy lap, new-born, in smiles he lay.

And thou, oh Dream, that com'st her sleep to cheer,
   Oh take my shape, and play a lover's part;
Kiss her from me, and whisper in her ear,
   Till her eyes shine, 'tis night within my heart.

—————o—————

CORINNA.

By Dean Swift. Written, 1712.

This day (the year I dare not tell)
   Apollo play'd the midwife's part;
Into the world Corinna fell,
   And he endow'd her with his art.

But Cupid with a Satyr comes:
   Both softly to the cradle creep;
Both stroke her hands and rub her gums,
   While the poor child lay fast asleep.

Then Cupid thus: " this little maid
   Of love shall always speak and write."
" And I pronounce," (the Satyr said,)
   " The world shall feel her scratch and bite."

DARK ROSALEEN.

Translated from the Irish, by JAMES CLARENCE MANGAN.

O MY dark Rosaleen,
  Do not sigh, do not weep!
The priests are on the ocean green,
  They march along the deep.
There's wine. . . .from the royal Pope,
  Upon the ocean green ;
And Spanish ale shall give you hope,
  My dark Rosaleen !
  My own Rosaleen !
Shall glad your heart, shall give you hope,
Shall give you health, and help, and hope,
  My dark Rosaleen !

Over hills, and through dales,
  Have I roamed for your sake ;
All yesterday I sailed with sails
  On river and on lake.
The Erne, ...at its highest flood,
  I dashed across unseen,
For there was lightning in my blood,
  My dark Rosaleen !
  My own Rosaleen !
Oh ! there was lightning in my blood,
Red lightning lightened through my blood,
  My dark Rosaleen !

All day long, in unrest,
  To and fro, do I move,
The very soul within my breast
  Is wasted for you, love !
The heart. . . .in my bosom faints
  To think of you, my queen,
My life of life, my saint of saints,
  My dark Rosaleen !
  My own Rosaleen !
To hear your sweet and sad complaints,
My life, my love, my saint of saints,
  My dark Rosaleen !

DARK ROSALEEN.—*Continued.*

Woe and pain, pain and woe
  Are my lot, night and noon,
To see your bright face clouded so,
  Like to the mournful moon.
But yet.....will I rear your throne
  Again in golden sheen ;
'Tis you shall reign, shall reign alone,
  My dark Rosaleen !
  My own Rosaleen !
'Tis you shall have the golden throne,
'Tis you shall reign, and reign alone,
  My dark Rosaleen !

Over dews, over sands
  Will I fly, for your weal:
Your holy, delicate white hands
  Shall girdle me with steel.
At home.....in your emerald bowers,
  From morning's dawn till e'en,
You'll pray for me, my flower of flowers.
  My dark Rosaleen !
  My fond Rosaleen !
You'll think of me through daylight's hours
My virgin flower, my flower of flowers,
  My dark Rosaleen !

I could scale the blue air,
  I could plough the high hills,
Oh, I could kneel all night in prayer,
  To heal your many ills !
And one.....beamy smile from you
  Would float like light between
My toils and me, my own, my true,
  My dark Rosaleen !
  My fond Rosaleen !
Would give me life and soul anew,
A second life, a soul anew,
  My dark Rosaleen !

DARK ROSALEEN.—*Continued.*

O ! the Erne shall run red
   With redundance of blood,
The earth shall rock beneath our tread,
   And flames wrap hill and wood,
And gun-peal, and slogan-cry,
   Wake many a glen serene,
Ere you shall fade, ere you shall die,
   My dark Rosaleen !
   My own Rosaleen !
The Judgment Hour must first be nigh,
Ere you can fade, ere you can die,
   My dark Rosaleen !

———o———

THE BIVOUAC.

By Charles Lever.

Air.—*" Garryowen."*

Now that we've pledged each eye of blue,
   And every maiden fair and true,
And our green island home—to you
   The ocean's wave adorning,
Let's give one hip, hip, hip, hurra !
   And drink e'en to the coming day,
      When squadron square
      We'll all be there !
To meet the French in the morning.

May his bright laurels never fade,
   Who leads our fighting fifth brigade,
Those lads so true in heart and blade,
   And famed for danger scorning ;
So join me in one hip, hurra !
   And drink e'en to the coming day,
      When squadron square
      We'll all be there !
To meet the French in the morning.

THE MAN FOR GALWAY.

By Charles Lever.

To drink a toast,
A proctor roast,
　Or bailiff, as the case is;
To kiss your wife,
Or take your life
　At ten or fifteen paces;
To keep game cocks, to hunt the fox,
　To drink in punch the Solway,
With debts galore, but fun far more;
　Oh, that's " the man for Galway."
With debts, &c.

The King of Oude
Is mighty proud,
　And so were onest the Caysars;
But ould Giles Eyre
Would make them stare,
　Av he had them with the Blazers.*
To the divil I fling ould Runjeet Sing
　He's only a prince in a small way,
And knows nothing at all of a six-foot wall;
　Oh, he'd never " do for Galway."
With debts, &c.

Ye think the Blakes
Are no " great shakes;"
　They're all his blood relations;
And the Bodkins sneeze
At the grim Chinese,
　For they come from the Phenaycians.
So fill to the brim, and here's to him
　Who'd drink in punch the Solway;
With debts galore, but fun far more;
　Oh! that's " the man for Galway."
With debts, &c.

* This generally implies the arbitrement of the "*duello,*" blazers being a figurative term for pistols; but in the present case, the *Blazers* allude to a very break-neck pack of hounds, so called.

GOUGAUNE BARRA.

By J. J. Callanan.

THERE is a green island in lone Gougaune Barra,
Where Allu of songs rushes forth like an arrow;
In deep-valleyed Desmond a thousand wild fountains
Come down to that lake, from their home in the mountains;
There grows the wild ash; and a time-stricken willow
Looks chidingly down on the mirth of the billow,
As, like some gay child, that sad monitor scorning,
It lightly laughs back to the laugh of the morning.

And its zone of dark hills—oh! to see them all bright'ning,
When the tempest flings out its red banner of lightning,
And the waters rush down, 'mid the thunder's deep rattle,
Like clans from their hills at the voice of the battle;
And brightly the fire-crested billows are gleaming,
And wildly from Mullagh the eagles are screaming.
Oh! where is the dwelling in valley, or highland,
So meet for a bard as this lone little island?

How oft, when the summer sun rested on Clara,*
And lit the dark heath on the hills of Ivera,
Have I sought thee, sweet spot, from my home by the ocean,
And trod all thy wilds with a Minstrel's devotion!
And thought of thy bards, when assembling together
In the cleft of thy rocks, or the depth of thy heather,
They fled from the Saxon's dark bondage and slaughter,
And waked their last song by the rush of thy water!

High sons of the lyre, oh! how proud was the feeling,
To think, while alone through that solitude stealing,
Though loftier minstrels green Erin can number,
I fearlessly wak'd your wild harp from its slumber,
And glean'd the gray legend that long had been sleeping
Where oblivion's dull mist o'er its beauty was creeping,
From the love which I felt for my country's sad story,
When to love her was shame—to revile her was glory!

* Cape Clear.

GOUGAUNE BARRA.—*Continued.*

Last bard of the free! * were it mine to inherit
The fire of thy harp, and the wing of thy spirit—
With the wrongs which, like thee, to our country have bound
        me—
Did your mantle of song fling its radiance around me,
Still, still in those wilds might young liberty rally,
And send her strong shout over mountain and valley;
The star of the west might yet rise in its glory,
And the land that was darkest be brightest in story!

I soon shall be gone ;—but my name may be spoken
When Erin awakes, and her fetters are broken ;
Some Minstrel will come, in the summer eve's gleaming,
When Freedom's young light on his spirit is beaming,
To bend o'er my grave with a tear of emotion,
Where calm Avon-Buee seeks the kisses of ocean,
And plant a wild wreath, from the banks of that river,
O'er the heart, and the harp, that are silent for ever. †

————o————

OH, TELL ME, SWEET KATE.

By Lady Morgan.

Oh tell me, sweet Kate, by what magical art
   You seduced ev'ry thought, ev'ry wish of my soul,
Oh tell how my credulous fond, doating heart,
   By thy wiles and thy charms from my bosom was stole.

Oh, whence, dangerous girl, was thy sorcery, tell,
   By which you awaken'd love's tear and love's sigh ; —
In thy voice, in thy song, lurks the dangerous spell?
   In the blush of thy cheek, or the beam of thine eye?

* He must have meant Moore, from the context.

† This melancholy aspiration of the patriot poet was not realized ; his grave
is in a foreign land.

DRY BE THAT TEAR.

By RICHARD BRINSLEY SHERIDAN.

DRY be that tear, my gentlest love,
　Be hushed that struggling sigh;
Nor seasons, day, nor fate shall prove,
　More fixed, more true, than I:
Hushed be that sigh, be dry that tear,
Cease boding doubt, cease anxious fear—
　　　Dry be that tear

Ask'st thou how long my love shall stay,
　When all that's new is past?
How long, ah! Delia, can I say,
　How long my life shall last?
Dry be that tear, be hushed that sigh,
　At least I'll love thee till I die—
　　　Hushed be that sigh.

And does that thought affect thee, too,
　The thought of Sylvio's death,
That he, who only breathed for you,
　Must yield that faithful breath?
Hushed be that sigh, be dry that tear,
Nor let us lose our heaven here—
　　　Dry be that tear.

———o———

THE CHAIN OF GOLD.

By SAMUEL LOVER.

OH, Moina, I've a tale to tell,
　Will glad thy soul, my girl;
The King hath giv'n a chain of gold
　To our noble-hearted Earl.
His foes they rail'd, the Earl ne'er quail'd,
　But with a front so bold,
Before the King did backward fling
　The slanderous lie they told;
And the King gave him no iron chain,
No—he gave him a chain of gold!

THE CHAIN OF GOLD.—*Continued.*

Oh, 'tis a noble sight to see,
   The cause of truth prevail;
An honest cause is always proof
   Against a treach'rous tale.
Let fawning false ones court the great,
   The heart in virtue bold,
Will hold the right in pow'rs despite
   Until that heart be cold:
For falsehood's the bond of slavery;
   But truth is the chain of gold.

False Connal wed the rich one,
   With her gold and jewels rare,
But Dermid wed the maid he lov'd,
   And she clear'd his brow from care.
And thus, in our own hearts, love,
   We may read this lesson plain—
Let outward joys depart, love,
   So peace within remain:
For falsehood is an iron bond,
   But love is the golden chain!

ST. PATRICK'S DAY IN MY OWN PARLOR.

By J. F. Waller.

Air.— " St. Patrick's Day."

THE white and the orange, the blue and the green, boys,
 We'll blend them together in concord to-night;
The orange most sweet amid green leaves is seen, boys—
 The loveliest pansy is blue and white.
   The light of the day
   As it glides away,
Paints with orange the white clouds that float in the west,
   And the billows that roar
   Round our own island shore
Lay their green heads to rest on the blue heaven's bosom,
 Where sky and sea meet in the distance away.
As Nature thus shows us how well she can fuse 'em,
 We'll blend them in love on St. Patrick's Day.

The hues of the prism, philosophers say, boys,
 Are nought but the sunlight resolved into parts;
They're beauteous, no doubt, but I think that the ray, boys,
 Unbroken, more lights up and warms our hearts.
   Each musical tone,
   Struck one by one,
Makes melody sweet, it is true, on the ear—
   But let the hand ring
   All at once every string—
And, oh! there is harmony now that is glorious,
 In unison pealing to heaven away;
For union is beauty, and strength, and victorious,
 Of hues, tones, or hearts, on St. Patrick's Day.

Those hues in one bosom be sure to unite, boys;
 Let each Irish heart wear those emblems so true;
Be fresh as the green, and be pure as the white, boys,—
 Be bright as the orange, sincere as the blue.
   I care not a jot
   Be your scarf white or not,
If you love as a brother each child of the soil;
   I ask not your creed,
   If you'll stand in her need
To the land of your birth in the hour of her dolors,
 The foe of her foes, let them be who they may;
Then, " FUSION OF HEARTS, AND CONFUSION OF COLORS !"
 Be the Irishman's toast on St. Patrick's Day.

LEAVE US A LOCK OF YOUR HAIR.

By J. F. Waller, LL.D.

Air.--" The Low-backed Car."

The night is fresh and clear, love,
 The birds are in their bowers,
  And the holy light
  Of the moon falls bright
 On the beautiful sleeping flowers.
Oh! Nora, are you waking?
Or don't you hear me *spaking?*
You know my heart is breaking
 For the love of you, Nora dear.
Ah! why don't you speak, Mavrone?
Sure I think that you're made of stone,
 Just like Venus of old,
 All so white and so cold,
But no morsel of flesh or bone.

" There's not a soul astir, love,
 No sound falls on the ear,
  But that rogue of a breeze
  That's whispering the trees
 Till they tremble all through with fear.
Ah! them happy flowers that's creeping
To your window where you're sleeping,
Sure *they're* not chid for peeping
 At your beauties, my Nora dear.
You've the heart of a Turk, by my *sowl,*
To leave me perched here like an owl;
 'Tis treatment too bad,
 For a true-hearted lad,
To be sarved like a desolate fowl.

" You know the vow you made, love—
 You know we fixed the day;
  And here I'm now
  To claim that vow,
 And carry my bride away;
So, Nora, don't be staying
For weeping, or for praying—
There's danger in delaying—
 Sure maybe I'd change my mind

LEAVE US A LOCK OF YOUR HAIR.—*Continued.*

For you know I'm a bit of a rake,
And a trifle might tempt me to break——
   Faix, but for your blue eye,
   I've a notion to try
What a sort of ould maid you'd make."

" Oh ! Dermot, win me not, love,
   To be your bride to night :
     How could I bear
     A mother's tear,
   A father's scorn and slight?
So, Dermot, cease your sueing—
Don't work your Nora's ruin,
'Twould be my sore undoing,
   If you're found at my window, dear."
" Ah ! for shame with your foolish alarms—
Just drop into your own Dermot's arms :
   Don't mind looking at all
   For your cloak or shawl—
They were made but to smother your charms."

And now a dark cloud rising
   Across the moon is cast,
     The lattice opes,
     And anxious hopes
   Make Dermot's heart beat fast:
And soon a form entrancing,—
With arms and fair neck glancing,—
Half shrinking, half advancing,
   Steps light on the lattice sill;
When—a terrible arm in the air
Clutched the head of the lover all bare,
   And a voice, with a scoff,
   Cried, as Dermot made off,
" WON'T YOU LEAVE US A LOCK OF YOUR HAIR? "

FAIR-HILL'D, PLEASANT IRELAND.

FROM THE IRISH.

TAKE a blessing from the heart of a lonely griever
    To fair-hill'd, pleasant Ireland,
To the glorious seed of Ir and Eivir,
    In fair-hill'd pleasant Ireland,
Where the voice of birds fills the wooded vale,
Like the mourning harp o'er the fallen Gael—
And, oh! that I pine many long days' sail
    From fair-hill'd, pleasant Ireland!

On the gentle heights are soft sweet fountains,
    In fair-hill'd, pleasant Ireland;
I would choose o'er this land the bleakest mountains
    In fair-hill'd, pleasant Ireland—
More sweet than fingers o'er strings of song,
The lowing of cattle the vales among,
And the sun smiling down upon old and young,
    In fair-hill'd, pleasant Ireland!

There are numerous hosts at the trumpet's warning,
    In fair-hill'd, pleasant Ireland;
And warriors bold, all danger scorning,
    In fair-hill'd, pleasant Ireland —
Oh, memory sad! oh, tale of grief!
They are crush'd by the stranger past all relief;
Nor tower nor town hath its native chief,
    In fair-hill'd, pleasant Ireland!

——o——

THE WIND AND THE WEATHERCOCK.

BY SAMUEL LOVER.

THE summer wind lightly was playing
  Round the battlement high of the tow'r,
Where a vane, like a lady, was staying,—
  A lady vain perch'd in her bow'r.
To peep round the corner the sly wind would try;
But vanes, you know, never look in the wind's eye;
  And so she kept turning shily away :—
  Thus they kept playing all through the day.

The summer wind said, " She's coquetting :
    But each belle has her points to be found ;
Before evening, I'll venture on betting,
    She will not then *go* but *come* round ! "
So he tried from the east, and he tried from the west,
And the north and the south, to try which was best ;
    But still she kept turning shily away :—
    Thus they kept playing all through the day.

At evening, her hard heart to soften,
    He said, " You're a flirt, I am sure ;
But if vainly you're changing so often,
    No lover you'll ever secure. "
" Sweet sir, " said the vane " it is you who begin ;
When *you* change so often, in *me* 'tis no sin ;
    If you cease to flutter, and steadily sigh,
    And only be constant—I'm sure so will I. "

BRIDGET CRUISE TO CAROLAN.

FROM THE IRISH.

OH! tempt not my feet from the straight path of duty,
 Love lights a meteor but to betray!
And soon wouldst thou tire of the odorless beauty,
 If grew not esteem upon passion's decay.
Then cease thee—ah, cease thee to urge and to pray!
I may not, I cannot, thy suit is in vain!
For filial affections a daughter restrain,
 And worthless were she who had slighted their sway.

Oh! how couldst thou trust for connubial affection
 The bosom untrue to its earliest ties?
Or where were thy bliss when, on sad recollection,
 I'd sink, self-condemn'd, self-abash'd from thine eyes?
Then cease thee—ah, cease thee!—'tis fated we part!
Yet, if sympathy soften the pang of thy heart,
I will own to this bosom far dearer thou art
 Than all that earth's treasure, earth's pleasure supplies.

But where am I urged by impetuous feeling?
 Thy tears win the secret long hid in my breast.
Farewell! and may time fling the balsam of healing
 O'er wounds that have rankled, and robbed thee of rest.
Yet lose not, ah, lose not, each lingering thought
Of her who in early affection you sought,
And whose bosom to cheer thee would sacrifice aught
 But love to a parent, the kindest and best.

——o——

THE SILVERY LEE.

RIVERS are there great and small,
 Romantic, too, the course of many,
With coated crag and foamy fall;
 But never river saw I any
 Half so fair, so dear to me,
 As my own, my silvery Lee.

Much I've heard about the Rhine,
 With vineyards gay, and castles stately;
But those who think I care for wine
 Or lofty towers, mistake me greatly:
 A thousand times more dear to me
 Is whiskey by the silvery Lee.

THE SILVERY LEE.—*Continued.*

The Tagus, with its golden sand,
  The Tiber, full of ancient glory,
The Danube, though a river grand,
  The Seine and Elbe, renowned in story,
    Can never be so dear to me
    As the pure and silvery Lee.

'Tis not the voice that tongues the stream,
  In winter hoarse, in spring-time clearer,—
That makes my own sweet river seem
  Above all other rivers dearer;
    But 'tis her voice, who whispers me,—
    " How lovely is the silvery Lee!"

——o——

THE TWISTING OF THE ROPE.

Translated from the Irish, by E. WALSH.

WHAT mortal conflict drove me here to roam,
Though many a maid I've left behind at home;
Forth from the house where dwelt my heart's dear hope,
I was turned by the hag at the twisting of the rope!

If thou be mine, be mine both day and night,
If thou be mine, be mine in all men's sight,
If thou be mine, be mine o'er all beside—
And oh, that thou wert now my wedded bride!

In Sligo first I did my love behold,
In Galway town I spent with her my gold—
But by this hand, if thus they me pursue,
I'll teach these dames to dance a measure new!

GRACE NUGENT.

By Carolan.

Translated by Samuel Ferguson.

Brightest blossom of the spring,
Grace, the sprightly girl, I sing;
Grace who bore the palm of mind
From all the rest of womankind;
Whomsoe'er the fates decree,
Happy fate for life to be,
Day and night my Coolun* near,
Ache or pain need never fear.

Her neck outdoes the stately swan,
Her radiant face the summer dawn;
Ah, happy thrice the youth for whom
The fates design that branch of bloom!
Pleasant are your words benign,
Rich those azure eyes of thine;
Ye who see my queen, beware
Those twisted links of golden hair!

This is what I fain would say
To the bird-voiced lady gay †—
Never yet conceived the heart
Joy that Grace cannot impart:
Fold of jewels, case of pearls!
Coolun of the circling curls!
More I say not, but no less
Drink your health and happiness.

---

* Coolun means a fine head of hair, and the term is often used as one of endearment.

† This "bird-voiced lady" (how sweet the epithet!) was a fair daughter of the Nugent of Castle Nugent, Columbre.

THE GIRLS OF THE WEST.

By Charles Lever.

Air.—" *Thady ye Gander.*"

You may talk, if you please,
Of the brown Portuguese,
But, wherever you roam, wherever you roam,
You nothing will meet
Half so lovely or sweet
As the girls at home, the girls at home.
Their eyes are not sloes,
Nor so long is their nose,
But between me and you, between me and you,
They are just as alarming,
And ten times more charming,
With hazel and blue, with hazel and blue.

THE GIRLS OF THE WEST.—*Continued.*

They don't ogle a man
O'er the top of their fan
Till his heart's in a flame, his heart's in a flame
But though bashful and shy,
They've a look in their eye
That just comes to the same, just comes to the same.
No mantillas they sport,
But a petticoat short
Shows an ankle the best, an ankle the best,
And a leg; but, O murther!
I dare not go further,
So here's to the West, so here's to the West.

WHEN MY OLD HAT WAS NEW.

By Thomas Moore.

When my old hat was new, now thirty-six long years,
I was at the review of the Dublin volunteers.
There have been brought to pass with us a change or two
They're altered times, alas, since my old hat was new.

Our parliament did sit then in our native land:
What good came of the loss of it I cannot understand,
Although full plain I see, that changes not a few
Have fallen on the country since my old hat was new.

*　　*　　*　　*　　*　　*

The nobles of our country were then our neighbors near,
And our old squires and gentry made always jolly cheer.
Ah! every night at some one's house or other's was a crew
Of merry lords and commoners, when my old hat was new.

They're altered times entirely, as plainly now appears,
Our landlord's face we barely see pass once in seven years.
And now the man meets scorn as his coat is green or blue,
We had no need our coats to turn when my old hat was new.

THE BELLS OF SHANDON.*

By Rev. Francis Mahony.

With deep affection
And recollection
I often think of
   Those Shandon bells,
Whose sounds so wild would
In the days of childhood,
Fling round my cradle
   Their magic spells.
On this I ponder
Where'er I wander,
And thus grow fonder,
   Sweet Cork, of thee;
With thy bells of Shandon,
That sound so grand on
The pleasant waters
   Of the river Lee.

* Shandon Church is an odd-looking old structure in the City of Cork.

THE BELLS OF SHANDON.—*Continued.*

I've heard bells chiming,
Full many a clime in,
Tolling sublime in
   Cathedral shrine;
While at a glibe rate
Brass tongues would vibrate;
But all their music
   Spoke naught like thine.
For memory dwelling
On each proud swelling
Of thy belfry, knelling
   Its bold notes free,
Made the Bells of Shandon
Sound far more grand on
The pleasant waters
   Of the river Lee.

I've heard bells tolling
Old " Adrian's Mole " in
Their thunder rolling
   From the Vatican,
And cymbals glorious
Swinging uproarious
In the gorgeous turrets
   Of Notre Dame ;
But thy sounds were sweeter
Than the dome of Peter
Flings o'er the Tiber,
   Pealing solemnly.
Oh ! the bells of Shandon
Sound far more grand on
The pleasant waters
   Of the river Lee.

There's a bell in Moscow,
While on tower and kiosk O !
In Saint Sophia
   The Turkman gets,
And loud in air
Calls men to prayer
From the tapering summits
   Of tall minarets.

THE BELLS OF SHANDON.—*Continued.*

Such empty phantom
I freely grant them ;
But there is an anthem
   More dear to me—
'Tis the bells of Shandon
That sound so grand on
The pleasant waters
   Of the river Lee.

———o———

AVONDHU.

By J. J. Callanan.

Oh Avondhu I wish I were,
As once, upon that mountain bare,
Where thy young waters laugh and shine
On the wild breast of Meenganine.
I wish I were by Cleada's * hill,
Or by Glenruachra's rushy rill.
But no ! I never more shall view
Those scenes I loved by Avondhu.

Farewell, ye soft and purple streaks
Of evening on the beauteous Reeks ; †
Farewell, ye mists, that loved to ride
On Cahirbearna's stormy side.
Farewell, November's moaning breeze,
Wild minstrel of the dying trees ;
Clara ! a fond farewell to you,
No more we meet by Avondhu.

No more—but thou, O glorious hill,
Lift to the moon thy forehead still ;
Flow on, flow on, thou dark swift river,
Upon thy free wild course for ever.
Exult young hearts, in lifetime's spring,
And taste the joys pure love can bring ;
But, wanderer, go, they're not for you—
Farewell, farewell, sweet Avondhu.

* Cleada and Cahirbearna (the hill of the four gaps) form part of the chain of mountains which stretch westward from Mill-street to Killarney.

† Magillicuddy's Reeks, in the neighborhood of Killarney.

COME ALL YOU PALE LOVERS.

By Thomas Duffett.

Come all you pale Lovers that sigh and complain,
While your beautiful Tyrants but laugh at your pain,
　　Come practice with me
　　To be happy and free,
In spite of Inconstancy, Pride or Disdain.
　　　I see and I Love, and the Bliss I enjoy,
　　　No Rival can lessen, nor envy destroy.

My Mistress so fair is, no Language or Art
Can describe her Perfection in every part,
　　Her mien's so Gentil,
　　With such ease she can kill:
Each look with new passion she captives my heart.
　　　I see, &c.,
　　　No rival, &c.

Her smiles, the kind message of Love from her eyes,
When she frowns 'tis from others her Flame to disguise,
　　Thus her scorn or her Spite
　　I convert to delight,
As the Bee gathers Honey wherever　she flies.
　　　I see, &c.,
　　　No rival, &c.

My vows she receives from her Lover unknown,
And I fancy kind answers although I have none,
　　How Blest should I be
　　If our Hearts did agree
Since already I find so much Pleasure alone.
　　　I see, and I love, and the Bliss I enjoy,
　　　No Rival can lessen nor envy destroy.

THE BOYS OF THE IRISH BRIGADE.
By Mrs. Gore.

WHAT for should I sing you of Roman or Greek,
  Or the boys we hear tell of in story?
Come match me for fighting, for frolic, or freak,
  An Irishman's reign in his glory;
For Ajax, and Hector, and bold Agamemnon
  Were up to the tricks of our trade, O,
But the rollicking boys, for war, ladies and noise,
  Are the boys of the Irish Brigade, O!

What for should I sing you of Helen of Troy,
  Or the mischief that came by her flirting?
There's Biddy M'Clinchy the pride of Fermoy,
  Twice as much of a Helen, that's certain.
Then for Venus, so famous, or Queen Cleopatra,
  Bad luck to the word should be said, O,
By the rollicking boys, for war, ladies and noise,—
  Are the boys of the Irish Brigade, O!

What for should I sing you of classical fun,
  Or of games, whether Grecian or Persian?
Sure the Curragh's the place where the knowing one's done,
  And Mallow that flogs for diversion.
For fighting, for drinking, for ladies and all,
  No times like our times e'er were made, O,
By the rollicking boys, for war, ladies and noise,
  The boys of the Irish Brigade, O!

———o———

KATTY MOONEY.
By Blewitt.

I COURTED Katty Mooney, dear,
  A girl so neat and cosey;
Her eyes they were so bright and clear,
  Her lips were ripe and rosy.
I bought a pig to live with us,
  I got a stick to mind it;
'Twas a beauty too, but, like the rest,
  It carried its tail behind it.
            Och, hubbaboo, och phillaloo,
              Wasn't I a spooney,
            Ochone, ochone, to grunt and groan,
              And all for Katty Mooney!

KATTY MOONEY.—*Continued.*

Och, we were glad when we made one,
  In love we made a dozen;
But very soon she brought to town
  Her thirty-second cousin:
I made him eat, I made him drink,
  With compliments he lined me,
But the reason why I ne'er could think,
  Till he stayed one day behind me.
                    Och, hubbaboo, &c.

I don't know why that I went back
  I wisht I hadn't seen thim,
For they were giving smack for smack,
  And the pig was sitting between thim;
He ran away, och hubbaboo!
  May the devil catch and bind him,
And my wife may go to the devil too,
  If they leave the pig behind thim.
                    Och, hubbaboo, &c.

OH! DON'T YOU REMEMBER?

By Samuel Lover.

Oh! don't you remember the beautiful glade,
Where in childhood together we playfully stray'd,
Where wreaths of wild-flowers so often I made,
        Thy tresses so brightly adorning?
Oh! light of foot and heart were then
The happy children of the glen :—
The cares that shade the brows of men
        Ne'er darken childhood's morning.

Oh! who can forget the young innocent hours
That were pass'd in the shade of our home's happy bow'rs,
When the wealth that we sought for was only wild flow'rs,
        And we thought ourselves rich when we found them?
Oh! where's the tie that friends e'er knew,
So free from stain, so firm, so true,
As links that with the wild-flowers grew,
        And in sweet fetters bound them?

————o————

BY CŒLIA'S ARBOR.

By R. B. Sheridan.

By Cœlia's arbor, all the night,
    Hang, humid wreath,—the lover's vow ;
And haply, at the morning's light,
    My love will twine thee round her brow.

And if upon her bosom bright
    Some drops of dew should fall from thee,
Tell her they are not drops of night,
    But tears of sorrow shed by me.

AH! CRUEL MAID.

By R. B. Sheridan.

Ah, cruel maid, how hast thou chang'd
  The temper of my mind !
My heart, by thee from love estrang'd,
  Becomes, like thee, unkind.

By fortune favored, clear in fame,
  I once ambitious was ;
And friends I had, who fanned the flame,
  And gave my youth applause.

AH! CRUEL MAID.—*Continued.*

But now, my weakness all accuse,
  Yet vain their taunts on me ;
Friends, fortune, fame itself, I'd lose,
  To gain one smile from thee.

And only thou should not despise
  My weakness, or my woe ;
If I am mad in others' eyes,
  'Tis thou hast made me so.

But days, like this, with doubting curst,
  I will not long endure—
Am I disdained—I know the worst
  And likewise know my cure.

If false, her vows she dare renounce,
  That instant ends my pain ;
For, oh ! the heart must break at once,
  That cannot hate again.

ILLUSTRATIONS.

	PAGE.
Adieu to Innisfail	140
"And often in those grand old woods."	85
Brickeen Bridge	35
Fermoy	155
Gerald Griffin	332
"God Save Ireland,"	53
"I'm sitting on the Stile, Mary."	84
"I saw thy form in youthful prime."	277
Killarney	216
Mallow Castle	105
Miss Fanny Parnell	297
Mitchellstown Castle	248
Mr. Grattan addressing the Irish Parliament	259
Muckross Abbey	121
Robert Emmet	286
Savourneen deelish Eileen oge	443, 444, 445, 446, 447
Shemus O'Brien	407
Silent, O Moyle	322
Sloperton Cottage	310
The Donnybrook Jig	437
The Jaunting Car	341
The Irish Jaunting Car	13
The Irish School-master	25
The Pretty Girl milking her Cow	44
The Twig of the Shannon	454
The Woods of Caillino	416
The Winding Banks of Erne	59
"When the Moon is on the waters."	191

INDEX.

Angel's Whisper... 32
Adieu to Innisfail... 140
A Place in thy Memory, Dearest................................ 149
Annie, dear.. 196
A Soldier, a soldier to-night is our Guest.................... 202
A New Year's Song... 209
And must we part?... 253
Avenging and Bright... 264
After Death... 296
A True Story,—called Molly Bawn.............................. 321
As a Beam o'er the Face of the Waters........................ 326
After the Battle.. 347
At the Mid Hour of Night...................................... 353
A Lamentation... 359
A Munster Keen.. 412
A Spinning-Wheel Song... 453
A Sigh for Knockmany.. 458
Avondhu... 487
Ah! cruel maid.. 492
Bowld Sojer Boy... 7
Banks of Banna.. 8
Barney Brallaghan's Courtship................................. 9
Bugaboo,.. 20
Blackbird... 23
Boys of Kilkenny.. 55
Boyne Water... 68
Banks of Clody.. 70
Brennan on the Moor... 77
Buncheen of Lucharoe.. 87
Bantry Girl's lament for Johnny............................... 115
Billy O'Rourke.. 124
Bumpers, Squire Jones... 177
Barney Avourneen, I won't let you in.......................... 223
Bouchelleen Bawn.. 265
By that Lake whose Gloomy Shore............................... 269
Believe me, if all those endearing young charms............... 283
Burning of the Emigrant Ship.................................. 298
By Memory Inspired.. 305

Before the Battle.. 375
Between my sleeve and me.. 378
Barney O'Hea.. 386
Bad luck to this marching... 392
Bryan O'Lynn.. 393
Bridget Cruise.. 435
Bridget Cruise to Carolan... 480
By Cœlia's arbor.. 491
Cushla Machree..(Before the sun rose,).............................. 14
Cate of Araglen... 15
Cruiskeen Lawn.. 17
Croppy Boy.. 29
Come back to Erin... 33
Cushla machree..(Dear Erin, how sweetly,).......................... 39
Colleen Rue... 42
Come all you young fellows.. 80
Come to me darling, I'm lonely without thee......................... 76
Clare's Dragoons.. 170
Come to Glengariff, come.. 200
Convict of Clonmell,.. 233
Come, rest in this Bosom.. 266
Come o'er the Sea... 271
Come, send round the Wine... 336
Come back to me... 354
Cœlia's my foe.. 462
Corinna... 466
Come all you pale Lovers.. 488
Dear Land... 10
Deserter's Meditation... 26
Dear Irish Boy,... 28
Dawning of the day.. 52
Dublin Bay, or Roy Neill.. 63
Don't Marry... 95
Drinane Dhun.. 109
Dear Little Shamrock.. 160
Dear Harp of my Country... 208
Drink to Her.. 276
Drimin down dilis... 304
Dermot O'Dowd... 381
Darling old Stick... 414
Digging for Goold... 420
Dear Old Ireland.. 427
Dance light, for my heart it lies under your feet, love............. 457
Dark Rosaleen... 467
Dry be that tear.. 473

Erin's Lovely Home.. 12
Eileen Aroon... 34
Emigrant's farewell to Ballyshannon............................ 58
Exile of Erin,.. 62
Enniskillen Dragoon,... 134
Eibhlin a ruin,... 234
Erin ! the Tear and the Smile.................................. 274
Erin ! Oh, Erin !... 335
Eveleen's Bower.. 353
Four-leaved Shamrock... 43
Faithless Bride... 81
Flaming O'Flanagans 153
Farewell, my gentle Harp....................................... 201
Feast of O'Rorke... 205
For I am Desolate... 221
Farewell to my Harp.. 251
Farewell, but whenever.. 260
Fly not yet.. 268
Fill the Bumper fair.. 289
Fineen the Rover... 343
Father Land and Mother Tongue.............................. 379
Farewell, Bessy.. 413
Fair-hill'd, pleasant Ireland................................... 478
Groves of Blarney... 5
Gille Machree... 18
Gallant Hussar,.. 38
God Save Ireland.. 53
Gra gal machree... 92
The Green Flag... 162
Green above the Red... 164
Gael and the Green,.. 166
Garryowen.. 198
Glas-en-gorach... 219
Go where glory waits thee...................................... 228
Go ! forget me.. 246
Green were the fields... 434
Gougaune Barra... 471
Grace Nugent... 482
He tells me he loves me... 72
Hibernia's lovely Jean... 138
He said that he was not our Brother......................... 204
How Dear to me the Hour...................................... 268
Honor the Brave... 327
Has sorrow thy young days shaded.......................... 352
How oft, Louisa... 114

Hy-Brasail—The Isle of the Blest........................ 419
Hours like those.. 430
Had I a heart for falsehood framed................................ 433
Irish Jaunting Car,..(My name is Larry Doolan)........ 13
I'm a ranting, roving blade..... 21
Irish Shore.................. 22
Irish Schoolmaster.. 24
Irish Girl.. 31
I breathe once more my Native air... 45
Irish Stranger...... ....— .. 51
I love my Love in the Morning. ....,......... 69
Irish wife,.................................. 133
Irish Molly........... 148
Irishman's Shanty................................. 150
Irish Maiden's Song............................. 201
It is not the Tear at this moment shed............................... 210
If I had thought thou couldst have died................................ 211
I would not die................... 227
Irish Reaper's Harvest Hymn.................... 242
Inis Eoghain.......................... ....— 245
I Love but Thee.............................. 271
I saw thy form.. 276
It's little for Glory I care....... 287
I'd mourn the Hopes that leave me...................................... 288
I'll never forget that, Ma'am......... 293
I saw from the Beach.. 301
I'm not myself at all..... 324
I'm very happy where I am. 340
It may be yet... 362
I leave you to guess.... 383
Inspiring fount of cheering wine....................... 418
I was the Boy for bewitching them........................... 456
Johnny I hardly knew ye.. 48
John O'Dwyer of the Glen 104
Kathleen O'More... 65
Kitty Clare.. 106
Kitty Tyrrell... 144
Kathleen Mavourneen...................................... 165
Kate Kearney... 181
Kitty of Coleraine......... 185
Kate of Garnavilla,... 195
Killarney... 215
Katey's Letter 217
Kitty Maclure... 316
Kathleen and the Swallows,................................. 300

Kitty Creagh... 409
Kathleen Ny-Houlahan................. 450
Katty Mooney........... 489
Lough Erne's Shore........ 74
Lament of the Irish Emigrant 85
Lady and the Farmer,......... 93
Lovely Land of Dreams 108
Love Not... ....•.......... 111
Lads Who live in Ireland 118
Low-backed Car........ 123
Lamentation of General James Shields............ 125
Limerick Races,................... 126
Lament of Grainne Maol................................. 172
Let Erin Remember the days of Old....... 203
Lament of Morian Shehone for Miss Mary Burke...................... 220
Lament for the Milesians...... 236
Love and the Novice..................... 270
Larry O'Gaff... 319
Love's Young Dream.................................... 325
Lanty Leary........... 345
Live in my Heart and pay no Rent..................... 372
Lady mine.......................... 398
Limerick is beautiful...... 465
Leave us a lock of your hair 476
Molly Asthore.................................... 262
Maid of sweet Gortein 64
Matilda Heron's Celtic Song..................... 67
Memory of the Dead...................................... 79
Molly Bawn 82
Molly Carew 98
Maid of Skreen.......... 132
Molly Brallaghan..................................... 156
My Emmet's No More ... -------------------------., 157
My Land 163
Mountain Dew,.------------------------------------- 197
Mary Machree... 203
Mother, He's going away 222
My Mary of the Curling Hair............................ 229
Mary le More... 284
Mary, I believed thee True......... 291
Mary O'Mara.. 308
My Connor................................... 329
My dark-haired girl..................................... 345
Mary of Tipperary. 354
Mo Craoibhin Cno.... 363

My Mountain Home.................................... 374
My Mother Dear.. 374
Mild Mabel Kelly......................,................................ 410
Mairgread ni Chelleadh.................. 422
Mary Draper.................... 429
Mauryeen..... 441
My Native Town................................. 448
Ned of the Hill.. . 50
Norah Machree 117
Norah, the Pride of Kildare 146
New St. Patrick's Day..................... 147
Norah O'Neill......................... 161
New Irish Emigrant..... 167
Native Swords......... 214
Nora Creina..... 252
No, not more welcome.. .. 264
Norah's Lament... 347
Never despair..... 309
Native music......................... 370
Now can't you be aisy...... 449
O'Donnell Abu 49
O ! say my brown drimmin........... 89
Old Ireland, you're my darling 137
Oh ! Erin, my country.. 143
Once I had a true love..... 189
Oh ! the Marriage.................................. 218
O'Brien of Ara....................... 250
Oh, blame not the Bard......... 267
One Bumper at parting................................. . 275
Oh, Lady fair. 285
Oh, think not my spirits.. 291
Oh, 'tis sweet to think..... 292
O, Molly, I can't say you're honest......................... 307
Oh ! where's the slave... 314
O'Byrne's Bard to the Clans of Wicklow.................... 318
Oh ! the Shamrock........ 330
Oh, give me thy hand, fair Lady... 350
O'Donovan's Daughter................................ ... 356
Oh ! had we some bright little Isle.. 367
Oh, Judith, my dear... 411
Oh ! once we were illigant people.......................... 450
Oh, yield, fair lids 466
Oh, tell me, sweet Kate.... 472
Oh ! don't you remember 191
Paddy Hagerty's old Leather Breeches........ 46

Peggy Bawn 73
Paddy Carey 100
Patrick Sheehan.. 120
Potteen, good luck to ye, dear 127
Paddy's Wedding... 129
Pat Malloy.. 169
Paddies evermore........ 174
Paddy McShane's Seven Ages................................... 226
Pretty girl of Loch Dan.. 231
Paddy O'Rafther.. 300
Paddy's Island of Green...................................... 386
Paddy's pastoral Rhapsody.................................... 389
Peggy Browne... 397
Phelim O'Neile...... 435
Robin Adair 41
Roy Neill, or, Dublin Bay.................................... 63
Rejected Lover,.. 96
Rakes of Mallow,... 105
Rory of the Hills.. 113
Rambler from Clare,.. 116
Rising of the Moon,.. 154
Rory O'More.. 187
Recruiting Song of the Irish Brigade. 199
Roisin Dubh.. 247
Rich and Rare were the Gems she Wore........................ 283
Remember the glories of Brien the Brave...................... 368
Sweet Castle Hyde.. 27
Soggarth Aroon,.. 40
Star of Slane.. 66
Shan Van Voght... 71
Shanduine,..(Old man).. 88
Sailor Boy,.. 97
Shamrock Shore,.. 110
Shannon's Flowery Banks,..................................... 123
Streams of Bunclody,... 130
Steer my bark to Erin's Isle................................. 136
Since I've been in the army.................................. 145
Stand together... 176
Shamrock and the Lily.. 183
Song of Moina the Maniac..................................... 188
Sons of Hibernia... 193
Songs of our Land.. 194
Song of an Exile..(In Ireland 'tis evening,)................ 212
Song of an Exile.. (Farewell, and for ever,)................ 223
Serenade... 243

She is far from the land.. 255
Sleep, my babe, sleep... 312
Sublime was the warning................... 315
Silent, O'Moyle.. 322
Song of the galloping O'Hogan.. 331
Secrets were not meant for three 346
Soft on the ear..,........ 355
Sally....................................... 373
Shemus O'Brien........................ 401
Sweet Seducer............................ 423
Savourneen Deelish Eileen Oge......... 443
St. Patrick's Day in my own Parlor........................... 475
The Cow that ate the Piper 35
Terence's Farewell.. 83
Trust to Luck...................................... 119
That rogue Reilly.. 131
The savage loves his native shore................................ 135
Tim Finigan's Wake....................................... 152
Tell me, Mary..................................... 158
The Suit of Green,....................................... 159
The Welcome... 182
The tie is broke, my Irish girl............................... .. 186
The Lost Path,....................................... 207
The forsaken maid....................................... 213
The Mother's Lament......... 221
The Emerald Isle..(Alas ! border minstrel,).............. 221
The Emerald Isle..(Of all the nations under the sun,).... 225
The night was still 230
The leaves so green,.. 237
The Grave of McCaura.................................... 240
The Fairy Child.. 241
The mi na meala now is passed................................ 244
The Desmond................................... 249
The Minstrel Boy,.. 253
The Meeting of the Waters...................................... 254
The Harp that once through Tara's halls........... 255
The County of Mayo................................. 256
The Patriot Mother.. 257
The Man who led the van of Irish volunteers.............................. 258
Though the last glimpse of Erin with sorrow I see................ 260
The Poor Man's labor's never done.................................... 261
There's not a word......... 272
'Tis the Last Rose of Summer.............................. 278
The rocky road to Dublin...................................... 279
The Land of the West,..............,,, .,,.,............... 281

PAGE.

The White Cockade.. 281
The Irish Mother in the Penal days................................ 282
There's nothing true but Heaven.................................. 284
The Fisherman's Daughter.. 294
Take back the Sigh..... 295
The time I've lost in wooing...................................... 302
'Tis gone and for ever.. 306
The boatman of Kinsale.. 309
Through grief and through danger.................................. 311
The Flower of Finae... 313
The Fairy Isle.. 317
The Sister of Charity,.. 333
The Emigrant Mother,.. 335
The Bridal of Malahide,... 337
To Ladies' Eyes... 339
The Jaunting Car,... 341
The young May moon.. 342
The Letter.. 344
The Minstrel's walk... 348
The fair hills of Ireland,.. 357
The girl I left behind me... 358
The new Moon.. 360
The Valley lay smiling before me.................................. 361
The Fairy Tempter... 364
The Lupracaun ; or Fairy Shoemaker................................ 365
This life is all chequered.. 367
The Wild Geese.. 371
The Blarney... 371
The sorrowful Lamentations of Callaghan, Greally and Mullen....... 376
The Snow.. 378
The hour before day... 382
The Pilgrim Harper.... 383
The May-Dew... 384
The Meeting of Friends and the Meeting of Foes.................... 385
There's no such Girl as mine...................................... 390
The Fairy Boy... 390
The Avenger... 394
The Lamentation of Hugh Reynolds.................................. 395
The Burial of Sir John Moore...................................... 396
The Geraldine's Daughter.. 397
True Love can ne'er forget.. 399
The Nightcap.. 400
The Woods of Caillino... 417
The Brigade at Fontenoy... 424
The Irish Dragoon... 426

	PAGE.
'Tis a bit of a thing that a body may sing	430
The winter it is past	432
The Donnybrook Jig	437
The Haunted Spring	441
The Twig of the Shannon	454
The Boyne Water	459
The Bivouac	469
The Man for Galway	470
The Chain of Gold	473
The Wind and the Weather-cock	478
The Silvery Lee	480
The Twisting of the Rope	481
The Girls of the West	483
The Bells of Shandon	485
The Boys of the Irish Brigade	489
Up for the Green	112
Under the Rose	349
Wexford Heroes	56
Willy Reilly	90
Widow's Pig	94
Whistling Thief	102
Widow Machree	107
Wearing of the Green	139
Widow Malone	142
Whiskey	180
When the Moon is on the Waters	190
When Erin first rose	192
Woman of Three Cows	238
When first I met thee	263
War Song of O'Driscol	265
When daylight was yet sleeping	273
When he who adores thee	287
What the bee is to the flow'ret	290
We may roam through the world	303
While gazing on the Moon's Light	311
Weep on, weep on	323
When first I over the mountain trod	328
When and where	351
What will you do, love	388
When your beauty appears	415
Waiting for the May	463
When my old hat was new	484
Young Riley	103
You'll soon forget Kathleen	158
You remember Ellen	273
Yes and No	369

PUBLICATIONS

OF

P. J. KENEDY,

Excelsior Catholic Publishing House,

5 BARCLAY ST., NEAR BROADWAY, NEW YORK,

Opposite the Astor House

Adventures of Michael Dwyer........................	$1 00
Adelmar the Templar. A Tale.................	40
Ballads, Poems, and Songs of William Collins	1 00
Blanche. A Tale from the French..............	40
Battle of Ventry Harbor......................	20
Bibles, from $3 50 to	15 00
Brooks and Hughes Controversy...	75
Butler's Feasts and Fasts....................	1 25
Blind Agnese. A Tale.......................	50
Butler's Catechism.........................	8
" " with Mass Prayers............	30
Bible History. Challoner...................	50
Christian Virtues. By St. Liguori...........	1 00
Christian's Rule of Life. By St. Liguori.......	30
Christmas Night's Entertainments.......	60
Conversion of Ratisbonne................	50
Clifton Tracts. 4 vols...	3 00
Catholic Offering. By Bishop Walsh.............	1 50
Christian Perfection. Rodriguez. 3 vols. *Only complete edition*...........................	4 00
Catholic Church in the United States. By J. G. Shea. Illustrated......................	2 00
Catholic Missions among the Indians........	2 50
Chateau Lescure. A Tale....................	50
Conscience; or, May Brooke. A Tale.............	1 00
Catholic Hymn-Book.......................	15
Christian Brothers' 1st Book.................	13

Catholic Prayer-Books, 25c., 50c., *up to* 12 00

☞ Any of above books sent free by mail on receipt of price. Agents wanted everywhere to sell above books, to whom liberal terms will be given. Address

P. J. KENEDY, Excelsior Catholic Publishing House, *5 Barclay Street, New York.*

Christian Brothers' 2d Book	$0 25
" " *3d* "	63
" " *4th* "	88
Catholic Primer	6
Catholic School-Book	25
Cannon's Practical Speller	25
Carpenter's Speller	25
Dick Massey. An Irish Story	1 00
Doctrine of Miracles Explained	1 00
Doctrinal Catechism	50
Douay "	25
Diploma of Children of Mary	20
Erin go Bragh. (Sentimental Songster.)	25
El Nuevo Testamento. (Spanish.)	1 50
Elevation of the Soul to God	75
Epistles and Gospels. (Goffine.)	2 06
Eucharistica ; or, Holy Eucharist	1 00
End of Controversy. (Milner.)	75
El Nuevo Catecismo. (Spanish.)	15
El Catecismo de la Doctrina Christiana. (Spanish Catechism)	15
El Catecismo Ripalda. (Spanish)	12
Furniss' Tracts for Spiritual Reading	1 00
Faugh a Ballagh Comic Songster	25
Fifty Reasons	25
Following of Christ	50
Fashion. A Tale. 35 Illustrations	50
Faith and Fancy. Poems. Savage	75
Glories of Mary. (St. Liguori.)	1 25
Golden Book of Confraternities	50
Grounds of Catholic Doctrine	25
Grace's Outlines of History	50
Holy Eucharist	1 00
Hours before the Altar. Red edges	50
History of Ireland. Moore. 2 vols.	5 00
" " O'Mahoney's Keating	4 00
Hay on Miracles	1 00
Hamiltons. A Tale	50
History of Modern Europe. Shea	1 25
Hours with the Sacred Heart	50
Irish National Songster	1 00
Imitation of Christ	40

Catholic Prayer-Books, 25c., 50c., *up to* 12 00

☞ Any of above books sent free by mail on receipt of price. Agents wanted everywhere to sell above books, to whom liberal terms will be given. Address

P. J. KENEDY, Excelsior Catholic Publishing House,
5 Barclay Street, New York.

Irish Fireside Stories, Tales, and Legends.
(Magnificent new book just out.) About 400 pages
large 12mo, containing about 40 humorous and pa-
thetic sketches.   12 fine full-page Illustrations.
Sold only by subscription.   Only.................... $1 00
Keeper of the Lazaretto. A Tale............... 40
Kirwan Unmasked. By Archbishop Hughes..... 12
King's Daughters. An Allegory 75
Life and Legends of St. Patrick........ ...... 1 00
Life of St. Mary of Egypt... 60
     "   "   *Winefride........................* 60
     "   "   *Louis.......................* 40
     "   "   *Alphonsus M. Liguori.............* 75
     "   "   *Ignatius Loyola.* 2 vols............ 3 00
Life of Blessed Virgin................ 75
Life of Madame de la Peltrie.................. 50
Lily of Israel. 22 Engravings 75
Life Stories of Dying Penitents............... 75
Love of Mary 50
Love of Christ 50
Life of Pope Pius IX........................... 1 00
Lenten Manual......................... 50
Lizzie Maitland. A Tale........ 75
Little Frank. A Tale..................... 50
Little Catholic Hymn-Book........ 10
Lyra Catholica (large Hymn-Book)............... 75
Mission and Duties of Young Women........ 60
Maltese Cross. A Tale..................... 40
Manual of Children of Mary................. 50
Mater Admirabilis........................ 1 50
Mysteries of the Incarnation. (St. Liguori.).... 75
Month of November......... 40
Month of Sacred Heart of Jesus............... 50
     "   "   *Mary.................................* 50
Manual of Controversy....................... 75
Michael Dwyer. An Irish Story of 1798........... 1 00
Milner's End of Controversy................... 75
May Brooke; or, Conscience. A Tale... .. .. 1 00
New Testament....................... 50
Oramaika. An Indian Story...................... 75
Old Andrew the Weaver...................... 50
Preparation for Death. St. Liguori........... 75

Catholic Prayer-Books, 25c., 50c., up to 12 00
   ☞ Any of above books sent free by mail on receipt of price. Agents
wanted everywhere to sell above books, to whom liberal terms will be given.
Address
    P. J. KENEDY, Excelsior Catholic Publishing House,
       5 Barclay Street, New York.

Prayer. By St. Liguori..........................	$0 50
Papist Misrepresented..........................	25
Poor Man's Catechism........:............;.....	75
Rosary Book. 15 Illustrations..................	10
Rome: Its Churches, Charities, and Schools. By Rev. Wm. H. Neligan, LL.D......................	1 00
Rodriguez's Christian Perfection. 3 vols. Only complete edition...........	4 00
Rule of Life. St. Liguori..............	40
Sure Way; or, Father and Son........... ...	25
Scapular Book...................................	10
Spirit of St. Liguori............................	75
Stations of the Cross. 14 Illustrations..........	10
Spiritual Maxims. (St. Vincent de Paul)........	40
Saintly Characters. By Rev. Wm. H. Neligan, LL.D..	1 00
Seraphic Staff........	25
" *Manual,* 75 cts. to......................	3 00
Sermons of Father Burke, plain..........	2 00
" " " gilt edges.	3 00
Schmid's Exquisite Tales. 6 vols...............	3 00
Shipwreck. A Tale	50
Savage's Poems...	2 00
Sybil: A Drama. By John Savage................	75
Treatise on Sixteen Names of Ireland. By Rev. J. O'Leary, D.D............................	50
Two Cottages. By Lady Fullerton.......	50
Think Well On't. Large type...................	40
Thornberry Abbey. A Tale.....................	50
Three Eleanors. A Tale.........................	75
Trip to France. Rev. J. Donelan................	1 00
Three Kings of Cologne.......................	30
Universal Reader..............................	50
Vision of Old Andrew the Weaver.............	50
Visits to the Blessed Sacrament................	40
Willy Reilly. Paper cover......................	50
Way of the Cross. 14 Illustrations..............	5
Western Missions and Missionaries...........	2 00
Walker's Dictionary...........................	75
Young Captives. A Tale..................	50
Youth's Director..............................	50
Young Crusaders. A Tale......................	50

Catholic Prayer-Books, 25c., 50c., up to 12 00

☞ Any of above books sent free by mail on receipt of price. Agents wanted everywhere to sell above books, to whom liberal terms will be given. Address

P. J. KENEDY, Excelsior Catholic Publishing House, *5 Barclay Street, New York.*

CPSIA information can be obtained at www.ICGtesting.com
Printed in the USA
LVOW09s1605011014

406780LV00008B/371/P

9 781241 244521